Chinese Immigrants,
African Americans,
and Racial Anxiety
in the United States,
1848–82

THE ASIAN AMERICAN EXPERIENCE

Series Editor
Roger Daniels, University of Cincinnati

*A list of books in the series appears at
the end of this book.*

Chinese Immigrants, African Americans, and Racial Anxiety in the United States, 1848–82

NAJIA AARIM-HERIOT

University of Illinois Press

URBANA AND CHICAGO

♾ This book is printed on acid-free paper.

Library of Congress Cataloging-in-Publication Data
Aarim-Heriot, Najia.
Chinese immigrants, African Americans, and racial anxiety in the
United States, 1848–82 / Najia Aarim-Heriot ; foreword by Roger
Daniels.
p.   cm. — (The Asian American experience)
Includes bibliographical references (p.) and index.
ISBN 0-252-02775-2 (cloth : alk. paper)
1. Chinese Americans—Social conditions—19th century.
2. Immigrants—United States—Social conditions—19th century.
3. Chinese Americans—Legal status, laws, etc.—19th century.
4. African Americans—Social conditions—19th century.
5. African Americans—Legal status, laws, etc.—19th century.
6. United States—Race relations—Political aspects.
7. United States—Politics and government—1849–1877.
8. United States—Politics and government—1877–1881.
9. Racism—United States—History—19th century.
I. Title. II. Series.
E184.C5A17   2003
305.8'00973—dc21   2002005249

For my mother and father,
Rabha El Khalssi and Jelloul Aarim,
whose courage and love inspired this work,
and for all the scholars who strive to link their
intellectual work to pursuits for social justice.

I want a home here not only for the negro, the mulatto and the Latin races; but I want the Asiatic to find a home here in the United States, and feel at home here, both for his sake and for ours.

—Frederick Douglass, "Composite Nation"

Contents

Foreword by Roger Daniels   *xi*

Acknowledgments   *xiii*

Introduction   *1*

1. Racial Nativism in America until 1850   *15*

2. The Beginning of the Negroization of the Chinese
   in California, 1850–53   *30*

3. "The Copper of the Pacific" and "The Ebony of
   the Atlantic": Race Relations, 1854–60   *43*

4. Race Relations in the Civil War Era   *63*

5. Congressional Reconstruction and the
   Race Questions, 1865–69   *84*

6. Americans and the Chinese Question, 1865–69   *103*

7. Chinese Labor in the South and New England, 1865–70   *119*

8. Chinese Immigrants, African Americans, and the Retreat
   from Reconstruction, 1870–74   *140*

9. Race Relations in California, 1870–74   *156*

10. Intensification of the Anti-Chinese Movement, 1874–80   *172*

11. The Politics of Racism in the Chinese Exclusion
    Debates, 1879–82   *196*

    Conclusion   *215*

    Notes   *229*

    Bibliography   *261*

    Index   *277*

Foreword

ROGER DANIELS

UNTIL FAIRLY RECENTLY, most historians treated the Chinese Exclusion Act of 1882 and the fourteen other pieces of legislation that modified it until its repeal in 1943 as minor if ugly events in American history. In the last two or three decades, the act has come to be seen as the hinge on which all subsequent American immigration policy turned and the foundation stone of American immigration law. In this stunning new work, a young historian argues convincingly that there were important and ongoing connections between anti-Chinese and anti-Negro attitudes, connections that became even more striking in the Reconstruction and post-Reconstruction eras. She has demonstrated—in greater and more convincing detail than any previous author—not only that Negrophobia and anti-Chinese attitudes were inextricably linked but also that the "Chinese question," as contemporaries styled it, played a far more significant role in Reconstruction politics than has previously been recognized.

A unique aspect of this work is the way in which she traces the relationships between the evolution of anti-black and anti-Chinese thought and rhetoric. These matters have almost always been treated separately. Her work is thus a contribution, not only to the historiography of the Asian American experience but also to the history of American race relations generally and the political history of both the Reconstruction Era and the Gilded Age. It examines these topics in California and on the national scene.

The author, Najia Aarim-Heriot, who has taught at the Fredonia campus of the State University of New York since 1998, is a most unusual American historian. Born in Morocco of Moroccan parents who emigrated to France when she was three, she grew up in Toulouse and got her secondary education and first university degrees there in British and American studies before going on to Grenoble for the equivalent of an M.A. in British studies. She then remigrated, alone, to Morocco, where she taught courses in both British and American civilizations as well as English as a second language at University Moulay Ismail in Meknès. During the early 1990s, she alternated between teaching in Morocco and studying American history at Temple University in Philadelphia, where she earned a Ph.D.

She writes that her "experiences as a person with shifting and/or multiple immigrant identities have resulted in my interest in the questions of immigration, the consequences of diasporas, immigration and new forms of citizenship, ethnic and race relations, and, above all, the ethics of immigration policies. Growing up in France, I was fully aware of the latent xenophobic forces and of the convergence of French ethnic and racial patterns with those of countries (like the United States) that had a long history of 'absorbing' a variety of racial and ethnic groups." She believes that her work demonstrates that much of the recent historical and sociological scholarship on "whiteness" has had a Eurocentric focus. *Chinese Immigrants, African Americans, and Racial Anxiety in the United States, 1848–82* serves notice that such narrowness needs to be reconsidered.

Acknowledgments

WHEN I ENTERED Temple University's Ph.D. program in history in 1990, I wanted to research a topic that would allow me to address the complex questions of immigration and race—for academic and personal reasons. Kenneth K. Kusmer, my dissertation adviser, was my first ally in this project. I thank him for his invaluable criticism, his guidance, and his enthusiasm. I also thank him for his good humor and for extending himself in innumerable ways to support my work. Although my student days are over, I am still truly obliged to him for camaraderie, professional encouragement, and continued assistance. I am also grateful to the other members of my dissertation committee and other faculty members at Temple University for their constructive criticism and encouragement.

From the start of the publication project in 1998, knowing that Roger Daniels, editor of the Asian American Experience Series, would be the editor of this book eased my mind. Daniels was a committed and responsive editor. He read the whole manuscript closely at various stages and helped me shape my 880–page dissertation into a book—a daunting task, indeed. He gave scrupulous attention and rigorous and enlightening criticism to the manuscript. John David Smith read the whole manuscript and counseled me on various parts, notably (but not exclusively) on chapters about race relations in the Civil War and Reconstruction eras. Both reviewers' sharpness of eye and vigor of mind came at a time when those properties needed to be revived in the author. Many thanks to Michele May and Laurie Matheson, who steered the book to completion with perceptive suggestions, and to the editorial, production, and marketing staff at the University of Illinois Press for their patience, diligence, and expertise. I am especially grateful to Jane Mohraz, who prepared the copyedited manuscript with meticulous attention.

I also thank Kirk Heriot, who entered my life in the last leg of this project, though not too late for him to lend crucial support to my project. Kirk read the entire manuscript. Without him, the overwhelming task of cutting yet another eighty pages of text would have been even more "painful." He not only helped me prune down the manuscript but also responded to the text with insightful comments, intellectual support, and a wealth of historical reflections.

I have profited immensely from the great body of scholarship in Asian American and African American history as well as race relations studies. This book rests on the work of such scholars as Roger Daniels, Sucheng Chan, Ronald Takaki, Stuart Miller, George Fredrickson, Henry Tsai, Stanford Lyman, Charles McClain, Alexander Saxton, Ping Chiu, Michael Omi, Howard Winant, Edna Bonacich, David Roediger, John Hope Franklin, John Higham, Eric Foner, Paul Finkelman, Leon Litwack, Eugene Berwanger, and Jacque Voegeli. Their inspirations have shaped much of my thinking on this project.

This book owes a great deal to so many. Moulay Ismail University, Temple University, the Balch Institute, and SUNY College at Fredonia provided either financial support or invaluable periods of uninterrupted researching and writing, which helped in the development and completion of this project. I am greatly indebted to the dedicated librarians in special collections at the Bancroft Library in San Francisco, the Library of Congress, and the Balch Institute in Philadelphia, as well as the interlibrary loan staffs at Temple University and SUNY College at Fredonia for their time, expertise, and assistance in providing innumerable documents.

Working on this book has been consuming. I owe a number of apologies to relatives, friends, and colleagues, who found me divided in attention over the last eight years. Thanks to my colleagues in Fredonia and in Morocco, who cheered me at critical moments and offered advice and comments. The support of friends and relatives in France, Morocco, and the United States has been invaluable. Many thanks to my relatives and friends who tolerated my obsession and managed to help me keep my sanity. They provided inspiration by seeing promise throughout this project, even when I despaired of ever completing it. Without their love, support, and steadfast commitment, this book would not have been possible.

Chinese Immigrants,
African Americans,
and Racial Anxiety
in the United States,
1848–82

Introduction

[The] crusade against the Chinese will have to go on till it reaches a
climax of mischief and unreason that must be followed by
reaction, and then we shall wonder at our folly. . . .
—*Sacramento Daily Union,* July 1, 1870

Opposed as I am to Chinese immigration, wishing to see the
contact of that people with ours cease as soon as possible, I do
desire to see expelled from our statute books this flagitious and
ferocious legislation. . . .
—Cushman K. Davis (Republican from Minnesota), *Congressional
   Record,* November 2, 1893

THE OMISSION OR marginalization of Asians from the canon of American
immigration history buttressed the notion of America as a nation of immigrants of European stock and trivialized the Chinese (and, more generally,
Asian) exclusion movement and the Chinese American experience.[1] In the
last three decades, however, a number of important works have provided new
insight into the Asian American experience in the United States.[2] Unlike earlier interpretations, these valuable contributions are based on the assumptions that Chinese immigration was, for the most part, not very different from
that of other groups and that Chinese immigrants were motivated by the
same goals that brought the overwhelming majority of Europeans to the
United States.[3] By looking at Chinese immigration as a typical transnation-
al migration, these studies have supplied ample evidence that Chinese immigration was an important feature of U.S. immigration history and that
Chinese immigrants should be viewed as subjects and shapers of their history
rather than as passive objects. One of the major studies is Charles McClain's
legal history, *In Search of Equality* (1994), which chronicles the nineteenth-
century conflicts between the Chinese and white American officialdom in
California. McClain establishes that the Chinese mounted legal challenges
to virtually every disadvantage imposed on them by the state of California

and the federal government. Many of these cases contributed to the molding of American constitutional jurisprudence.[4]

Because the new scholarship has focused on documenting the Chinese perspective, however, it has paid little attention to the forces behind the rise of Sinophobia in the United States. This book seeks to contribute to the recent historiography of Chinese immigration by reassessing the historical origins of the Chinese exclusion movement and its culmination in the first racially based immigration act. It does so by providing a new interpretive framework for understanding the American reaction to the Chinese, from their arrival in California in 1848 to the passage of the first Chinese Exclusion Act in 1882.[5]

The first scholarly work that focused on the rise of Sinophobia in the United States was *Chinese Immigration* (1909), by Mary R. Coolidge, an activist scholar.[6] Coolidge's main argument was that the anti-Chinese movement originated in a fund of prejudice combined with economic grievances and specific political circumstances in the late 1860s. The movement became organized in California only after 1869, when an economic depression, the even division of voting strength between the two major parties, and labor unrest made Chinese immigration a convenient and expedient issue for labor leaders and politicians. In the 1860s, California labor leaders used the anti-Chinese feelings of their union members to establish for themselves a strong bargaining position and to win political favor from politicians eager to seize the issue of Chinese immigration in their quest for votes. As Californians shifted their efforts to achieve restriction from Sacramento to Washington, D.C., in the 1870s, the fortuitous circumstances that had allowed the Chinese issue to become a politically viable issue in California began to operate at the national level.[7] Notwithstanding the pathbreaking quality of Coolidge's well-documented analysis, her explanation for the treatment of Chinese immigrants in nineteenth-century California contains several misconceptions, rooted in her ideological biases against the working class and organized labor and her contempt for political demagogues. A considerable number of the anti-Chinese agitators, she claimed, were Irish Catholics or white southerners.[8] Besides this, restriction was a matter of regional policy, to which Congress and the executive branch reluctantly acquiesced. National anti-Chinese legislation, she maintained, was passed on the eve of close national elections, "against a disapproving majority in the East." "The clamor of an alien class [Irish] in a single state [California]," Coolidge concluded, "taken up by politicians for their own ends was sufficient to change the policy of a nation and to commit the United States to [a policy of] race discrimination at variance with our professed theories of government...."[9]

For three decades, Coolidge's study remained the only comprehensive treatment of Chinese immigration in the United States. During that time, however, the "Chinese question" found its way into histories of the labor movement in California. While most of these studies generally supported Coolidge's interpretation of the role of organized labor and the working class in the anti-Chinese movement, they provided a reevaluation of the significance of anti-Chinese activities for the growth of labor unionism in California. These activities were often interpreted as an essential factor leading to the cohesiveness, growth, and strength of California's labor movement.[10]

In 1939, Elmer Sandmeyer's *Anti-Chinese Movement in California* set out to reappraise the circumstances leading to anti-Chinese legislation. Overall, Sandmeyer's explanation upheld Coolidge's assumptions about the anti-Chinese campaign as a phenomenon centered in the Far West and radiating throughout the country by the late 1870s and as a movement dominated by labor organizations until the political climate made the Chinese question a possible campaign issue.[11] In other respects, however, Sandmeyer's monograph revised Coolidge's indictment of American labor. The Chinese had come to the United States with customs that were, he thought, incompatible with American norms. Because the Chinese refused to acculturate, they were responsible for the conditions under which they lived in California, especially the "segregating effect of racial prejudice and antagonism."[12] To a larger extent, though, the roots of the anti-Chinese movement were in deeply felt economic grievances. Sandmeyer argued that interracial conflict and violence were thus caused by the serious threat that Chinese laborers posed to the prevailing wage scale. This was because the Chinese, unlike European immigrants and white Americans, were accustomed to "a lower standard of living developed through generations of meager income."[13] Notwithstanding the subjectivity of her explanation, Coolidge had provided substantial evidence that the economic argument behind the call for Chinese exclusion—namely, that Chinese labor was so cheap that it caused the lowering of living standards for whites—was questionable. Thirty years later, Sandmeyer's study buttressed the importance of the "cheap labor" theme in the rise of American Sinophobia.

Sandmeyer's thesis had a profound influence on the historiography of Chinese immigration. For a long time, no one questioned whether Chinese labor was cheaper or how and why American workers reached the conclusion that their livelihood was jeopardized by the competition of Chinese labor. It was not until the 1960s that two studies successfully challenged the assumption that the anti-Chinese movement was for the most part economically motivated. The first was Ping Chiu's analysis of the role of Chinese labor in the early economic development of California. His study shows that from 1850 to 1880, the

white labor market in California remained "relatively insulated from the income and job competition of [the Chinese]." Why, then, did white workers
regard Chinese laborers as competitors? Chiu's answer was that the anti-Chinese movement originated in the displacement of an aggressive behavior from
an actual source of frustration to a substitute target—the Chinese. Following
the incorporation of California's economy into the national market in the
1870s, Chiu concluded, white workers fell victim not to Chinese competition
but to "a long-run shift to the mass-produced and mass-distributed goods."
The impersonal forces of the postbellum economic depressions were also too
complex for workers to understand, and the presence of Chinese laborers offered a readier explanation for the gap between expectation and reality.[14]

The charge of cheap labor was then taken to task by Alexander Saxton in
The Indispensable Enemy (1971). In this influential revisionist history of the
relationship between Sinophobia and California's labor movement, Saxton
argued that American labor's hostile reception to the Chinese stemmed not
so much from economic reasons as from ideological patterns of thought and
behavior. Anti-Chinese antagonism was rooted in the political ideology of
the Jacksonian Era. Despite its professed egalitarian ideology, the labor movement of that period had room for only white men. By the time the Chinese
arrived in California, racial thinking was part and parcel of the "ideological
baggage" of white migrants (both native and European-born) to the West.
Having set up the ideological context, Saxton explained the role of the anti-
Chinese movement in the development of nineteenth-century western politics. The rabid Sinophobia in California, he argued, originated in labor organizers' desperate need for a rallying tool and Democrats' need for an
expedient issue to rehabilitate their party. As a labor organizational tool,
"anti-Orientalism" resulted in the emergence in California of a strong labor
movement with political ambitions. The success of the anti-Chinese campaign in the labor movement convinced Democratic leaders of the enormous
potential of the Chinese issue. The Democrats manipulated the Chinese
question so successfully that by 1867 in California and 1875 in the nation at
large, anti-Chinese politics was successful politics. In essence, Saxton concluded, the Chinese laborers were the "indispensable enemies" of American
labor and political organizations.[15]

It is significant that the conceptual framework in all these analyses focuses on California. They offer only a tenuous connection between anti-Chinese
hostility in the West and the nationalization of the Sinophobic campaign.
Coolidge's and Sandmeyer's studies leave the impression that westerners
foisted their anti-Chinese attitudes on easterners who, until then, had been
sympathetic or indifferent to the Chinese. Sinophobia was thus a "sectional

disease," which became national only after the passage of the national exclusion law. Although Saxton also focused on California's labor movement,
he did try to put the anti-Chinese agitation in a national context by tracing
its roots to the ideology of Jacksonian democracy. In his analysis, however,
Jacksonian ideas about work and politics did not mature before the late 1860s,
that is, long after anti-Chinese agitation in California had started. Saxton also
accounted for the nationalization of the Chinese issue by relating it to the
decline of abolitionist thought. This interpretation, however, neglected the
existence of Sinophobia prior to this declension. Furthermore, all these studies stressed that Californians regarded Chinese laborers as a problem. It is not
clear why the Chinese, rather than Hispanic, African American, or European
laborers, were seen as the unacceptable economic competitors and chosen
as the perfect scapegoats.

In addition to not accounting satisfactorily for the nationalization of the
Chinese question, these studies do not explain the intensity of the reaction
against the Chinese at the regional and national levels. This failure can be
attributed to their concentration on the policy of exclusion and on the labor community. It is highly debatable, however, whether the working class
could have imposed a national policy of exclusion without the tacit acqui-
escence of policymakers and the rest of the citizenry. It is also a mistake to
think that legislation would be enacted for the benefit of the working class.
The other significant problem in these works is their deemphasis on the severity of the law. The 1882 Chinese Exclusion Act was more than a restriction law. All Chinese laborers, skilled and unskilled, were banned from the
United States. That there were exempt classes (e.g., Chinese merchants and
students) should not deflect attention from the fact that immigration is,
above all, a movement of laborers. The excepted classes stood for a different
movement, which was essential to international trade relations and America's "civilizing mission." In an America eager to have a share of the fabled
China trade, to disallow the entry of Chinese merchants would have made
no commercial sense. Besides this, the prosperity of Chinese merchants in
the United States depended largely on the growth of the Chinese labor community, which included most of their patrons. As the number of Chinese
laborers decreased, so would the number of merchants. As for students, the
transitory character of their sojourn and their use as potential Americaniz-
ing agents on their return to China explain, to a large extent, why they were
among the classes not affected by the ban. Hence, the 1882 act was an *exclusion* act, for all intents and purposes. Apart from not giving enough attention to that aspect of the law, these early histories disregarded the fact that
outright exclusion constituted only one facet of the oppression of Chinese

6 *Introduction*

people in the United States. The stringency and scope of the anti-Chinese laws, both local and national, demonstrate that there was much more to them than a simple reaction to a potentially large population of Chinese economic competitors. It is important to remember that when the Chinese Exclusion Act was passed, denying Chinese men and women entry, there were a little over 100,000 Chinese in America. In the next forty years, the United States opened its Atlantic gate to about 27 million European immigrants.

Unlike the previous authors, Stuart C. Miller did not restrict his investigation to the western region. His approach involved, among other things, looking at the anti-Chinese movement in the United States the other way, that is, from east to west rather than west to east. In *The Unwelcome Immigrant* (1969), Miller offered a persuasive revision of the early interpretations, particularly their regional concentration. His major argument was that a nationwide and well-established anti-Chinese prejudice, rather than the lobbying of a single state, provided the impetus for Chinese exclusion. His study demonstrates that the American image of China was negative long before the first Chinese laborers landed in California in the nineteenth century. The main dynamic in the American response to Chinese immigration was shaped by these negative images, which derived from the stereotyped accounts of "inside dopesters" (travelers, traders, and missionaries). Miller's refutation of the "California thesis" is very well encapsulated in his conclusion that "Californians did not have to expend much effort in convincing their compatriots that the Chinese in America would make undesirable citizens." "For decades," he explained, "American [inside dopesters] had developed and spread conceptions of Chinese deceit, cunning, idolatry, despotism, xenophobia, cruelty, infanticide, and intellectual and sexual perversity."[16] Miller's intellectual history is an enlightening contribution to our awareness of the full spectrum of American perceptions of the Chinese and China. It provides new possibilities for undertaking the task of evaluating the nature and impact of anti-Chinese opinions on both regional and national policies—that is, the behavioral dimension of American antagonism toward the Chinese.

Common thought generally assumes that prejudice leads to or causes discrimination, automatically and infallibly. However, if this were always true, individual and institutional discrimination against the Chinese would have been carried out from the very beginning of the interaction between Euro-Americans and Chinese immigrants, and Chinese exclusion would have been codified in the antebellum period. To understand the singular Chinese experience in the United States, it is essential to shift the focus from the prejudicial attitudes to a thorough examination of what was made of these prejudices. In the thirty-four years between the arrival of the Chinese and the passage of the exclusion act, anti-Chinese prejudice and discrimination were not constant but were changing and variable, depending on a number of situational factors. The historical circumstances surrounding the early experiences of Chinese immigrants explain why what seemed impossible in the 1850s became reality in 1882.

The American society that the Chinese entered in the critical decade preceding the Civil War was an inegalitarian, multiracial society. From the beginning of European settlement in America, Eurocentrism, competition for scarce resources, and an unequal distribution of power had shaped a two-tiered racial hierarchy, which in turn had shored up the establishment of white supremacy. When the Chinese joined the thousands of Argonauts in 1849, the subordination of Native Americans and African Americans was such that almost all white Americans believed that these groups could not be assimilated into an integrated American nation. It is thus reasonable to assume that the starting point in explaining Chinese exclusion lies in the racist ideology that was deeply embedded in American society and had actually served to color the Chinese stereotype.

Until the 1830s, American nationality had been defined in ideological terms as the commitment of individuals to the principles of liberty, equality, and republicanism. The American creed, however, was not color-blind. It excluded African Americans and Native Americans from the American body politic. Beginning in the 1840s, many developments gave rise to an effort to redefine American identity. In the East, the massive influx of Irish and German immigrants signified that American citizenship had to be redefined in ethnic terms. Meanwhile, westward expansion heightened nationalism, intensified sectionalism, and again raised questions about the status of Native Americans and African Americans. The annexation of the Southwest with its large Mexican population and the influx of Chinese immigrants complicated further the process of redefining American nationality in racial terms.

The complex history of ethnic and race relations in the decades following the Mexican-American War (1846–48) demonstrates that one should be wary of hasty, simplistic, or rigid historical models and sequences. As Tomás Almaguer's analysis of the historical origins of white supremacy in California shows, the experiences of the racial groups there followed divergent courses.[17] Native Americans were subjected to violent pogroms and were ruthlessly segregated on reservations. Anti-Chinese sentiment led to an active and sometimes violent campaign against them. Meanwhile, a significant shift in racial thought concerning the indigenous Mexicans led to their incorporation as "whites." White supremacy, the common source of the unequal treatment of these groups, led to distinct racist actions. By emphasizing white supremacy and the economic, political, and cultural contestations of racial status in California, Almaguer's impressive study highlights the weaknesses of earlier interpretations of race relations in the American West. The major problem with his interpretation, however, lies in the fact that he has neglected African Americans in his analysis, dismissing their experience in a four-page section entitled "Neutralizing the Presence of Blacks in Anglo California."[18] In fact, "neutralization" was a process that applied to all nonwhite groups, albeit under different forms and in different degrees. Moreover, the historical experiences of all racial groups in California were based on the very attitudes that had caused the subordination of blacks.

Though building on earlier explanations of the Chinese exclusion movement, this monograph takes a different perspective. It does so by placing the Chinese interaction with Americans in the context of an acute consciousness of race. In writing about settlement in the western territories, American historians have largely neglected the antebellum legislation that aimed to restrict the right of free blacks to the liberties accorded all white Americans and European immigrants, to come and go and to dispose of their person as they pleased.[19] They have treated the Chinese exclusion movement in a vacuum and failed to see the common threads in the experiences of African American migrants and Chinese immigrants to the American West. Basic to an understanding of the depth and breadth of the American response to Chinese immigration is the need to place this response within the broad context of race relations in the United States, especially within the backdrop of the conscious and continuous reconstruction of who could "belong" to the expanding American community. The processes of racial identification and categorization concerned all the people in the United States. The location and relocation of all people—regardless of their origin (European, African, Asian, or Native American) and regardless of their status (slave or free, citizen or alien)—were part of the same process of racial formation.[20] From this perspective, the anti-Chinese movement that ended in a dramatic change in national immigration policy was not an aberrant phenomenon. Rather, it brought immigration law into line with the hierarchical racial ranking that had been central to the organization and reproduction of the Euro-American social world. For at least sixty years before the Chinese arrived in California, racist thought had informed the criteria by which membership of the American community was determined.

The nineteenth-century history of Chinese immigration unfolded during a period of intensifying sectionalism, which culminated in major changes in race relations, especially between African Americans and white Americans. The thesis of this book is that the best way to reconstruct the dynamics of the

Chinese exclusion movement, at the regional and national levels, is to relate it to the dynamics of black-white relations. This study thus eschews the thoroughly explored theme of the relation between the anti-Chinese movement and labor organizations. As mentioned earlier, the prominence given to the role of labor and economics in the explanation of the anti-Chinese movement is defective in that it cannot account for the intensity of the "flagitious and ferocious legislation" against Chinese immigrants, from individual to institutional discrimination and from individual and collective violence to legislation banning their entry and naturalization and attempting to deny them basic civil and human rights. By giving disproportionate emphasis to the alleged impact of the Chinese on the workplace and white laborers, traditional

E PLURIBUS UNUM EXCEPT THE CHINESE

Before the Chinese, there were two excepted groups—Native Americans and African Americans. The passage of the Chinese Exclusion Act added yet another contradiction to the "inclusive" motto by bringing immigration law into line with the racial organization of the Euro-American social world. (Source: *Harper's Weekly*, April 1, 1882, 207. Courtesy of the Library of Congress)

histories have given insufficient attention to a more significant and devastating aspect of the Chinese stereotype. It was the notion that, like African Americans, Chinese immigrants could *not* assimilate into American society and that their presence would lead to greater heterogeneity and latent racial strife.

In many ways, the anti-Chinese movement was merely a continuation of the earlier extreme polarization between whites and nonwhite groups. This book contributes to a better understanding of the rise of Sinophobia by knitting the fragmentary history of race relations in America. The diversity of the West put a formidable strain on the "simpler" varieties of anti-black and anti-Indian racism, simpler because they were thought to be firmly in place after generations of racial contests. The anti-Chinese movement indicates that, as westerners and easterners contemplated the addition of "a new color upon the loom," they concluded that Chinese exclusion was essential for preserving their self-definition as citizens of a white American nation.[21] At the same time, this exclusion served to shore up the essential unity of nonwhite humanity.

From the time of their arrival in 1848, Chinese immigrants were singled out for particular treatment. The marginalization of the Chinese from the large and diverse immigrant community can be traced to their "racialization," that is, the extension of a sense of absolute biological and cultural difference that rendered their presence in California and in the United States at large a problematic one.[22] The separation of the Chinese from European immigrants was buttressed by their relegation to the "nonwhite" category—more particularly, their "Negroization."[23] The early pattern of relations between the Chinese and Americans exhibited many parallels to the relations between African Americans and white Americans. In the antebellum period, the measures abrogating the rights of Chinese immigrants duplicated laws that had been designed to limit the access of blacks to the same opportunities afforded whites and to legitimize their degraded status in American society—North and South. The conflation of the two groups was reflected in the fact that they shared two fundamental discriminatory measures, which put them outside of the political and social community and made them legally disabled: their ineligibility for citizenship and the inadmissibility of their testimony in civil and criminal cases. Within a few years of the Chinese arrival in California, the long-established racial proscription of African Americans was used successfully by Californians to discriminate against Chinese immigrants. The anti-Chinese rhetoric was an almost verbatim repetition of the anti-black rhetoric. The perception of Chinese inferiority and servility originated in a similarly negative perception of African Americans.

In the antebellum period, both African Americans and Chinese immigrants were viewed as an undesirable and degraded labor element. While African Americans were stigmatized as slave or unfree labor, regardless of their status, the Chinese were stigmatized as cheap labor, "coolies" (involuntary contract laborers or imported laborers), or servile and unfree labor, irrespective of their free immigration to and free labor status in the United States. The charge of "coolieism" was taken for granted in some traditional histories, which saw the Chinese exclusion movement as a rational, indeed reasonable, measure for the protection of the dignity of labor and white workers.[24] One of the many problems with this interpretation is, of course, that the charge of coolieism was included in the panoply of anti-Chinese stereotypes only after the familiar catchphrase "slave/unfree" labor had been used to denote the alleged undignified nature of Chinese labor. In the antebellum North, a strong belief in "free labor" and the need to protect its concomitant social values provided the ideological underpinning of the westward movement. That both blacks and Chinese were not embraced in the free labor ideology is evident in the repeated attempts to exclude both groups, using the smoke screen of unfree/imported labor or, in the light of contrary evidence, cheap and degraded labor.

Despite the common pattern of their oppression in California, there were important differences in the experiences of African Americans and Chinese immigrants. The more numerous Chinese population was perceived as a greater threat than African Americans. Under some circumstances, race antipathy was subordinated to economic necessity. Interestingly, when economic conditions in California dictated it, a slot opened for the Chinese rather than African Americans. Unlike African Americans, Chinese immigrants were regarded as a pool of labor, whose presence could be strictly regulated by American authorities. Another significant difference in the treatment of both groups lay in the shift in attitudes toward African Americans in the final years of the Civil War. As Republican and Union leaders became more receptive to black civil rights, they remained adamantly opposed to the extension of similar rights to the Chinese.

The period from emancipation to the passage of the Chinese Exclusion Act in 1882 was critical. In a nation going through a reconstruction process after a civil war in which race had been an important factor, the enactment of a racially based immigration policy was, of course, of great significance. Such action highlights the need for a thorough reappraisal of racial thought in the postbellum period. Generally, the historiography of postbellum racial politics is inadequate. The scant attention to the Chinese question in the category "Reconstruction" in the historiography is paradoxical in view of its prominence in the congressional debates over Reconstruction. Furthermore, by neglecting these debates, historians of the Chinese exclusion movement have enshrouded the nationalization of the Chinese question in conceptual fog. To ignore the tortuous course of the Chinese question in the transitional Reconstruction years is to ignore an important facet of the multicultural and multiracial American past. In this book, then, I attempt to dispel the notion that Reconstruction involved the attempt by the nation to resolve the problems associated with a biracial nation. The evidence shows that, throughout Reconstruction, the "Negro problem" and the Chinese question were harnessed together. The presence of the Chinese at that time put an enormous strain on the efforts of the Republican majority to follow a course of action that adhered to its professed egalitarian creed.

My examination of the Chinese question in postbellum congressional politics calls into question important assumptions about Republican racial ideology. The intent of the framers of Reconstruction has been a controversial topic. Whether historians have stressed the conservatism or radicalism of Republican Reconstruction policies, they have usually neglected the wrangling about the implications of these policies for race relations in the Pacific states. These bitter arguments exposed the abstract nature of the Republican majority's commitment to racial equality. As they expressed their misgivings about the immigration of the Chinese, conservative and even some radical Republicans found themselves referring to African Americans' unfitness for self-government and their inferiority. It was, however, in their treatment of the Chinese issue that the Republican majority demonstrated unequivocally the limits of its commitment to racial equality. Michael L. Benedict has argued that Republicans, in formulating Reconstruction policies, were limited by a basically conservative view of the Constitution and of what they could do in the South.[25] However, my analysis of the congressional debates during Reconstruction shows that, in handling the Chinese question, Republicans deliberately promoted a conservative, indeed reactionary, policy aimed at narrowing the future course of action for the incorporation of the Chinese in California and in the country at large. In that respect, the debates over naturalization in July 1870 brought to light in a dramatic way the rift within Republican ranks, between the few radicals (far ahead of their time), who saw the essence of the party in its devotion to equality for both African Americans and Chinese immigrants, and the conservative majority (whose racial ideas typified societal norms), which saw it in a more limited and practical commitment to equality for African Americans only. By opting to keep the word *white* in the naturalization statute of 1870, the Republican majority placed the Chinese in the category of persons ineligible for full membership in the newly defined biracial nation.

The vote against the naturalization of the Chinese exposed the persistence and ascendancy of a racist ideology in a political scene dominated by a Republican majority and the role of that ideology in the Chinese American experience. The subsequent retreat from "Radical Reconstruction" affected both African Americans and Chinese immigrants. From 1879 to 1882, the debates on the Chinese exclusion bills revealed not only the dramatic implications of the Republican retreat from Reconstruction but also the fact that the improved status of African Americans was critically undermined by the unequal treatment of the Chinese. The passage of the Chinese Exclusion Act reflected the extent to which racial politics had regained respectability in the national political discourse in the late 1870s.

This book is the first full-scale examination of the relationship between the Chinese question and the Negro problem. It chronicles the successive manifestations of anti-Chinese sentiment and behavior in connection with the evolving status and situation of African Americans, from slavery to emancipation and from Reconstruction to post-Reconstruction. It is, in many ways, a contribution to the new historiography of the Chinese American experience, which seeks to incorporate more fully Asian Americans in the canon of American immigration history. It rectifies some of the conceptual and historiographical deficiencies of American immigration history and race relations studies by tracing the relation between Chinese immigration and the dynamics of American race relations. The connection between immigration and nativism in traditional immigration histories has for the most part focused on the experiences of the "New Immigrants"—southern and eastern European immigrants—at the turn of the century.[26] The rise of anti-Chinese nativism, although it formed an important precedent for the later movement to restrict European immigration, has received far less attention. Within the race relations historical category, studies of the African American experience have dealt extensively with anti-black attitudes and behavior, but they have rarely related these attitudes to the racial confrontations between European Americans and other peoples of color. Race relations studies have often neglected the great racial diversity in America by focusing exclusively on black-white relations. It is evident, however, that the dynamics of race relations in the United States has always been too complex to be contained within a white-black dichotomous framework. The premise of this book is that the patterns of black-white relations functioned as a pacesetter in the encounter between the Chinese and white Americans—that is, until Chinese exclusion reversed the dynamic and Chinese–white American relations influenced black-white relations.

Much insight will be gained by examining the similarities and differences in white American attitudes toward Chinese immigrants and African Americans and by looking at the significance of the shifts in racial attitudes across time in California and the country at large. To achieve a thorough account of the historical origins of the Chinese exclusion movement, this narrative moves back and forth between a western and national focus. From that perspective, the 1882 Chinese Exclusion Act was the culmination of thirty-four years of unequal treatment of the Chinese in the western region and sixteen years of hesitant progress on the part of the Republican majority toward the civil rights of the Chinese and its resistance to granting them citizenship rights. Less than fifteen years before the act, the overwrought reaction of easterners to the use of Chinese laborers in the Southeast and Northeast is indicative of the anti-Chinese prejudices in those regions. The anti-Chinese movement was thus a coherent and continuous movement involving not only California, its working class, labor organizers, and political demagogues, but also eastern workers and labor reformers, California and U.S. justices, northern and southern congressmen, and presidents of the United States. The book also moves back and forth between the black and Chinese experiences to trace the complex racialization of the Chinese in California and in the nation at large and the essential role of black-white relations in shaping Chinese–white American relations.

This comparative history of race relations in nineteenth-century America demonstrates that racial anxiety over America's destiny as a "composite nation"—to use Frederick Douglass's expression—was the most significant factor in the rise of Sinophobia in the United States and in the racialization of its immigration policy.[27] The same concern led to the broadening of the movement into an "Asiatic" exclusion drive and, insofar as blacks were concerned, their relegation to second-class citizenship. Not until the mid-twentieth century would American society confront squarely the heterogeneity of its population and begin the piecemeal dismantling of its discriminatory legislation against African Americans and Asian Americans. The current debate over the large-scale immigration of non-Europeans (mostly Asian and Latin American) in the past three decades is reminiscent of the nineteenth-century debate on Chinese immigration. Behind the familiar smoke screen of economic and political arguments lies the sad reality that the process of reconciling America with its multiracial identity has yet to be completed. This book might help raise fundamental questions about this resurgent nativism. Obviously, the Chinese exclusion acts were repealed without sufficient thought about the "folly" that took hold of the nation. Before going down the path of "mischief and unreason" again, let us revisit the past in the hope that we may not go full circle.

1. Racial Nativism in America until 1850

The population of the United States consists of natives of
Caucassian origin....
—William H. Seward (Whig from New York), *Congressional Globe*,
   March 8, 1850

We desire only a white population in California....
—*Californian*, March 15, 1849

THE REVOLUTIONARY ERA initiated the first major debate over American
nationality. To legitimize their separatist move, Americans claimed a new
identity that set their nation apart from Europe. They defined themselves as
a republican people, committed to the principles of liberty, equality, and self-
government. This republican creed was, however, far from color-blind. It excluded two classes from the body politic and from the protection of person
and property that represented the condition of civil liberty under U.S. citizenship. While Native Americans were regarded as members of "foreign nations," enslaved Africans were degraded to a condition of nonhumanity by
being reduced to three-fifths of a person for federal representation. One year
after the ratification of the Constitution, the 1790 Naturalization Act granted the right of naturalized citizenship to "free white persons."[1] This limitation confirmed the convergence of race and national citizenship and of race
and rights, or lack thereof.

Nonwhite groups were the foils of Americans' early self-definition as
"white only." When the issue of extending slavery into the western territories emerged, the equation of America with whiteness and its corollary, "the
bitter, malignant, and cruel prejudice against color," were so pervasive that
a white contemporary complained that "the American people are emphatically a *Negro-hating* people."[2] The racial undertone of American nationalism could be seen in the legal and social fabric of each section. In the South,

it found expression in the increased stringency of the "Peculiar Institution" and in the restrictions placed on free blacks, who were required by local laws to register with the police and to carry their certificates of freedom at all times.[3] In the North, African Americans were often subjected to a system of discrimination that effectively blocked their access to the social, economic, and political opportunities afforded whites. Fearing an increase in the number of fugitive slaves and free blacks in their communities, some northern states attempted to discourage black settlers by requiring them to register their certificates of freedom at a county clerk's office and to present bonds guaranteeing that they would not disturb the peace and become public charges. Efforts to control the effects of black migration included total or partial disfranchisement—as in New Jersey, Connecticut, Pennsylvania, and New York—and school segregation. It was, however, in the free midwestern territories that the harshest anti-black laws (outside of the South) were passed—for example, legislation that absolutely prohibited black migration.[4]

The status of northern African Americans raised the murky subject of the nature of citizenship, state and national, and whether it included free blacks. Article 4, section 2, of the Constitution provides that "[t]he Citizens of each State shall be entitled to all Privileges and Immunities of Citizens in the Several States." Had free blacks been considered citizens, the laws restricting their mobility in the country should have been held unconstitutional. The issue did not capture national attention until the Missouri controversy in 1820. One provision of the proposed constitution of Missouri called for the exclusion of free Negroes, causing anti-slavery forces to try to prevent the admission of Missouri as a slave state. They failed and had to settle for the Missouri Compromise.[5] Missourians agreed, however, not to enforce their anti-black law against Negroes from the free states.

Although the questions of black citizenship and migration rights were not seriously discussed in Congress until the late 1850s, they were taken into judicial consideration earlier. Some of the most important constitutional issues from 1830 to 1860 involved the interpretation of the commerce clause (article 1, section 8, of the Constitution), which gives Congress power to regulate commerce with foreign nations and among the several states. One main area of commerce pertains to the influx of immigrants to the United States. Interestingly, critical cases about state immigration laws involved a discussion of the migration rights of African Americans. One such case concerned a South Carolina statute on seamen. Like other southern Negro seamen acts, this statute drastically restricted the activities of alien black sailors (mostly British), requiring their imprisonment while in port. The South Carolina statute was particularly resented because it required the sailors or the masters of the ships to pay the costs of detention. Failure to do so could result in the sale of the sailors into slavery.[6] The statute was declared unconstitutional by Attorney General William Wirt in 1824 for being in violation of the exclusive power of Congress to regulate commerce with foreign nations—in that case, Great Britain. In 1831, however, a different opinion was given by Attorney General John M. Berrien of Georgia, who decided that the statute was a legitimate exercise of the police power of the state, which was protected by the Tenth Amendment of the Constitution. Wirt and Berrien restricted their judicial reasoning to the regulation of states' rights, but Roger B. Taney, who succeeded Berrien, transcended the issue at hand, British sailors' rights, to discuss the status and rights of free American Negroes. In his 1832 opinion, Taney used the same racial argument that he would proclaim from the bench of the Supreme Court twenty-five years later in *Dred Scott v. Sandford.* The African race, even when free, was everywhere "a degraded class." The privileges that Negroes enjoyed, he added, were "accorded to them as a matter of kindness and benevolence rather than of rights." Hence, they were not intended to be embraced in any of the provisions of the Constitution. No power could or should induce southern states to surrender their right to exclude free blacks. Faced with this setback, Britain turned to negotiations with individual states to protect its black mariners. By the early 1840s, the seamen laws were enforced exclusively against American blacks from northern states.[7]

These judicial opinions were not used to legitimize the constitutionality of excluding free Negroes from nonslave states, however. When delegates at the Iowa constitutional convention proposed an outright Negro exclusion provision in 1844, they were persuaded to remove the article by federal officials in the territory who cited possible congressional disapproval. The next year, however, Florida was admitted as a slave state with a Negro exclusion clause in its constitution. Obviously, Congress had drawn a line between slave and nonslave states. Notwithstanding this, state laws restricting the migration of free blacks in the Midwest were retained and remained unchallenged.

In the 1840s, the Supreme Court was presented with two cases involving immigration statutes, the so-called *Passenger Cases.* One case, *Smith v. Turner,* came from New York, and the other, *Norris v. City of Boston,* came from Massachusetts. Both states justified the imposition of a tax on immigrants as an effort to curb the immigration of undesirable classes and to raise money to pay for the support of foreign paupers. Starting in 1843 and 1844, respectively, the cases attracted considerable attention from all sections of the country, notably because of the analogy between the statutes and the state laws restricting the interstate movement of blacks. Although the issue was European immigration, the Supreme Court justices and counsel often raised the question of black mobility in their judicial reasoning. Counsel arguing for the constitutionality of the statutes justified them as police measures rather than as regulations of commerce. The police powers of each state, they argued, embraced the power to exclude migrants liable to constitute a danger to its welfare. If the statutes were unconstitutional, one counsel asked, then "on what principle [could] the laws expelling or forbidding the introduction of free negroes be sustained?"[8]

In February 1849, by a margin of one vote, the Supreme Court held that the state laws were unconstitutional because they involved the regulation of foreign commerce, a sphere that belonged to the federal government. The justices made clear in their opinions, however, that states could exclude Negroes. On the majority side, the focus was on black migration in the slave states. Justice James M. Wayne declared that the Court's opinion should not be construed by southern states as a loss of their right to turn away free blacks. A correct interpretation of the Constitution, he went on, would guard against any attempt to test such power.[9] On the minority side, Justice Taney upheld the immigration laws as a reasonable exercise of the police power reserved by the states. The Court, he noted, had already decided that a state might remove *any* person it wished.[10] If so, it might refuse their entrance. It was in fact more sensible to exclude them than to admit and later expel them. Determined to go beyond the subject of state regulations at ports of entry, Taney discussed the legality of a state exclusion law imposed on citizens of another state. Such a measure, he declared, would be unconstitutional, because all citizens of the United States had "the right to pass and repass through every part of it without interruption, as freely as in [their] own states." A state entry tax would be inconsistent with the rights of citizens as members of the Union. To prevent any misinterpretation, though, Taney intimated that his intention was not to assert the rights of noncitizens. Whereas he would oppose any attempt by any state to exclude a "citizen of another state," he would defend the power of any state to decide whether immigrants or Negroes should be permitted to enter and reside therein. Taking exception to the majority opinion, he warned that it could be used to disallow the efforts of a slave state to protect its domestic security by banning "cargoes of negroes from Jamaica, Hayti, or Africa."[11]

Neither Wayne nor Taney delivered opinions on the right of American Negroes to come and go as they pleased in the free states and territories. Nor did either man address the critical question of black citizenship. It would be eight more years before Taney would expressly draw a racial boundary in his legal construction of national citizenship in *Dred Scott*. The historical significance of the *Passenger Cases,* however, is that they implicitly sanctioned the discriminatory measures against African Americans who moved from state to state or territory. While the minority opinion put aliens, slaves, free blacks, convicts, and paupers in one category of people with no constitutional rights, the majority opinion differentiated between aliens, whose fortune depended on Congress, and slaves, free blacks, convicts, and paupers, whose rights or lack thereof were decided by the states. In short, the cases established the dual doctrine of nationalism for foreign immigration and states' rights for Negro mobility.

Accordingly, the movement to restrict free blacks continued unabated. In the South, a major reason for their exclusion was the fear that their presence might foster yearnings for freedom and provide leadership for slave revolts. In a system built for two—free and slave, white and black, respectively—the free Negro was perceived as a threat to the social order. In the American West, the drive to exclude blacks originated in the desire to actualize an exceptional region—not only "free" but also all-white or nearly so. The adherence to racial homogeneity was pronounced in the late 1840s. The Mexican-American War (1846–48) and the subsequent annexation of territories in northern Mexican land were interpreted as the playing out of America's "Manifest Destiny." When transposed in biological terms, this conquest signified the superiority of the Anglo-American over the "inferior races" of Mexico. The discussion about the racial traits of Mexicans turned back to the racial makeup of American society. John Sullivan's article "Annexation" (1845) is often quoted for its use of the expression "Manifest Destiny." However, Sullivan did more than encourage American imperialism. He offered his solution to the race problem in America: the Spanish and Indian populations of Central and South America afforded "the only receptacle capable of absorbing that [Negro] race whenever we shall be prepared to slough it off."[12] By virtue of its annexation, however, the northern Mexican territory would not qualify as a possible host region for blacks. The racialization of the political discourse over annexation was swiftly transferred to the slavery extension issue, providing a new occasion to convey the immutable "alien status" of Africans in America. The territorial acquisition, most of it south of the Missouri Compromise line, threatened the political balance between North and South. In the struggle that ensued, moral and principled opposition to slavery was rare and voiced mostly by abolitionists. To most anti-expansionists, the problem was not that slavery was an inhumane institution but that its extension would affect the political equilibrium, economic opportunities for whites, and social and racial homogeneity.

As they emphasized the need to protect the welfare of free white men, anti-expansionists made clear the incompatibility of not only slave and free labor but also black and white labor. The degrading effect of black labor was a very compelling argument in the late 1840s. After the incremental abolition of slavery in the North, changes in race relations had brought northern blacks into direct competition with white laborers. White workers reacted in much the same way fellow laborers in the South had. From South Carolina to Texas, white mechanics had petitioned legislative bodies for laws restricting the employment of slave and free black operatives, whom they charged were unfair competitors depressing wages. While cordial relations could be found occasionally, hostility, erupting sometimes into violence, was more common. In the North, too, white laborers were prompt to show their resentment of blacks in their workplaces.[13] Many studies have evidenced the economic plight of free blacks in the antebellum North and West: the existence of a dual labor market, their displacement from skilled and unskilled jobs by not only native but also foreign-born (mainly Irish) workers, and the low occupational mobility of all black laborers.[14] The concentration of black workers in the lowest-paid unskilled occupations was, however, interpreted as a problem of adjustment to the new industrial environment. The racial stereotype of African Americans as lacking skills, industry, thrift, and independence was often used to justify exclusionary or discriminatory practices. This ideological offensive found expression in an ethos that defined black labor as intrinsically inferior to white labor and black economic competition as unfair and underhanded. From this perspective, any black progress in white trades was assumed to lower the social status of whites.[15]

There were more severe forms of discrimination against blacks than the denial of jobs, education, or housing. Racial violence was quite common in the antebellum northern cities. Two of the most virulent episodes occurred in the summer of 1834 in New York and Philadelphia. By that time, segregation typified black-white relations in virtually all areas of social life in both cities. Racial segregation was a fact of life in all free states, where it served to ensure that blacks kept "their place" as a subordinate class. Of the many reasons that contributed to the riots in July and August 1834, some contemporaries saw the economic factor as the most critical. However, recent studies have demonstrated that black laborers were in no position to compete with the rioters, whose rivals for jobs were actually white immigrants.[16] More important than real or perceived economic grievances, a deeply ingrained prejudice turned free blacks into the convenient target of displaced aggression. In New York, Negrophobia was exacerbated by a hatred of abolitionists and their supposed advocacy of racial equality. The rioters' first acts of aggression were the disruption of the abolitionists' integrated celebration of Independence Day and attacks on white abolitionists and their property. The ugliest violence, however, was precipitated by a rumor that a black priest had officiated at an interracial marriage. Incensed, rioters spilled over into the Sixth Ward, attacking its large black population. For some time before the riot, anti-abolitionists had inflamed New Yorkers with accusations that abolitionists wanted to force amalgamation on whites. The race riot was partly a form of sexual vigilantism—an attempt to abort the abolitionists' "repugnant" program of debasement of the white race. The leading abolitionists' disclaimer that they had any desire to promote intermarriage was to no avail. In Philadelphia, too, fear of amalgamation contributed to the racial prejudice that stimulated the mob attacks on racially integrated establishments, although the riot there was to a greater extent the result of a breakdown in the racial order, which required that blacks accept a subordinate status. The major targets of the rioters were propertied Negroes.[17]

These race riots set a precedent for a string of racial disturbances in the antebellum North. A common feature of all these riots was the lack of compassion for the victims in the larger communities' responses. In Philadelphia, when the rioters shifted their activities from destruction of property to "hunting the nigs," only a few voices were raised to condemn their fiendish brutality.[18] In most riots, the black communities were blamed for the outbreaks, for perpetrating amalgamation or forgetting that the Negro's place should be inferior to that of the least favored white man. These riots cannot be dismissed as the irrational or pathological behavior of a few disturbed individuals. The slow intervention of the police and the reluctance to punish the guilty after the events show that acts of aggression against blacks did not offend the sensibilities of the white communities.

In 1834, the Philadelphia investigation committee stated that the most active among the rioters had sought to intimidate the colored population in an attempt to compel them to leave.[19] Would African Americans find a refuge in the American West, the "region of freedom and democracy"? Chances were slim. Very shortly, white western settlers embraced an inegalitarian belief system that mirrored its eastern counterpart. In the late 1840s, several western states and territories organized constitutional conventions and passed laws that drew a racial distinction as the basis for granting settlers the right of entry and full citizenship privileges. The discussion about the status of blacks at these conventions was so infused with racist comments that it was clear many westerners did not want them as slaves or free persons. If the West was to be a preserve for "free white laborers," then the migration of free blacks must be checked too. While most restriction laws were hardly enforced and midwestern states had continuous growth in their black population, the statutes revealed an antipathy toward black migration. These restrictions on native blacks should be juxtaposed with the unqualified incorporation of white migrants. Western states were actively encouraging European immigration and the migration of white Americans. The assimilation of aliens was made easy by the naturalization law, which required them to live in the United States for five years before they could be naturalized.[20] While naturalization gave new Americans all the rights of a citizen, immigrants did not have to wait for five years for all such privileges. When the Constitution was adopted, it recognized not only citizens of the United States but also citizens of each state. To enjoy the rights and privileges conferred by citizenship, one must reside in a state and comply with the rules and regulations of that state. States were thus entitled to bestow almost all the rights of citizenship without naturalization. The right to vote for national legislators especially was a right conferred and regulated by state laws.[21] In the western territories, while Negroes were barred from the ballot box, the franchise was open to resident aliens after a short residence—less than five years—in an effort to build communities and prepare for statehood.

American advance across the continent reinforced the ideology of white supremacy. In the course of a complicated process involving such paradoxes as liberty and slavery and democracy and racism, expansionists reinforced the comforting stereotype connecting whiteness with Americanness. Settlement in California during the gold rush has to be seen against this backdrop of racial enmity against blacks and other nonwhite groups.

California was a singular frontier. The Mexican-American War of 1846 had reenacted the old practice of American progress through conquest and subordination. The annexation of northern Mexico was, however, an anomaly in the pattern of domination because of its substantial population. In 1846, the American West was a complex meeting ground, a point where three Americas intersected: Native America, Hispanic America, and Anglo America. An earlier contest for cultural dominance had led to the settlement of populations from colonial Mexico between 1769 and 1821. Native Americans were then dispossessed of their lands and enslaved. After independence was won from Spain in 1821, the Mexican government slowly expanded the definition and privileges of citizenship to include Native Americans. In California, Mexican settlers began to voice their own territorial identity in the early 1830s. In 1834, emancipation of Indians and secularization of the California missions were enacted, and Californios (native-born Californians of Spanish ancestry) obtained from the Mexican government control of the countryside. As citizens, Native Americans were granted the right to claim a share of mission land, but they did not regain their right to the precolonial territory that the church had held in trust for them during the mission period.[22] On February 2, 1848, the Treaty of Guadalupe Hidalgo, ending the Mexican-

American War, sealed the second territorial conquest of the American West. The victorious United States absorbed the region's 75,000 Spanish-speaking inhabitants and its 150,000 Native Americans and increased its territory by one million square miles.

Besides the successive conquests, the early history of Anglo-American California was greatly influenced by a particular industry: mining. California offered wealth through the direct exploitation of mineral resources rather than the laborious development of land and provided the most fluid social structure in the West. The announcement of the discovery of surface gold in a mill stream near Sutter's Fort in January 1848 precipitated a great influx of migrants from Latin America, Asia, and Europe, as well as other parts of the United States. The absence of a statute excluding African Americans from California encouraged the migration of not only free blacks but also slaveholders, who brought in their slaves. Very early, though, white miners rallied against the importation of slave labor in the mining districts. By March 1849, about six months before the first great inrush of gold seekers, American miners made clear their sentiment that slave *and* free black labor should be barred from the state.[23] By July 1849, local miners' resolutions stipulated that Negroes were not privileged to work in the mines, which were intended for "American citizens." According to William Shaw, a British gold seeker, the mere presence of African Americans in a mining party was sufficient to bar the whole party from mining. Whatever their condition, he said, blacks were thought to be in a state of slavery to whites.[24] Anti-black attitudes were not confined to the mining class. As early as March 1849, newspaper editors in San Francisco voiced their support of the miners' demand for black exclusion.[25]

Six months later, during the constitutional convention in Monterey, the question of statehood was entwined with political issues surrounding the Negro question. The newly drafted California Constitution made clear that the state would not offer equal opportunities to African American settlers. The forty-eight delegates at the convention voted speedily and unanimously to ban slavery from the state.[26] The ensuing debate over a proposition to exclude free blacks from California verified the racial rather than humanitarian basis of this prohibitory clause.[27] The exclusion proposition was made by Morton McCarver (Democrat), who deemed the nonadmission of Negroes necessary because the whole purpose of banning slavery would be defeated if free blacks were allowed to settle in California.[28] In a short time, his supporters agreed, California would be filled with Negroes. These delegates pointed to the "riots" arising from "the habitation of negroes among the whites" in the East to demonstrate that the black and white races could not associate without mutual harm. They further expressed their misgivings about allowing free blacks to settle in California, because no population "could be more repugnant . . . or injurious to the prosperity of the community, than free negroes."[29] While some delegates objected to black migrants because of their alleged depravity, idleness, dependent nature, and shiftlessness, others brought a contradictory indictment against them.[30] In a vituperative speech in support of McCarver's proposition, Oliver Wozencraft (Whig) described free blacks as "living laboring machines," with their attendant evil: the degradation of labor. He urged not only black exclusion but also the expulsion of all Negroes already in the state. Failing to enact an exclusion clause would be construed as an invitation to a "black tide." He concluded his diatribe with his conviction that the Negro race was a "discordant element" in the United States and that its social sphere was in "the boundless wastes of its native land [Africa]."[31]

Amid this adverse trend, three delegates rose to restrict exclusion to former slaves or to strike the proposal altogether. William Shannon (Whig), Kimball Dimmick (Whig), and Edward Gilbert (Democrat) argued that, given the cost of the passage to California, very few Negroes could afford to come. They further explained their opposition to McCarver's measure on the grounds of principle, consistency, and expediency. Shannon asserted that "free men of color have just as good a right . . . to emigrate here as white men." Dimmick exposed the inconsistency of proclaiming the extension of the privileges of free institutions to all classes in the Bill of Rights and then, in another section, debarring one class of people from entering the state. Gilbert rebuked his colleagues for proposing to exclude individuals, "simply because [they are] black." If the California Constitution bore the stigma of Negro exclusion, he warned, it would be rejected by Congress. As he closed his rebuttal, however, Gilbert exposed the abstract nature of his commitment to egalitarianism. His feelings against Negroes were strong, he confessed, for his whole education had tended to make them repugnant to him. To achieve statehood, however, prejudices had to be set aside. Notwithstanding their call for a "free" and "liberal" constitution, these three delegates were not racial egalitarians. Hence, while they welcomed "Negro citizens" from the northern states, they opposed the introduction of blacks who had previously been slaves. The admission of such citizens, they explained, was a matter of not humanitarian rights but "expediency."[32]

The argument about the unconstitutionality of the measure caused many delegates to think that exclusion could better be accomplished by law after statehood.[33] As the debate over the second reading of the exclusion clause proceeded, opponents made it plain that their motivation was their eagerness for statehood ratification, not racial equality.[34] After reconsideration, the exclusion clause, which had first been adopted, was removed by a vote of 31 to 8.[35]

After the state convention adjourned, the first state assembly moved to prohibit the entry of African Americans. The motion was buttressed by the opening address to the legislature of Democratic governor Peter H. Burnett on December 21, 1849. Confident that California could reach perfection as a great white community, Burnett warned that, unless the legislature excluded free blacks, the state would be swamped with "swarms of this population to our shores." He assured the legislators of the constitutionality of an exclusion provision because blacks were not granted equal status by the U.S. and California constitutions. He went on to ask for consistency. Because blacks were denied social and civil equality, it was better to exclude them than force them to live in a degraded position.[36] Spurred by this speech, the state assembly passed a bill barring the migration of free blacks into California. In the Senate, though, the bill met some opposition. While a few senators deplored the prejudices of Governor Burnett and other advocates of exclusion, the majority of the opponents to the bill argued that legislation was unnecessary because African Americans would not migrate in large numbers. The bill was ultimately rejected by a single vote, 13 to 12.[37]

Racial inequality was, however, displayed in a host of restrictive measures. The state constitution excluded blacks from the privileges of state citizenship by reserving the right to vote to "white male citizens." The first legislature passed anti-black measures similar to those of some other free states. Black testimony in court was disallowed by a criminal statute in 1850.[38] One year later, African Americans were prohibited from testifying in civil cases.[39] In 1850, an act banned all marriages between whites and Negroes or Mulattos.[40] The following year, blacks were denied the right to homestead on public land, and black children were excluded from public schools.[41] All in all, African Americans in California had to cope with the same infringements that they had known in many of the free states east of the Rockies. California had drawn a familiar racial fault line, the ideological residue of which was equating "Californian" with "white."

The unprecedented diversity in California, however, was to put a distinctive strain on intergroup relations. With the exception of Native Americans, the population of California before the gold rush was very small: about 15,000, including 7,000 Californios, 6,000 Americans from the United States, and 2,000 foreigners.[42] The discovery of gold in January 1848 stimulated a massive immigration. The census figures for 1850 indicate that the foreign-born population of the state numbered 21,802 and the American-born 70,795. In the 1850s, immigration increased, but migration from other parts of the United States remained the major source of growth of the state's population. Out of 379,994 residents in California in 1860, 61.44 percent (233,466 residents) were native-born, while 38.56 percent (146,528) were foreign-born. While the national ratio for 1860 was 86.83 percent native-born to 13.16 percent foreign-born, many states and territories other than California had a comparatively high proportion of alien residents—for example, 25.8 percent and 35.69 percent in New York and Wisconsin, respectively, and 30.10 percent and 31.66 percent in the territories of Nevada and Utah.[43] More significant than the size of California's immigrant population was its diversity. In 1850, aliens in California were mostly Europeans, including 3,050 English, 2,452 Irish, 2,926 Germans, 1,546 French, and over 2,540 from other states and principalities in Europe. Numerically though, Mexicans (6,454) surpassed all other national groups. Of the remaining population, the census listed 660 Chinese and 2,100 immigrants from various locales in Latin America, Asia, the Pacific Islands, and Africa.[44] Notwithstanding this heterogeneity, there was a common line in the stories of all newcomers to California, be they American or foreign-born. They were all voluntary and transient migrants, drawn to California by the lure of gold. They saw their stay in California as a sojourn rather than a permanent relocation. They were intent on achieving one goal only—strike it rich and return home to resume their former lives, wealthier than before.

This "mercenary" purpose soon stimulated a debate over the desirability of permitting foreign prospectors to carry away the treasure of California. Very early, a sense of proprietary claim was expressed by prominent American public figures. In 1849, for example, General Persifor Smith, who assumed charge of the military forces in California, issued a circular to all American consuls in Pacific ports declaring that he would exclude from the mines as "trespassers" all those who were not citizens of the United States. This measure was in violation of not only congressional policy regarding free immigration and the right of foreigners to mine but also the judicial decision in the *Passenger Cases* delivered three weeks before Smith's circular.[45] It was therefore not carried out. Smith's and other officials' efforts to exclude or restrict foreigners, however, served to foster violence against foreigners in the mining fields. By the winter of 1849, American miners were not only drawing up proclamations demanding the withdrawal of aliens from the mines but also organizing raids on foreign camps.

These practices went on despite the stipulation in the state constitution that "[f]oreigners who are, or may hereafter become *bona fide* citizens of this State, shall enjoy the same rights . . . as native born citizens."[46] There was, however, no liberal motive behind this incorporation of foreigners within California social and political structures. Aware of the limit of their prerogatives so far as aliens were concerned, the drafters of the constitution had confined their discussion about migration to the issue of the admissibility of African Americans. Interestingly, this debate shed light on the expedient nature of the inclusion of foreigners. In the course of their argumentation against the exclusion of blacks, Dimmick and Gilbert denounced the inconsistency of the delegates' anti-black position and their hands-off policy toward foreigners. Asking the delegates to consider "the miserable natives" from the Islands of the Pacific and "the refuse of population from Chili, Peru, [and] Mexico," Gilbert wondered why the delegates had not inserted a provision preventing them from "polluting the soil of California." These immigrants were, in his opinion, "as bad as any of the free negroes of the North, or the worst slaves of the South."[47] No delegate raised his voice to defend the character of foreigners. The delegates did not take any action against foreigners, however, because they believed that this was a legislative rather than a constitutional matter.

When the first state assembly gathered in December 1849, it moved to prohibit the entry of not only African Americans but also foreigners. Of the two waves, however, foreign immigration was considered the more urgent matter. American miners had petitioned the state legislature for relief, expressing their frustrations with alien miners (over 20,000) rather than African Americans, who constituted fewer than 1 percent of the total population in California. In March 1850, state senator Thomas J. Green (Democrat) responded by recommending the passage of a bill that would impose a monthly tax on foreigners for the privilege of working the mines.[48] Meanwhile, state representative George B. Tingley (Whig) submitted a report on the effect of immigration. In very strong terms, he called for the exclusion of all immigrants from California, finding them vicious, indolent, dishonest, and degraded.[49] Foreign miners were no longer simply "trespassers"; they also represented a social, political, and cultural threat. In response to Tingley's report, the legislature attempted to pass a law for the eviction of all foreigners from the placers. When informed that such a course of action was one for the national government alone to handle, the legislature enacted Green's bill, requiring foreign miners to pay a monthly tax of twenty dollars.[50]

At first glance, the use of the generic term *foreign* in the foreign miners' license tax and in the resolutions of American miners seems to indicate that nativism in California during the gold rush was an expression of indiscriminate xenophobia. Evidence of prejudice can be found regarding all foreign groups. All were subjected to acts of violence and were, in theory, included in the category "foreign" in the mining legislation. There were, however, dissimilarities in the early experiences of immigrant groups in California. American miners and officials generally objected to specific groups: Latin Americans and Pacific Islanders.[51] Evidence of the selectiveness of anti-foreign hostility can also be found in the foreign miners' tax, which was levied against all foreigners but was vigorously enforced against only some groups. While the report from the state comptroller does not give the nationality of the miners from whom the tax was collected, the reportage on the violence in the mining districts following the attempt to collect the tax sheds some light on the victimization of specific groups. Most accounts reveal the concentration of violence in the southern mines, where the foreign population was made up largely of Latin Americans. Nothing much is said about the collection of the tax in the northern counties, where foreigners were more scattered and mainly from Europe.[52]

American enmity toward foreigners was discriminating. Coexisting with the nativism that originated in the avaricious thirst of white Americans for "their" gold was another form of xenophobia, whose distinctiveness was reflected in the differential treatment of foreigners. Nonwhite foreigners were more liable to be opposed. While there were individual attacks on white alien miners, mob attacks on them were rare. Moreover, white foreigners were all gradually incorporated within the white American group.[53]

While the antagonism between white Americans and white immigrants subsided, hostility toward Hispanic Americans increased. From the earliest interaction, American officials and miners had deemed the presence of Latin Americans objectionable. The ethnic and racial diversity in California prior to U.S. occupation had called for a revision of American racial formation. To ease the annexation of northern Mexico, the American government set terms that were acceptable to the Mexican government, notably the incorporation of the Mexican population. Articles 8 and 9 of the Treaty of Guadalupe Hidalgo provided that the Mexican citizens who elected to remain in the American Southwest and chose not to retain their original allegiance to Mexico were automatically granted the title and rights of citizens of the United States. The treaty virtually incapacitated the Hispanophobic delegates at the California constitutional convention in 1849. They accordingly moved to grant Mexicans citizenship rights. The issue of the applicability of the provision, however, precipitated a heated debate. In the initial proposition, citizenship rights were given to "every male citizen of Mexico" who elected to become a U.S. citizen under the treaty. An amendment was offered by a delegate who argued that one very important word—*white*—had been omitted. Alluding to the racial prerequisite for citizenship imposed on all other applicants, he asked that Mexicans be placed on the same footing with all others. This amendment was censured by a prominent Californio, Noriega de la Guerra, who stated that many dark-skinned Californios would be deprived of citizenship merely because of their color. He was assured, however, that the word would serve to exclude only "the inferior races of mankind"—the African and Indian races.[54] The amendment was adopted, and the final article provided for the enfranchisement of "[every] white male citizen of the United States, and every white male citizen of Mexico."[55]

This legal "whitening" of the Californios did not change the popular and collective image of Mexican Americans as "nonwhite" and inferior.[56] Furthermore, this redefinition applied only to Mexicans residing in the annexed territories prior to their acquisition. Mexicans and other Latin American immigrants did not benefit from this incorporation. American miners refused to distinguish between Spanish-speaking Americans and Latin American immigrants, all of whom they regarded as "interlopers" or "peons"—that is, quasi-slaves. The racialization of all Hispanics proved to be resistant to the legal construction of Californios' whiteness. The philosopher Josiah Royce's assessment of American-Mexican relations in nineteenth-century California confirms that the inclusion of Americans of Mexican ancestry in the white category did not reflect a decline in race prejudice. Considering American aggressiveness toward Latin Americans a "disgrace," he described the situation in these cynical terms: "the life of a Spanish American in the mines in the early days . . . was apt to be a little disagreeable. It served him right, of course. He had no business, as an alien, to come to the land that God has given us. And if he was a native Californian, a born 'greaser' then so much the worse for him. He was so much the more our born foe; we hated his whole degenerate, thieving, landowning, lazy, and discontented race." A "Greaser," Royce added, would be convicted on very moderate evidence, because one could see guilt plainly written "in his ugly swarthy face, before the trial began."[57] This indiscriminate hostility toward all Spanish-speaking Americans suggests a racial rather than a simple economic motive.

Before Chinese immigrants arrived in California in great numbers, the special targeting of African Americans and Latin Americans for discrimination amounted to an attempt to make whiteness the test of access to the mines and to California at large.

2. The Beginning of the Negroization of the Chinese in California, 1850–53

[The Chinese] are amongst the most industrious, quiet, patient
people among us. . . . [They] seem to live under our laws as if born
and bred under them, and already have commenced an expression
of their preference by applying for citizenship. . . . Hats and other
American garments succeed and soon the chief distinction consists
in the copper color, the narrow angular eyes, the peculiar gibberish
and beardless faces.

—*Daily Alta California*, May 12, 1851

BY THE END OF 1849, only a few hundred Chinese had come to seek their
fortune in California. In 1851, however, the outbreak of the Taiping Rebellion
against the Manchu dynasty plunged China into fifteen years of civil war and
social unrest. This rebellion originated in the economic depression that had
been plaguing China since the 1839–42 Opium Wars with Britain. Forced to
pay large indemnities to the Western imperialist powers engaged in these wars,
the Qing government had imposed heavy taxes on the peasants. Unable to pay,
most of them had lost their land and migrated to the coastal provinces of
Guangdong (Kwangtung) and Fujian (Fukien). This situation was aggravated by a series of natural disasters that caused food shortages. Emigration became an important safety valve for the growing and impoverished population along the coast. Paralleling these push factors, rumors of easy wealth in
California caused a movement of Chinese emigrants from the Guangdong area
to the "Golden Mountains," their name for California. Other destinations for
Chinese emigrants were the West Indies and Latin America.

In the nineteenth century, there were two categories of Chinese emigrants:
free emigrants and contract laborers. Contract laborers formed the more
important part of Chinese emigration. The contract labor system was very
early dubbed "cooly [coolie] trade" by the European participants in it. The
term *cooly* originates in an ancient Urdu-Hindustani word meaning "hire"
or "hireling." Prior to its use in China, the term had designated an unskilled

laborer in India. The coolie trade started as a means to contract for and send Bengalese and other East Indian indentured servants to various parts of the British colonial empire.[1] In China, where the word *coolie* assumed the meaning of "bitter strength," the trade began in the late 1840s with the shipment of Chinese laborers under contract with foreigners to the West Indies and Peru.[2] In the early 1850s, British and American official documents began to expose the atrocities of the Chinese coolie trade: the recruitment under coercion and fraud, the detention in barracoons (called "pigpens"), the horrors of the transoceanic passage, and the extreme exploitation in the country of destination. The coolie trade was particularly harsh in Cuba and Peru, where, through the mid-1870s, only one coolie in ten survived the perils of the voyage and the abuses of employment and returned home.[3] The enormities of the trade were such that some American officials likened it to slavery. This, however, did not prevent American and British vessels from participating in this lucrative trade, carrying coolies to various destinations in the West Indies and Latin America, until the British and American governments legislated against the trade in 1855 and 1862, respectively.

Chinese immigrants to California were *not* coolies but free emigrants under the credit-ticket system.[4] Although this system was technically a form of contract, it differed from the contract/coolie labor system because it did not involve coercion and because emigrants entering such contracts were required to work for their creditors only until their debt (two hundred dollars) had been refunded. Thereafter, they were free to go where they wanted and work for whom they desired.[5] Chinese immigration to California was thus a speculative operation by moneyed parties. In that sense, the Chinese were not much different from other Argonauts. In California during the gold rush, both foreign and American miners were digging gold under contracts with parties who contacted them while they were still at home.[6] Like most miners, the Chinese were young men intent on acquiring a fortune and returning home to enjoy it with their families. Like other miners, they soon organized benevolent institutions and mutual aid societies.[7] Most Chinese immigrants came from the Kwangtung area, a region divided into several well-demarcated districts. When they arrived in California, they were asked to join the district association that was an extension of the one at home. The main functions of the associations were to assist newcomers, arbitrate disputes between members, collect debts owed by immigrants to creditors at home, and help in dealing with American authorities. By the 1860s, the several district associations organized a coordinating council, popularly known as the Chinese Six Companies.[8]

Soon after the Chinese appeared on the California scene in 1848, they were initiated into the reality of white supremacy and its corollary, the dual or split labor market. Faced with prejudice and discrimination, many African Americans in California had turned to menial trades that were not coveted by white laborers and to which whites referred as "nigger work," such as cooking, laundering, and unskilled labor.[9] So long as they opted for such occupations, they were safe from harassment. In 1850, when their number was still small, the Chinese followed the pattern of African Americans' economic adjustment. They concentrated in the lower-paid activities that did not lead to conflict with white laborers. By doing so, they became essential to the comfort of white laborers, and it was not uncommon to read positive reportage on them. When the Chinese ventured into mining activities, though, they faced the same opposition as other nonwhite miners.

In an address to the California legislature on January 7, 1852, Governor John McDougal (Democrat) described the Chinese as "one of the most worthy classes of our newly adopted citizens," and he recommended a system of land grants to encourage their immigration.[10] McDougal's call for Chinese immigrants was, however, based on the understanding that they would settle in the flooded lands of the San Joaquin Valley. While he anticipated the successful reclaiming of these inhospitable districts by the Chinese, he did not allude to their potential employment in the more profitable mining and urban occupations. McDougal's choice of Chinese rather than European immigrants for that hard work indicates his belief in the inferior status of nonwhite labor.

Labor was scarce in California during the gold rush, and contract labor was used as a means to stimulate migration. In the early 1850s, however, the contract labor system outside of mining proved to be a failure. The temptation of the mines was so great that inducing workers to stay in regular employment was almost impossible. Where labor could be secured, moreover, it demanded very high wages. Besides the magnetism of the mines, the impossibility of coercion and the ease with which all labor contracts could be set aside were two other causes for the failure of contract labor in nonmining fields in California.[11] What California needed was a form of contract labor that would be vulnerable to quasi-coercive measures. Of course, Chinese laborers in California could not be degraded into servitude. One facet of their incorporation, however, could parallel that of slaves: they could be deemed "outsiders." Set apart from the rest of the community, in law and in practice, they could be treated differently from all white laborers, native and foreign-born. This choice of Chinese rather than European immigrants recalls yet another choice—that of blacks over white indentured servants for indeterminate bondage. In both cases, white ethnocentrism was a critical factor.

Another important aspect of Governor McDougal's proposition was his selection of Chinese rather than African Americans, Californians of Mexican ancestry, or Latin Americans from neighboring countries.[12] The Treaty of Guadalupe Hidalgo had incorporated Californios as equals. They could therefore not be—at least, not openly—regarded as "outsiders" in the sense described above. Unlike Mexican Americans, Latin American groups could be subjected to discriminatory measures with impunity. From their early interaction with white Americans, however, it was clear that American settlers and officials were not eager to encourage the immigration of Latin Americans. Obviously, such immigration would have resulted in the increase of the population of Hispanic origin, threatening Anglo dominance. Chinese immigrants were also preferable to black Americans. During the California constitutional convention in 1849, McDougal had revealed a strong animosity toward slaves and free blacks.[13] Two years later, his refusal to incorporate African Americans in a pool of manual labor indicated his persistent aversion to any policy that would increase their numerical strength in the state.

On March 6, 1852, two months after McDougal advised the legislature to turn to China to solve the state's labor shortage, Senator George B. Tingley (Whig/Free Soil Democrat) introduced a bill to enforce in California long-term (up to ten years), fixed-wage, labor contracts made in China between Chinese laborers and Chinese capitalists.[14] Tingley had been a staunch exclusionist in the first assembly, calling for the exclusion of all foreigners.[15] In 1852, his bill reflected the essential role of nonwhite laborers in the economic structure, doing what whites would not do. For the business class and its representatives in the legislature, the enforcement of Tingley's labor contracts was the perfect plan. Chinese contract laborers could constitute a pool of cheap labor, the presence of which would be strictly regulated by American authorities. Above all, labor contracts would guarantee the transitory nature of Chinese immigration.

Originally designed to solve the labor problem in the state, the bill provoked a fierce reaction among white Californians. The mining regions were shaken by a series of forceful evictions of Chinese miners, and the bill was condemned at meetings in urban and mining districts. The Tingley bill and the overwhelming opposition to it are very important. Until then, the currents of feelings expressed by American miners and their elected officials had fed on one another and stimulated a strong animosity toward foreign, especially nonwhite, miners. However, the bill was not so much a challenge to the prevailing negative views about these miners as it was an attempt by the ruling classes to renegotiate the admissibility of one specific group (the Chinese) and its role in California. Central to this development was Tingley's proposal for a narrow policy of exploiting the Chinese.

A bipartisan select committee reported favorably on Tingley's bill. However, a minority report by the only dissenter in the select committee, Senator Philip A. Roach, gave expression to latent Sinophobic feelings. In 1846, President James K. Polk had appointed Roach U.S. consul to Portugal. Three years later, Roach headed for California, where he became a prominent citizen, occupying several official positions, including state senator. In 1867, he would become the editor of the Democratic organ, the *Examiner,* and six years later, after his reelection to the state senate, he would be sent to Washington to secure anti-Chinese legislation. On March 20, 1852, a younger Roach declared that the chief hope for California's progress—free labor—would be dashed by Chinese contract laborers. He expounded on the theme of unfair economic competition by stigmatizing Chinese labor as cheap because it possessed a low standard of living. The Tingley bill, he argued, was a law by which the surplus and inferior population of Asia would be brought into competition with American labor. Roach used the phrases "Chinese contract labor" and "Chinese labor" interchangeably. In his report, the differences between Chinese and European-American labor were self-evident: Chinese labor was unfree and inferior; European-American labor was free and superior. By setting the Chinese apart from white foreign laborers, Roach replayed the script of an older drama, involving the dichotomy between free white labor and unfree black labor.

Despite his prejudices, Roach recognized the urgent need for cheap labor in certain enterprises, such as draining swamps, cultivating rice, and planting sugar, cotton, and tobacco. He had no objections to the introduction of Chinese laborers in these occupations. Obviously, his adverse reaction to the Tingley bill did not stem from a principled opposition to contract labor. Roach went on to recommend that the Chinese be excluded from all "honorable" branches of activities because they should remain the preserve of American mechanics. Adverting to the dangers of amalgamation and Chinese pagan beliefs, he insisted that admission as contract laborers should not entitle Chinese immigrants to the privileges of citizenship.[16] Roach certainly hoped that the exclusion of the Chinese from citizenship would fix their social position as inferior to whites and would make them unable to negotiate better working conditions.

Despite the committee's favorable majority opinion, the Tingley scheme was laid to rest under an indefinite postponement, which was eventually accepted by an overwhelming majority of the assembly.[17] Neither the miners nor the legislature would let go of the issue, however. One month later, the Assembly Committee on Mines and Mining Interests called the legislature's attention to the concentration of vast numbers of members of "Asiatic races," denouncing them as "a preeminent evil threatening the well-being of the mining districts."[18] As servile labor imported by foreign capitalists, the Chinese not only demeaned American labor but also deterred the migration of white Americans and Europeans. Furthermore, the committee pointed out that the cultural incompatibility of the Chinese was such that absolute prohibition would soon be necessary. At this moment, though, the committee asked the legislature to enact a new foreign miners' license law that would exempt foreigners who would declare their intention of becoming American citizens.[19]

Beneath this proposition to extend complimentary mining rights to non-Americans was a tacit exclusive trend. Given the strong bias against the Chinese in the report, the committee obviously wished to make the license law bear more heavily, if not exclusively, on them. This is apparent in the use of "intended naturalization" as a factor for exemption. When set against the backdrop of federal and state naturalization rulings, it is doubtful whether all foreigners could have availed themselves of their right to be exempted by expressing, sincerely or not, their intention to become American. In 1852, when the Chinese became the target of Californian nativism, their eligibility or disqualification for citizenship had not yet been the subject of a judicial decision.[20] However, some Californians believed that they were ineligible for citizenship under federal and state laws. This opinion was based on the racial requisite for naturalized citizenship in the Naturalization Act of 1790 and a similar criterion for suffrage in the California Constitution. While the California Constitution granted suffrage to "white males," the main qualification for U.S. naturalization was that the alien be a "free white person." In the spring of 1850, white miners in Tuolumne County decreed that only Americans and Europeans who intended to become citizens be allowed to mine in the district.[21] Not all Californians were convinced that the Chinese were ineligible for citizenship. Some senators, for example, supported Senator Roach's recommendation that the Chinese be expressly prohibited from becoming citizens.[22]

The assembly report was followed by a special message from Democratic governor John Bigler. Stirred by a feeling of "urgency," Bigler called for immediate and extraordinary measures to check the "tide of Asiatic immigration." He reported the widely held belief that the "Chinese coolies" were bound to long contracts of servitude at nominal wages, while their families were retained as hostages in China. In addition to being transient partakers of California's gold, the Chinese had "the vices of all ages." In this message, the notion that the unrestricted immigration of "Chinese coolies" would lead to the submergence of American civilization found its first official expression. California's only recourse, as Bigler saw it, was to stop immigration from China. Considering possible constitutional objections, he held that states had the right to prevent the entry of dangerous classes. As to California Chinese residents, he urged the legislature to ask Congress to pass an act prohibiting "coolies" from laboring in the mines. In the meantime, legislators should set up a taxation program that would fall exclusively on the Chinese.[23] This could be considered the earliest articulation of the 1870s Sand Lot agitators' notorious battle cry "The Chinese Must Go."

Bigler's message was symptomatic of a growing public sensitivity to immigration. Although Chinese immigration had been low prior to 1851, it suddenly increased in 1852. The figures of Chinese arrivals in San Francisco for 1848, 1849, 1850, and 1851 are, respectively, 3, 325, 450, and 2,716. The figure for 1852 soared to 20,026.[24] On March 5, 1852, one day before the Tingley bill was introduced into the legislature, the *Daily Alta California* stated, "The character of the immigration daily pouring on to our shores is a subject in which every good citizen feels a deep and intense interest." During the controversy over the Tingley bill in and out of the legislative chambers, newspapers kept the public constantly informed about the influx of Chinese migrants. Three days after Bigler delivered his message, the *Alta* announced that "in one day, two ships from Hong Kong had brought an addition of 525 to our already large Chinese population." On May 4, 1852, the *Alta* concluded that there was strong public sentiment against admitting Chinese laborers into the country.

Official anti-Chinese statements played a major role in legitimizing violence in the mining districts. Some American miners were satisfied that their decision to bar "the Chinks" from their mines was generally endorsed by their representatives. The "heathen" Chinese, they declared, were "getting to be altogether too plentiful in the country." "If not molested," they added, "they would soon overrun the country." The Chinese were also becoming impudent, taking up claims and appropriating water "without asking leave." The Chinese assumption that they were entitled to the same privileges as whites was particularly objectionable to white miners. As a forty-niner bluntly put it, the Chinese were not looked upon as human beings. Some American miners were, however, willing to put aside their prejudices or indignation at "uppity Chinese" for economic reasons. They would allow the Chinese to mine worked ground, provided they purchased it at a high price from a white owner. Despite their titles to the ground, however, the Chinese were sometimes chased off their claims under penalty of being shot.[25]

This powerful fund of Sinophobic attitudes prompted a swift response in the state legislature. On May 4, 1852, the legislators enacted two measures. The first was a new foreign miners' license tax.[26] The 1850 exorbitant tax (twenty

dollars) had resulted in a massive exodus of Latin American miners and subsequent losses in profits for businesses and local authorities.[27] The legislators
reduced the license fee to three dollars per month, hoping that it would encourage the Chinese to stay and contribute to the revenue of the local and
state treasuries. An important feature of the new measure was that it required
a foreign miner to have a license to prosecute or defend any action in a California court. While the law was dubbed *An Act for the Protection of Foreigners,* it actually reinforced some of the conditions that had led to abuses. From
the start, the enforcement of the foreign miners' tax law had been conducive
to sporadic fraud and violence by some official collectors, who extorted
money from miners holding licenses under the pretext that they were forged,
and by men masquerading as collectors. Not infrequently, acts of resistance
were crushed by violence. The new measure then deprived foreign miners
who had been victimized by lawless elements of their civil rights. The license
law was compounded by a stringent immigration act, providing for a "commutation tax."[28] The act required vessel owners arriving at California to report all foreign passengers on board and allowed the mayor of San Francisco
to obtain a bond of five hundred dollars from every master of a vessel for
every alien landed in California. This was to indemnify the city from any
expense incurred for passengers. The bond could be commuted by the payment of five dollars per passenger. The act was, in practice, a tax imposed on
the passengers, because the vessel owners simply added a five dollar fee to
the price of the passage. While there was no direct mention of the Chinese
in the act, the Chinese contributed a disproportionate share of the commutation tax levied at the port of San Francisco.[29]

This legislation marks a turning point in the early interaction between
white Californians and Chinese immigrants. From the moment Tingley introduced his bill, events raised the presence of the Chinese to a statewide issue that transcended the question of mining privileges and rights. In this first
debate on the Chinese question, mining and immigrating in California became more explicitly than ever the right of people of European descent. The
alarmist picture of California being flooded by "Asiatic contract laborers"
helped form a collective image of the Chinese as thoroughly incompatible
with Euro-American free society. Like Africans and Latin Americans, whatever their number, the Chinese simply by their presence constituted a problem. Anti-Chinese officials were only partially motivated by economics. They
were, in fact, willing to use Chinese laborers, provided they were formally
excluded from the mines and denied most of the rights of white immigrants.
This readiness to exploit Chinese labor demonstrates that they opposed not
contract labor per se but the social implications of the Chinese presence.

Their prejudices are obvious in their call for Chinese exclusion and the deportation of the Chinese already in California.

The fear of a tide of Chinese immigrants was an important theme in the racialization of the Chinese question. This fear had, of course, a significant precedent in the fear of a "black tide." In both cases, white American hostility was sustained by the perception of black migration and Chinese immigration as illegitimate intrusions. As a group of American miners put it before they attempted to expel a company of miners that included one Chinese and a few African Americans, they had previously declared that "coloured men were not privileged to work in a country intended only for American citizens."[30] Or, as a forty-niner stated in 1852, Americans were confident that the Chinese had "no rights that a white man [was] bound to respect."[31]

The conflation of African Americans and Chinese immigrants is apparent not only in Tingley's proposal to use the Chinese as contract laborers but also in the opposition to his bill. The characterization of Chinese labor as essentially "unfree" and "contract labor" was not random. It can be traced to the free labor ideology, which had been used to dichotomize "unfree black labor" and "free white labor" and to justify discriminatory measures against blacks. In California, one tenet of this ideology, the inferior status of nonwhite labor and people, prompted Tingley to regard the Chinese as a work force particularly fit for the menial jobs essential to economic prosperity. The violent reaction to his bill makes sense when it is set against the backdrop of antagonistic feelings toward black mobility and labor. The words used by opponents of Chinese laborers were the same words used by midwesterners opposing black migration. When legislators referred to the condition of depravity of Chinese labor, they were repeating anti-black rhetoric. In their diatribes, the freighted hallmark of black labor as "inherently unfree and degraded" was simply shuttled over to the Chinese. Like black labor, Chinese labor was allegedly liable to supplant white labor, not because of its superiority but because of its inferiority. Last but not least, the legislators racialized the Chinese issue unequivocally when they presented their anti-Chinese legislation as an effort to avert the anticipated hazard of a mixed population—that is, the political, social, and economic ruin of California.

This Negroization of Chinese immigrants was denounced as early as May 1852 by Norman Asing (also As-sing), a San Francisco resident of Chinese origin. An 1849 arrival, Asing had become a prosperous merchant and restaurateur and a spokesperson for Chinese immigrants. In an open letter to Governor Bigler, Asing began by observing that Americans had degraded Negroes, holding them in involuntary servitude. Now, it seemed that they wished to place the Chinese in a similar subordinate position. While Chinese people happened "to have been a little more tan" than Americans, Asing noted, the Chinese might compare with many of the European races.[32]

In the minds of California legislators, however, the Chinese and Negro questions were closely connected. In addition to enacting a foreign miners' license tax and the commutation tax aimed at the Chinese, California legislators showed their concern for black migration from the East. Compared with the increase of Chinese immigrants, that of black migrants was negligible. The African American resident population rose from 962 in 1850 (including Latin American blacks and Kanakas) to 2,206 in 1852.[33] Blacks constituted only 1 percent of the state population, yet their presence was considered an imposition. The legislators were aware that most black residents were slaves or former slaves who had won, legally or not, their freedom in California. The problem was thus not so much excluding free black migrants as it was regulating slavery in the state. The first action of the legislature in April 1852 was to enact a fugitive slave law.[34] The law provided that Negroes who had been brought to the state as slaves and those who had escaped in California prior to its admission into the Union could be reclaimed by their masters as fugitives. Not only could slaveholders continue to bring their slaves into California, work them, and later return them to the South, but they were even allowed to sell them if they could not afford the expense of their return passage.

To a large extent, the law was intended to restrict the black population. This was made explicit two months later in a California Supreme Court opinion concerning a case involving the reclaiming of three free blacks by their former master—*In the Matter of Carter Perkins and Robert Perkins*. Sustaining the constitutionality of the California fugitive slave law, the court declared that it shared Californians' concern about the increase in the number of fugitive slaves and free Negroes, "in view of the pernicious consequences, necessarily resulting from this class of inhabitants." The court had no doubt that the desire to purge California of these "festering sores upon the body politic" entered into the legislature's passing the fugitive slave act.[35] When the defendants were remanded to their former master, African Americans in California realized that, under the law, even free blacks were at the mercy of fraudulent charges. Discouraged, some migrated to Canada, Mexico, or Central America during the three years that the law was in effect. The majority, however, remained and organized a protest movement, whose primary goal was to obtain suffrage rights and the right to present testimony in court. They presented the first of a number of petitions to the state assembly demanding the right to testify. The assembly refused to receive it for fear of "tarnishing" its *Journal* with such an "infamous document."[36] The state legislature then turned its attention to migration. A harsh Democratic bill providing for the prohibition of black migration and the forced deportation of black residents from California did not pass, however. It suffered the same fate as the earlier exclusion bills. It was delayed and was still in the legislature when it adjourned.[37]

Partly because of the hostile mining legislation and partly because of the discovery of gold in Australia, Chinese immigration to California decreased dramatically from 20,026 in 1852 to 4,270 in 1853. That same year, the return migration figure was 4,421. Nevertheless, anti-Chinese agitation in the mines continued unabated, and several anti-Chinese bills were introduced in the legislature. One of the bills stated that "[n]o Asiatic, or person of Asiatic descent" could work in the mines. Another bill providing for the increase of the mining license tax emphasized that nothing in the act should be construed as securing foreign miners, "who from their color, nature, and education can never become citizens of the United States, against the liability of being ousted from any mining claim by citizen miners of this state."[38] Most members of the Committee on Mines and Mining Interests to which the bills were referred took exception to these harsh bills. Rejecting the apprehension about a Chinese invasion as completely groundless, its majority report hinted that the miners' tax was a major source of revenue for the state. Pointing to the ruinous effect that a prohibitive license fee would have on the state economy, the committee urged only a one dollar increase.[39] Accordingly, the state legislature enacted a new law providing for the suggested increase and a second act authorizing the translation of the act into Chinese.[40]

The Chinese were not oblivious to the nature of Sinophobic feelings in California. In 1853, the heads of the Chinese district associations in San Francisco contacted the Assembly Committee on Mines and Mining Interests to apprise it of their point of view. While they did not object to the foreign miners' tax, they deplored that the state often withheld the protection implied in the payment of taxes. They offered compelling evidence that, in numerous instances of violent attacks on Chinese by white miners, the local courts had not accepted the testimony of Chinese witnesses because of the color of their skin. While they criticized the harassment of their compatriots, the Chinese leaders were careful not to question the American racial arrangement. In an attempt to discontinue the association of the Chinese with African Americans, they stressed that, in the eyes of the law, the Chinese were foreigners. As such, they should be subject to the same laws as other aliens and granted equal privileges and protection.[41]

Meanwhile, some groups were voicing their concern that attacks on the Chinese were endangering the state economy and destroying the hope of ever getting a large portion of the Chinese and East Indian trade. Meetings were held in San Francisco, which invariably ended with a set of resolutions ex-

posing the economic motivations of their authors. In January 1853, for example, Henry H. Haight (who would become governor of California in 1867
and a vocal Sinophobe) resolved "[t]hat we regard with pleasure the presence of great numbers of [Chinese immigrants] among us, as affording the
best opportunity of doing them good, and through them of exerting our
influence upon their native land."[42]

More important than these resolutions, though, were the lectures delivered during these meetings by the Reverend William Speer, a staunch advocate of Chinese interests.[43] A returned missionary from China, Speer was the
state's most prominent Presbyterian minister and missionary from 1852 to
1857.[44] In his lectures, Speer generally presented the practical advantages of
Chinese immigration in California. Pointing to the labor shortage in the
western region, he reminded his audiences that the toiling millions of Europe, who had helped build the eastern states' economy, were barred from
California by natural obstacles. Providence had thus sent these "Asiatic
multitudes," to build California's railroads, dig its canals, tunnel its mountains, and construct its houses, churches, and prisons. Although Speer contemplated a range of activities for the Chinese, as servants, agriculturalists,
mechanics, fishers, and miners, he insisted they would always be "sub-work-
ers," laboriously reaping, under American supervision, the golden harvest
gathered by American citizens. Insofar as mining was concerned, racial animosity stemmed from Chinese diligence in accumulating gold. To settle the
problem, Speer suggested that the Chinese occupy only the poorer diggings.[45]

Chinese labor offered more than the opportunity to solve the labor shortage in California. It also had, in Speer's opinion, the potential of solving the
Negro problem. He predicted that millions of Chinese servants would one day
supersede the use of Negroes throughout the country. Viewing Chinese immigration as a fortunate compensation for the impending settlement of American blacks in Africa, he envisaged a prosperous future for the American South
as a result of Chinese labor. Transcending the economic argument, he developed an early version of the "White Man's Burden" theme. The Chinese were
a heathen people, trembling "with a thousand horrible or absurd fears and
superstitions." Like the "Sons of Ham" before their coming to America, the
"Sons of Han" were spiritually and intellectually degraded beings. Carried
away by missionary zeal, Speer concluded that "[God] has selected us to be
the agents of the regeneration of the two dark continents of heathenism. He
sends three millions of the ignorant sable sons and daughters of the one to
be schooled here, and in due time to be returned to their torrid clime. . . . As
this race approaches the completion of its education the opposite door is
opened. [The Oriental race] . . . is brought to seek of us the same boon."[46]

Speer's lectures had the effect of signifying the Chinese as closer to African Americans than to European immigrants. While the Chinese community leaders had striven to approach the Chinese question as an immigration issue, not a racial one, Speer's vision of a Chinese labor pool performing the "drudgery of life" in an America free of African Americans seemed to conjure up the grafting of a new and problematic racial presence.

3. "The Copper of the Pacific" and "The Ebony of the Atlantic": Race Relations, 1854–60

Our people want none but the white race among us; we do not want Negroes or Chinese.
—Senator William M. Gwin, *Congressional Globe*, May 18, 1858

ADVOCATES OF Chinese immigration were soon the target of attacks from the main organs in San Francisco, notably the *Daily Alta California*. A majority of the California assembly, the paper stated in 1853, had decided that the interests of American miners were subservient to those of commerce. American laborers, however, would not always tolerate the "motley mass of beings," with whom they had nothing in common, that capital had forced upon them. They would eventually drive the Chinese from the mines and their supporters from the legislature.[1] Although the *Alta* had praised the Chinese as "industrious and honest servants" in 1851 and 1852, the paper now described them as "miserable, ignorant Asiatics, as thick as the frogs of Egypt."[2] Weeks later, they were portrayed as servile coolies, living on rats, lizards, and shellfish.[3] In June 1853, the paper deplored the country's liberal immigration policy. Alluding to the "Illinois Black Law" of 1853, which forbade the entry of free blacks, the editor suggested that a similar law be passed against the Chinese. Every reason used against tolerating free blacks in Illinois, he stated, may be argued against enduring the Chinese in California. The Chinese, he added, had "most of the vices and few of the virtues of the African and they are numerous in both town and country."[4]

Anti-Chinese attitudes were given a decisive boost in 1854. That year, 16,084 Chinese arrived at San Francisco (up from 4,270 in 1853), while only 2,339 returned to China. Talk of an imminent Asian invasion resumed in the state legislature. The foreign miners' licensing requirement was amended to exempt all those who had declared their intention to become American citizens.[5] Then the legislature passed a resolution requesting California's congressmen to seek federal authorization for a capitation tax on all natives of China and Japan arriving at San Francisco.[6] This second measure confirmed that California was taking a racial rather than a simply xenophobic stand. While the Chinese constituted a significant racial component in California, Japanese immigration was almost nonexistent. But the two groups were lumped together for no other reason than that they belonged to the despised "Asiatic races."

This racialization of Chinese immigration was reinforced in *People v. Hall* (1854).[7] As noted earlier, many acts of violence against Chinese immigrants had gone unpunished because of local courts' ruling that Chinese testimony was inadmissible. In October 1853, George W. Hall was found guilty of the murder of a Chinese miner, Ling Sing, in Nevada County. Three Chinese and a Caucasian had testified on behalf of the state. The counsel for the defendant appealed the verdict on the ground that the testimony of the Chinese witnesses should have been denied. The question of Chinese testimony went to the California Supreme Court. Writing for the majority was Chief Justice Hugh C. Murray. A Democrat at the time of the decision, Murray later joined the Know-Nothing party and was nominated by that party for reelection as justice of the state supreme court in 1855.

Citing the 1850 California criminal statute that provided that "[n]o black . . . shall be allowed to give evidence in favor, or against, a white man," Murray argued that the framers of the statute used "black" as a generic term. Had it not been the case, Africans and Pacific Islanders would be admitted to testify against white citizens upon their arrival in the country. Moreover, the exclusion of "domestic negroes" could not be consistent with "a policy that [turned] loose upon the community the more degraded tribes of the same species." To validate his interpretation further, Murray relied on the federal law that provided for the naturalization of "free white persons" only. He concluded that while "white" excluded black, yellow, and all other colors, the term *black* should be construed as the opposite of white or Caucasian. Excluding blacks therefore entailed the debarment of all non-Caucasians. To diverge from this reading, Murray warned, would only foster unsound public policy. Admitting Chinese testimony would trigger the need to grant the Chinese all the rights of citizenship. In closing, Murray hinted at the danger inherent in the immigration of a race of inferior people, "differing in language, opinions, color, and physical conformation." As expected, Murray delivered his opinion that the testimony of the Chinese had been received improperly and that the judgment ought to be reversed.[8]

Now that the Chinese were legally denied access to the witness stand, criminal assaults on them became common and were usually unpunished for want of evidence. The Chinese reaction to *People v. Hall* was quick. Attacking the decision in an open letter to Governor Bigler in June 1855, a prominent merchant expressed the Chinese community leaders' outrage at the conflation of the Chinese with blacks. The merchant was especially concerned about the domestication of Chinese immigration as a racial rather than an immigrant issue.[9] African Americans were also prompt to interpret *People v. Hall* as a serious blow to their efforts to obtain the right to testify.[10]

Despite the decrease in Chinese immigration in 1855 and the higher return migration (3,473 departures for 3,329 entries), violence shook the mining regions in that year. The disturbances were in response to new economic circumstances. Until 1853, mining had provided many American miners with high incomes and substantial profits. Subsequently, rich surface mines became scarce, and wages and profits fell rapidly. Insufficient rainfall in 1854 and 1855 made it difficult for the miners to work the placers to their best advantage. They often had to rely on water companies. Meanwhile, technological changes brought about the rise of company mining. Following the ascendancy of quartz and hydraulic mining, the pioneer-miner-prospectors found it harder to compete successfully or even to survive, unless they accepted menial labor in a mining company.[11] Blaming the Chinese for their loss of status, American miners were convinced that their exclusion would reverse the depressing trend. In response to a plethora of anti-Chinese petitions and proceedings of miners' meetings, both legislative houses impaneled select committees to examine the petitions and make recommendations. The two most influential reports issued by the committees were the assembly's "Majority Report" and the senate's "Minority Report." Both stated in strong terms their desire to protect the laboring poor of America from the "immense hordes of Asia."[12]

Transcending the issue of mining rights, the two reports contained the full range of anti-Chinese stereotypes: biological and social nonassimilability, servility, shiftlessness, dishonesty, and depravity. Until then, the assembly report stated, America had welcomed only "peoples of kindred lands," who could be admitted on terms of equality. To extend the same hospitality to the Chinese who were so different in "physical organization" would injure Americans without benefiting the Chinese. Since the Chinese could never enjoy the rights and privileges of citizens and because of the natural animosities between the races, the Chinese would constantly be abused by vicious citizens.[13] A similar argument was used by some opponents of black migration. Out of "friendship" and "compassion" for Negroes, they insisted that it was better for them to stay in the South rather than move north or west where they would become "legal and social outcast[s]."[14] Both reports also stressed that amalgamation with the Chinese was "impossible, and repugnant to every feeling of decency and propriety." Americans and Chinese could not even reside in the same neighborhood "in consequence of [the] loathsome and filthy habits [of the Chinese]."[15]

Two months prior to the disclosure of the reports, Governor Bigler's annual message to the legislature had made numerous references to the danger of amalgamation with the Chinese because of their inferiority, slavishness, immorality, and stagnation. He had thus entreated legislators to take decisive measures against them.[16] Until 1854, only a few state officials had expressed their belief that California could enact a policy of exclusion. That year, however, the legislature had urged the state's representatives in Congress to seek federal approval for the enactment of such policy.[17] By 1855, the Assembly Select Committee on Foreign Miners was unwilling to wait for such approval because of its conviction that California had "*full, complete,* and *exclusive control* of all *police* regulations within her limits." The state thus had the right to determine who should be admitted and who should be excluded. Referring to the restrictions placed on African Americans in several western states, the committee was satisfied that its prohibition of the Chinese would have a precedent.[18] Besides this, the legal construction of the Chinese as "nonwhite" in *People v. Hall* rendered them, according to the committee, ineligible for citizenship.[19]

Compelling evidence of the racialization of the Chinese can also be found in the committees' recommendations. While both expressed their aversion to any social relation with the Chinese, the assembly committee was the more radical, calling for a policy similar to that regarding African Americans. Outright exclusion was only one part of the solution to the "vexing Chinese Question." Some members of the committee went a step further in their eagerness to avert the barbarian threat to their hearthstones, calling for the deportation of the Chinese residing in California. While they conceded that the Chinese could be of a great advantage in the reclamation and cultivation of the Tule lands, they insisted that not until white Americans became incapable of upholding their government and supporting their communities would it be time "to import Chinese, Malays and Negroes" to do that which Americans did not have the virtue to do for themselves.[20]

The senate's "Minority Report" similarly insisted that legislation was urgently needed to prevent America from being filled with "the millions of surplus population there is in China." Its authors were unwilling, however, to jeopardize trade prospects with China and revenue from the foreign miners' tax. Pointing out that the mining licensing tax was an essential source of revenue, they suggested that the Chinese already in California be left alone.

As to future immigration, though, they advised that a head tax of fifty dollars be imposed on each new immigrant. The amount was purposefully high so that Chinese laborers would be unable to raise the passage money and also the capitation tax.[21] The recommendation was soon enacted into the *Act to Discourage the Immigration to This State of Persons Who Cannot Become Citizens Thereof.*[22] By 1855, then, the California legislature, probably feeling in a strong position after *People v. Hall,* set out to frame an immigration-restriction policy that distinguished between European and Asian aliens. The act was, however, strongly opposed by the state's commissioner of immigrants, who informed the legislature that the capitation tax was unconstitutional. Merchants and shipping companies joined him in protest and threatened to test the act in court. This was done in 1857 in *People v. Downer,* which summarily voided the act.[23] Besides this frontal attack on Chinese immigration, the foreign miners' license tax law of 1853 was amended, providing for an increase in the license fee to six dollars per month after October 1, 1855, and for additional increases of two dollars per month each succeeding year.[24] On the one hand, the legislature was counting on the law to bring in more revenue for the near future. On the other hand, there was hope that, by the time the increase became unbearable and Chinese miners chose to leave, the state would be able to do without this source of revenue.

In the midst of such adversity, the Chinese merchants published a protest, in which they expanded some of the arguments they had used in their message to the Committee on Mines and Mining Interests in 1853. Falling short of criticizing the American racial order, they again expressed their shock at being subjected to the same treatment as Negroes. Could it be possible, they asked, that they were classed with that race?[25] Governor Bigler, to whom the merchants' complaint was addressed, did not respond, but Hinton R. Helper offered his crude answer to the question. This North Carolina "anti-slavery racist" would become a leading Republican polemicist following the publication of *The Impending Crisis of the South* (1857), his inflammatory call for the overthrow of the planter class and the removal of all African Americans from America.[26] After an apprenticeship to a North Carolina storekeeper, Helper had migrated first to New York and then to California, with the hope of making a quick fortune. Both attempts had ended in failure. Back in the East, Helper sought to discourage westward migration by exposing the "scandalous truths" about California's "barbarous civilization" in two travelogues—*The Land of Gold* (1855) and *Dreadful California* (1855).[27]

It was especially the image of California as a homogeneous region that Helper wished to correct. Describing the San Francisco population as one of the most diverse that ever occupied space, he averred that such a complete human menagerie could never be integrated into a harmonious whole. Like many, he had looked forward to finding a white sanctuary in the West. His hope had been shattered, however, by the presence of African Americans, Mexicans, Native Americans, and Chinese immigrants. Helper's diatribe focused not so much on the first three groups, because they knew their proper place in America, as it did on the Chinese, whom he described as a "legion of fiends" and "vermin."[28] In *Dreadful California,* Helper devoted a whole chapter to the "Celestials" or "xanthous children of the flowery land." Arguing that they held themselves aloof from Americans and would not identify their interests with America, Helper could not understand why these "semi-barbarians" were permitted to work the mines in California. The Golden State should be reserved for Americans and European immigrants. In any case, he was certain that, like blacks, the Chinese would become "subordinate to the will of the Anglo-Americans."[29] Drawing from his experience as a southerner that suggested racial diversity brought with it "strife and conflict of feeling," he concluded he "should not wonder at all, if the copper of the Pacific yet becomes as great a subject of discord and dissension as the ebony of the Atlantic."[30]

Helper's concern that the American population was too heterogeneous even before the arrival of the Chinese was shared by many Californians, as well as some easterners. In the early 1850s, the negative reports of American traders, missionaries, and diplomats in China had already greatly influenced the development of a negative image of China and the Chinese in the East.[31] While the opposition to the Chinese in California until 1854 was expressed in both economic and cultural terms, eastern editorials had been more concerned about the cultural, social, biological, and political incongruity of the Chinese. The prospect of a massive Chinese immigration therefore awakened their apprehension that it would radically alter the American character. As early as 1854, some eastern editors were calling for legislation that would deny the Chinese the right of naturalization. In 1854, the Whig editor of the *New York Tribune,* Horace Greeley, expressed his "grave fears" over admitting immigrants from China. The Chinese pouring into the sparsely populated California, he lamented, were "uncivilized, unclean and filthy beyond all conception." The men were "lustful and sensual in their dispositions," while every Chinese female was a "prostitute of the basest order." Chinese immigration, Greeley stressed, was peculiar in another sense. Unlike European immigrants, who were gradually fusing with Americans into one homogeneous people, the Chinese would forever remain distinct. Hinting at the black experience in America, Greeley declared that, despite the nation's commitment to republican principles, practice had shown that two different races could not occupy the same territory on terms of equality. The Americans would thus inevitably become "the virtual, if not the nominal, masters of the Chinese." Far from objecting to Californians' bigotry, he was thankful to them for attempting to exclude the Chinese "flood of ignorant and filthy idolaters."[32] Published two months before *People v. Hall,* this harsh editorial demonstrates the broad-based nature of the racialization of the Chinese in the mid-1850s.

In California, while the recent anti-Chinese measures had the effect of reducing immigration and driving away a substantial number of Chinese miners, the Chinese issue remained the subject of a heated debate. In 1856, two new mining reports reflected the intensity of the hostility toward the Chinese.[33] The senate report stated that the presence of the Chinese was "a putrefying sore upon the body politic—in short a nuisance."[34] Denouncing the "mercenary" objective of Chinese laborers and stressing their inferiority, the assembly report concluded that whether they were sojourners or settlers, they could add nothing to the wealth and glory of the state. The problem was not demographic. The consequences of Chinese immigration would be the same, regardless of numbers. What the state needed was the addition of "white men, with their wives to breed children; and not Chinese, either with or without wives."[35]

Deploring the fact that the removal of Chinese residents in California was beyond the power or financial ability of the state, the assembly report recommended that further Chinese immigration be banned from the country at once. The question was whether California had the right to pursue a policy of exclusion. Although the Immigration Act of 1855 was still in effect, the committee members were aware that charges of unconstitutionality had been brought against it. By virtue of natural law, they declared, California was sovereign and the sole judge of who may be admitted. Instead of using the measures against black migrants in the western states, they based their arguments on the U.S. Constitution. Although they could find no express provision that Congress had the power to prohibit aliens from immigrating, they were satisfied that it recognized this power in article 1, section 9: "The migration or importation of such persons as any of the States now existing shall think proper to admit, *shall not be prohibited* by the Congress prior to the year 1808." To them, the article established the right to admit or exclude aliens of not only the United States but also individual states, each in the sphere of its sovereignty.[36] The quoted section of the Constitution, whose purpose was to bar the importation of African slaves in the United States after 1808, was seen as a precedent for Chinese exclusion. The committee also used the *Passenger Cases* (1849) to shore up its contention that California had the right to exclude aliens. Out of the multiple opinions in the cases, the committee quoted Chief Justice Roger B. Taney's dissenting opinion. Taney had argued that if a state could expel undesirable persons, then it could exclude them in the first place. Furthermore, he had verified that, under the Constitution, Congress did not have the power to compel a state to receive aliens, whom it may be the policy or pleasure of the United States to admit.[37]

In an attempt to thwart the expansive anti-Chinese forces, the Reverend William Speer addressed a pamphlet to the California legislature in behalf of Chinese immigrants.[38] He insisted that excluding the Chinese would be detrimental to the economic interests of the region. Other regions might also benefit from Chinese labor. The South was in need of a substitute for slave labor, which had become increasingly "unpleasant and unproductive." Looking at the Chinese as the solution to the agitation over slavery and the Negro, he contemplated an American South freed from the "manifold and continued burdens of slavery." In his vision, African Americans were singularly absent, and the Chinese were the hardy and efficient tillers of the soil for southern planters and the active and intelligent porters for New Orleans and Charleston merchants.[39]

By 1856, while rabid Sinophobes called for outright exclusion, liberal and even pro-Chinese elements favored a restriction policy. Speer himself concluded his "humble plea" with a recommendation that the capitation tax be kept so that the number of Chinese immigrants would not be too great.[40] On April 19, 1856, the state legislature retained that tax, but it repealed the 1855 Foreign Miners' License Act to reset the license fee at four dollars—down from six dollars—and repeal the automatic increase.[41] Obviously, the Chinese would be tolerated as taxpayers.

The mid-1850s were important years in California politics and that of the nation at large because of the sudden rise of the American party.[42] The new party burst onto the American political scene in 1854. Its members were dubbed "Know Nothings" because they would always respond "I know nothing" to questions about their secret order. In the three decades preceding their ascent to power, the United States had experienced major transformations, notably population shifts, industrialization, growth of cities, and sectional strife. These changes brought with them their share of social problems. Unable to comprehend the underlying causes of these social ills, native-born Americans linked the increase in moral and political corruption, violence, crime, and pauperism to the large influx of immigrants. America had received 3,153,198 immigrants from 1790 to 1850, but in the five years from 1850 to 1855 the number amounted to 1,879,828. Besides the numerical factor, most of these recent immigrants had different ethnic backgrounds, especially German and Irish.[43] American nativists reacted to their loss of status by exploiting religious and ethnic prejudices, accusing immigrants of overstocking the

labor market, degrading labor, and undermining political and moral institutions. In their early days in the 1830s and 1840s, eastern nativists focused
on some political action and individual or mob acts against Catholic institutions and immigrants. In the 1850s, when slavery deeply divided Democrats
and ultimately led to the destruction of the Whig party, political nativism
became a powerful force. The American party organized very quickly in
major cities in 1854. Within a year, the Know Nothings had elected eight governors, more than a hundred congressmen, the mayors of major cities, and
thousands of other local officials in California, New York, Massachusetts,
Connecticut, New Hampshire, and Rhode Island.[44]

In September 1854, California Know Nothings carried the election in San
Francisco, the only city in which they had organized. One year later, they
elected their entire ticket of state officers, and they gained a majority in both
houses.[45] Thus, at the beginning of 1856, Democratic rule in California ended, and the Know Nothings dominated state and local politics. Studies of
nativism have usually excluded or devoted very little attention to California
nativism, often branding it as a different form of nativism.[46] To be sure, a
cursory reading of the American party resolutions would suggest that California Know Nothings were neither anti-foreign nor anti-Catholic. In their
1855 platform, for example, they called for "universal religious toleration" and
a "judicious revision of the laws regulating naturalization." At the same time,
though, they rejected a candidate they had nominated upon finding out that
he was a Catholic. Naturalized citizens in California felt threatened enough
that they established Freedom's Phalanx to protect immigrants and naturalized Americans from the Know Nothings.[47] A closer look at the nativist
movement in California verifies the Know-Nothings' abhorrence of the
Chinese and Californios. Regarding Californios, the American party platforms in 1855, 1856, and 1857 contained many planks that posed a potential
threat to Spanish-speaking Americans, especially their hold on their lands,
culture, religion, and political power.[48] Similarly, the absence of expressly anti-
Chinese resolutions does not signify that the Know Nothings were indifferent to the Chinese question. Besides political nativism, Know Nothingism
also manifested itself in individual and mob actions by overzealous members or sympathizers. As early as September 30, 1854, the *Daily Alta California* observed that the Know Nothings had formed a branch in almost every
mining town. The next year, American miners made particularly vociferous
demands for the restriction of Chinese miners and sometimes engaged in
violent action to achieve it. The 1855 Democratic-led assembly reacted to the
situation by legislating against the Chinese. In 1856, the policies adopted by
the Know-Nothing majority in the assembly pointed to the continuity of anti-

Chinese sentiment. The Know Nothings did not reverse the policies of their Democratic predecessors. They, too, favored European immigrants. At their 1856 state convention, they heartily welcomed all the honest and industrious immigrants who came to American shores to escape European despotism.[49]

Eastern Know Nothings were not indifferent to the situation in California. Representative Nathaniel P. Banks, for instance, expressed his serious concern over Chinese immigration. A former soldier, Banks was elected to Congress from Massachusetts as a coalition Democrat in 1853, only to become a champion of Know Nothingism in 1854.[50] Three years later, he would cast aside his nativist association and accept the Republican nomination for governor. In December 1854, however, he gave a long speech in the House of Representatives in support of the American party's position on naturalization. Know Nothings were in general very resentful about the voting power of naturalized Americans, blaming them for the prevalent corrupt political practices. For Banks, the only way to maintain the integrity of the government was to enact his party's proposal that the period of residence before immigrants could apply for naturalization be extended from five to twenty-one years. Banks mulled over the probability of a massive immigration from not only Europe but also Asia. "Look to the East, to China, India, Japan," he said, and you will see six hundred million potential immigrants. Who, he asked, would be able to check the tidal wave from Asia, when California was only ten or twelve days away by steamship? The *Passenger Cases* made it impossible for individual states to do so. If the Chinese came, the law asked that they be admitted. This, however, did not mean that they should be granted citizenship. Anticipating the duality of immigration policy in the 1880s, he wondered, "[Are] we to have another extension of judicial decrees . . . [that] shall determine what affinities of race, and color, and blood, make it impossible for men ever to participate in the powers of government?"[51]

Less than a month later, another prominent Know Nothing, William R. Smith from Alabama advised eastern legislators to forget for a moment the German and the Irish and turn their attention to the appalling picture in the West. He urged, "See the stream of emigration from the Celestial Empire to California! What are we to do with disciples of Confucius? . . . How long . . . will it be before a million of Pagans . . . claim the privilege of voting for American Christians, or against American Christians? How long before a pagan shall . . . mingle in the councils of this Government?" There was, he cried out, no law to prevent a Chinese from becoming a citizen. "*The American party,*" he stressed, "*demands a law to prevent it.*"[52]

The decline of the American party was as rapid as its meteoric ascent to power. Although nativists had attempted to submerge the sectional cleavage over slavery, they soon had to take a stand. When they did, they created the conditions that led to the destruction of their party. By the late 1850s, sectional tension culminated in violence in Kansas, where free-soil and pro-slavery forces clashed following the Kansas-Nebraska Act of 1854, which permitted a local option on slavery. The act was the signal for a bitter congressional battle, which ultimately caused the split of the Democratic party, the demise of the Whig party, and the emergence of the new Republican party. In Michigan and Wisconsin, mass meetings against the act led to conventions, which in turn led to the regular formations of the Republican party in other midwestern states—especially Ohio and Indiana—and in New England. The antislavery Whigs threw in their lot with the new party in 1855. The other Whig faction gave up the party and attempted to take control of the Know-Nothing party. Meanwhile, the Democrats divided into three factions: the "Independent Democrats" opposing the act, the southern or slave Democrats, and a third force attempting to reconcile the other two factions. While anti-slavery Whigs made up the bulk of the Republican party, Independent Democrats, Free Soilers, members of the Liberty party (abolitionists), and Know Nothings supplied further strength to it.[53] In its 1855 national convention in Philadelphia, the American party sundered in a majority group favoring the Kansas-Nebraska Act and a minority group opposed to it. California took the majority view—pro-slavery and pro-states' rights. In 1856, the Know Nothing party began to wane, largely because of its members' position on slavery. The new Republican party also contributed to the demise of the party by alluring several of its members. As Tyler Anbinder has noted, the frequency with which some Know Nothings became prominent Republicans showed the relative ease with which this transition occurred.[54]

The Republicans were thus a coalition of moderate and radical members. The avowed abolitionists were in the minority, and the larger group was composed of cautiously moderate members, who aimed to prevent slavery from spreading into the western territories. In the years following the creation of the party, some abolitionists did try to promote a more comprehensive program than the mere nonextension of slavery. It was clear, however, that any such program would be a political liability for the party and for the few radical members in the party. Putting aside their ideological differences during the national organization of the party in 1856, the radicals gave their support to the Republican platform, which focused on nonextension and the Kansas controversy. A corollary to the theme of opposition to the extension of slavery was the embrace of the free labor ideology.[55] Republicans agreed that free labor was degraded by slave labor and that the extension of slavery in the territories would dissuade free labor from migrating there. While most abolitionist Republicans affirmed the right of African Americans to participate as free laborers in the marketplace, conservative Republicans frequently used the "free labor" watchword to divert attention from the role of free blacks outside the slave states. The main impulse of these Republicans was, according to the *New York Tribune,* "a desire to secure the new Territories for Free white labor, with little or no regard for the interests of negroes, free or slave."[56] Despite the limitations of the Republican program, the radical Republicans kept the inhumanity of slavery and the essential humanity of the slave in the foreground. They contributed greatly to the expansion of new protections and rights for free blacks in the North.[57] They also fought the attempts by northern Democrats to deprive African Americans of certain basic rights, including the right to migrate and to testify in court.

In California, the issue of black migration emerged again in 1857 with yet another unsuccessful attempt to exclude free blacks and fine any person bringing in or freeing a slave in the state.[58] The senate and assembly lineup stood at 18 Democrats, 11 Americans, and 3 Republicans, and 60 Democrats, 8 Americans, and 11 Republicans, respectively. When the Republican legislators tried to secure the right of African Americans to testify in court against whites, they failed by an overwhelming majority. The bill they submitted would have had the effect of reversing *People v. Hall,* thus extending testimony rights to the Chinese. While it is not possible to determine the Republicans' intent, some evidence shows the conflation of black and Chinese rights in the minds of many supporters of blacks' right to testify. From 1855 on, the petition campaigns organized by the African American community for the repeal of the anti-testimony laws had included a substantial number of white residents. Simultaneously, some signers had begun to add "not Chinamen" or "not Chinese" next to their names, indicating their objection to a repeal of the testimony restriction on the Chinese.[59]

On the eve of the U.S. Supreme Court decision in *Dred Scott v. Sandford,* the legal position of free blacks in the western states was varied, depending on geographic and demographic factors and the strength of the Republican party. A Republican electoral victory in Iowa in 1856 led to improvements in the rights of African Americans; in strongly Democratic states and territories, such as Illinois, Indiana, California, and Oregon, the legal position of African Americans either worsened or remained unchanged. Presumptions of racial inferiority were, however, pervasive and unqualified by geography. The opinion delivered in *Dred Scott* on March 6, 1857, gave little hope for any progress toward racial justice in the nation.[60] Chief Justice Roger B. Taney, who delivered the majority opinion held that Congress had no power to prohibit slavery in the territories and that African Americans were not included under the word *citizens* in the Constitution. To arrive at this conclusion, Taney provided a skewed historical review of the status of African Americans, which ignored the variations in their status.[61] That African Americans were unfit to associate with the white race and undeserving of any rights that white people were bound to respect had been such a "fixed and universal" opinion, he stated, that the delegates at the constitutional convention of 1787 could not have intended to include them in the political community they had created. The restriction of naturalization to free white persons, anti-Negro state and federal legislation, and the conduct of the executive constituted further evidence that blacks were but "property" and that there could be no such thing as a free territory. Regarding the "free states," Taney observed that African Americans there still occupied the status of a degraded class, whose members could not be citizens within the meaning of the Constitution.[62]

Dred Scott was assailed by many political leaders and editors in the East.[63] Editors were influential in causing several Republican legislatures and state conventions to challenge the decision by stating that color did not disqualify a resident from citizenship. The racial reasoning, which sustained the relegation of blacks to an inferior caste, was not a significant source of objection, however. The majority of the Republicans were primarily incensed at Taney's turning upside down years of efforts at compromise by setting the slavery issue beyond the reach of legislative action. Had Taney confined his argument to the question of black citizenship, as Leon Litwack has noted, he might have gone unchallenged.[64] His conclusions merely verified existing anti-black state and federal practices sanctioned by both Democrats and Republicans.

Dred Scott is recognized as a key event in the history of black-white relations. What is generally not understood, however, is that the decision that African Americans could have no claim on American law or privileges struck a severe blow to other groups. In the East, Negrophobes were satisfied that Taney's ruling had "fixed the *status* of the subordinate [Negro] race *forever.*"[65] Meanwhile, several African American leaders deplored that the decision was further evidence that the Negro could be nothing but an alien, disfranchised, and degraded class. In the West, however, some political leaders interpreted *Dred Scott* as a wide-ranging ruling affecting not only blacks but all other nonwhites. This was made clear during the Oregon constitutional convention in 1857. The predominantly Democratic delegates barred African Americans from militia service and voting. Of great significance during the debates over suffrage was the close association of the Negro and Chinese questions. While the delegates agreed that elections should be "free and equal," a delegate specified that this "did not mean Chinese or niggers." The delegates thereafter wrote in the constitution that "no negro, Chinaman, or mulatto, shall have the right of suffrage."[66]

Unable to agree on a black exclusion article, the delegates opted for a separate article to be submitted to the people of Oregon. As they discussed the referendum phrasing, some delegates expressed their desire for a homogeneous community, free from the demoralizing presence of Negroes and Chinamen. Using the free soil and free labor themes, several delegates complained that if Chinese immigration continued, "no white man would inhabit [the mining counties of the state]." Therefore, they would vote to "couple Chinamen with Negroes." Significantly, the proportion of nonwhites in Oregon in the 1850s was only about 1 percent of the total population.[67] The delegates referred the black exclusion measure to the voters but preferred to deal with the Chinese issue themselves. Oregonians voted overwhelmingly to prohibit slavery (75 percent) and to bar the migration of free blacks (89 percent).[68] Accordingly, article 1, section 36, of the Oregon Constitution provided that no Negro or mulatto not residing in Oregon at the time of the adoption of its constitution would be allowed to come and settle in the state. While the delegates did not expressly provide for Chinese exclusion, they incorporated discriminatory clauses against the Chinese. Section 32 of the bill of rights empowered the legislative assembly to regulate the immigration of persons not qualified to become citizens of the United States. It was, however, in the article on miscellaneous provisions (article 15, section 8) that the delegates expressly discriminated against the Chinese. "No Chinaman," it prescribed, "shall ever hold any real estate or mining claim, or work any mining claim therein."

Oregon was the only free state ever admitted with a black exclusion provision in its constitution. It is equally important that Oregon received congressional approval of its racialization of Chinese immigration. In the debate over the admission of Oregon, Senator Benjamin F. Wade (Republican from Ohio) remarked that Oregon's constitution separated the Chinese from other immigrants. This was "a novelty," he stated, which would sound rather harsh if the provision had stated that "no Englishman" or "no Frenchman" should be entitled to certain rights. One singular element in the constitution, he noted, was that on every occasion that they are mentioned, "the constitution put Chinamen, negroes, and mulattoes on precisely the same footing."[69] While no senator alluded to the fact that Oregon's anti-Chinese measure might be a violation of the exclusive power of Congress to regulate commerce, Senator John P. Hale (Republican from New Hampshire), a sharp critic of the *Dred Scott* decision, objected to the Chinese clause in the Oregon Constitution for its violation of U.S. treaty obligations to China.[70]

Not surprising, the Oregon statehood bill had the full support of the West Coast delegations. Senator William M. Gwin (Democrat from California) was satisfied that the decision to not allow the Chinese to have an abode in Oregon agreed with the sentiment of all westerners. Until *Dred Scott,* Gwin lamented, Californians had wrongly thought that the power to exclude the Chinese was lodged in Congress and that they could not prohibit Negroes from entering their state. *Dred Scott* had finally confirmed the scope of the police powers of the states. Bemoaning the tardiness of that decision, he went on to speculate that if the *Dred Scott* decision had been rendered in 1849, Californians would have prohibited "all the degraded races."[71]

For Gwin, *Dred Scott* had cleared the path for the enactment of discriminatory legislation against all nonwhite groups. Another significant manifestation of this reasoning emerged in the 1858 senatorial campaign in Illinois. Representing the young and vigorous Republican party, Abraham Lincoln engaged in seven formal debates with Stephen A. Douglas, the incumbent candidate. Although Douglas won the election, Lincoln's defeat was a "slip and not a fall"—as Lincoln himself put it. Lincoln was relatively unknown outside of Illinois before 1858, and the campaign contributed to his nomination as the Republican candidate in the 1860 presidential election. In the 1858 debates, both men assured their audiences that they would not afford the Negro full equality with the white man. However, while Douglas was satisfied with the inferior status of blacks, Lincoln anticipated the time when all Americans would be free and Negroes would have an equal chance to advance *to the limit of their capabilities.*[72]

To a large extent, *Dred Scott* was at the heart of the matter in the campaign debates. Both men had expressed their opinion on the case a few months earlier. Douglas had fully endorsed the decision, describing the conflict raging over it as a "naked issue between the friends and the enemies of the Constitution." Lincoln, on the contrary, had questioned the legitimacy of the decision because it was not in accordance with legal expectations and was based on erroneous historical facts. Furthermore, because the decision had not been unanimous, he had thought that it could not be binding in the branches of government until all constitutional issues were settled.[73] The 1858 debates provided a perfect forum for discussing *Dred Scott.* Although Justice Taney had drawn a rigid distinction between black and white residents of the United States as far as the exercise of constitutional rights was concerned, Douglas went one step further. On July 9, 1858, in the opening speech of his campaign at Chicago, he upheld Taney's contention that the American government was founded on the white basis. Douglas's racial concerns were not limited to the Negro problem, however. Amalgamation with all "inferior races" had to be prohibited to preserve the purity of American blood. In California, this could mean legislating against the Chinese. Douglas did not believe that "the cooley imported into [America] must necessarily be put upon an equality with the white race." An ardent defender of states' rights, he argued that California was free to deny the Chinese rights that could possibly be conferred upon them in Illinois.[74] In his reply the following day, Lincoln did not address Douglas's pronouncements about the Chinese. Rather, he reiterated his belief that the Declaration of Independence linked "the hearts of all patriotic and liberty-loving Americans." Significantly, he described these Americans narrowly, as men descended by blood from the framers of American democracy or from latter-day European immigrants.[75] As he stumped the state of Illinois, Douglas went on expounding his white supremacist beliefs.[76] On September 15, he held the third joint debate with Lincoln at Jonesboro. In his opening statement, Douglas remarked that when the signers of the Declaration of Independence proclaimed all men to be created equal, they meant "white men," not "the negro, the savage Indians, the Fejee, the Malay, or any other inferior and degraded race." Here again, Lincoln failed to take the broad and lofty ground of equality for all residents in America, irrespective of their race.[77]

In California, events following *Dred Scott* proved that some Democrats construed it as fixing the status of both blacks and Chinese immigrants. Early in 1858, two immigration bills were introduced in the legislature almost simultaneously. The first required all African Americans to register to prove their residence and to carry their registration papers at all times. Failure to produce such proof could lead to their auction for six months' labor, followed by their removal from the state at the end of this period. There was no provision for readmitting black residents who had left the state and intended to return. This anti-black migration bill passed the assembly overwhelmingly. In the senate, however, an amendment was added to exempt African Americans already residing in the state. The bill was then sent back to the assembly, where it died.[78]

Black migration to California had been extremely low throughout the 1850s. While the black population increased by 185.2 percent between 1852 and 1860—from 2,206 to 4,086—it remained at 1 per cent of the population in both censuses.[79] Chinese immigration was comparatively very high. Arrivals for 1855, 1856, and 1857 amounted to 3,329, 4,807, and 5,924, respectively. The censuses for 1852 and 1860 indicate a 356.13 percent increase of Chinese residents—from 9,809 to 34,933. By 1860, Chinese immigrants amounted to 9.19 percent of the state population.[80] In the course of the debate over black exclusion, the perception of the greater threat posed by Chinese immigration caused the legislature to consider a Chinese exclusion bill. This bill was as unconstitutional as the 1855 capitation tax law. Like the anti-Negro bill, the anti-Chinese measure was very harsh, providing for the prohibition of all immigrants of "Mongolian blood." Except when driven by bad weather, any person landing or allowing such immigrants to land was liable to a heavy fine, imprisonment for three to twelve months, or both. The unequivocal racialization of the immigration policy was evident in the captioning of the law: *An Act to Prevent the Further Immigration of Chinese or Mongolians to This State.*[81] Although the act was declared unconstitutional the next year, it was clear that the Chinese were the target of an attempted policy of exclusion rather than restriction.

As the Chinese followed the trail of gold and other work opportunities in the territories of the Pacific Northwest—Oregon, Washington, Idaho, and Montana—they met with similar white hostility, resulting in the same pattern of violence and Sinophobic legislation. Though the Chinese were not excluded from these territories, mining taxes were levied on them. In some localities, they were excluded from buying or holding title to placer mines; in others, taxes were levied on all their trading operations. All the territories barred the Chinese from testifying in court when white persons were a party, and all but Montana denied them the franchise.[82]

By the end of the first decade of Chinese immigration, the long-established unequal treatment of African Americans had extended to Chinese immigrants in California and the Pacific Northwest. Both groups were experiencing serious forms of discrimination, which put them outside the political and social community and made them legally disabled. The denial of the right to testify was especially destructive to the security of Chinese miners in their persons and property. The ineligibility of the Chinese for naturalized citizenship had not been codified, but their collective image was such that in 1853 the *Daily Alta California* expressed the widely held opinion that the Chinese were neither free nor white and were therefore not eligible to become citizens.[83] By the time *People v. Hall* reached the state supreme court in 1854, Chief Justice Murray could declare as a matter of dictum that the Chinese could become neither voters in California nor citizens of the United States. Three years later, *Dred Scott* placed racist westerners in a strong position, as they interpreted the decision as disqualifying African Americans and the Chinese from the privileges of U.S. citizenship. Of all immigrant groups, the Chinese and other Asians alone passed into the category of aliens barred from citizenship, a status they now shared with American-born blacks. This racialization was reflective of a deficit model that originated in a legally constructed disability. The relegation of the Chinese to the status of an inadmissible class was thus ascribed to their ineligibility for citizenship rather than an act of racial injustice. This rationalization was to play a decisive role in the experiences of the Chinese and, more generally, Asian immigrants to the United States for the next century. By resorting to this legal disqualification—"ineligible for citizenship"—both Congress and the courts could largely avoid addressing directly and meaningfully the thorny issue of the convergence of race (whiteness) and citizenship.

The ideological underpinning of the nexus of whiteness and citizenship lay in the perception of a condition of inferiority habitual to all nonwhites. Insofar as the Chinese were concerned, this prejudicial attitude was not unique to California, where the majority of the Chinese settled. In the Northeast, reports from Americans in China had resulted in shaping the image of the Chinese as the essentialized depraved pagan.[84] In the Southeast, the anti-Chinese imagery derived from these reports as well as from consideration of Chinese coolie labor in the West Indies and Latin America. Concerned about the labor shortage in their region, editors of influential southern journals and delegates at southern commercial conventions discussed the need for additional labor to supplement the existing black labor force. The potential sources of labor included the Chinese, East Indians, and Africans. By the late 1850s, however, southerners had made up their minds that reopening the slave trade in Africans was preferable to initiating a trade in coolies.[85] In California, anti-Chinese prejudices were, to a large extent, an extension of the response to the collective image of African Americans. The charge of unfair economic competition or "coolieism" was but a borrowing from the earlier stigmatization of black labor as inherently unfree.

This conflation of Chinese immigrants and African Americans was, of course, blatant in the statements that adverted to the Negro question to justify the call for Chinese exclusion. The Negroization of the Chinese went a step further, however, when the Chinese were described as patient, docile, loyal, and humble by their sympathizers[86] or as inferior, impure, and immoral by their detractors.[87] This set of contradictory stereotypes had been and still was applied to blacks. Among some commentators, the racialization of the Chinese culminated in the formation of the image of a "Negroid Chinese." In 1857, the *Lippincott's Geographical Dictionary of the World* described the affinities between black and Chinese phenotypes. "In thickness of lips, flattened nose and expanded nostrils," it stated, "[the Chinese] bear a considerable resemblance to the Negro."[88] One year later, *Harper's Weekly,* the rapidly expanding magazine designed primarily for middle- and upper-class readers, published a series of vignettes on the Chinese from a correspondent in Hong Kong. The "Chinese coolies," the correspondent averred, were a miserable and brutish set, "half-horse, [and] half stevedore." "Celestial ladies," he went on, were either small-footed "quasi-crippled" wives or "splay-footed" concubines. Looking down on the Chinese women's hairstyles, bound feet, and manner of dress, he was convinced that only men who had a taste for "the baboon-like faces of Hong-Kong women" would find them attractive. This vignette was supplemented with a large illustration, representing Celestial ladies with Negroid features.[89] Earlier descriptions of Chinese women in America had presented them more as "exotic curios," "queer and diminutive specimens of the human family," than as disgusting or simply grotesque beings.[90] Within a few years of their arrival in California, a new dimension was gradually added to the Chinese woman stereotype. In California, a predominantly male community during the gold rush, prostitution thrived as a stratified service industry, involving foreign and native-born

This portrait of Chinese women with Negroid features was accompanied by a long racist description of "Celestial ladies" by a correspondent in Hong Kong. (Source: *Harper's Weekly*, January 30, 1858, 68. Courtesy of the Library of Congress)

women, white and nonwhite. By the late 1850s, an estimated 85 percent of the Chinese women in San Francisco worked as prostitutes.[91] Writing on the alleged depravity of Chinese females in California, a writer for the *Hutching's California Magazine* declared in 1857 that, "though with complexions in some instances approaching fair, their whole physiognomy indicates but a slight removal from the African race."[92]

Relegating the Chinese to the status of the "inferior Negro race" meant that in all matters, from immigration and testimony rights to education and intermarriage, the restrictions placed on blacks were extended to the Chinese. In 1854, the school authorities in San Francisco established a separate "colored school" for black children.[93] One year later, Paul Hubbs, the state superintendent of education, made a public statement that black children were naturally inferior to white children and that the public school systems in California would permit "no mixture of the races."[94] By the end of the year, the Sacramento City Council issued a report that defended its mayor's stand against using state school appropriations to establish schools for blacks. The report expressed the fear that providing schools for Negroes would oblige them to instruct Chinese children as well.[95] In 1858, following the controversy over the attendance of a light-complexioned black girl at the only high school in San Francisco, many expressed the opinion that a wise policy would be to impose social distinctions between whites and all inferior races.[96] That same year, Andrew J. Moulder, the state superintendent of public instruction, voiced his opposition to the attempt to force Negro and Chinese children into white schools. His opposition was instrumental in framing the California school law of 1860, the first school law that expressly discriminated against nonwhite children. The act excluded Mongolians and Negroes from the public schools and provided for separate schools for nonwhite children.[97] In the lengthy and impassioned debate over the education of nonwhite children, the amalgamation battle cry was used to justify segregation and attack real or imagined proponents of integration. The issue of common schools, Moulder declared, could be reduced to preserving the supremacy and purity of Caucasian blood or allowing schools "to become tenanted by blacks alone."[98] In the community at large, amalgamation was also deemed unacceptable. In 1860, the 1850 law prohibiting marriages between blacks and whites was amended to include a ban on intermarriage between whites and Chinese. By setting up group boundaries between whites and nonwhites, this antimiscegenation law sought to preserve racial categories and maintain the hierarchical racial order. The significance of this legal form of sexual vigilantism is reflected in the fact that it would take longer to strike down antimiscegenation laws than any other racial restriction.

4. Race Relations in the Civil War Era

The place of the black man in the older States will soon be filled up
by foreign immigrants, who, in filling the vacuum, will give no
shock to the sensibilities of a kindred race or endanger the future
peace of the country. . . .
—Senator James H. Lane, *Congressional Globe*, February 16, 1864

BY THE LATE 1850s, the nation was more than ever before preoccupied by
the issues of slavery, states' rights, and secession. As rival passions fed violence, Republicans set out to clarify their position. They assured the elector-
ate that their party alone could bring back law and order and preserve the
Union. They insisted that their constitutional obligation was to abide by the
law of the land and accommodate slavery where it existed. Theirs was an opposition to the *spread* of slavery, not to slavery itself. Curbing slavery's spread
was, however, not the Republicans' primary motivation. Most historians now
argue that fears for the survival of the Republic were of greater significance
than the slavery extension issue. "Slave power," whose alleged goal was the
nationalization of slavery, was thus perceived as a major threat to Republicanism. Beginning in 1856, Republican propaganda would draw on the slave
power conspiracy theory to expound the progress of the sectional conflict
and to propose a program that would save the Republic.

While Republicans portrayed the sectional crisis as a contest between slave
power and Republicanism, Democrats viewed it as a contest between democracy and the "party of anarchy and disunion." In the political campaigns that
ensued, Democrats were the first to use race as a key issue. Through name-
calling, they stirred up racial fears with such consistency that Republicans
were forced to take a position. They did so by stressing that their party was
"the white man's party."[1] Soon after Congress convened in 1859, Republican
professions of allegiance to white supremacy became daily utterances in the
two chambers. Except for a few abolitionists, even the Republicans who had
responded with bravado to earlier Democratic accusations that their party
was the party of "Amalgamists" and "Negro Worshipers" now softened their

rhetoric and repudiated their initial response that it was more important to get rid of slavery than to preserve the Union.[2] Especially in the West, many Republican spokesmen objected to the expansion of slavery, because it would result in barring free labor. In their pronouncements about the stigma attached to labor in a slave society, however, they made little or no distinction between free blacks and slaves.[3] Obviously, the underlying tenets of the Republican free labor ideology were still based on the close associations of blacks with slavery and free labor with white labor. The attempt to rebut the Democratic image of Republicans as proponents of the "Africanization" of the territories does not account for the anti-black emphasis of some Republicans. Their declarations revealed their belief in the inferiority of blacks and their incompatibility with American free society and institutions.

These prejudices were explicit in some Republicans' calls for resettling blacks as the best solution to the race problem. In 1858, a group of Republican leaders from the border states and the West introduced legislation to subsidize black colonization in Latin America. "Negro deportation," they claimed, would prove that Republicans did not wish to set blacks free among white southerners to be "their equals and rulers." In the border states especially, they added, espousing colonization was essential to building a Republican party base among poor whites. In the West, colonization would promote racial homogeneity. Besides this, they argued, given the impossibility of racial equality in America, it was better for free blacks to be colonized in a country where they could have political rights and dignity.[4] Republicans from the border states were the first to endorse publicly colonization plans. The significant presence of African Americans in their states, they explained, made race relations a vital question, not a mere political abstraction. It should be noted, however, that these Republicans' advocacy of colonization did not antagonize most other Republicans. Even some of the men who would become radicals in the 1860s (for example, Salmon P. Chase, Benjamin F. Wade, Thaddeus Stevens, and Samuel C. Pomeroy) favored the scheme at one time or another.[5] In the late 1850s, most Republicans were aware of the great potential of endorsing colonization.

By 1860, Republican racial attitudes differed from those of Democrats only insofar as they suggested that blacks were a subclass rather than a nonclass. As Victor J. Voegeli has noted, Republicans' abhorrence of human bondage went hand in hand with their aversion to living among large numbers of blacks.[6] Abraham Lincoln himself shared many of the opinions of his contemporaries. The physical differences between blacks and whites were so great, he had argued during the 1858 Illinois senatorial campaign, that the two races could never live together on terms of equality. While he regarded slavery as an "injustice" and an immoral system violating the precepts of Christianity and humanity, he was also aware of the racial phobias of white Americans.[7]

Lincoln's election in 1860 was the signal for the secession of southern states and civil war. The question of the status of the African American was then deemed as secondary compared with the problem of preserving the Union. Lincoln's response to Horace Greeley's famous "Prayer of Twenty Millions" made this clear. "My paramount object in this struggle," he stated, "is to save the Union, and is not either to save or destroy Slavery."[8] A few weeks later, however, Lincoln issued the Emancipation Proclamation, which freed the slaves residing in areas of insurrection. Prompted by a discouraging military situation, the proclamation was a political and military move aimed at appeasing the radical Republicans and keeping the border slave states from joining the Confederacy. Lincoln also hoped that the Emanicaption Proclamation would win the North the support of the international community.[9] Meanwhile, Lincoln continued to disclaim notions of racial parity, explaining to a group of African Americans that "harsh as it may be," white Americans had a "natural disgust" for blacks and were unwilling "for you freed colored people to remain with us."[10]

As Republicans advanced haltingly to the belief that emancipation was necessary to further the cause of the North, they were not insensitive to their constituents' opposition to such policy. Prior to the war, local exclusion laws and federal and state fugitive slave acts had discouraged black migration and had held the number of African Americans in the western region to a tiny percentage. When the war broke out, the anxieties over a possible "black deluge" resumed and were intensified by some western Democrats' propaganda. Democrats used three phrases to sum up the alleged consequences of emancipation: "racial amalgamation," "Africanization of America," and "Free Negroism."[11] In response, Republicans denied that their party would jeopardize the current racial balance of power in the North. "The battles of freedom," a Republican leader crudely stated, aimed to prevent the "white laboring classes" from coming into competition with "negro labor, whether free or slave."[12] Above all, Republicans labored to prove that fear of a massive black migration was groundless. They kept repeating that it was bondage rather than freedom that was driving blacks into the North. Once slavery was abolished, not only would African Americans remain in their native South, but those residing in the North would rush south.[13] In a final attempt to assuage the racial worries of their constituents, Republicans pointed to their plans for colonizing free blacks. While emancipation made the destiny of African Americans an issue affecting the future of postbellum America, the official adoption of black expatriation afforded little promise of a revolutionary solution to the problem of America as a racially diverse society. Indeed, Republican policy reinforced the popular conviction that African Americans had no place in the nation and body politic for which the North was fighting. On December 1, 1862, in his second annual message, President Lincoln presented a plan for gradual, compensated emancipation coupled with voluntary expatriation after freedom. In it, he denied that emancipation would send the freed blacks north. Once the slaves were freed, he predicted, they would work for their former masters for wages until "new homes [could] be found for them in congenial climes and with people of their own blood and race." Lincoln supplied yet another deterrent to a colored people's invasion of the North. "[In] any event," he asked, "can not the North decide for itself, whether to receive them?"[14]

In California, as everywhere else, sectional bitterness and strife had occupied public attention and racialized the political discourse since the late 1850s. During the 1859 gubernatorial campaign, Leland H. Stanford, the Republican nominee, clarified the position of his party. Stanford was a prosperous merchant who had begun his political career as a Whig with strong feelings against slavery. In a few years, he would become one of the Central Pacific Railroad "Big Four" and one of the largest employers of Chinese laborers. In 1859, Stanford responded to Democratic attacks by pledging his support for white supremacy. Unlike the midwestern and northeastern states, where public attention was on the implications of the war for the status of African Americans, California was beset with a more complex race relations situation. Stanford therefore added that he preferred "free white citizens to any other class or race."[15] By so doing, he sounded the traditional Californian association of African Americans and Chinese immigrants.

As the North and South girded for war, the near-passage of the California black exclusion bill and the passage of the Mongolian exclusion bill in 1858 demonstrated that racism in California was not going into abeyance. African Americans expressed their displeasure with the pending exclusion bill by holding "indignation meetings." As a final expression of protest, about six hundred blacks emigrated to Victoria, British Columbia, draining an already small black community.[16] The increase in the black population, which amounted to only two dozen in the preceding year, was trifling compared with the influx of 5,924 Chinese immigrants at San Francisco in 1857.[17] While the Mongolian exclusion act was not enforced and was soon held unconstitutional by the state supreme court,[18] the foreign miners' license law was still in effect. By 1859–60, two-thirds of the Chinese in California lived in the mining districts. Meanwhile, independent miners, mostly whites, started a mass exodus. In 1863 alone, some 20,000 miners left the state to participate in a gold rush outside California. Subsequently, anti-Chinese agitation in the mining districts was rare, and the legislature revised the foreign miners' license law to make it more profitable.[19]

The success of the mining tax led to attempts to tax other occupations undertaken by Chinese laborers. In April 1862, the legislature passed a more comprehensive exploitation measure entitled *An Act to Protect Free White Labor against Competition with Chinese Coolie Labor, and to Discourage the Immigration of the Chinese into the State of California.*[20] The act imposed a monthly capitation tax (the Chinese police tax) of $2.50 on all persons of the Mongolian race over seventeen except those who had taken out licenses to work in the mines and those who were operating businesses or were engaged in the production and manufacture of specific crops. The Chinese police tax is a highly significant piece of legislation in at least two respects. First, racial antipathy was evident in the setting apart of not only Chinese immigrants but also all persons of the "Mongolian race" as special targets of taxation and as undesirable immigrants.[21] In 1860, about 39 percent of California's residents were foreign-born. This figure represents the high-water mark in the ratio of foreign-born to the total population from 1850 to 1920.[22] Even so, population was still considered to be California's greatest need. The transcontinental railroad itself was desired principally to facilitate migration to the region. Hence, anti-Chinese sentiment and policy paralleled an eager desire for American-born and European-born migrants. The second important element in the 1862 act lay in the use of "free white labor" in its caption. By adopting such phraseology, California legislators expanded the eastern ideologies of "whiteness" and "blackness" that originated in the free labor paradigm. In California, the emphasis was on a fundamental incompatibility of *free white* labor and *Chinese* labor. In that respect, the 1862 act could be said to be the first formal expression of this new ideological construction opposing "whiteness" to "Chineseness" or rather (with a view to a possible immigration of other Asian groups) "Mongolianness."

Historical evidence shows that neither Chinese miners nor the Chinese laborers who gradually drifted into the cities displaced white labor. Chinese miners continued to take up claims that had been worked and then abandoned by white diggers. In 1862, a joint select committee of the California legislature reported that the Chinese were providing the unskilled and cheap labor that American entrepreneurs needed to create skilled and highly paid jobs for white laborers.[23] Like African Americans in the East, Chinese laborers were performing the menial labor that served to upgrade the employment positions of white laborers—American and European-born. The refutation of Chinese labor competition often seemed to imply that any infiltration of

Chinese labor in a field of occupation held by white laborers was objectionable. In September 1859, the hostile reaction to the introduction of a few Chinese in the hitherto all-white cigar-making trade had made this sentiment very clear. While the number of Chinese employed in the trade was still negligible, the Cigar Makers' Association of San Francisco expelled employers who were hiring Chinese and called for a boycott on their products.[24] Two months later, the People's Protective Union was organized to represent the interests of the cigar manufacturing business class. The union agitated against "forcing" Chinese labor into the cigar trade sporadically for a number of years, but it failed in its efforts to exclude the Chinese. The number of Chinese cigar makers was minute before 1864, and the trade itself was thriving despite a dearth of labor, unlike the situation in the mining districts at the height of anti-Chinese agitation.[25]

During the agitation, the cigar makers staked their claim to their workplace by permeating their complaints with racial meaning. The resolutions of the People's Protective Union echoed the arguments of white Americans, who were raising the specter of the degradation of American civilization with the emancipation of African Americans. The Chinese were thus condemned as socially, morally, and politically inimical to the general welfare and manifest destiny of America.[26] The rights of the white industrial classes were endangered by Chinese labor, which the union called "cooly labor" or "enslaved Chinese labor." Like African Americans, the Chinese were deemed to be "an unassimilative and enslaved human element."[27] The frequent equation of coolieism and slavery was only partially aimed at conjuring up familiar stereotypes of slavery. The People's Protective Union also described Chinese workers as cheap laborers or apprentices hired by greedy or ignorant white employers, thereby acknowledging that Chinese laborers were not "slaves." In the same way that the slavery theme was used east and west of the Rockies to signify the inferiority of *all* black labor, coolieism served to indicate the inherently inferior status of *all* Chinese labor.

Accordingly, the racial reasoning in the 1862 Chinese Police Tax Act demonstrates that the limitations of the free labor outlook also applied to the Chinese. Not all Californians, however, agreed with the attitudes behind the racialization of the Chinese. For John Archbald, the author of a pro-Chinese pamphlet, the separation between "white and colored skins" was arbitrary and irrational. He argued that Americans had made two serious mistakes in the course of their history. The first had been to receive the Ethiopic race and retain it in slavery. Then, on coming in contact with the Chinese, Californians had made the error of judging them by the color of their skin rather than their attainments and capabilities. Even though Chinese and blacks were not the same color, Americans had lumped the two groups together, denying them both fundamental civil rights. While Archbald stood for political and social justice for all races, he did not favor complete racial equality. Striving to reassure his readers that they should not fear granting political rights to the Chinese, he stressed that even if they were admitted to citizenship, they would remain "patient drudges," rarely dreaming of themselves as equal to white Americans. Archbald was then cautious to explain that "political unity" would not lead to amalgamation. Although Americans had come into extensive contact with the Negro race, he noted, there had been no important admixture of blood. He was therefore confident that the Chinese and the African could live among Americans for centuries without any important amount of amalgamation taking place.[28]

This was not the opinion of Arthur B. Stout. In 1862, this prominent physician and future member of the State Board of Health, published a pamphlet in which he sought to prove that the ingress of the Chinese in California would ultimately lead to self-destruction.[29] He warned that mixture of blood was the inevitable consequence of the presence of different races in the same locality. As of 1862, Stout estimated that the blending of the Caucasian, Aboriginal American, and Negro had produced twenty-three inferior hybrids. Bad blood was thus multiplying its kind to the detriment of the Caucasian race. In the eastern states, he lamented, the transplantation of the black "cancer" was so perfected that eradication was impossible. Tears, he prophesied, would be shed in California when in addition to the Indian and Negro amalgamation, "the Chinese, Japanese, Malays and Mongolians of every caste, shall have . . . given origin to their countless varieties of hybrid creatures." The only way to prevent such a calamity was to enact a state exclusion law. As to the Chinese residing in California, he proposed that they be denied permanent domicile, elective rights, and titles to land and that their employment be discouraged.[30]

Stout concluded by evoking the irrepressible conflict between the forces of civilization and barbarism. On January 10, 1862, California Republican governor Leland Stanford's inaugural message sounded the same alarm. Stanford predicted that unless something was done to check Chinese immigration, "the question which of the two tides of immigration meeting upon the shores of the Pacific shall be turned back will be forced upon our consideration." His statements are significant because of his political affiliation and his employment of Chinese laborers on the Central Pacific Railroad a few years later. As he took office in 1862, he expressed his belief that the settlement of an inferior race in California was to be discouraged by every legitimate means. He would therefore confer with the legislature in any constitutional action to discourage the immigration of the Asiatic races. Echoing expressions of white opposition to blacks in several states, he stated that the presence of a degraded class in California would repel desirable immigration.[31]

After Stanford's message, the legislature appointed a committee to confer with prominent Chinese merchants in San Francisco and to report back to the full body on the wisdom of allowing a large influx of Chinese laborers. Interestingly enough, the committee's report issued on March 11, 1862, congratulated the state on the presence of the Chinese. There were 50,000 worthy Chinese laborers in the state, who were contributing significantly to the state revenue from taxes and to shipping, farming, and mechanical interests. The committee denied there was any competition between Chinese and white laborers, and it could not find any grounds for the allegations that the Chinese were a servile, immoral, and criminal class. In fact, reprehensible behavior had been the hallmark of Americans. The Chinese merchants had provided the committee with a list of eighty-eight Chinese who had been murdered by white men, only two of whom had been brought to justice. The committee went on to urge granting naturalization to the Chinese already in California and inducements for others to come. It also insisted that it would be advantageous to lighten the financial burden imposed on the Chinese, to refrain from enacting new oppressive statutes, and to maintain friendly commercial relations with China.[32]

The pro-Chinese attitude in this report is reminiscent of the 1853 report of the Committee on Mines and Mining Interests (see chapter 2), which had also put forward the economic contribution of Chinese immigrants to the state revenue and exposed the harsh treatment of Chinese miners. There was, however, one major difference between the two reports. Unlike the 1853 report with its emphasis on the Chinese question as an immigration matter, the 1862 report was dealing with it as a *domestic racial* issue. The discussion was no longer about the admission and mining privileges of a foreign group but about the more fundamental subject of Chinese settlement in California and the relation of Chinese immigrants to white Americans. The 1862 committee was confident that white Americans had nothing to fear from a race so "contemned" and "restricted": "[The Chinese] are denied privileges equal with other foreigners; they cannot vote nor testify in courts of justice, nor have any voice in making our laws, nor mingle with us in social life." "We adopt none of their habits," the committee added, "form no social relations with them, but keep them separate and apart, a distinct inferior race." While it is difficult to assess the committee's true sentiments, it obviously presented the subordination of the Chinese as evidence that no particular action was necessary.[33]

Despite the potency of the committee's arguments, the larger body of legislators did not feel any need to conciliate Chinese immigrants. Rejecting its report in toto, the assembly adopted a long statement listing three major complaints: Chinese labor was servile; it was brought into unfair competition with white labor; and the Chinese were a demoralizing and unassimilative race.[34] The legislators then enacted the previously mentioned Chinese Police Tax Act, forbidding Chinese access to all but a few specific fields of labor, unless they paid a monthly tax for the privilege. Chinese labor employed in the production of sugar, rice, coffee, or tea were exempt from taxation. Obviously, the authors of the Chinese Police Tax Act saw a connection between the growth of produce and nonwhite people. This relationship had long been established in the case of African Americans in the South, where it was assumed they were more adept at raising plantation crops than any other pursuit.

While Californians were willing to establish a system of plantation work for the Chinese, they did not seek to include African Americans in the scheme. In fact, the issue of black settlement was raised again in 1862 when a bill to repeal the anti-Negro testimony laws of 1850 and 1851 was introduced by the Republicans in the legislature.[35] In the debate that ensued, although some Republican legislators showed some concern for the state's black population, the majority emphatically rejected the notion of full equality before the law. Their proposal, they affirmed, was only a "mild reform," certainly not a proposition to elevate blacks to a position of social equality with whites.[36] Despite a Republican majority in both chambers, the bill failed to pass. Obviously, the Republicans did not close ranks. Showing their disaffection with the state of race relations in California, 242 black residents petitioned Congress in 1862 to settle them in a country where their color would not be a badge of degradation. It seemed to be the policy of the state and the nation, they commented, to discourage the increase of persons of color in their midst and to use every legal means to induce those among them to emigrate.[37]

In the early 1860s, the tendency to group African Americans and Chinese together was manifest in the fact that laws restricting education, miscegenation, and testimony were still affecting both groups. In Congress, however, California congressmen chose to dissociate the two groups. A case in point was Representative Aaron A. Sargent, a Republican. In June 1862, Sargent proposed an amendment to a tariff bill, providing for the increase of the tariff on clean rice. Sargent explained that the measure would primarily affect the 50,000 Chinese residing in California, because they were the main consumers of imported cleaned rice. To Thaddeus Stevens (Republican from Pennsylvania), the amendment amounted to asking Congress to countenance California's racially motivated policies and undermine the right of the Chinese to settle in California. Thereafter, Sargent used an argument that he thought would win him the support of all eastern Republicans but instead attracted intense scrutiny. He conceded that although the peculiar form of American slavery did not exist in China, the basic relationship by which the control of one individual belonged to another existed there and was imported in California. If this were true, Horace Maynard (Republican from Tennessee) asked, why did Californians not emancipate the "Chinese slaves"? Sargent's response was that only Negroes were worthy of emancipation because they were infinitely superior to the Chinese. His comments on the Chinese became increasingly vitriolic. California, he asserted, had been overrun by a "people of strange tongue, vile habits [and] impossible of assimilation." Instead of upbraiding Californians for doing what they could to discourage Chinese immigration "in the mild form of taxation," congressmen should support their effort, Sargent declared.[38]

Sargent's proposed amendment was rejected, but it was important because it was California's first attempt to nationalize the Chinese issue. In the midst of a civil war during which race relations was an important factor, the congressmen's skepticism about the existence of "Chinese slavery" in California and their disregard of the alleged immorality of the Chinese reinforced their professed principled opposition to the oppression or exclusion of any "particular class," their euphemism for "race."

Meanwhile, an important test case was brought before the California Supreme Court, resulting in a victory for the Chinese. In June 1862, Lin Sing, a Chinese resident, brought suit before a magistrate for a refund of the tax levied on him under the Chinese Police Tax Act.[39] Arguing the state's case before the court was Attorney General Frank M. Pixley, who later became prominent in the anti-Chinese movement. Pixley argued that the act was a legitimate exercise of the state's police power. The California court rejected his reasoning, affirming that the tax on the Chinese was similar to a tax that discriminated against imports. By singling out the Chinese for oppressive taxation in the hope of decreasing their immigration, California was interfering with foreign commerce. The act was declared unconstitutional and repealed.[40] Anti-Chinese forces had obviously gone too far. Governor Stanford conceded that the statute was "stringent and oppressive." In his annual message to the legislature in 1863, he expressed his confidence that the legislature should be able to pass a substitute, which would be constitutional and would have "the object desired, the discouragement of Chinese immigration and not its total prohibition."[41]

On January 1, 1863, the inclusion of emancipation in the northern war strategy resulted in a renewed barrage of Democratic propaganda about a large-scale black migration to the North and West and the attendant problems of amalgamation and black-white labor competition.[42] Within the Republican ranks, after an initial burst of enthusiasm for the proclamation, the discouraging military situation and the increasing virulence of anti-black attitudes caused midwestern Republicans to either play down or virtually ignore it.[43] In the months following its promulgation, the opposition of white laborers to African Americans working in their trades, especially as a strike-breaking element, often resulted in violence in the North.[44] In April 1863, violent racial conflict erupted between white and black longshoremen on the New York waterfront. The following month, the hiring of black longshoremen to reduce wages led to a new outburst and the discharge of African American laborers.[45] Similar incidents between white and black laborers took place in other northern cities. In these early conflicts, the attacks were often confined to the workplace, where blacks were perceived as a threat to economic security.

A few weeks later, however, the popular reaction to the Conscription Act of May 1863 revealed the deeper roots of the opposition to African Americans. The enforcement of conscription led to minor disturbances in several cities, including Boston and Troy. In New York, it led to the most violent civil disorder in nineteenth-century America, with a death toll of at least 105.[46] For three days, until Union troops arrived from Gettysburg, New York was under the control of mobs. During the first day, much of the violence bore the stamp of rioters conducting a demonstration against the inequitable provisions of the Conscription Act. The second day, however, the riot entered a new, more murderous and destructive phase and expanded into a bloody race riot, encompassing both community and workplace. Native and foreign-born white laborers set out to assault all the groups they considered to be exploitative—especially, African Americans, whom they held responsible for the loss of control over their jobs. As the riot drew to a close, the violent purges of black tenement districts and the horrific slaughter of African Americans were reminiscent of the vicious attacks perpetrated on blacks during the earlier mob actions of the nineteenth century.

As Iver Bernstein has argued, the New York draft riots were indicative of a citywide campaign to erase the black community.[47] Like earlier race riots, the 1863 attacks were designed to induce or compel African Americans to remove themselves from the city or, at least, the rioters' districts. They showed that white laborers would not accept any challenge to the segmentation of labor that had hitherto kept blacks out of the white sectors of the economy. Like anti-Chinese actions in California, these riots also demonstrated that African Americans served as a convenient scapegoat for white laborers who sought to make sense of the structural changes affecting their livelihoods.[48] The evidence shows that psychological sexual fears were also important elements in the racial violence. Attacks on racially mixed couples and white women keeping company with black men were perpetrated by several riot-ers, men and women, who were, according to the *New York Herald,* "ambi-tious to regulate the races and prevent amalgamation." This form of sexual vigilantism was, however, not limited to white-black relationships. One ri-oter, for example, was caught while he was trying to destroy the property of a man keeping house with a "squaw."[49] After the general exodus of blacks from the Fourth Ward, the Chinese residents were next to meet the wrath of the crowd. Urged by a speaker who described the Chinaman as a "modifica-tion of the negro," the rioters turned against the few Chinese peddlers sus-pected of having liaisons with white women.[50]

The rioters partially achieved their aims. While conscription resumed peacefully in August, there was a decline in economic rivalry between blacks and whites. After the riots, editorials noted that employers were reluctant to restore their black employees to their old jobs. By the end of the summer, though, the thriving economy and a dearth of labor led to the relaxation of some of the racial tensions.

As the war drew to a close, the Democrats, especially in the West, remained firm in their opposition to emancipation and any public policy aimed at improving the legal standing of black Americans—including the creation of the Freedmen's Bureau, the removal of racial distinctions from state and federal laws, and the enfranchisement of African Americans. Meanwhile, the Republican majority began to express solicitude for black Americans, whom they increasingly included in their discussion of postbellum America. In Congress, opinion turned against the colonization projects of the Lincoln administration, which were now condemned as "extremist folly" and "haz-ardous and disgraceful." In July 1864, Lincoln signed an act repealing all the acts relating to black colonization.[51] In that same year, the debate over the Thirteenth Amendment demonstrated that a substantial number of Repub-licans had reconciled themselves to universal emancipation on the soil, that is, not tied to colonization abroad. In most western states, the changing atti-tudes of Republicans could be seen in their support of measures to foster legal equality. Many of these states began the long process of removing civil re-strictions against African Americans from their statute books.

There were many reasons for the softening of racial attitudes in the latter stages of the war. The hope of ultimate northern triumph, the growing ani-mosity toward the South, the increased agitation of radicals, the compassion-ate reaction to racial violence in the North and South, and the growing sense of the righteousness of emancipation all played a major role in this devel-opment. Furthermore, the actions of African Americans themselves consti-tuted an essential element in speeding up the cause of freedom. As laborers on the abandoned southern plantations and as soldiers, African Americans had demonstrated their fitness for living "intelligently and productively as a free people." Northerners were also relieved that the dreaded influx of blacks from the South had not materialized.[52]

The Republican solicitude was not without limits. While abolitionists insisted that the freedmen's postwar status should be equal to that of white men, few in Congress were willing to go that far. In 1864, the major concerns of Republicans, even radical ones, were to render emancipation unassailable, to extend equality before the law to freed blacks, and to effect Unionists' control of the new southern governments.[53] All these goals, most Republicans thought, could be accomplished without going beyond the extension of basic civil rights for freed blacks in the South. Insofar as northern blacks were concerned, whites had established that they did not favor complete racial equality. On the eve of the Civil War, blacks in the North constituted only 2 percent of the population, and only 6 percent of that small number could vote. It would have been unreasonable to expect a dramatic change in race relations after the war. The racial prejudices of the Republican congressmen were, after all, indicative of a tenacious belief in inequality. The limited racial agenda of the Republicans at this juncture in the war reflected a certain continuity in northern racial thinking and policies. In western states, where African Americans won legal rights protecting their lives and property, the majority of Republicans were still unwilling to break down *all* racial disabilities. In California, for instance, the anti-black testimony laws were repealed as early as 1863,[54] but legislators specifically dissociated the question of the legal status of African Americans from that of their political and social standing, and they excluded other civil rights, notably suffrage.

Above all, most Republicans seemed to be engaged in a concerted effort to keep African Americans in the South. Some extreme elements made various suggestions for setting apart sections of the South or the West for Negroes. Pointing to the imminence of universal emancipation, Senator James H. Lane of Kansas reminded his fellow Republicans that the North objected to the Negro as a laborer and that it abhorred amalgamation. He proposed that the "4 million good [Negro] citizens" be planted at the door of Mexico, where they would be able to govern and care for themselves.[55] Like the deportation plans, these domestic colonization schemes were rejected by the Republican majority, which deemed them patently impossible and unnecessary.

While blacks were not systematically prevented from leaving the South, neither the federal government nor the different humanitarian groups formed any plans to help southern blacks move north or west. In most cases, the central government actually participated in or sanctioned policies that resulted in the confinement of African Americans within their native South. These efforts started as early as 1862 when federal troops under the command of General Benjamin F. Butler occupied New Orleans. To discourage contrabands, Butler ordered that "vagrant slaves" be moved to the plantations of loyal citizens and put "under the charge of the planters and overseers," with the help of military units as "guards and patrols to preserve order." In 1863, General Nathaniel P. Banks took over the wartime program of the Union army in Louisiana. Like Butler, Banks believed that coercive labor codes were necessary to prevent idleness among freed blacks. He shaped a wage labor program whereby freedpersons were contracted for a year's work and forbidden to leave the plantation without the written permission of their employers. Banks's program was denounced by abolitionists as the "Government Establishment of Slavery in New Orleans."[56] Notwithstanding, the majority viewpoint in the northern press rallied to Banks's approach. This early attempt at fashioning a "free labor" program in the South is significant for at least two reasons. Public opinion in the North did not see a fundamental contradiction between the free labor ideal and coercive labor codes insofar as freed blacks were concerned. Lincoln's administration itself agreed with Banks's views that freed blacks needed to be forcibly inculcated with the habits of free labor through compulsion and contract. Furthermore, it was obvious that emancipation from slavery would not entail emancipation from plantation labor or from the South. Under Butler and Banks, blacks were forced to return to the plantations and work as field hands under the control of their former masters.[57]

To a large extent, the labor-military programs were structured to facilitate the political reconstruction of the South by ensuring economic and social stability. To let the market regulate conditions would have threatened such stability by encouraging black mobility. The reluctance to reverse the practice of sealing African Americans within the South can be further demonstrated in four unsuccessful attempts. In April 1864, Senator Garrett Davis (Democrat from Kentucky), a notorious opponent of black rights, proposed a radical expansion of the abolition bill to provide for the distribution of African Americans among all the states and territories in proportion to their white population. This proposal was, of course, an obstructionist and expedient measure. In that same year, Senator Waitman Willey (Republican from West Virginia) offered an amendment to the Freedmen's Bureau bill, requesting the cooperation of northern governors and municipal authorities in schemes to find employment for African Americans in their localities. In January 1866, Senator Lyman Trumbull (Republican from Illinois) proposed a measure extending the jurisdiction of the Freedmen's Bureau to refugees and freed blacks all over the country.[58] Earlier, in December 1863, Secretary of Interior John Usher had offered a plan to settle African Americans in the Far West. Conceding the reality of extreme anti-black prejudice throughout most of the free states, Usher believed that "Negro labor was in great demand" in the West, where it might be used in constructing the Pacific railways.[59] While radical Republicans applauded such initiatives, moderate Republicans were usually adverse to them.

These discarded schemes of voluntary and assisted black migration were concurrent with congressional approval of a federal law to encourage immigration. This law provided for the enforcement of labor contracts made by immigrants to the United States in foreign countries. Immigrants would be allowed to pledge the wages of their labor for a term not exceeding twelve months to repay the expenses of immigration. After the enactment of the law in July 1864, several emigrant companies were established to help in immigrant labor recruitment and control. Setting up offices in many European countries, these companies received the assistance of American consular officials, who served as disseminators of information about opportunities in the United States and as recruiting agents.[60]

While the act was not expressly racially exclusive, it was construed as applying to European immigrants only. Two years earlier, Congress had given Chinese emigration special consideration when it passed *An Act to Prohibit the "Coolie Trade" by American Citizens in American Vessels*.[61] It seems appropriate to say a word about the coolie trade. In the early 1850s, the U.S. Congress paid only scant attention to the emigration of Chinese indentured laborers to the West Indies and Latin America, notably Cuba and Peru. In fact, it failed to respond to the dispatches of U.S. commissioners to China about the abuses of the traffic, the participation of American vessels in it, and the legal difficulties they had in trying to regulate the trade.[62] In February 1856, Peter Parker, the U.S. minister plenipotentiary to China sent a report to Secretary of State William L. Marcy about the "revolting and inhuman atrocities" of the coolie trade in the hope of receiving specific instructions for regulating the trade in coolies on American vessels.[63] Parker did not receive any response, and Americans continued to engage in the trade. William Reed, who succeeded him, also sought to gain U.S. support for repressing the coolie trade by American vessels. Hindered by the absence of legal authority, he proposed to build a regulatory policy based on the Act of Congress of April 20, 1818, which prohibited the importation of slaves in the United States. This act defined slaves in broad terms as persons of color from Africa or any other foreign country who were forcibly transported to be held to service of labor.[64] Reed was confident that the law could apply to the coolie trade, because the

Chinese were "persons of color" and because coolie emigration was under coercion, with no provisions for the laborers' return to China. In March 1859, however, Reed was advised by the U.S. attorney general that he could not use the 1818 law to control the coolie trade and that only Congress could provide legislation to restrain American involvement in the traffic.[65]

Between 1847 and 1859, some 51,000 Chinese coolies were transported to Cuba in American holds. On the eve of the Civil War, discussion over American participation in the coolie trade gained a new momentum. In 1859, John E. Ward, the new commissioner to China, expressed his alarm that regulations issued by other nations would ultimately cause the trade to pass into American hands.[66] These concerns resonated with Republican legislators, who set out to regulate this other "species of slavery." Meanwhile, in the North and the South, editorials and articles described at length the brutalities of the coolie trade and appealed to Congress to stop American merchants and shipmasters from participating in the trade.[67]

It is important to note that, all this time, American officials in China insisted that the coolie trade had nothing to do with the voluntary emigration of Chinese laborers to California. When Congress finally moved to legislate against Americans engaged in the coolie trade, this distinction was inscribed into the Coolie Act of February 19, 1862, which prohibited American citizens and foreigners residing in the United States from transporting "Chinese coolies" to any foreign country.[68] Although the act failed to give an authoritative definition of the term *coolie,* the explanations about the trade offered by the drafter of the bill, Thomas D. Eliot (Republican from Massachusetts), precluded the existence of coolieism in the United States. The main purpose of the bill, he stated, was to put an end to American participation in the trade in coolies to Latin America and the West Indies. Accordingly, section 4 of the act stated that the act should not be construed to apply to or affect any free or voluntary emigration of Chinese subjects. Not only did the bill distinguish between coolie labor and Chinese voluntary emigration, it also sought to make sure that the act could not be used to ban Chinese free emigration.[69]

There was, however, an important stipulation in the Coolie Act that reveals the legislators' desire to enable American officials to check a possible immigration of coolies into the United States. It required that all Chinese emigrants to the United States obtain a certificate by the U.S. consular agent at the port of embarkation verifying the voluntary nature of their emigration. Two years later, when Congress passed the 1864 Immigration Act validating labor contracts made by (European) emigrants, it was careful to condemn any contract "creating in any way the relation of slavery or servitude."[70] Although this clause served to reinforce the ban on coerced contract labor in the Coolie Act of 1862, it did not require a certification system for emigrants. Moreover, the 1864 Immigration Act established that, unlike Chinese laborers, European immigrants could legally come to the United States on *contracts*. The racialization of this policy was further demonstrated when the provisions of the Coolie Act of 1862 were extended to the Japanese and all Orientals in 1869.[71] To conclude, it is plain that the Chinese occupied a singular position. Although it had been decided that a statute aimed at restricting Negro slaves could not apply to Chinese coolies, the 1864 Immigration Acts indicated that the Chinese were considered a separate class of immigrants. This confusing situation would lay the basis for the unequal treatment of the Chinese in the next decades.

In searching for a remedy to labor shortages in the North and Midwest in the 1860s, both the federal and state governments expressly sought European rather than Chinese immigrants, and they deliberately turned away from a solution at hand, that is, black labor. In the Far West, too, a similar choice was made. When Secretary of Interior Usher proposed that Congress provide for the settlement of African Americans in the Far West to work on the Central Pacific Railroad, he made the astonishing statement that this was a section of the country "where the objection to color does not exist."[72] To be sure, California did not ring as openly and profusely with anti-black statements as some legislative bodies in the Midwest did. Yet there were enough anti-black and anti-Chinese public statements to belie Usher's opinion. California representatives did not hide their racial hostility.[73] Usher was, of course, wrong to assume that Californians would gladly open their state to blacks. One reason that California legislators had pressed for reforms for African Americans earlier than other states was their growing conviction that blacks would remain an insignificant proportion of the state population. Besides this, all three parties in California—Republican, Unionist, and Democratic—never stopped upholding the white man's preeminence over the Chinese and African Americans.

The buildup of the work force of the Central Pacific Railroad (CPR) revealed both the tenacity of racial prejudices and their adaptability to economic exigencies. In 1864, the CPR management faced an acute shortage of labor. Following a general exodus to the newly discovered silver and quartz mines in Nevada, white laborers were in very short supply. Among those who stayed, many were considered shiftless and liable to abandon construction work at the news of a gold strike. In February 1865, following a wage strike among Irish laborers, Charles W. Crocker, the CPR partner in charge of construction, introduced 50 Chinese into the work force. What began as an experiment, for the Chinese were thought to be too frail to perform heavy construction work, turned into a great boon. The management was so satisfied with them that within six weeks, between 2,000 and 3,000 more Chinese were hired. By 1869, when the Central Pacific line was almost completed, the labor force included 10,000 men; 90 percent were Chinese common laborers and 10 percent Irish and American foremen.[74]

Despite the enormous proportion of Chinese laborers, the construction of the railroad went peacefully. This was because the employment of the Chinese did not cause the displacement of white laborers. In general, white workers had a strong aversion to the work performed by the Chinese because they considered it a dangerous and dirt-shoveling job. Besides this, Chinese labor increased opportunities for many white laborers by allowing them to be upgraded to supervisory positions.[75] The hiring of Chinese laborers, then, did not upset the racial order in the western house of labor. In the early months of construction, neither blacks nor Chinese were seriously considered for employment. Only when white laborers failed to meet the demand did the CPR management decide to experiment with the Chinese. Twelve years later, as he reflected on labor relations on the CPR, Crocker concluded that the Chinese were "a mighty good substitute for white labor, when you could not get such labor."[76]

The low net gain of Chinese immigration in 1865 (799) and the net losses of 871 in 1866 and 205 in 1867 demonstrate that most of the Chinese who formed the CPR work force were not fresh immigrants. In those three years, the Chinese population in California was over 50,000. Yet it is questionable whether this availability accounted for the choice of Chinese over African Americans in February 1865. There were then a little more than 4,000 blacks in California. Despite the interest in the transcontinental railroad that blacks expressed in their 1865 California State Convention of Colored Citizens and despite their pointing out the possibility of transporting up to 20,000 freed blacks to California to work on the railroad, the CPR management made the decision that Chinese immigrants rather than African Americans would be used to build the Pacific railroad. This policy was a repetition of the eastern pattern that favored European immigrants over African Americans. It was also the materialization of the earlier state attempts to use Chinese immigrants rather than blacks or Latin Americans to develop the land of California. An early plan to import thousands of "Mexican peons" to work on the Central Pacific Railroad failed because of a strong, adverse public sentiment.[77]

Despite the aversion to both Chinese and African Americans in California, there were variations in the treatment of both groups. In the 1860s, African Americans in California constituted less than 1 percent of the state population, and Chinese immigrants almost 9 percent.[78] While Republican and Union leaders were becoming more receptive to civil rights for the small black community, they remained opposed to them for the larger Chinese group. In 1863, testimony rights were extended to African Americans exclusively, leaving Mongolians, Chinese, and Indians still legally disabled.[79] The legal separation of African Americans from the Chinese was, however, incomplete. Neither African Americans nor the Chinese could become citizens and vote; nor could their children attend public schools. One month after the amendment of the testimony laws, it became unlawful for any school district to admit any prohibited person to its schools—that is, any Negro, Indian, or Mongolian.[80] With respect to economic opportunities, white Americans viewed both African Americans and the Chinese as a degraded and undesirable labor element. When economic necessity in California dictated it, however, a slot would open for the Chinese, provided they accepted the most menial work. Indeed, mass employment of Chinese immigrants rather than blacks on railroad construction in California and the Pacific Northwest occurred without any hostility on the part of white labor, at least until the work was completed. In mining and other occupations, however, they encountered resistance and restrictions everywhere.[81]

When the Chinese proved to be the most efficient and dependable laborers on the CPR, former governor Leland Stanford, founder and president of the CPR, put aside his earlier calls for a decisive action against the "inferior [Chinese] race." In a report to President Andrew Johnson in October 1865, Stanford declared that the Chinese were "quiet, peaceable, patient, industrious, and economical" and "ready and apt to learn all the different kinds of work required in railroad building."[82]

On June 24, 1867, however, the Chinese proved wrong Stanford's and the other magnates' stereotyped notions of the Chinese as nonaggressive and incapable of getting organized. That day, some 2,000 Chinese engaged in tunnel work "walked out as one man," sending the management into a panic. The main organizing tool behind the strike was a placard circulated among the Chinese a day or two before the strike. Never before had the management witnessed such discipline and order in a strike.[83] In their placard, the Chinese set forth their claims to higher wages, a more moderate day's work, and, last but not least, the abrogation of "the right of the overseers of the company to either whip or to restrain them from leaving the road when they desire to seek other employment."[84] In addition to revealing the extent of the exploitation of Chinese railway laborers, these demands exposed the singular status of Chinese laborers as closer to African Americans in the South than workers in the North—black or white. In the North, the grievances listed by the Chinese had been redressed over several periods of workers' struggles. In the postbellum South, however, cries of "abolition of whipping," "freedom to quit," and "reasonable pay scale and working day" were still voiced by black workers, whose economic rights were harshly restricted by their former masters. The Chinese did not experience the most extreme outrages perpetrated on southern blacks—such as fraud, extreme violence, and murder. However, they, too, faced restrictions and whippings. Most black codes in the postbellum period still authorized whipping, the stocks, or the treadmill for freed blacks' offenses.[85] In the course of the institutionalization of slavery, whipping had become restricted to enslaved persons—male and female. In the postbellum period, whether the whip was used in the "freed" South or in the West with the sanction of the CPR management, it was perceived as a badge of white authority. For both Chinese railroad builders and black agricultural laborers, whippings and coerced labor were used as a form of social control and to degrade and impress upon them that they were powerless. Although some Republicans raised their voices against the southern labor codes as a "new slavery," they did not express any concern for the Chinese who were subjected to these archaic measures that were more fit for an unfree system of labor than a society advocating liberty of contract in a free market.

Far from being conscience-stricken, the CPR management was interested only in laying as much track mileage as possible before the CPR encountered the westward-moving Union Pacific. It therefore could not afford a protracted strike. The management had two options when Chinese workers went on strike: break the strike or recruit a strike-breaking element, that is, a group of laborers that would be below or as inferior as the Chinese. Mark Hopkins, one of the partners, inquired about the possibility of transporting ten thousand African Americans to replace the strikers. Collis P. Huntington, another partner, assured him that there would be no problem getting all the Negro laborers he wanted. He could arrange for their transportation from the East at a low rate. "How many thousand shall I send?" Huntington asked.[86] Crocker chose the more economical solution of breaking the strike by using oppressive means. The Chinese were isolated, and their food supply was cut off. One week later, the strike collapsed. The message was clear. Chinese laborers were tolerated only so long as they accepted the exploitative terms of their employment. Moreover, they could expect no support from white laborers' organizations, which made no comment on the strike.

At the celebration of the completion of the transcontinental railroad, Charles Crocker paid tribute to the Chinese laborers. "The early completion of this railroad," he stated, had been in a great measure due to the fidelity and industry of Chinese laborers. Eight years later, in 1877, he praised them as the essential contributor to the material prosperity of California. However, Crocker was prompt to explain that while he had no objection to the presence of the Chinese in the United States, he believed that they should be restricted to the most menial jobs.[87] Like other capitalists, Crocker viewed the Chinese only as a cheap, expendable, and replaceable form of labor. It was a labor that could be dismissed after use, as when Chinese laborers were pushed aside at the ceremony at Promontory Summit on May 8, 1869, or when a commentator attributed the successful completion of the CPR to the commingled blood that flowed in the veins of Californians—French, German, English, and Irish.[88]

PACIFIC RAILROAD COMPLETE.

Following the completion of the Pacific railroad, some raised the specter of amalgamation. As in the case of African American males, racial amalgamation was viewed as an assault on white male honor and the racial order. (Source: *Harper's Weekly,* June 12, 1869, 624. Courtesy of the Library of Congress)

5. Congressional Reconstruction and the Race Questions, 1865–69

[There] are reasons for giving the ballot to the black man of the
South which do not exist for giving the ballot to the Chinaman in
California, or the black man in Ohio or anywhere else.
—Senator James W. Patterson, *Congressional Globe*, June 6, 1868

ON APRIL 9, 1865, the war of rebellion came to an end with the forces of
unionism, national sovereignty, and emancipation victorious on the bat-
tlefield. The resentment fanned by the war was not abated by the defeat of
the South, however. Republicans soon realized that former Confederates still
adhered to their philosophy of state sovereignty and their racial customs. By
the end of 1865, the fruits of the northern victory were already endangered,
and the process of restoring the southern states to the Union had become the
problem of preserving the principles for which the war had been fought.[1]

The intent of the framers of Reconstruction has been the subject of a heated debate. While some have maintained that the Republicans were only slight-
ly interested in the welfare of the African American and were primarily driven
by their desire to keep the South under their control, others have argued that
the Reconstruction amendments originated in a genuine interest in the fate
of African Americans.[2] Two major studies have provided a new understanding of the complex forces that shaped the decision-making process of the
congressional Republican majority. In *A Compromise of Principle* (1974),
Michael Les Benedict laid to rest the notion that the Republican majority in
Congress was either monolithic or very radical. For most Republicans in 1865,
he wrote, the essence of the party had become its devotion to "equal rights"
or racial justice. In practical terms, however, these abstract fundamentals
brought radicals into sharp conflict with conservative Republicans. While
radicals insisted that southern blacks be given a meaningful role in the political life of the restored states, conservatives believed that the party should
proceed with extreme moderation. The conservatives differed from the rad-

icals in the strength of their commitment to carrying out these abstract principles when balanced against other considerations. Despite their differences, however, Republicans acted in harmony because of a common perception of political practicality. Very early in the Thirty-ninth Congress, the Republican majority pursued a conservative Reconstruction policy. After President Johnson's obstinacy and southern resistance, the majority moved increasingly toward a radical agenda. From 1863 to 1869, Benedict concluded, "[m]ost Republicans never had to choose between political expediency and political morality, for to a large extent the political fortunes of the Republican party were best served by fulfilling its liberal ideological commitments."[3] In *Reconstruction* (1988), Eric Foner took issue with the emphasis on the conservative basis of Reconstruction. "Despite all its limitations," he wrote, "[c]ongressional Reconstruction was indeed a radical departure, a stunning and unprecedented experiment in interracial democracy," and the enfranchisement of blacks was "an astonishing leap of faith." The tragedy, though, was that "the lofty goals of civil and political equality were not permanently achieved."[4]

Was Reconstruction aimed to promote a national "experiment in interracial democracy"? Did, as Foner suggested, the enfranchisement of African Americans mark "a powerful repudiation of racial thinking"? In their interpretation of Reconstruction, historians have generally focused on the political disagreements among Republicans regarding southern Reconstruction and the status of African Americans. They have ignored the acrimonious discussions about the larger implications of the extension of civil and political rights to African Americans. As a matter of fact, the congressional debates over Reconstruction opened up the second debate on the subjects of citizenship and naturalization in the nation's history. In this debate, the question was whether not only blacks but all other nonwhites, most notably the Chinese, could and should be granted citizenship. Looking at this important aspect of the congressional debates, this chapter provides a more comprehensive account of race relations in postbellum America and sheds new light on the Republicans' attitudes toward race.[5]

In December 1863, Abraham Lincoln announced his Reconstruction plan. It provided a general amnesty to all southerners (with the temporary exception of high officials of the Confederacy), who would take an oath pledging future loyalty to the government and acceptance of the wartime measures eliminating slavery. When 10 percent of the voters in 1860 took the oath in any state, they could set up a state government. In July 1864, angered at the mildness of Lincoln's program, the Republican majority passed a far more drastic Reconstruction plan. Lincoln, however, disposed of it with a pocket veto. After Lincoln's assassination, Andrew Johnson inherited the controversy over Reconstruction. A southerner and former slaveholder, a Democrat before he had been placed on the Union ticket with Lincoln in 1864, Johnson became the head of a Republican administration at a time when partisan passions, long held in restraint, were about to prevail. Johnson revealed his plan of Reconstruction soon after he took office. Amnesty would be granted to all who would take an oath of allegiance. The conditions for readmittance were that a state should revoke the ordinance of secession, ratify the Thirteenth Amendment, and repudiate all Confederate debts. By the end of 1865, the seceded states were all "reconstructed." When Congress reconvened in December 1865, however, Republican leaders refused to seat the southern congressmen from the states that the president had restored. They declared that Congress needed to know about conditions in the postwar South. Accordingly, they set up a joint committee to investigate these conditions and to advise Congress in developing a Reconstruction policy of its own. The period of "congressional" or "radical Reconstruction" had begun.

Ratified on December 6, 1865, the Thirteenth Amendment to the Constitution changed African Americans from chattel property to a status still not defined yet implicitly within civil society. Southerners were quick to note that while blacks' membership in the national community was established, this classification did not explicitly make them citizens or entitle them to equality before the law. Strictly speaking, the amendment was a mere abrogation of slavery. Accordingly, former Confederate states passed the "black codes" of 1865 and 1866, which drastically limited the rights of newly emancipated blacks. While the codes varied somewhat in their provisions, they generally prohibited African Americans from holding office, voting, serving on juries, or testifying in court except against other blacks. They were often required to possess passes in moving from place to place. If they refused to work, they could be fined and hired out to work by labor contractors. They were largely restricted to rural residence and to cultivation of the soil, without the right to purchase or own it, and they were often excluded from gainful occupations.[6] In January 1866, this defiant behavior led Republicans to take effective measures to protect freed blacks in the South. Senator Lyman Trumbull (Republican from Illinois) proposed a civil rights bill conferring citizenship on "all persons of African descent born in the United States" and declaring illegal any discrimination in civil rights or immunities among the inhabitants of all the states and territories of the United States, when these were made on account of race, color, or previous condition of slavery.[7] Trumbull explained that "civil rights" in a republican state included certain fundamental rights—namely, the natural rights to life, liberty, and property and the right "to make and enforce contracts, to sue, be parties, and give evidence, to inherit, purchase, lease, sell, hold, and convey real and personal property, and to full and equal benefit of all laws and proceedings for the security of person and property." These rights did not, however, involve political or voting rights.[8]

The objection of Senator Peter G. Van Winkle (conservative Republican from West Virginia) to Trumbull's bill precipitated a long and impassioned discussion on the definition of citizenship. Trumbull had explained that the legal basis for his bill was that the Thirteenth Amendment had given Congress the right to pass laws eliminating state laws that denied some persons rights common to all other people.[9] To Van Winkle, the amendment had bestowed no rights beyond the abolition of slavery; hence, there was no constitutional ground for the passage of the pending civil rights bill. "The position [of persons of the Negro race] is certainly anomalous," he commented. He insisted that all the current prohibitions against African Americans—not counted among "We the People" by the framers of the Constitution, excluded from citizenship by most states, and forbidden to come within the borders of some states for permanent residence— would be of no effect if they were citizens. The only way to bestow citizenship on African Americans was thus a constitutional amendment. Before such a step was taken, he warned that it was important to assess the implications of such an amendment. This question of citizenship, he argued, involved not only the Negro race but also other inferior races residing on the Pacific Coast—an obvious hint at Chinese immigrants.[10]

Subsequently, some senators worried that Trumbull's bill might be used to confer citizenship on other groups. Among them, Senator Edgar Cowan (conservative Republican from Pennsylvania) asked whether the bill would have "the effect of naturalizing the children of Chinese . . . born in [the United States]." He was particularly concerned about the consequences that the citizenship clause would have on the Pacific Coast. If the Chinese were given political rights as citizens, he warned, California would soon belong to the Mongolian rather than Indo-European race. Cowan's inquiry was met by Trumbull's erroneous argument that under the naturalization laws, the children born in the United States of Chinese parents were citizens. Since the law made no distinction on the basis of race, he explained, "the child of an Asiatic is just as much a citizen as the child of a European."[11] In 1866, however, neither the naturalization laws nor the U.S. Constitution defined the citizenry. The assumption was that the English common law rule of *jus soli* was in effect. Under *jus soli*, a person born in the United States is, by virtue of that fact alone, a citizen of the United States. Obviously, as the debate demonstrated, this doctrine was not thought to apply to African Americans. Chief Justice Taney's ruling in *Dred Scott v. Sandford* (1857) that blacks could never be citizens of the United States had yet to be completely invalidated. Senator Cowan's remarks reveal that, like African Americans, Chinese were not thought to be included within the bounds of *jus soli.*

In the following two months, Trumbull had to defend his bill against bipartisan attacks. He made plain that the bill was designed to confer *some* civil rights on *all* persons, not merely to abolish discrimination against African Americans. His bill was then amended to include "all persons born in the United States" rather than "all persons of African descent born in the United States."[12] Tying this new version of the bill to the abolition of the black codes, Trumbull managed to rally round him the Republican majority, which was satisfied that the bill did not include political privileges. The tiny Democratic delegation, even with the aid of some ultraconservative Republicans, was unable to stop the passage of the bill by a comfortable margin.[13] In the House, the Republican majority concurred with Trumbull's interpretation that the Thirteenth Amendment gave Congress the authority to ensure equal protection for all persons. In the course of the debate, however, House Republicans provided a narrow definition of the term *civil rights* that excluded not only political rights but also schools, jury service, and miscegenation from its ambit.[14]

The bill was vetoed by President Johnson, who explained that, besides lacking a constitutional basis, the bill was objectionable because it would operate in favor of all the colored races and against the white race. The first section of the bill, he noted, conferred citizenship on all persons in the United States, including what he called the "excepted races": the Chinese of the Pacific states, Indians subject to taxation, the people called Gypsies, "as well as the entire race designated as blacks." It was not sound policy to make the entire colored population citizens of the United States while eleven states were unrepresented in Congress. Moreover, the bill proposed to discriminate against not only white southerners but also "large numbers of intelligent, worthy and patriotic foreigners." Nonwhite foreigners were, of course, not included in the latter category. Johnson found it unfair that African Americans should be granted citizenship by a single legislative enactment while worthy foreigners had to undergo a probation of five years.[15]

The Republicans in the House had no problem mustering a two-thirds majority to override the president's veto (122 to 41). In the more conservative Senate, the vote was close (33 to 15).[16] For the Republicans, the lesson of this first contest was that it was necessary to introduce a constitutional amendment embodying the principles of the Civil Rights Act, so that the act could be neither repealed nor declared unconstitutional.

In his expository speech about the proposed Fourteenth Amendment, Senator Jacob M. Howard (Republican from Michigan), a consistent radical, stressed two major provisions: citizenship derived from birth (*jus soli*) and a "privileges and immunities" clause.[17] The first point was the occasion for another rancorous discussion about the citizenship of nonwhite groups. Senator Cowan took the opportunity to ride his favorite hobbyhorse, calling for some limitation of the term *citizen of the United States.* With no such limitation, he argued, California would be in great danger of being overrun by the Mongolian race. As he saw it, the amendment would undermine the right that California and all other states claimed to exclude undesirable persons. When Cowan shifted his attention away from the Pacific Coast, it became clear that the amendment hit him closer to home. His state (Pennsylvania) was "infested with Gypsies,"[18] a class of people who, in his opinion, constituted an "imperium in imperio." There was no doubt in his mind that the Chinese presented a singular menace. Unlike the "pestiferous Gypsy," the Mongolian was not only equal to the white American but perhaps superior. Nobody, he continued, should doubt the superior industry, skill, and pertinacity of the yellow race.[19]

When Senator John Conness (radical Republican from California) took the floor, Cowan expected him to support his position. Far from agreeing with Cowan, Conness scolded him and all other Republicans who had been deprecating the civil rights bill and the pending amendment because of their alleged pernicious implications for California. The citizenship proposition in the amendment related to the children begotten of Chinese parents, not to Chinese immigrants, he stressed. These children, he said, constituted a very small portion of the population in California. "Notwithstanding the proximity to the Celestial land," he added, the progeny of the Chinese could never become substantial because Chinese men brought their wives to America in very limited numbers. Californians, he averred, were not troubled at all with the Chinese in their midst. Before closing his rebuttal, Conness warned that adding the Chinese question to the current debate would only complicate the political agitation about the status of the African American.[20]

Cowan and Conness showed the split in the Senate Republican majority over extending citizenship and civil rights to African Americans exclusively or to all nonwhites. Earlier in the House, William Niblack from Indiana, one of the most learned and respected Democrats, had exposed this lack of consensus by taking to task William Highby (Republican from California). Highby had expressed his strong support for a constitutional amendment that would provide for the citizenship and civil rights of African Americans. When asked by Niblack whether this amendment would apply to the Chinese in his state, Highby abruptly responded that if the central government would annul the treaty with China, Californians could simply get rid of the Chinese, whom he described as a pagan and immoral race. That Highby was known to be a radical made him a good target for Niblack. If, as Republicans claimed, citizenship and civil rights were a simple question of manhood, Niblack quipped, how could Highby use morals and religion to deprive the Chinese of their rights as human beings? Did the Negro not belong to a similarly defective race? "Why should [the Chinese] not receive the same right as the negro?" he asked. Highby's reply was that, although African Americans were once pagans, they were now as "native" as any of the representatives in the House. In presenting American nativity as the rationale for Negro rights, Highby did not realize the flaw in his argument. If American nativity sufficed to make African Americans citizens, Niblack reasoned, then the children born of Chinese parents in the United States were citizens too. Highby lost his temper, hammering awkwardly that he need not give any more reasons to justify the exclusion of the Chinese.[21]

For three months after this exchange, the question of citizenship remained a moot point dividing Republicans. On May 30, 1866, when Senator Howard proposed inserting the *jus soli* doctrine in the Fourteenth Amendment, he hoped to prove that Republican racial policies were consistent. That same day, when Senator Conness rose to defend the Chinese against Cowan's censure, it was clear that he rendered the Republican party a valuable service. Unlike Cowan, he had not put the concerns and prejudices of his state above the interests of the party.

The second significant provision in the proposed Fourteenth Amendment was contained in the "privileges and immunities" clause. Using broad language, the first statement in the clause prohibited the states from infringing on the privileges, immunities, and rights to due process and equal protection of the law, which Americans enjoyed as citizens of the United States. The second statement extended "due process of law" and "equal protection of the laws" to *all persons,* regardless of whether they were citizens. In his expository speech, Senator Howard explained that extending protection to all persons would do away with the injustice of subjecting any class of persons to a code not applicable to another.[22] Without it, the operation of the privileges and immunities clause insofar as noncitizens were concerned would be uncertain. Indeed, the category of "noncitizens" in 1866 included not only aliens but also African Americans. Naturalization laws distinguished between aliens on the basis of race. So far as blacks were concerned, while Republicans could easily rebut the racist harangues of some Democrats, they had to consider the reasoned constitutional objections to their claim that African Americans were entitled to be citizens of the United States.[23] Accordingly, a clause about the immunities and privileges of *citizens* of the United States might have had no effect on both African Americans and nonwhite aliens. At this juncture, though, Howard expressed his concern for African Americans rather than nonwhite aliens. "Is it not time," he asked, "that we extend to the black man . . . the poor privilege of the equal protection of the law?"[24]

Equally important in the Fourteenth Amendment was a section devoted to the basis of representation in the House. Prior to 1865, enslaved African Americans had counted for three-fifths of a person in apportioning representation. Under the leadership of Representative Thaddeus Stevens from Pennsylvania, the Republicans set out to prevent the increased voting strength that the newly enlarged population base gave southern Democrats. Stevens proposed that wherever African Americans could not vote, they would be excluded from the population base. While most Republicans supported his motion, a few radicals rejected it on the grounds that it would fail to secure voting rights for African Americans and that it would extend congressional approval to the principle of disfranchisement by leaving the decision on suffrage to the states.[25]

More than any other issue, black suffrage demonstrated the fluctuations in Republican racial thought. Four years of war had not purged the racial prejudices of many Republicans and their constituents. Thorough racial egalitarians were in the minority. As in the antebellum period, the Republican majority was reluctant to grant political privileges to African Americans. Only in New England (excluding Connecticut) were blacks allowed to vote. In the calculations of the Republican majority, however, racial animosities weighed less heavily than the hope of attaining dominance in the South with the help of African American votes. Notwithstanding this, black suffrage was a touchy issue. From 1865 to 1868, a number of state referenda on black suffrage in northern and western states indicated a lack of support for black suffrage.[26] Accordingly, Stevens's proposed amendment would maintain the status quo in the North and permit Republicans to build up majorities in the South with or without the votes of African Americans. Moderate Republicans were satisfied that the preservation of the states' right to grant suffrage would allow their states to keep their own restrictive laws. The limitation of the moral principle of the Republican majority was also obvious in its reluctance to enfranchise other nonwhite groups. Congressman Roscoe Conkling (Republican from New York), for example, called for vigilance to ward off the probability of "unbridled suffrage." California, he observed, "may let her Chinese and half-breeds vote, Oregon her Indians, and any State its aliens."[27]

Stevens's amendment was included in section 2 of the Fourteenth Amendment. On June 13, 1866, the amendment was accepted as a partisan measure, with two-thirds of each chamber concurring in its passage. In the fall elections of 1866, Republicans connected black suffrage with the restructuring of the Union under Republican hegemony. They endorsed black suffrage in the South, but they shied away from advocating universal black suffrage. The Republican party won an overwhelming electoral victory over the Democrats, which the Republicans interpreted as an endorsement of their moderate Reconstruction program, especially the sharp distinction between civil and political rights, the extension of civil rights to all persons, and the Fourteenth Amendment as the terms of Reconstruction for the southern states. The Democrats were not yet ready to capitulate, however. With the support of President Johnson, all southern states except Tennessee rejected the Four-teenth amendment. The Republican majority responded by passing the Re-construction Acts of 1867, which divided the South into five military districts and laid out the conditions for readmission to the Union: essentially, the drafting of new constitutions providing for manhood suffrage and the ratifi-cation of the Fourteenth Amendment.[28]

The debate over the Reconstruction bills focused on protecting southern black males in their exercise of the franchise. It also involved the larger ques-tion of race relations in the United States. James A. Johnson (Democrat from California) objected that this new policy would result in incorporating as citizens not only "the pet negro but also . . . the filthy Chinese."[29] James Beck (Democrat from Kentucky) held that the Negro was as unfit for political rights as the Chinaman and the Indian.[30] Senator James Patterson (conser-vative Republican from New Hampshire) argued that southern insubordi-nation dictated the imposition of universal suffrage in the South. Anywhere else, though, voting privileges should be conferred solely by the states. To explain this double standard, he turned to California and its large number of Chinese residents. If the vote was extended to them, they would have the power to determine any election.[31]

In their 1868 platform, the Republicans made their party's stand on black suffrage unequivocally clear. While they called for the "guaranty by Congress of equal suffrage to all loyal men at the South," they stressed that the ques-tion of suffrage in the loyal states belonged to the people of those states. Meanwhile, the Democrats discredited Reconstruction policies, charging that, instead of restoring the Union, the Republican party had subjected ten states to military despotism and Negro supremacy. They also denounced the ty-rannical prescription of Negro suffrage in the South while the majority of the other states denied their black population the right to vote.[32] Notwith-standing this, the Republican party won the 1868 presidential election, with a majority of electoral votes: 214 for Ulysses S. Grant and 80 for Horatio Sey-mour. The popular vote was 52.71 percent to 47.29 percent. Together with the surprising strength of the Democratic party in many northern and western states, such as Connecticut, New Jersey, New York, Indiana, Oregon, and California, the popular vote was close enough to dispel any notion that the Republicans were unbeatable. Although the Republican platform had promised not to interfere with northern suffrage qualifications, when Congress met after the election, Republican leaders made proposals for a constitutional amendment that would provide for universal black male suffrage. As the drafts for the amendment were considered, Republican leaders now emphasized their party's commitment to equality for all African Americans and now admitted that Negro enfranchisement was required.[33] Gradually, conservative Republicans' objections to universal suffrage decreased. It was clear that the Reconstruction program had to be consolidated while they still dominated the state legislatures. If they failed to do so before the next legislative elections, the Democrats might make suffrage a campaign issue and achieve a comeback on the national political scene. As Senator Waitman T. Willey (Republican from West Virginia) put it, Negro suffrage "will remove him [the Negro] from the arena of national politics."[34]

Even before Willey's prediction could be tested and as the debate over the Fifteenth Amendment proceeded, the African American was actually withdrawn from the discussion, which shifted to the Chinese on the West Coast. It started when Senator George H. Williams (Republican from Oregon) proposed that each state regulate the right of suffrage under the supervising power of Congress. Universal suffrage, he warned, would create the conditions for a change in the naturalization laws and would deliver the nation to "the political filth and moral pollution" of Asiatic immigrants. Williams concluded with a diatribe against Chinese paganism, devotion to absolutism, and nonassimilation; in short, they were constituting "an imperium in imperio—China in the United States."[35] Williams's vehement rhetoric is significant in the light of his otherwise strong support of Reconstruction. In 1857, as a leading member of the Democrat-led constitutional convention of Oregon, Williams had helped shape the discriminatory measures against nonwhite residents.[36] Beginning his political career as a Democrat, he had eventually become a northern Democrat opposed to slavery. During the Civil War, he joined the Republican party and was elected to the U.S. Senate in 1864. As a member of the Joint Committee on Reconstruction and a backer of the radicals against President Johnson, Williams had demonstrated his intransigent support of Negro rights. Notwithstanding, his anti-Chinese attitude had endured.

Williams's crude Sinophobic appeals provided ammunition to the Democrats, who were quick to seize the opportunity to argue that race should remain a qualification for voting.[37] Senator James A. Bayard from Delaware, a veteran of the Democratic power structure on Capitol Hill, expounded that race should remain a major exception to the general truth that the powers of government should be entrusted to the people at large. History, he argued, had proved that whenever two races were so dissimilar as to prevent their fusion, political equality ended in racial conflict or in mongrelization. It was not in the American South, however, but on the Pacific Coast that a war of the races was imminent, he predicted. There, with the help of a universal suffrage amendment, "the effete civilization of the Chinese" would soon have political control of the region. Bayard then admonished California's Republican senators, Conness and Cornelius C. Cole, for not supporting Williams and for solacing themselves "under the delusion that the Chinese are not and will not become citizens."[38]

In the following debate, Williams took the lead in the effort to exclude the Chinese from the suffrage amendment. As Senator Cole assumed the function of presiding officer, Williams proposed to insert the word *natural-born* before the word *citizen* in the amendment. As he saw it, the proposition agreed with the Republican principle that neither Congress nor any state could discriminate against any citizen on the basis of race, color, or previous condition of servitude. It would, however, allow western states to deprive persons born in China or Japan of the elective franchise or the right to hold office. What was more, he continued, it would "leave it with the States to declare that persons born in Asia or in Africa should not exercise political power within the several states." So far as Africans were concerned, Williams explained that his proposition would hardly be operative because not many Africans would ever immigrate.[39]

It is significant that no Republican senator expressed any sympathy for the Chinese or the potential African immigrants. The suffrage amendment pending in the Senate could hardly reflect a repudiation of racial prejudice. It was, as Henry W. Corbett, a conservative Republican from Oregon, stated, a measure to protect African Americans' and Republicans' interests *in the South.* Shifting his attention to the Pacific Coast, he assailed Chinese suffrage on the grounds that it would encourage their immigration. Like Williams, he was concerned that the Chinese threat reached the very foundation of American institutions.[40] Senator Frederick T. Frelinghuysen from New Jersey conjoined in part with the two senators from Oregon. He did not support Chinese suffrage because he did not favor taking steps backward into the slough of ignorance and vice; however, he believed that exclusion from the franchise should not find its way in the Constitution but rather should be attended to in the naturalization laws.[41]

The diversity of the Republicans' racial attitudes was again exposed by the Democrats, who prided themselves on being consistent in their demands for racial exclusion and in harmony with the wishes of the country's founders. The Declaration of Independence, Senator Garrett Davis (Democrat from Kentucky) recalled, embraced neither the Negro nor the Indian. It was therefore only natural to object to "Negro and Mongolian government." While he conceded that the prospect of a vast Chinese immigration was alarming, he also called the attention to the fact that the Chinese were "a vastly superior race to the negro." Their efficiency as laborers in the West was a fact known to all, Davis stressed.[42] Senator Davis was a notorious minority party militant, who stoutly resisted all efforts to change the status of blacks. Not infrequently, he had been criticized by less intransigent Democrats, including Senator Thomas A. Hendricks from Indiana, a politician known to be pragmatic and moderate. Early on in the debate over black suffrage, Hendricks had actually given his support to qualified black enfranchisement in the South.[43] In his rebuttal of the Republican position on the Chinese question, however, he proved to be just as prejudiced as Davis.[44] Following a long harangue about the inferiority of the black race, Hendricks expressed his amazement at the Republicans' proposition to exclude the Chinese—who came from a higher civilization—on the ground of their paganism. Christian religion, he stated, was not a qualification for voting in any state. Befuddled by this defense of the Chinese, William M. Stewart (radical Republican from Nevada) asked Hendricks whether he was in favor of naturalizing and enfranchising the Chinese. Of course, Hendricks was not; he was in favor of white voters only. Having established the consistency of his argument, he concluded that Republican racial policy was governed by expediency. Most of these states had very few blacks, but they had large numbers of Chinese. It suited certain purposes that the suffrage be extended to the Negro, but it did not suit other purposes that it be extended to the Chinese.[45]

While Williams's amendments failed miserably, receiving only a few votes, the debate that ensued demonstrated that the lack of support of the Republican majority did not stem from a principled opposition to racial injustice. That same day, on February 8, 1869, Senator Howard offered to confine the suffrage amendment to "citizens of the United States of African descent." Only two Republican senators objected to the proposition. While Senator George Edmunds (conservative Republican from Vermont) acknowledged that it was expedient for the black-white relations, he was still of the opinion that any amendment to the Constitution should be "broader than one race and be longer in its duration and application than any limited period." Senator Willard Warner (radical Republican from Alabama) was worried that Howard's proposition failed to secure to all persons their rights. As it stood, it lacked a stipulation about the rights of "citizens of Irish and German ancestry."[46]

Warner did not allude to the burning case of Chinese immigrants. Nor did two of the three West Coast legislators who expressed their support for Howard's amendment. The third, Senator Cole from California, was satisfied that the amendment would effectually remove the subject of Chinese immigration from the debate. Unlike the senators from Oregon, he did not anticipate any great difficulty arising from such immigration. The Chinese were so wedded to their native country, he argued, that they were reluctant to apply for citizenship. Why, then, did he approve of a suffrage amendment that implicitly excluded the Chinese? Simply because, as he put it, the "Chinese Question" had excited so "much feeling on the part of Senators *not from the Pacific Coast* [emphasis added]" that it was liable to upset the course of the debates. The question facing the Senate, he explained, was whether persons of African descent residing in the United States—not foreigners—should be enfranchised.[47]

James R. Doolittle, the controversial Republican senator from Wisconsin, was not duped. Doolittle had taken a prominent part in politics as a Democrat until 1856, when he identified himself with the Republican party and became one of the staunchest proponents of the doctrine of no compromise with the slave states. Elected to the Senate in 1857 and serving there until 1869, he became increasingly critical of Reconstruction policy. Holding that the radical Republicans had violated the Constitution by keeping the southern states out of the Union, he became an able supporter of President Johnson. To be sure, many Republicans believed that Doolittle had betrayed the party. However, his comment that the Reconstruction scheme was "a double-faced thing," looking "with a black face to the South and with a white face to the North,"[48] was the cause of embarrassment within Republican ranks. To Doolittle, the attempt to narrow the scope of the amendment from "citizens" to "native-born citizens" stemmed from an irrational fear of Chinese citizenship and suffrage. The Chinese, he argued, were known to all senators "as far in advance of the African" in point of civilization. If senators wanted to carry out the egalitarian principle, he remonstrated, why did they not extend the same privileges to the industrious Chinese as those extended to the "African"? Sooner or later, he predicted, Republicans would have to stand on the principle one way or another. Of course, Doolittle was not a racial egalitarian. He never spared words to express his contempt for the attempts to force southern governments into the "African's hands." All through his exposition, he kept referring to black Americans as Africans, thereby signifying their symbolic banishment from *his* America. He also offered his long-advocated nostrum—black emigration—to the quandary in which the country found itself. So far as the Chinese were concerned, notwithstanding his praise of their industry and frugality, Doolittle adverted to the imminent invasion of the Pacific Coast. The senator from Wisconsin was thus against granting suffrage to both African Americans and the Chinese.[49]

Howard's amendment was rejected in a vote of thirty-five to sixteen.[50] This did not, however, end the debate on the Chinese. The following day, Charles Sumner (radical Republican from Massachusetts) proposed a new amendment to broaden the scope of the suffrage amendment: "The right to vote and hold office shall not be denied or abridged by the United States, nor by any State, on account of race, color, or previous condition of servitude." Senators Oliver P. Morton (Republican from Indiana) and Doolittle were the first to object to this attempt to impose complete egalitarianism. Morton protested that the amendment would make the Chinese eligible to vote, despite their noncitizen status. Doolittle contended that, if the amendment was passed, Congress would have total power over citizenship. By a simple act of a majority, it could strike the word *white* from the naturalization laws. When Sumner reminded him that he had already submitted a bill for that purpose before the Committee on the Judiciary, Doolittle conjured up images of social equality between the Chinese and Americans of European descent, the unfortunate consequence of Sumner's "sledge-hammer blows at this terrible word 'white.'"[51]

The colloquy between Doolittle and Sumner increased the fears of anti-Chinese senators. As the debate progressed, Sinophobic feelings became more clamorous. At this juncture, Sumner began to draw back, explaining that his amendment would not supersede the racial naturalization restriction. Morton was prompt to counter that the phrase "citizen of the United States" was "put in to protect us against Chinamen." Without the word *citizen,* the suffrage clause would include all persons, regardless of race or color. This egalitarian trend, he went on, would inevitably find its way in the naturalization laws. The result would be a deluge of Chinese immigrants. China, he recalled, was an immense hive of several hundred million human beings. In a year, he estimated, they would outnumber all other groups on the Pacific Coast and take political control of the whole region.[52]

Under this assault that presented Chinese exclusion from citizenship as a protection of national integrity, Sumner justified his move by his desire to bring American laws in harmony with the principles enshrined in the Declaration of Independence, especially its color-blindness. When he realized that his call for a higher moral ground did not impress his fellow Republicans, Sumner acknowledged that he had opened "an immense debate" and that the prospect of a Chinese invasion should be of concern. He therefore decided not to press further the passage of his amendment.[53]

Thinking that the Pacific delegation was in a strong position because of Sumner's retraction, Senator Corbett resubmitted his amendment expressly excluding the Chinese from citizenship. It was high time, he proclaimed, senators nipped the Chinese question in the bud or admitted that they were prepared to abandon the Pacific states to the Chinese. He was satisfied that the current naturalization laws excluded the Chinese, who as "copper-colored people" were regarded as a *colored race*. Senator Stewart shared Corbett's concern about Chinese immigration. Unlike him, however, he had faith in the senators' perspicacity. When his colleagues learned the facts about the Chinese, they would agree with the impropriety of naturalizing them, he contended. It was not, however, the most opportune moment for such a discussion. For now, Republicans had to pledge their support for black suffrage.[54]

In the midst of these more or less frank appeals to racial prejudice, two senators took the floor to vindicate the rights of the Chinese. Pointing to the fact that the senators had been in session for twenty-seven hours, Simon Cameron (Republican from Pennsylvania), a constant radical, deplored that they were not a bit closer to a conclusion than when they had started the session. Filled with consternation at the discussion about "the poor Chinaman," he sought to correct the misrepresentation of Chinese immigrants. The Chinese, he stated, should be praised because they had enriched the Pacific slope with their toil. If, as the West Coast congressmen maintained, the Chinese did not want to become citizens, what harm could they cause? he asked. It was, in his opinion, imperative that Republicans put aside their fear of that "simple, frugal people, lest they should destroy their liberties," and pledge their unwavering support for a suffrage amendment that would include all persons. Following him, Trumbull elaborated on the censurable position of the anti-Chinese members. Was it not paradoxical, he asked, that at the same time they sought to carry out the great principles of human rights by including "the Hottentots and cannibals from Africa," some Republicans were proposing a clause against the subjects of the oldest empire of the earth? Trumbull was positive that Corbett's amendment expressly excluding the Chinese from citizenship would not obtain any considerable support. He was right. The amendment was summarily rejected.[55]

This rejection did not lay the Chinese question to rest. Next, Senator Henry Wilson (radical Republican from Massachusetts) proposed to forbid discrimination in voting based on not only race but also property, education, creed, and *nativity*. This new amendment at once gained the support of a few Republicans, who felt that a broad suffrage amendment would be more accept-

able to their constituents than one providing for black suffrage only. It, however, drew the fire of a great number of Republican senators representing
northern and western states, whose constitutions limited the right to vote or
hold office based on any one of these grounds.[56] James W. Patterson (Republican from New Hampshire) objected to abolishing literacy tests, which were
used in his state to "exclude Hottentots," whom he regarded as unfit for self-
government. Wilson took him to task, reminding him that the question of
whether African Americans should be enfranchised was already settled so far
as their party was concerned. The pending discussion was about *aliens,* he
insisted—specifically, "the people who come here from western Europe, who
are of our race, [and] who are naturalized in the United States." Obviously,
Wilson was intimating that Patterson should be careful not to drag up the
Chinese question again in the discussion. Patterson chose to ignore him and
asked if a literacy test would be necessary to help California guard its institutions against "the flood of Asiatic barbarism."[57]

Ensuing debates in the Senate and the House displayed the deep disagreement within the Republican majority, prompting the Republican leaders to
offer an amendment providing for the suffrage of African Americans only.
West Coast Republicans reiterated their objection to any amendment that did
not guarantee Chinese exclusion from suffrage and citizenship.[58] Wilson's
amendment passed by a very narrow margin in the Senate and was overwhelmingly defeated in the House.[59] The final draft of the amendment
banned discrimination against *citizens,* based on race, color, or previous condition of servitude. It received a large majority in both houses—39 to 13 in
the Senate and 145 to 44 in the House.[60] The amendment was, however, rejected by a number of northern and western states. Its ratification as the Fifteenth Amendment on February 3, 1870, was made possible by the votes of
reconstructed southern states.

By 1870, then, the Republican party had erected the basic structure of its
Reconstruction program in the form of two amendments, which conferred on
African Americans civil and political rights that, in principle, no state could
thereafter deny them. The Reconstruction debates were, however, marred by
the persistence of racial animosity and prejudices toward all nonwhites, the
Republicans' hesitant progress toward political rights for African Americans,
and the limitations of the Republican crusade for equality. Black civil and political rights were achieved only as a result of long battles between Republicans
and Democrats and, more critically, among Republicans themselves. As during the antebellum and Civil War periods, the question about the rights of
African Americans was clearly subordinated to the more essential aim of ensuring the hegemony of northern political, economic, and social institutions.

Whether they have stressed lofty ideals or political expediency, the conservatism or radicalism of Republican Reconstruction politics, historians have generally neglected the wrangling over the implications of Reconstruction for the race-relations situation affecting the Pacific states. The angry discussions over the Reconstruction amendments confirm that, except for a few radicals, the Republican majority did not adhere to racial egalitarianism. Despite the rhetoric of equal rights irrespective of race, color, or previous condition of servitude, the interjection of the Chinese question in the debates caused Republicans to slip into uneasy contradictions. The abstract nature of the egalitarian creed of the Republican majority was thus exposed throughout the debates over the status of Chinese immigrants in the United States. As they expressed their misgivings about the Chinese, conservative and some radical Republicans found themselves referring to black inferiority, barbarism, and unfitness for self-government. Despite its enfranchisement of African Americans, the Republican majority was still far from accepting their full incorporation into the American social and political structure.

It was, however, in the treatment of the Chinese issue that the Republican majority demonstrated unequivocally the limits of its commitment to racial equality. Significantly, the Chinese question entered national politics in 1866 as a *racial* issue rather than an immigration issue. In their formulation of Reconstruction, Republicans were certainly limited by a basically conservative view of the Constitution and what they could do in the South. However, they inscribed in the Fifteenth Amendment a phraseology that was aimed to narrowly circumscribe the future course of action for incorporating the Chinese in the United States. As they set out to amend the Constitution and provide a catalyst for significant changes in American law and race relations, they deliberately promoted a conservative framework that they hoped would enable them to set the pace of social change. While the Fourteenth Amendment verified the Republicans' commitment to extending equal protection under the law to all persons, the liberal construction of the next amendment should not deflect attention from the fact that the choice of the word *citizens* over *persons* originated in the Republican majority's desire to maintain a legal basis for a racial prerequisite in the naturalization laws. The words "race, color, or previous condition of servitude" in the amendment applied to *blacks in America,* not "copper-colored" immigrants. The integration of African Americans did not mean that nonwhiteness no longer mattered. Had the Republican majority been genuinely committed to interracial democracy, it would have countenanced the abolition of racial discrimination for "persons," be they citizens or resident aliens. As they argued about the propriety of extending equal rights to aliens, the Republicans used a line of reasoning that culminated

in the strict separation of aliens along racial lines, white and nonwhite, European and Asian. Their refusal to come out for equal rights for the Chinese was
not prompted by economic motivations. The theme of "coolieism" was hardly
used by anti-Chinese congressmen. To be sure, a few stressed the mercenary
motives of "the sojourning Chinamen." Others deplored the industriousness
and frugal habits of the Chinese, which made them dangerously competitive.
Yet the major charge leveled at Chinese immigrants was cultural. The Chinese
were objectionable because of their color, paganism, and barbaric culture.
What was more, their "exhaustless numbers" made them a formidable threat.
Despite the "superiority" of Anglo-Saxon culture, Republicans feared it could
not withstand the invasion of millions of Asians.

The Democrats were prompt to point out the inconsistency of the Republican position. Of course, their objections did not stem from a humanitarian concern. As they taunted the Republicans, they generally exposed their
racial antagonism to all nonwhites, including the Chinese. In essence, they
declared that while California and the Pacific Coast risked being overrun by
the multitudes of "copper-colored barbarians," the American South was already afflicted with four million "Hottentots." If a pagan and inferior culture was a determining factor for discrimination, then both the Chinese and
African Americans ought to be excluded from citizenship. While some Republicans met this trenchant criticism by distinguishing between the Hottentots in Africa and American Negroes or by referring to the limited number of African Americans, the Republican majority made clear that the special
solicitude bestowed on African Americans was inspired by their potential key
role as a solid Republican voting bloc in the Reconstruction plan. In that
scheme, the Chinese question proved to be a major complication and oftentimes an embarrassment.

While radicals were far ahead of their time, the Republican majority was
more in harmony with social norms. In the society at large, negative perceptions of blacks and Chinese had survived the war and continued to influence
American society—north and south, east and west. These prejudices inspired
a torrent of racist books and articles about the status of freed blacks in America. While antebellum Negrophobic literature had been somewhat qualified
by a strain of paternalism, the postbellum literature revealed an extreme and
undisguised contempt for and hatred of the Negro.[61] An important new consideration in some of these publications was their comprehensive approach
to race relations in America.

Of all the racist writings of the postbellum period, none was more gross-
ly offensive than Hinton Helper's virulently racist 479–page diatribe—*Nojoque* (1867). In the 1850s, Helper had castigated the presence of nonwhites

in what could have been a pristine white West (see chapter 3). In *Nojoque,* he expressed his wish to rid America of "Negroes, Mulattoes, Chinese, and Indians!"[62] America was divided in two, he argued: a thriving North, "white with Anglo-Saxons and Anglo-Americans," and a poor South lagging behind, "cursed with a tenantry of hell-hatched and hell-doomed Ethiopians." What the South needed, he insisted, was white immigrants. Before welcoming them, however, it was essential to open at once the back doors in the South and the West for the speedy exit of all the black and copper-colored races.[63] Helper's vicious attacks also extended to the white "conspirators," or "Black Republicans" whose Reconstruction plan had betrayed the most important prewar tenet of the Republican party as the white man's party. Americans had to remove these "white traitors" and give full power to such "White Republicans" as James Doolittle and Edgar Cowan.[64]

6. Americans and the Chinese Question, 1865–69

> The Chinaman, like the negro, is to be the prolific author of a hundred thousand speeches in the *Congressional Globe.* The Chinaman, like the negro, is to be mobbed in the streets of a hundred American cities. The Chinaman, like the negro, is to be rioted against by the makers of orphans and the burners of asylums.
>
> —*New York Independent,* August 19, 1869

IN CALIFORNIA, as in the nation at large, Reconstruction dominated politics in the postbellum years. Of all the issues related to it, black suffrage was a dramatic rallying point for partisans on both ends of the political spectrum. In 1866, the California Democrats and Republican Unionists adopted resolutions regarding Reconstruction policy. As expected, the Democrats praised President Johnson's refusal to endorse black suffrage and his support for the right of states to decide who should vote. The Republican Unionists took an opposite stand. Early in the war, national and regional leaders of the Republican party had worked to create a broad coalition of all the groups that supported the war. In particular, they had tried to attract the "War Democrats" (northern Democrats who supported Lincoln's policies). In California, too, the Union party was little more than the Republican party and a small fringe of War Democrats. After the war, some Democrats returned to their first allegiance. In 1866, the Union party endorsed the Fourteenth Amendment and any other "radical" action of Congress for the reconstruction of the southern states. It did not, however, take a position on black suffrage outside the South.[1] Furthermore, the stormy debate in the national legislature over the applicability of the provisions of the Fourteenth Amendment to the Chinese was not taken up by California politicians. Only later would the full impact of the amendment on relations between Americans and Chinese immigrants be felt.

In the campaign of 1867, the black suffrage issue took on a new meaning as it melded with the Chinese question into the larger issues of race and labor relations in a multiracial state. While Chinese immigrants never ceased to be subjected to oppressive legislation and individual acts of violence, there was actually no statewide clamor against them in 1865 and 1866. There were many reasons for that. First, the attention of Californians was on the restoration of the Union and the role of the African American in it. Second, the immediate postbellum years in California were very prosperous. Workers were in great demand, and wages were fairly high. It was also a period of rapid organization of trade unions and material progress for white laborers.[2] So far as Chinese laborers were concerned, the decline in the mining industry forced them to move to other branches of labor. They found employment as railroad laborers, servants, and farm hands, where they did not compete with American laborers. Third, the decline in Chinese immigration to California in 1865 and 1866 explained the dormancy of the anti-Chinese campaign.[3] Finally, Republican governor Frederick F. Low took exception to the "illiberal and barbarous" treatment of the Chinese. A native of Frankfort, Maine, Low arrived in San Francisco in 1849. He was elected to Congress in 1861 and elected governor as a Republican Unionist in 1863. As governor, Low distinguished himself as a defender of the Chinese against racial bigotry. In January 1867, he presided over a banquet held to commemorate the opening of steamship service with China and stated that Americans must learn to treat the Chinese decently instead of allowing them "to be abused, robbed, and murdered without extending to them any adequate remedy."[4]

Soon, however, the agitation against the Chinese intensified. As Chinese laborers started to move into the cities and into manufacturing, American laborers began to express their opposition to their employment. In February, tension erupted in a riot in San Francisco. A crowd of about four hundred white laborers injured a dozen Chinese, destroyed their barracks at a job site, and threatened to storm two other companies employing Chinese laborers.[5] This outburst of violence was reminiscent of anti-black violence in the urban East, notably the mob actions in New York's seaport during the Civil War. The Chinese attacked in the riot had been hired as a cost-cutting measure. The California rioters' objective was similar to that of the New York white longshoremen. It was to enforce a standard wage rate by imposing an "all-white" rule and by terrorizing those who dared challenge that rule. The arrest and conviction of ten men who had participated in the disturbance was followed by an organizational effort to achieve the exclusion of the Chinese. In March 1867, the Pacific Coast Anti-Coolie Association was formed to protect American labor from Chinese competition, resist by legal means the furtherance of Chinese immigration, and encourage the removal of Chinese immigrants already in California. Within a few weeks, branches were established in each of the twelve wards of San Francisco and other parts of the state. Three months later, a state convention of anti-Chinese clubs was held in San Francisco.[6]

This early urban anti-Chinese movement is significant in at least two respects. With the exception of the building and cigar-making trades, none of the trades represented in the Anti-Coolie Association was in direct competition with the Chinese.[7] The competition theme was thus used as a rallying point by skilled American laborers who were in no way competing with Chinese laborers. In that respect, this anti-Chinese movement was not different from some anti-black labor activities in the East. Of significance, too, were the drastic anti-Chinese resolutions that demonstrated racial animosity rather than economic competition, real or imagined, was the dominant motive of the white laborers' mobilization. As in racial conflicts in the East, nothing short of total exclusion from the white labor fields was acceptable.

Although the Anti-Coolie Association did not achieve its exclusion goal, it succeeded in shifting the attention from the Negro question to the Chinese question during the 1867 gubernatorial campaign. At its outset, the officers of the Anti-Coolie Association sent a letter to the four candidates for the Union nomination requesting their views on the Chinese question. Three of them expressed very succinctly their opposition to Chinese labor as a form of slavery. The leading aspirant, George Gorham, later dubbed "George Coolie Gorham" by his adversaries, began by stressing his opposition to all forms of slavery, including coolieism and peonage. Unlike the other candidates, however, he distinguished between voluntary and involuntary Chinese immigration. While he was willing to remedy the evil of coolieism, he insisted that if, as he understood it, the avowed object of the anti-Chinese movement was an attempt by white Americans and aliens to prevent the employment of Asian men, then he disapproved of the movement on the grounds of policy and principle. A believer in the universal brotherhood of man, he insisted that no man of whatever race had a better right to labor than any other man. He admonished the Anti-Coolie Association for its disregard of America's obligations to its Chinese trade partners. Gorham was also convinced that the "Asiatic brethren" would contribute further to the prosperity of California.[8]

Gorham's liberal response was the occasion for a barrage of anti-Union rhetoric from Democratic ranks. Whereas Democrats had until then deprecated the Union's advocacy of black equality, they now focused on both African American and Chinese equality. The assumption was that black suffrage would lead to Chinese suffrage and result in thorough racial equality. As tension mounted, Gorham's position on Chinese immigration became a liability for his party. Accordingly, the Union platform in April 1867 took a strong

This 1867 political satire was aimed at the California Republican gubernatorial nominee, George C. Gorham, because of his espousal of voting rights for African Americans, Chinese immigrants, and Native Americans. (Courtesy of the Library of Congress.)

position against the "importation" of Chinese or any other people of the Mongolian race into America. The delegates resolved that the presence of the Chinese in California was so injurious to American labor that legal means should be sought to restrict their immigration. They also recognized congressional Reconstruction as a wise policy. Still, no word about black suffrage in California.[9] On June 19, 1867, the Democrats held their state convention, resolving to defeat the Reconstruction Acts and the doctrine of universal suffrage and confirming their opposition to the influx of Mongolian laborers. It was, they felt, the duty of the California legislature to petition Congress for the enactment of restrictive legislation. As they saw it, Reconstruction measures in the South would inevitably affect the status of the Chinese in California. If put into practice, they would result in granting suffrage to African Americans and Chinese immigrants, thereby causing, in their words, "the degradation of the white race and the speedy destruction of the government."[10] By July 1867, the Union party coalition disintegrated. While a group of Republican Unionists established themselves as an affiliate of the original national Republican party, the other group deserted and joined the Democratic party. At their convention on July 16, the Republicans endorsed the action of Congress on the issue of impartial suffrage without distinction of color. Regarding the Chinese, they softened their position, opposing "coolie labor" and lending their support to voluntary immigration and protection for all free labor from whatever nationality it may come.[11]

In September 1867, the Democratic party swept the state, capturing the governorship and its administration, two of California's three congressional representatives, and a majority of twenty-two in the assembly. The Union party, however, had a majority of four in the senate. This political rehabilitation of the Democratic party after years of local and national reprobation was not an anomaly. The fall elections of 1867 brought about a sweeping majority of seats for the Democrats in the New Jersey and Ohio legislatures and one house in the New York legislature.[12] In these states, as in California, the voters expressed their disaffection with Republican policies, especially those designed to bring about racial equality.

As anti-Reconstruction feelings gathered momentum in California, the Chinese issue transcended the confines of a foreign-labor issue and was elevated to an equal status with the Negro question in the larger issues of restructuring the Union and structuring California. The conflation of the Chinese and black issues was made clear by the newly elected governor, Henry H. Haight. Born in Rochester, New York, in 1825, Haight had moved to California in 1849. In the early 1850s, Haight, who was a member of the Whig party, had regarded very favorably the presence of the Chinese in California, expressing his hope that it would lead to extensive trade with China. This liberal attitude eventually wore off, and, by the time he became a Democrat and was elected governor, Haight was convinced that "Republican radicalism" had been carried to excess. In his victory speech in September 1867, he attributed the Democratic victory to the extravagant interference of Congress in California's internal affairs, especially its attempt to populate California with Asiatics and force Californians to share their government with inferior races. In his inaugural address, he observed that national legislators believed that if the ballot was given to the Negro, it should be given to the Chinaman, too. There was, he stated, no truth in this assumption. Nor was there any soundness in the opinion that the extension of suffrage to black and Chinese residents was a matter of inalienable rights and justice or that African Americans and the Chinese needed the ballot to protect themselves. Haight contended that it was for the good of "Africans and Asiatics" that the elective franchise should be confined to whites. Otherwise, antipathy of race would enter political contests and lead to strife and bloodshed. Pointing to the South, where the imposition of black suffrage by military force was "corrupting the source of political power," he declared that he would never consent to give the inferior races in California the right to vote or hold office. While he professed that he was not motivated by prejudice, his arguments about black and Chinese impurity, brutal ignorance, and barbarism revealed his racial hostility. In closing, Haight conceded California's great need for immigrants to hasten the development of its resources; however, he specifically invited "white men, who will . . . meet the responsibilities and discharge the duties of freemen." Above all, Californians did not desire "an effete population of Asiatics" for their free state.[13]

Notwithstanding the governor's harangue, the delegates to the California political conventions in the first months of 1868 chose to focus on the pressing disagreement between the executive and Congress, which culminated in a resolution of impeachment of the president. While the Republicans denounced the course of action taken by President Johnson, the Democrats gave him their full support. As they condemned the "revolutionary" action of the radical majority in Congress, however, they reiterated their opposition to black and Chinese suffrage and to the importation of Chinese. At a meeting of the Republican Central Club of San Francisco, the Republicans approved of Reconstruction measures. None of their resolutions concerned Chinese immigration or the status and rights of the Chinese in America.[14]

In 1868, the "first Chinese mission to the Foreign Powers" diverted the attention from Reconstruction to Chinese-American relations and Chinese immigration. In 1867, Anson Burlingame, the first American minister to the Manchu court in Peking, had been appointed to be the Chinese government envoy to all the powers with which China had negotiated treaties, to promote "commerce and peace in the interests of the whole human race." Burlingame's mission arrived at San Francisco in April 1868. Burlingame was not unaware of the long history of anti-Chinese feelings in California. Expecting to meet a hostile population, he was instead cordially welcomed by a large crowd of people. The mission received numerous invitations for public appearances and private parties. At a grand banquet given by the leading citizens of the state, city officials, businessmen, merchants, and representatives of the Six Companies, Governor Haight himself bid the mission "a hearty welcome and God-speed," in the interest of progress, commerce, and humanity. While opinions about Chinese immigration differed, he added, there was no disagreement about the desirability of unrestricted commercial intercourse with China— that is, an extensive "interchange of products," not people.[15]

While the Chinese diplomats were feasted by the leading citizens of San Francisco, anti-Chinese riots and meetings were held by workingmen's and Democratic associations, which denounced the mission as base and pandering to "American and Oriental aristocracies."[16] The Burlingame mission felt encouraged, however, by the ovation of the official representatives, and it made its way across the country to Washington, where Burlingame met with Secretary of State William Seward. Seward seized the opportunity to revise the Chinese-American treaty of 1858. In late July 1868, he and Burlingame concluded the Treaty of Trade, Consuls, and Emigration.[17] Commonly known as the Burlingame Treaty, this compact was actually drafted by Seward, who stated that its primary purpose was to increase commerce between China and the United States,[18] by amplifying the trading privileges and consular rights established in previous treaties.[19]

As its title indicates, the treaty was also a migration treaty, providing for the rights of trade and residence of the Chinese in the United States—and, reciprocally, those of Americans in China. In fact, the importance of the treaty lay not in the commerce provisions but in the stipulations regarding migration rights. Two factors seem to have prompted Seward to insert an "emigration" clause. First he hoped to secure a plentiful supply of labor for the western states.[20] Then, like most of his contemporaries, Seward viewed access to the China trade as a guarantee of wealth, power, and prestige. But he was aware that, unlike Great Britain and France, the United States could not consider the commercial question as a matter of foreign affairs only. Given the presence of Chinese subjects in the United States, the increase in trade depended on maintaining good relations with the Chinese in China and at home. More than a by-product of commercial intercourse, the free immigration of the Chinese to America was, Seward argued, "the essential element of that commerce and trade."[21] Practical sense dictated that the new diplomatic agreement include provisions facilitating the exchange of commodities and the interchange of population.

The Burlingame Treaty contained two articles pertaining to the Chinese rights of migration to America. Article 5 recognized in sweeping terms "the inherent and inalienable right of man to change his home allegiance, and also the mutual advantage of free migration and emigration" of American citizens and Chinese subjects "for the purposes of curiosity, of trade, or as permanent residents." There was, however, one significant stipulation that "any other than an entirely voluntary emigration" should be reprobated, while both parties (the United States and China) agreed "to pass laws making it a penal offense" to take Chinese subjects "without their free and voluntary consent."[22] The prevention of involuntary emigration from China had been official policy since the 1862 Act to Prohibit the Coolie Trade. While the provision forbidding involuntary Chinese immigration in the treaty reinforced American commitment to the suppression of the coolie trade, it also reflected the apprehension that the treaty might be used to legitimize the introduction of coolies to the United States, especially in the South. Of great significance to anti-Chinese groups was the fact that the Burlingame Treaty implicitly acknowledged the possibility of an involuntary Chinese trade to the United States. Article 6 guaranteed that the Chinese subjects visiting or residing in the United States would enjoy the same privileges, immunities, and exemptions as those enjoyed by the citizens or subjects of the most favored nations; however, this egalitarian provision was critically qualified by the concluding sentence to the article: "But nothing herein contained shall be held to confer naturalization . . . upon the subjects of China in the United States."[23] An interesting concurrence was that in the 1860s and 1870s, the United States signed naturalization protocols with many European nations— for example, Belgium, Denmark, Great Britain, the North German Confederation, Sweden, and Norway. These conventions guaranteed to the citizens of these nations the right of naturalization.[24] The United States did not sign such a convention with China. Obviously, Chinese immigrants were not equal to the citizens of other most favored nations.

By expressly forbidding the use of the Burlingame Treaty to sanction the naturalization of Chinese residents in the United States, the provision may well convey that it was intended as a validation of the naturalization statute. It is, however, debatable whether the provision was inserted merely to confirm that Chinese naturalization could be decided only by complying with the naturalization statute. Similar treaties with other nations did not contain such clause, and, as noted, separate protocols had been signed to affirm the right of naturalization of European immigrants. Besides this, just one day before the ratification of the Burlingame Treaty, Congress passed *An Act concerning the Rights of American Citizens in Foreign States*, which proclaimed the universal right of expatriation and stated that, in recognition of this principle, "the U.S. government had received emigrants from all nations and invested them with the right of citizenship."[25] In view of this evidence, the withholding of the right of naturalization in the Burlingame Treaty was not a superfluous declaration. Rather, it served to reinforce the notion that Chinese immigrants did *not* figure as other immigrant groups. Most of the Burlingame Treaty negotiations between the American and Chinese legations and the discussions among the senators in Congress (who had to sanction the treaty) were confidential. Only later, in the course of the congressional debates on naturalization in 1870 (see chapter 8), would senators divulge their deliberate decision to exclude the right of naturalization from the provisions of the treaty. At any rate, the withholding of such a right should not be surprising given the concurrent dispute in Congress about the extension of citizenship to the Chinese as well as the African American. These debates demonstrate that the question of whether the Chinese were embraced within the intent and meaning of the naturalization statute was not an easy one. The treaty did nothing to settle the question. It did, however, make sure that the right of Chinese free immigrants to be received and invested with "rights and privileges" would not afford a basis for the argument that they were henceforth eligible for naturalization. Notwithstanding this, articles 5 and 6 would prove to be a powerful tool for the removal of Chinese civil disabilities and for their fight against discriminatory actions.

Throughout the country, the newspapers commented positively on the treaty. A very publicized reaction was that of Mark Twain, who discussed the treaty and its expected impact in a lengthy article in the *New York Tribune*. Twain was no stranger to Californians' abusive treatment of the Chinese. As a San Francisco resident, he had seen "Chinamen . . . maltreated in all the mean, cowardly ways possible to the invention of a degraded nature," and yet, had never witnessed a Chinese defendant righted in a court of justice. With the Burlingame Treaty, Twain was glad that the days of persecuting the Chinese were over. Article 6 especially "lifts a degraded, snubbed, vilified, and hated race of men out of the mud." While the best of California's citizens would extol the treaty, Twain predicted that it would excite much "weeping, and wailing, and gnashing of teeth" among the tormentors of the Chinese. At one sweep, the treaty had declared that these tormentors could not "beat and bang and set the dogs on the Chinamen any more." If they did, it would not be with impunity, for with article 6 "all the crippling, intolerant, and unconstitutional laws framed by California against Chinamen pass away." Announcing the atonement for past grievances, Twain could not help, however, expressing his misgivings about the redress of political iniquity. Chinese suffrage seemed somewhat unpalatable even to him. Drawing a significant parallel between the evolving status of African Americans and the changing status of the Chinese, he stated that the idea of making Negroes citizens of the United States was "startling and disagreeable to me, but I have become reconciled to it . . . and the ice being broken . . . I am ready now for all newcomers."[26]

As Twain predicted, the treaty was praised by the worthy groups in California.[27] Leading papers expressed their relief that the national government would force the state to extend the protection of the Fourteenth Amendment to the Chinese.[28] Regarding the naturalization stipulation in the treaty, one paper indicated that, despite the show of sympathy of the "good men" toward the Chinese, they still did not want to see naturalization conferred on them.[29] Twain was also right in his conjecture that other Californians would be incensed. After a number of protest rallies by labor and Democratic groups, a state anti-Chinese convention was held six months after the proclamation of the treaty. From then on, most anti-Chinese groups believed that the treaty had the effect of stimulating Chinese immigration and that its modification or abrogation would stop it altogether.

In the year following the Burlingame Treaty, the number of Chinese immigrants increased considerably, amounting to 11,085 in 1868—almost the total number for the four preceding years. In 1869, there were 14,994 new arrivals. Besides this influx of new immigrants, the release of Chinese laborers by the Central Pacific Railroad in April 1869 led to a greater Chinese visibility in urban manufacturing and construction industries and in agriculture. Although there is no evidence that the Chinese competed with white laborers, they soon became the target of persecution. This anti-Chinese agitation was, as Lucile Eaves and Ira Cross have both ably demonstrated, a by-product of the struggle between management and labor over the drastic wage reductions of the preceding years. It was then believed that the Chinese laborers would depress wages further and deprive white workers of their employment.[30]

No one did a better job of sounding the alarm against the invasion of "cheap coolies" than Henry George. Born in Philadelphia in 1839, George moved to California in 1857. He prospected for a while but was unsuccessful. He then began to work on newspapers in Sacramento and San Francisco. Frequently unemployed, he suffered desperate poverty. This early experience, which is somewhat reminiscent of Hinton Helper's earlier failure in California, was to color his thinking and writing in later years. In October 1868, George argued that of all the social evils brought about by the locomotive, the labor question was the most critical because it was rendered peculiarly complex by the proximity of the region to Asia.[31] In the spring of 1869, George addressed this labor question in a lengthy letter to the editor of the *New York Tribune,* and on May 1, 1869, the paper published it.[32] The letter recapitulated the arguments against Chinese immigration as they had developed in California during the preceding twenty years and in the national legislature during the last five years. George benefited, however, from a very powerful forum. Apart from having one of the largest circulation in the country, the *Tribune* was the paper of one of the founders of Republicanism, Horace Greeley.[33] It was also the paper that had published Twain's scathing attack on West Coast Sinophobia.

Opening with a section entitled "The Character of Asiatic Immigration," George described the tens of thousands of Chinese in the American West as "the thin end of the wedge which has for its base the 500,000,000 of Eastern Asia." As he proceeded with the economic aspect of the question, the Chinese "preeminence of numbers" remained a leitmotif. George was concerned that the Chinese had recently begun to engage in a variety of employments. He attributed these inroads to three major characteristics. The patience and imitative faculties of the Chinese, he argued, made up for their inferior physical and mental capabilities. Their submissiveness caused them to be "model laborers," unwilling to agitate and organize. George had thus consigned to oblivion the large-scale strike staged by the Chinese against the Central Pacific Railroad management in June 1867 and the traditional hostility of organized white workers to nonwhite laborers. Finally, their exceedingly low standard of comfort allowed the Chinese to undercut white workers.

As he shifted his attention from the economic to the cultural aspect of the Chinese question, George's racial prejudices became unmistakable. With the exception of African Americans, he stated, Americans had successfully melded into a homogeneous people. The Asian newcomers, George observed, differed from Americans "by as strongly marked characteristics as do the Negroes." He believed, however, that the Chinese would not "as readily fall into our ways as the Negroes." While the African brought to America was "a simple barbarian with nothing to unlearn," the Chinese had "a civilization and history of their own." George went on to predict that America was doomed with a permanent little China in its midst, inhabited by an army of "utter heathens, treacherous, sensual, cowardly, and cruel." The Chinese would not assimilate totally, as European immigrants had, or partially, as had African Americans. Like other advocates of Chinese restriction who compared African Americans with the Chinese, George did not elaborate on the extent to which blacks had assimilated. Turning to his final argument, George claimed that to give the franchise to the Chinese would put the balance of power on the Pacific Coast into their hands. The current political situation was not different from that of African Americans in the South. "Law or no law," George was sure that "the Chinese on the Pacific Coast could not vote, unless between lines of bayonets." Yet it would be wrong to assume that they would never vote. "Who could have dreamed ten years ago," he asked, "that the slaves of the South would now be the voters?" There was but one solution to the Chinese problem, he concluded: "Pluck them [the Chinese]" before they were firmly embedded.

One month later, George's diatribe was shored up by the publication of an article by Charles F. Adams Jr. (1835–1915), a railroad official, civic leader, and historian, who was the son of Charles Francis Adams, a diplomat and politician. Adams began with a full exposition of the corruption that was threatening American free institutions. The only way to protect the purity of the ballot, as he saw it, was to register voters carefully. Instead, he lamented, Congress was considering an extension of suffrage in an attempt to eradicate the vestige of caste in America. Universal suffrage, he warned, would introduce several pernicious influences into the body politic. One was the Negro, whose sudden enfranchisement was a "portentous experiment." A more dangerous element was the alien, especially the Asiatic. While he conceded that Chinese labor could hasten the development of America's material wealth, he warned that the contact with the semicivilized, ignorant, and inferior Asiatic races would "brutalize the inhabitants of the Pacific States more than the contact with the harmless African ever brutalized the South."[34]

George's and Adams's essays and the events surrounding their publication served to intensify the debate over Chinese immigration at the regional and national levels. In Congress, the Chinese question was causing additional discomfort and irritation among Republicans. Outside the national legislature, eastern publications had generally focused on black citizenship and black-white relations. Only once in the early debate had a major paper explicitly alluded to the threat to republicanism posed by newly freed blacks and Chinese laborers. In September 1865, the *New York Times* had opposed any extensive immigration of Asiatics to any part of the United States: "We have four millions of degraded negroes in the South . . . and if there were to be a flood-tide of Chinese population—a population befouled with all the social vices, with no knowledge or appreciation of free institutions or constitutional liberty, with heathenish souls and heathenish propensities . . . — we should be prepared to bid farewell to republicanism and democracy."[35]

But not until the Burlingame mission would other newspapers seriously consider the Chinese immigration issue. At that time, most of them entertained "extravagant expectations" about an immediate opening up of China to the commerce of the West.[36] These hopes had led the *New York Times* to qualify its earlier anti-Chinese position. While it still objected to the "racial mixture" of Americans and Chinese, it now believed that Chinese labor could greatly benefit America, *provided it remained in California.*[37] As the months passed, it was plain that the promise of a lucrative trade with China failed to materialize. The growing number of Chinese immigrants seemed to vindicate the charge that the treaty was but a "cheap labor treaty."

Within a few weeks of the publication of George's essay, major newspapers began to ponder the Chinese question from a *domestic* perspective, as a question of Chinese settlement in America.[38] The *New York Times* opened a barrage of articles in June 1869. Each day, the paper stated, the Chinese problem was becoming more prominent on the American scene. The pressing question was, "What should Americans do with John Chinaman?" According to "progressionists," Chinese immigration was a necessity and an economic advantage to the nation. They were fiercely criticized by "reactionists," who were alarmed that, before the close of the century, there could be as many Asiatics as Europeans on the Pacific Coast. The *Times* objected that the reactionists' position was based on their ignorance of the vast undeveloped resources of America. Besides, Chinese immigration could be a means of testing anew the Darwinian law of natural selection. "If the Anglo-Saxon is inferior," the paper declared, "it is time he made way for his betters, if he be superior, as he certainly is, then all other races . . . will only help do his inferior work for him." However, Chinese immigration involved more than a mere conflict of economic interests. Events in America were moving so fast that "before the affairs of the 'white man' and 'black man' are well settled, a new color comes upon the loom to be woven into the mighty national fabric. . . ." More than a simple question of immigration, the Chinese question was "the negro question all over again."[39]

A couple of months later, a short article bearing the striking title of "Our Celestial Negro" appeared in the *New York Independent*. It illustrated further the opinion that after the black man, "the yellow man" had become the figure of the day. Like the slavery question of the past, the *Independent* argued, the Chinese question would be at the center of fierce controversies in American politics.[40] In "The Coming of the Barbarian," E. L. Godkin of the *Nation* offered a less gloomy outlook. He believed that the demand for labor guaranteed the further admission of the Chinese, despite popular prejudice and prohibitory legislation. Capital would not consider the objections to the

Chinese that, in his opinion, were blown out of proportion by labor leaders and political demagogues. He asked how capital could relinquish such a "submissive, tractable, painstaking, economical [and] cheap" labor force. So much was to be gained from the Chinese, Godkin concluded, that restricting their immigration would be a severe blow to American progress. Regarding the Chinese influence on American politics, Godkin was satisfied that their presence afforded yet another reason for opposing universal suffrage.[41]

In essence, eastern editors were urging Americans to make the best out of Chinese labor. Given the negligible number of Chinese immigrants in the East, it is not surprising that they were cold to George's plea in behalf of the American worker. In California, however, the state's integration into the

THE LAST ADDITION TO THE FAMILY.

The hideous features of the Chinese baby in this illustration indicate in no uncertain terms the cartoonist's qualms about Columbia's maternal instinct and love in taking in this newest addition to the American family. (Source: *Harper's Weekly,* September 25, 1869, 624. Courtesy of the Library of Congress)

national economy had lowered the wage rates, prompting American laborers to resume their attacks on Chinese labor. George was therefore more
successful there, and his essay was received with delight by trade unions, anti-
Chinese clubs, and the local branch of the Democratic party.

Once more, the Chinese issue in California came rapidly to a focus, divert-
ing some of the passions that had flared since the proposal of the Fifteenth
Amendment, which made it illegal to deny *citizens* suffrage on the basis of
race, color, or previous condition of servitude. As noted earlier, many battles had been fought in Congress to limit its applicability to black Americans.
Notwithstanding, public opinion in California was that the Fifteenth Amendment might provide for Chinese suffrage. Hence, the implications of the
amendment for the status of the Chinese formed a great part of the Californians' reaction to it. The editor of the *San Francisco Daily Herald,* for example, lamented that, since the establishment of the radical doctrines of political equality for all races, "four million Mandarins" would soon add their
numbers to the four million blacks in the South.[42] The principles adopted
by the California Democrats at their convention in Sacramento in June 1869
echoed this projection of an imminent Chinese invasion. They opened their
platform with their confidence in the capacity of Californians to administer
and control their government "without the aid of negroes or Chinese." Carrying on with the reasons for their opposition to the Fifteenth Amendment,
they made it plain that, compared with Chinese equality, black equality in
California was a side issue. The amendment, they charged, was designed "to
degrade the right of suffrage; to ruin the laboring white man, by bringing
untold hordes of Pagan slaves . . . into direct competition with his efforts to
earn a livelihood; to build up an aristocratic class of oligarchs . . . maintained
by Chinese votes. . . ."[43]

Three weeks later, the Republicans held their state convention in Sacramento. Pledging to support the Fifteenth Amendment and the Grant administration, they resolved that the questions of rebellion, reconstruction, and
Negro suffrage had been settled once for all. Regarding Chinese immigration,
they adopted resolutions that indicated they were fully aware of the cross-
currents of opinion in the debate on the suffrage amendment in Congress.
"Unoffending immigrants from China," they declared, were entitled to full
protection and due process of law, as guaranteed by the Fourteenth Amendment. Yet they were unwilling to grant the Chinese suffrage in any form. After
endorsing the Fifteenth Amendment, they carefully added that they objected to any change in the naturalization laws. The Republicans finally concluded that the general prosperity of California would be greatly enhanced by
fostering commercial intercourse with Asia.[44]

The platform of principles adopted by the California Republicans made their party an easy target for criticism. James Gordon Bennett, the editor of the conservative *New York Herald*, seized the opportunity to lampoon Republicans, especially the "nigger-worshiping radicals of California." In a particularly crude and sarcastic editorial, he interpreted the Chinese question as a case of "Chickens [coming] home to roost." Republicans had gone for making all races equal, and now, he scoffed, they were alarmed at the consequences of their ultraradicalism. In California, Republicans had magnanimously given the suffrage "to the ignorant and brutal negro," but they wanted to deny it to the Chinese, "a far superior and more intellectual race than the Negroes." Bennett attributed this inconsistency to the lack of principle in the Republican egalitarian ideology. Were not northerners in favor of black suffrage because they had scarcely any Negroes among them? The California Republicans were "likely to have as large a dose of the Chinese as they had forced the Southern whites to swallow of the negro," he concluded.[45]

7. Chinese Labor in the South and New England, 1865–70

[Many] were thrown into some little excitement yesterday on the arrival of 13 Chinese. . . . [John Chinaman] is what we would call a cross between an African and an Indian.

—*Daily Arkansas Gazette* (Little Rock), June 19, 1870

JAMES BENNETT's article exposed the Republicans' descent from the high plane of their professed egalitarian ideals, but Bennett himself was not an egalitarian. He believed that Europeans were "at least ten times better than the Chinese."[1] This was an opinion that he shared with the California Republicans he had castigated a few days earlier. In their 1869 platform, they had vented their pride at the increasing immigration of white people from the Atlantic states and Europe.[2] Californians' preference for white immigrants rather than African Americans and Chinese immigrants was not at variance with national attitudes.

Anticipation of a vast black migration from the South to the North and West had played a major role in these two sections' resistance to black emancipation. In the months following Appomattox, the predicted influx of freed blacks did not occur. In the next years, there was only a trickle of African American migrants to the North. While geographic mobility among the freed blacks was impeded by southern whites' efforts to control labor, African Americans still retained some freedom of movement and took whatever opportunities they could to exercise that basic right.[3] They exercised it, however, mainly within the confines of the South. Given their lack of resources, long-distance moves were very difficult without assistance. Besides this, African Americans in the North were forced into an inferior position in the labor market. Where their labor was not needed, blacks were deemed an undesirable population.[4] In short, "despite the freedoms and half-freedoms" that the region outside the South offered, it still remained an inhospitable haven for the newly freed.[5]

In the North, the disinclination to induce blacks to migrate went parallel with the encouragement of European immigration with the 1864 Contract Labor Act. After the economic devastation and social disruption of the Civil War, southerners followed a similar exclusive policy. They looked to the northern states and Europe to secure a dependable labor force. Southern state legislatures passed laws creating bureaus of agriculture and immigration, which authorized them to dispatch agents in the North and Europe, permitted immigration under labor contracts, and fostered steamship connections with European ports.[6] Still, white migrants avoided the South. Besides the unstable situation after Appomattox, the major reasons for this lack of interest were the same as before 1865: fear of competition with black labor, fear of assuming the badge of inferiority by laboring with or replacing blacks, and the availability of preferable alternatives, such as homesteading in the West and industrial work in the North.[7]

The postbellum labor problem, as southern planters perceived it, was that the war and Reconstruction policies had eroded the labor pool necessary to maintain the plantations. During the summer and fall of 1865, freed blacks were in motion all over the South to rejoin families broken by slavery. Following this first impulse, African Americans demonstrated their desire for economic independence and their refusal to work in gangs. They demanded lighter work schedules and high wages, and they deserted one plantation for another that offered higher wages. They also struck for higher wages during periods of the year crucial to the welfare of the crops.[8] This assertive behavior confirmed in the planters' minds the notion that emancipation had rendered blacks intractable, unreliable, unstable, and dissatisfied with their work. The planters concluded that, unless freed persons were subjected to some degree of coercion, they would not work or would be less efficient than before the war.[9] Accordingly, the postbellum black codes contained labor provisions designed to replace the labor controls of slavery and limit the mobility of black people. As mentioned earlier, these codes were condemned by the Republican party. Ironically, though, many of the coercive labor rules were no different from those perfected by the Freedmen's Bureau itself. As rumors that African Americans were deserting the countryside and heading north became widespread in 1865 and 1866, some northerners also believed that methods of labor compulsion were necessary to inculcate blacks with "habits of free labor" *in their native South.*

The codes failed to relieve the anxieties of southerners, who decided that a new labor supply had to be obtained. As early as 1865, some thought they had found one in the Chinese. In 1865, southern newspapers printed many editorials and letters on the feasibility of Chinese labor. Many were reprinted time and again in the next five years. At that early stage, interest in the Chinese orig-inated in accounts of "Chinese coolie labor" in the West Indies.[10] One much quoted letter, for instance, attributed the increase in Cuban agricultural exports to the use of Chinese contract labor. Pointing to the similar climates and soil in Cuba and the American South, the letter concluded that John Chinaman would be more dependable and productive than the Negro. In another letter, an eminent jurist in Mobile, Alabama, proposed bringing in Chinese laborers from Cuba and China to work in fields of labor in which Caucasians were not likely to work.[11] Of course, the position of the Chinese was to be on the level of African Americans. The *De Bow's Review,* published in New Orleans, made this plain in an editorial entitled "Coolies as a Substitute for Negroes."[12]

While the discussion about the use of Chinese labor continued, the schemes to bring in large numbers of Chinese workers from the West Indies did not come to fruition. These efforts were hampered by some officials' fears that southerners intended to revive the slave trade under a new guise. The commissioner of immigration, in his annual report to Congress in Febru-ary 1866, expressed his concern over the attempted importation of "new races" to labor in the South. He insisted that, under the 1862 act prohibiting American participation in the coolie trade, U.S. policy was opposed to the importation of Chinese laborers into the South to serve under contracts sim-ilar to those in the West Indies. He concluded by encouraging southerners to try and work out profitable contracts with the freed blacks. If they failed in that enterprise, they should turn to "free foreign immigration."[13]

Significantly, the commissioner associated Chinese immigration to the South with involuntary immigration. This interpretation was certainly justified by southern publications that endorsed the use of coolie laborers in the West Indies and encouraged a similar practice in the South or that used the term *coolie* interchangeably with *Chinese workers.* In 1867, the recruitment of Chinese laborers seemed to confirm northerners' suspicions. Small groups of Chinese laborers had been brought from Cuba to work in Louisiana, Mis-sissippi, and Arkansas. In August of that year, the New Orleans district at-torney ordered the seizure of a ship coming from Havana with twenty-three Chinese aboard and the arrest of the ship captain and a labor contractor for violating the 1862 law against importing coolies.[14] As the case developed, sev-eral local papers exchanged opinions on it. In a highly publicized letter to the secretary of the treasury, a well-known planter and employer of Chinese la-borers denied the charge, arguing that the Chinese were voluntary laborers who had left Cuba after the expiration of their eight-year contracts. He in-sisted that the new contracts did not establish a relation of slavery or servi-tude. If these contracts violated the law, then he could not understand why the government was not forbidding the employment of the thousands of "Chinese contract laborers in California."[15] The district attorney dropped the charges after the U.S. vice-consul in Havana confirmed the free status of the Chinese. Southerners had scored an important victory. Two years later, the U.S. consul in China, Charles Goulding, was instructed by Assistant Secretary of State J. C. B. Davis that the credit system used by Chinese immigrants to the United States did *not* deprive them of the character of voluntary emigrants unless the contracts were vitiated by force or fraud. Subsequently, a major venture to procure Chinese directly from China resulted in the recruitment of about two hundred laborers and, eventually, a formal investigation about their status. Here again, the Chinese were proved to have come voluntarily.[16] Thereafter, southerners turned to California as a closer and less controversial place of recruitment.

In the summer of 1869, the completion of the transcontinental railroad and the praise accorded Chinese laborers for their contribution triggered off a renewed interest in the Chinese. In the *Southern Farmer,* a commentator presented Chinese labor as the panacea for the southern economic ills. In the matter of procuring labor, he stated, several considerations had to be kept in view: "[The] laborers must possess industry and willingness to work; they must be willing to work for moderate wages; [and] they must be able to work in our cotton, rice, sugar, and tobacco fields." He then asked, "Will the Irish, Scotch, Swiss or Germans fill the bill?" He did not think so, but he was confident that the Chinese would. The article went on to stress that the charges against the Chinese actually made them desirable for southerners. If the Chinese were ambitious for work, willing to work for low wages, and capable of adjusting to any avocation, it meant that they would be excellent "hoe hands or plowmen."[17] Claiming to sum up the views of most journals in Louisiana, the *New Orleans Commercial Bulletin* stated that the South should look to the "immense beehive of Asia" for the working muscle needed to develop its agriculture.[18]

While the *Southern Farmer* and *Commercial Bulletin* focused on the difficulty of securing white labor, other papers tied their discussion of Chinese immigration to the Negro problem. "Emancipation has spoiled the negro, and carried him away from fields of agriculture," the *Vicksburg Times* wrote. If the South wanted to ensure its prosperity, it had to "let the coolies come."[19] The *New Orleans Daily Picayune* advised to break down the "Negro monopoly of unskilled labor" by forcing blacks to compete with Chinese skillfulness and diligence.[20] In "The Chinamen and the Negroes," in July 1869, the *Picayune* argued that the proposed importation of Chinese labor originated in a concerted effort to meet new circumstances. "Our masters at the

North," it wrote, had decreed that the free Negro should be equal with whites in the field and the workshop. Accordingly, African Americans were now competitors in the labor market. Keeping out the Chinese would only slow the freedmen's apprenticeship. If blacks wanted to elevate themselves, they would have to learn the virtues of steadiness, patience, and frugality through trials, failures, and long sufferings.[21]

Other papers were more direct in their admission that the introduction of Chinese laborers in the South was intended to restore the traditional relation of the races. One paper, for example, emphasized the noncitizen status of the Chinese. "They never become naturalized," it stated, "[they] never vote and are not inclined to riots." The article concluded, "Better Shangee than Timbuctoo! Better a few years of Confucian philosophy than a cycle of Ashantee feticism."[22] Reproaching the freedmen for leaving the plantation for "politics and plunder," the *Vicksburg Daily Times* anticipated the time when the Chinese supplanted the Negroes on the American farm.[23] In Kentucky, an editor predicted that the coming of the Chinese would substitute the "work, nigger, or starve" tune for the "40 acres and a mule" motif.[24] In July 1869, a delegate to the immigration convention at Memphis, Tennessee, expressed his less crude opinion that no better scheme to control African Americans could be found than to introduce Chinese labor.[25]

The immigration convention at Memphis gathered two hundred delegates from Tennessee, Arkansas, Louisiana, Alabama, Georgia, South Carolina, Kentucky, and Missouri. One committee was formed to consolidate schemes for importing Chinese laborers into the South.[26] The delegates responded very enthusiastically to the committee's report on the suitability of Chinese labor to American southern economy and to various plans to bring Chinese laborers to their states. The convention adjourned with the expectation that a million dollars would be raised to further these plans. While the convention electrified the advocates of Chinese immigration, it did not alter the views of those who were skeptical about or opposed to the schemes. Despite the convention chairman's assertion that the introduction of the Chinese was not intended to harm the African American, southern Republicans remained convinced that it was a punitive measure to deprive blacks of their livelihood, force them into submission, and wrest power away from Republicans.[27] African Americans recognized very early that Chinese laborers were sought to reduce them to quasi-servitude and restore white supremacy in the South.[28] These views were best articulated by Frederick Douglass, who ascribed the call for Chinese immigration in the South to a combination of "pride, bitterness, and revenge" and concluded that southerners hoped that the "loss of the negro is to gain them, the Chinese."[29]

Whereas most southern Republicans shared a common suspicion of Chinese immigration schemes, Democrats were divided. Not all Democratic papers favored these plans. Some considered the Chinese poor substitutes for the former slaves. The Chinese coolies were "lazy, mutinous, obstinate and thievish," one paper declared. Others focused on the "peculiarities" and "vices" of the Chinese: their religious practices, superstitions, opium-addiction, and inclination for crime and prostitution.[30] As early as 1866, a strongly Democratic newspaper in Montgomery, Alabama, echoed Hinton Helper's prediction of 1857. "Soon," it announced, "the negro question will be lost in the Chinese question, and then will come up the perplexing question of [the] status [of the Chinese] in the community, his contracts, and his privileges."[31] In 1868, the *Journal and Guide* (Norfolk, Virginia) entreated white Virginians to prevent implanting another incompatible race in their state. Asiatic immigration, it warned, would amount to transplanting into the South millions of Asiatics, "who are to take the place of the negro as a retarder of our progress and a disturber of our peace."[32]

The *Journal and Guide*'s racial indictment of the Chinese was quoted in the leading journal of commerce in the South, the *De Bow's Review*. One year later, in 1869, William M. Burwell, the editor of *De Bow's*, published two major articles that recapitulated the southern Democratic opposition to Chinese immigration.[33] In "Science and the Mechanic Arts against Coolies," Burwell presented himself as a patriot and a planter, who thought it essential to transcend economics to comprehend the larger repercussions of introducing Chinese labor. A large Chinese population, he predicted, would of necessity be admitted to political and *social equality*. The mixing of the races would lead to the "Mongolising of the Americans." Quoting the *Baltimore Statesman*, he warned that in the not far distance, the population of America would have more "Chings and Changs" in their genealogical trees than "Smiths and Browns." Burwell believed that while the Chinese stood next to Africans in American estimation, in many respects, they were far below them. At least, Africans were "utterly ignorant," and so "docile [as] to be taught our own impressions." Asiatics, he noted, professed a superstition they would never surrender. Moreover, while they were physically unequal to Africans in their ability to labor, they were as repugnant when it came to ideas of a common race. Most southerners, Burwell concluded, were concerned that Chinese immigration would condemn the South to a new sectional curse.[34]

A few weeks later, "The Cooley-ite Controversy" stressed that the South had fought for a white man's government. There was thus no wisdom in going to Asia to supply the labor force, because the South was already "overloaded with darkies." It could take on no more inferior races without again risking that those races would turn their political and physical strength against the "autochtones." The article went on to argue that the solution to the southern labor crisis was right there in the South. While African Americans were as incongruous to the whites as the Chinamen were, blacks were "far more docile and respectable" than the "pagans and prostitutes of Asia." To be sure, blacks had been "soldiers for our enemies," but it was only natural that they should aid those who came to liberate them. Blacks were now convinced that their old masters were their "best friends." The author added that southern planters should exhort not only freedmen but also black women and children, who had withdrawn from the fields of labor after the Civil War, to resume their place in the work force. Planters should also encourage the organized "importation of surplus Negro labor" from old southern Atlantic states and the cities and states of the Mississippi Valley.[35]

Predictions of Chinese displacing African Americans came to nothing. By the fall of 1869, it was clear that interest in Chinese immigration had dramatically declined. A few experiments had proved the inadequacy of the planters' expectations that the Chinese would accept total submission to their employers and that they would be more efficient than or superior to black workers. Besides this, the high cost of transportation and other related expenses meant that Chinese labor was more expensive than southerners had anticipated. The planters' lack of means and Chinese disappointment with their experiences in the South only partially explain why the high hopes for a vast Chinese immigration into the southern agricultural areas came to nothing. An equally compelling reason was that the alarm sounded by Burwell and other critics in 1869 was quickly acted upon. Late that year, the governor and the commissioner of industrial resources of Alabama took a strong stand against Chinese labor. The governor argued that the impact the Chinese would have on the wages of native laborers justified their exclusion from Alabama. The commissioner went on to express his concern that the intrusion of this new racial element would only aggravate the southern race problem.[36] The *Dallas Herald* made a crude call for white immigrants: "We want neither niggers or Mongolians—we want white men."[37] Meanwhile, the Tennessee legislature passed an act to encourage immigration that contained a clause stating that nothing in the act should be construed as to authorize the importation of Chinese laborers.[38]

Despite the efforts of a few southerners to recruit Chinese laborers, only a trickle of migrants came. Notwithstanding this, the Chinese labor issue in the South stimulated a debate that left its mark on the national scene. Until then, the subject of Chinese immigration had been a California and partisan issue, with Republicans adopting a relatively liberal position and Democrats an intolerant one. When the issue arose in the South, it had the effect of temporarily dislocating party arrangements. The southern Democrats who advocated Chinese immigration were an embarrassment to California Democrats, who tried to ease the tension by charging that the scheme for importing Chinese laborers to the South was the work of "carpet-baggers from New England and from the Middle States."[39] In the South, meanwhile, anti-Chinese Democrats were presenting the southern interest in Chinese immigration as a fleeting infatuation. Even before the interest lessened as they had predicted, they realized that the Chinese question could be used to challenge the Republicans' professed belief in racial equality. When northern and southern Republicans condemned Chinese immigration to the South as coolie migration, southerners exposed the Republican double standard, "finding no fault" with Chinese immigration in California and yet opposing it in the South under the pretext that it was involuntary.[40]

More than the reaction to the Chinese experiment in the South, it was the response to the arrival of a few scores of Chinese laborers in Massachusetts on June 13, 1870, that revealed northern duplicity in handling the Chinese question. Exasperated by the demands of the Knights of Saint Crispin, the largest organization of workers in the country, Calvin Sampson, a shoe manufacturer in North Adams, Massachusetts, decided to hire Chinese laborers to break the Crispins' monopoly of labor. Sampson's interest in Chinese laborers came after several attempts to use white strikebreakers from neighboring manufacturing centers. Time and again, his new recruits frustrated him by joining forces with the Crispins. In the spring of 1870, Sampson dispatched his superintendent to San Francisco with instructions to engage Chinese laborers through a Chinese contract labor company. A few weeks later, seventy-five Chinese laborers arrived in North Adams, heading for Sampson's factory. In three months, they were able to produce a larger weekly aggregate of work than had the same number of Crispins. In one year, Sampson managed to save forty thousand dollars in labor costs.[41] While Sampson's labor difficulties were at an end, the northeastern press was ablaze with denunciations and defenses of the Chinese. The barrage of editorials in the next few weeks helped promote a sense of imminent crisis among easterners.

The reaction to North Adams was broadly defined along political and class lines, with the pro-labor press and representatives denouncing the introduction of Chinese labor and those representing business interests cheering the experiment as a legitimate response to labor intimidation and violence. Three days after the arrival of the Chinese, the *Springfield Republican* anticipated that the Chinese would free Sampson from the tyranny of the Knights of Saint Crispin. A few days later, an editorial in the *Boston Commonwealth* congrat-

ulated Sampson on refusing to accede to the dictates of a striking organization, whose practice was to rule or ruin.[42] A common line in these local editorials was their strong hostility to labor unions. The *New York Times* shared
that feeling. The North Adams Crispins, the paper averred, got what they
deserved for not being willing to work for sensible wages.[43]

Some of these papers also expressed their qualms about the consequences
of employing Chinese laborers. The *Springfield Republican*'s disquietude was
plain in its description of the Chinese as an "invading army of Celestials."
Sampson's experiment had "portents of a somewhat disturbing nature,"
according to the *Boston Evening Transcript,* which wondered if native strikebreakers from Maine could not have been used instead. While the editor of
the *Boston Commonwealth* praised the Chinese in North Adams for their rare
industry and high morality, he still found it hard to supplant native workers
with them.[44]

In June and July 1870, while the pro-capital press expressed its support for
Sampson's initiative and a somewhat ambivalent attitude toward the Chinese, labor led an unrelenting campaign against the Chinese shoemakers. As
Roger Daniels has observed, the reaction of eastern laborers and their leaders was predictable, accounted for by decades of white supremacist habits in
the American working class.[45] To be sure, some voices in the labor movement
were raised in defense of the Chinese.[46] Opposition to the Chinese, they
warned, served the interests of employers because it divided the working class.
Time and again, these labor leaders maintained that while they opposed the
"importation" of any worker, they still welcomed all "voluntary immigrants."
These advocates of labor solidarity were, however, in the minority. Significantly, some labor leaders who were in advance of others in their advocacy
of black and white unity chose to oppose Chinese labor. One such case was
Andrew C. Cameron, the editor of the *Workingman's Advocate* (Chicago) and
chairman of the platform committee of the National Labor Union (NLU),
whose anti-Chinese demands predated the North Adams incident. In February 1869, Cameron had anticipated a massive eastward migration of Chinese railroad laborers following the completion of the transcontinental railroad. In June, he had observed that the "Pagan rat-eaters" had already found
their way to St. Louis, Philadelphia, New York, and Chicago. His indictment
assumed a crude and racist tone, as when he cried out, "[Y]es, bring them
along, Chinamen, Japanese, Malays, and monkeys, make voters of them all;
acknowledge them as men and workers; mix them all up together, water down
the old Caucasian race." In the following months, the *Advocate* turned its
attention to the efforts to introduce "coolie labor" in the South as a substitute for Negro labor. Incensed, the *Advocate* insisted that it was "uncondi-

tionally opposed *under any circumstances,* to the project of peopling the Western and Southern states with the scum of the Chinese empire."[47]

When the seventy-five Chinese arrived in North Adams, labor mobilized and vociferously demanded their exclusion. Their campaign intensified until it culminated in protest meetings in not only Massachusetts but also New York, Pennsylvania, and Ohio. Oftentimes, these meetings were presided over by prominent labor leaders and public figures. Within a few weeks of the Chinese arrival, a large workers' meeting was held in Tremont Temple, Boston. Many speeches were made, the substance of which was embodied in a set of resolutions that welcomed voluntary laborers from every clime and pledged to extend the protection of law and equal opportunities to them in every field of industry but deprecated all attempts to introduce foreign con-

THROWING DOWN THE LADDER BY WHICH THEY ROSE.

The northeastern vehement resistance to the "experiment" in hiring Chinese laborers is reflected in this illustration and in the fact that Chinese immigration to the East remained inconsequential. (Source: *Harper's Weekly,* July 23, 1870, 480. Courtesy of the Library of Congress)

tract labor.[48] On the surface, these resolutions sounded workers' traditional opposition to the contract labor system. As noted, the 1864 Act to Encourage Immigration had authorized the federal government to enforce contracts made in foreign countries. Opposed to foreign labor contracting since its inception, American workers had intensified their agitation when employers began to use foreign laborers to thwart their strikes. In 1868, the law of 1864 was repealed by a clause in a consular and diplomatic act. Although foreign contract labor was no longer protected by the federal government, it remained fully legal and enforceable by state and local laws. Workers therefore resumed their campaign, calling for the outright prohibition of foreign labor contracting. Throughout this campaign, laborers and their unions lashed out at the importers rather than the imported,[49] unless the contract laborers were Chinese. Then, eastern workers used a language that sharply calls into question the nature of their opposition.

When the Chinese laborers arrived in North Adams, their status as contract laborers was legitimate. For one thing, their contracts had not been initiated abroad. The mercantile firm that had procured Sampson's Chinese laborers was a San Francisco company, the Kwong, Chong, Wing & Co., and the Chinese shoemakers had been residents of California prior to their contractual agreement with Sampson's superintendent. The terms of the contract signed by the superintendent and the Chinese business firm were published in the *Springfield Republican,* most certainly to demonstrate the legality of the operation.[50] While the pro-Sampson press defined the Chinese as contract laborers or simply laborers, the workers insisted on relegating them to the status of coerced and degraded labor. At their meeting in Tremont Temple, their spokesmen referred to the Chinese as "imported coolie labor used to a standard of rice and rats" and as a "servile class of laborers." Presenting themselves as "The Voice of Free Labor," they declared that their object was to prevent "the importation of coolie slaves."[51]

By 1870, the correspondence between servility and coolieism and between Chinese labor and coolie labor was a close one in California, where for about two decades Chinese laborers had functioned as foils against which white laborers measured themselves as "free workers." In the South, the postbellum inducements to stimulate Chinese immigration had reinforced the stigmatization of Chinese labor as coolie/unfree labor. Northerners bore a greater responsibility for this than did southerners. Together with some major public figures and organs of opinion, labor leaders had denounced the use of "Chinese coolies/quasi-slaves in the South" in no uncertain terms. During the 1869 NLU Convention, for example, the delegates had gone on record as unalterably opposed to "the importation of a servile race" of Chinese laborers contracted on foreign soil.[52] Southerners had usually rejected northern allegations that they were advocating a new slave system. They had insisted that the status of the Chinese in the South was similar to that of not only the Chinese in California but also the voluntary contract laborers imported from Europe by American emigration companies.[53] The northern argument eventually foundered for three reasons: the crucial want of rigid definitions of the terms *coolie, contract labor,* and *imported labor;* the legality of foreign and domestic labor contracting; and the inability to prove the "servility" of the Chinese imported into the South. Notwithstanding, northern coverage of southern interest in "coolie labor" helped cast the dark shadow of "unfree labor" over Chinese laborers.

The resolutions passed in Boston during the North Adams labor dispute demonstrate the northern workers' hasty acceptance of the equation of Chinese labor with servility. A few weeks after the meeting, in August 1870, they made the scope of their indictment clear. A group of Crispins carried their demands to the Fifth Annual Convention of the NLU in Cincinnati. By then, it was no longer the importation of coolie or contract labor they opposed but the immigration of all Chinese. "[The] presence in our country of Chinese laborers," the delegates resolved, was "an evil entailing want and . . . misery and crime on all other classes of the American people." They thus convinced the national organization to demand Chinese exclusion and the abrogation of the Burlingame Treaty.[54]

While the negative reaction of labor to the North Adams experiment is not surprising, the response of some radical Republicans and other labor reformers was unexpected. In their role as labor reformers, some Republicans had taken a firm stand against importing contract labor.[55] The North Adams incident could not be dealt with as a simple economic matter. In their handling of an issue that involved race and class, these labor reformers slipped into uneasy contradictions. Their initial response to the Chinese shoemakers was to play down their race and voice the traditional condemnation of contract labor as "the conspiracy of capital." Soon, however, their indictment would assume a more radical and racial tone.

Senator Henry Wilson (Republican from Massachusetts), for instance, first encouraged his state legislature and Congress to prohibit long-term contracts of Chinese imported labor. Gradually, though, his attacks became filled with racial animosity. Chinese labor was degraded labor, and his call for a prohibition of Chinese labor contracts broadened into a demand for immediate action to avert the "Mongolian invasion."[56] Wilson was known for his radicalism and labor stance in the postbellum period, and his collaboration with anti-Chinese forces is often attributed to his sympathies for American laborers and his attempt to woo the Labor Reform party for the upcoming senatorial election in Massachusetts in 1870. However, his political career evidences a consistent anti-Chinese position that shows the limitation of this explanation. Six months before the North Adams incident, Wilson had introduced a bill in Congress to break up what he called a "modern slave trade" of Chinese coolies to the American South.[57] Wilson was among the eastern Republicans who would later support the legislative efforts not only to prohibit or regulate Chinese immigration but also to oppose their naturalization. Obviously, there was more to his anti-Chinese attitudes than mere political expediency or labor sympathy. Wilson was elected to the Massachusetts senate in the 1840s; in 1853, he was defeated as the Free-Soil candidate for governor. In 1855, the Free-Soil party combined with the American party (Know Nothing party), and Wilson was elected senator of Massachusetts on the American party ticket in January 1855. This collaboration with the American party ended when he joined and became a prominent member of the Republican party. Notwithstanding his evolving radicalism in issues affecting Reconstruction and some aspects of labor, Wilson's anti-Chinese position smacks of a latent nativism.

Another significant case involved Wendell Phillips. A former abolitionist, Phillips had never failed to use the most uncompromising language for his advocacy of racial egalitarianism. Following black emancipation, he had spared no effort to fulfill the other part of his pledge: the extension of equal rights to African Americans. In 1869, Phillips urged Americans to be on vigilant guard. In rousing speeches and editorials, he warned that other racial conflicts were looming—this time involving the status of Chinese immigrants. Ignoring the economic argument in the opposition to the Chinese, he instead favored a line of reasoning that stressed human equality and political harmony. To Phillips, it was clear that the Chinese question would draw anew the color line into politics and be appended to the still unresolved Negro problem.[58]

In the following ten months, Phillips's weekly, the *National Anti-Slavery Standard,* included regular calls for civil and political equality for all people in America. The Chinese question, the *Standard* stressed, was a different part of the same troublesome "Race Question."[59] In April 1870, however, Phillips's commitment to Chinese rights seemed to falter. This happened just after the adoption of the Fifteenth Amendment, when he and former abolitionists concluded that the mission of the Anti-Slavery Society was fulfilled. Presiding over the last meeting of the society, Phillips declared that, with the Fifteenth Amendment, color had been washed out of the Constitution. However, Americans had yet to build a broader and more tolerant civilization. While Phillips reiterated his advocacy of black and Indian rights, his discussion of Chinese immigration revealed a certain ambivalence. "What will the surplus of four hundred millions of Chinese, floating upon our prairies, do in time to come?" he asked. "The Saxon and the Negro, facing John Chinaman," he answered, "will produce thirty years as tumultuous as those we have survived." "With that [Chinese] race," he predicted, "we are to come in conflict, immortal, aggressive as ourselves." Unlike his earlier discussions, Phillips did not close this one with his usual call for citizenship and equal rights for all as a requisite for social harmony. Rather, he concluded with the equivocating statement that "the very report of their coming had already frightened half of our Republican Senate out of their faith in universal suffrage."[60]

Over six weeks after North Adams, a long editorial published in the *National Anti-Slavery Standard* confirmed Phillips's misgivings about Chinese immigrants.[61] In it, Phillips lashed out at business interests who sought to use Chinese workers as a lever to control the American labor force. Unlike most abolitionists, Phillips was not indifferent to the demands of organized labor. Following emancipation, he had devoted much attention to many areas of social reform, notably labor reform. In 1869, the newly created Massachusetts Labor Reform party had managed to elect a senator and twenty-two representatives to the state legislature. The next year, the party entered the gubernatorial campaign with Phillips as its candidate. Although he conducted an active campaign, he suffered a severe defeat, mostly because his campaign lacked organization. In the 1870 campaign, Phillips gave his full support to workers' demands, including their call for the termination of "the forced importation" of Chinese labor. It is within the context of an increasing commitment to labor reform that Phillips's *economic* arguments against Chinese labor has to be assessed. In his July 30, 1870, editorial, Phillips began by offering his warm welcome to all the poor and oppressed of every race and stating his conviction that every immigrant must be admitted to citizenship and granted suffrage rights. Having said this, he turned his attention to the issue at hand, "the question of importing Chinese laborers." In what a historian has described as "tortured reasoning,"[62] Phillips strove to distinguish between *immigration* and *importation*. While "*immigration of labor*" was "*an unmixed good,*" he stated, "*importation of human freight*" was "*an unmitigated evil.*" If the Chinese had come to North Adams of their own free will, he would have welcomed them as a valuable addition to the mosaic of American nationality. However, the Chinese had been "imported" by the concerted action of capital to degrade American labor.

As he proceeded, Phillips's censure extended to the "imported laborers" themselves, and his line of reasoning was increasingly racial. Although he did praise the Chinese as "a painstaking, industrious, thrifty, inventive, self-respectful, and law-abiding race," his article was replete with critical qualifications. Immediately following his laudatory remark, he observed that the Chinese were "a little too much machines" and were in need of having their servile nature shaken out of them. The Chinaman, he explained, worked cheap because he was a "barbarian," who sought gratification of only the lowest wants. In contrast, the American demanded more, because the progress of Western civilization had made him "10 times as much a MAN." Phillips conceded that native workers had met similar competition from the Irish and German laborers. This interaction, however, never harmed them, because these laborers had come "in such natural and moderate numbers as to be easily absorbed." Looking at the seventy-five Chinese in North Adams as the vanguard of an invading army, he predicted that masses of Chinese would soon flood America "artificially" and with "unnatural rapidity" and would choke America's industrial channels. "An extended North Adams," he added, would enable the Sampsons of America to control "the ballot-box by their bond-servants," thereby imperiling the political system and checking social progress. Accordingly, Phillips believed that it would be premature to grant suffrage and naturalization rights to the Chinese. "[Give] us time, with only a natural amount of [Chinese] immigration," he finally entreated.

The North Adams scene afforded Edwin L. Godkin, the *Nation*'s editor, a good opportunity to criticize anti-Chinese Republicans and labor reformers. With characteristic irony, he commented that seventy-five Chinese shoemakers had plunged Republicans into considerable embarrassment. Having taken a firm stand on the doctrine of racial equality, they were now appalled at the prospect of having the strength of their position subjected to so serious a test as the influx of countless Chinese.[63] As Godkin saw it, Phillips's and other critics' contention that Chinese immigration was acceptable only if it was "spontaneous" was a matter of expediency. The catch to this prerequisite, he observed, was that if labor contracts were forbidden, the capitalist would import no Chinese, and the labor reformers would take credit for being first-class humanitarians and spread-eagle democrats and keeping the labor market for themselves.[64] Conceding that it might have been unwise to rush into the Burlingame Treaty, he believed that it was "too late to have Mongolian blood analyzed and the low condition of Chinese morals exposed." Americans had done so much crowing over the treaty that they could not now tell the Chinese that when they agreed to let them come here freely, they "never, never thought they would come." Godkin was a consistent advocate of unrestricted immigration, be it under contract or not. He believed that after 1865, no coercive labor could ever be established again. He thus rejected the charge of coolieism summarily: no matter what the Chinese were called at public meetings—coolies, peons, or slaves—they were, in practice, "as free as any Irish hodman in New York."[65] Godkin did not think that America could receive the Chinese only in driblets. America, he reminded anti-Chinese agitators, needed immigrants. Besides, he ridiculed the notion that the Chinese would come in hordes.

The demographic facts confirm Godkin's intimation that the Chinese question hinged not so much on quantitative facts as on qualitative factors. In June 1870, there were only 305 Chinese in the American East—broadly defined from the North Atlantic to the South Central region. The foreign-born population for the whole area was more than 5,250,000—including 67.5 percent from Ireland and Germany. After more than twenty years of Chinese immigration to California and the adjacent states and territories, the number of Chinese immigrants in the West was still fewer than 63,000. While Chinese immigrants accounted for 20 percent of the foreign-born population in the western region, they represented less than 6 percent of the population there.[66] Like Godkin, Victoria Claflin Woodhull, the editor of a journal supporting labor causes, woman suffrage, "social freedom," and socialism, believed that the numbers in which the Chinese could and would arrive were overstated. The apprehension about the probability of millions of Chinese labor competitors had, in her opinion, a significant precedent in the northern fear of a massive black migration.[67]

Even more crucial to the conflation of African Americans and Chinese immigrants was the use of terms indicating the singularity of Chinese labor. Until 1869, the eastern press had generally considered Chinese immigrants to the United States to be voluntary migrants. When the Chinese question became relevant to the Southeast, however, some easterners began to associate Chinese immigration there with involuntary immigration and their labor with another form of slavery. Three months before the Chinese shoemakers arrived in North Adams, the editor of the *New York Times* revealed this tendency in an article entitled "What Shall Be Done with John Chinaman?" In it, he established the close correspondence between coolieism and the southern region and between blacks and the Chinese. There was, he argued, "danger that John Chinaman [would] be preferred to the freedman." Having laid down the limited scope of the coolie problem in the United States, the editor then expressed his unwillingness to say to John Chinaman that he should not come unless he came on his own account. There was, in fact, nothing wrong in assisting the Chinese in coming to the United States.[68]

On the whole, the *New York Times* editorial dichotomized Chinese immigrants—the acceptable Chinese contract laborers in the West and the objectionable coolies in the South. Three months later, when the Chinese question arose in North Adams, the editor maintained that the Chinese shoemakers were not coolies. In a move reminiscent of the attempts by southern advocates of Chinese labor to relieve their efforts of the stigma of "coolieism," the northern pro-capital press emphasized that the contracting of the Chinese had been made in a legitimate California agency. Sinophobes, however, kept referring to the Chinese shoemakers as coolies contracted in China. By so doing, they were hoping that the national government would put an end to the experiment altogether. This hope was well encapsulated in the headline "Coolie Slavery. Why Are Not the Laws Prohibiting Coolie Importation Enforced by President Grant?"[69] On July 15, 1870, President Grant transmitted to Congress a report from Secretary of State Hamilton Fish verifying that the Chinese in the United States were all voluntary immigrants.[70] Because of the success of the anti-Chinese campaign in the East, however, Chinese immigration to the East remained inconsequential. Following North Adams, only two other experiments were made, the first in a laundry in Belleville, New Jersey, in September 1870 and the second at a cutlery factory in Beaver Falls, Pennsylvania, in 1872.[71]

While many Americans might have sincerely felt their world threatened by the imminent immigration of numerous Chinese laborers and the establishment of a degrading system of labor, the fact remains that no other group of foreign contract laborers suffered such extreme opposition. In their response to Chinese immigrants in their midst, many easterners proved to be no different from westerners. They, too, stigmatized the Chinese as "imported coolies," and they, too, saw Chinese laborers as mere pawns in the hands of domestic and foreign monopolists, whose goal was to degrade American labor to the social condition of slaves. The anti-Chinese resolutions passed by eastern laborers, Crispins and others, in the summer of 1870 were similar to those passed by westerners. What was more, their exaggerated reaction was used by westerners to underscore their comparatively restrained response to their Chinese problem. If "Massachusetts, with a population of over 1,300,000 was terrified by the appearance of seventy-five Mongolians," a speaker at a San Francisco anti-Chinese demonstration in July 1870 observed, then the West with its Chinese population amounting to about 9 percent was even more justified in its call for Chinese exclusion.[72]

In the East as in the West, the "yellow peril" and coolie themes were, to a large extent, a smoke screen masking racial fears. In the West, after years of antagonism had legitimized a racial discourse, Sinophobes were much more direct: the Chinese and their American employers were enemies of the social and racial compact. Their proposed solution was to hurl from their midst "this abominable clay-colored race."[73] In the East, anti-Chinese groups used economic rationalizations to shroud the racist cast of their opposition and make it somewhat respectable by defining it as a battle between capital and labor and between free and unfree labor. The racialization of the Chinese immigration issue in the East was sometimes unequivocal. In July 1870, the *American Workman* published a drawing of a coolie with a pigtail reaching to the ground. Over his shoulder, he carried a stick from which five dried rats were hung by the tail, with the caption "Coolie Food." In another issue, a drawing featured Simon Legree standing, whip in hand, in a barrack crammed with four-tiered bunks, a pigtail dangling over the end of each bunk. It was entitled "Coolie Slavery in Massachusetts."[74]

Another blatant example was that of John Swinton, who had been an abolitionist and the managing editor of the *New York Times* during the Civil War. Turning his attention to the labor movement, he would become one of the most eloquent labor editors of the 1880s. In June 1870, the *New York Tribune* published his letter to the editor about what he called the new issue of the day—"The Chinese-American Question." From the start, Swinton based his opposition to the influx of *all* Chinese immigrants on two main grounds: race and politics. In both cases, Swinton drew significant connections between Chinese immigrants and blacks. The American democratic-republican system of government, he explained, was based on popular intelligence and conscience. Regrettably, the system was currently severely tried by "vast and dense tainted hordes." Could Americans afford to add another menace to their liberties? Swinton's main concern, however, was race. The Chinese belonged to the Mongolian or yellow race, which, he asserted, was as radically different from the white race as the black race was. As he went on, he set about to inflame the latent sexual fears of his readers by asking them to consider the frightening consequences of allowing perverted and lecherous Chinese men to corrupt vast numbers of women in Massachusetts. The Chinese would bring "paganism, incest, sodomy and the threat of miscegenation to American shores." The survival and purity of the white race in America depended on excluding the Chinese and all other Mongolians. Addressing those who had doubts about the legitimacy of such policy, Swinton insisted that America was entitled to protect itself. Turning to those who had scruples because of their belief in "All Rights for All Men," he asked, Would it not be folly to include in this ideal the "myriads of debased Chinese pagans who are ready to swarm America"? Besides this, he remarked, was not such a lofty principle currently "subjected to modification, in its theoretical terms as well as in its practical application?"[75]

The principal locus of the revision of the ideal of equal rights was in Congress, where propositions to prohibit "coolie contracts" had been discussed since December of 1869. These propositions were by no means restricted to

West Coast or Democratic congressmen. One week after Senator George H. Williams (Republican from Oregon) introduced a bill to regulate Chinese immigration, Senator Henry Wilson introduced his bill to "regulate the importation of immigrants under labor contracts," notably the Chinese coolies.[76] Encouraged by this initiative from an eastern Republican, radical at that, congressmen from the West proposed several bills for the exclusion of coolie labor from the United States. The most extreme of these bills came from Representative James A. Johnson (Democrat from California), who submitted a resolution providing that the free importation and immigration of Chinese laborers should be discouraged by all lawful means.[77] Implicit in the statements of most legislators was the notion that coolies could be imported everywhere in the United States. A few days before the excitement over North Adams, for example, Senator William M. Stewart (Republican from Nevada) submitted a bill prohibiting labor contracts in an attempt to thwart plans to introduce coolie labor in the South.[78] In July 1870, in the midst of the agitation, he reintroduced his bill, urging the senators to pass his bill so that both the South and the North might be able to work out their problems with their free labor.[79]

Never before had Congress resonated with so many racist diatribes against the Chinese. Western congressmen especially propagandized their crude objections to Chinese immigration. According to Johnson, Chinese immigrants were the enemy of the future greatness of America, which could be secured only by preserving the Caucasian blood in its purity. Accordingly, his Chinese bill was much more than a coolie bill, providing also for the exclusion of "debased and abandoned [Chinese] females," whose presence corrupted the morals and health of American youths.[80] Senator Eugene Casserly (Democrat from California) averred that the immigration of Chinese coolies and prostitutes threatened America's Christian civilization.[81] It was, however, Senator Garrett Davis (Democrat from Kentucky), the intransigent foe of black rights, who offered the most extreme statements. Priding himself on having voted against the ratification of the "Chinese treaty," he was willing to vote for any bill that would keep the Chinese "pestilence" out. His harangue conflated the Negro and Chinese questions. Both groups, he charged, belonged to alien and hostile races capable of causing internal conflict in America. If it were practically possible, he would "eject the entire negro population from [America] and throw it back upon Africa." Blacks, he conceded, must remain in America, though. When a proposition was made to add "other hordes of the same species of man [as the Negro]," however, he was utterly opposed to it.[82]

In the antebellum period, easterners had apprehended the Chinese question as a tangential issue and had usually been unreceptive to western appeals to end Chinese immigration. In the postbellum period, the Chinese question—whether arising in the attempts of southerners to supplement or supplant black labor or in Sampson's fight with the Crispins—forced easterners to face the question squarely. The exaggerated reaction to the Chinese in the East seemed to vindicate western claims that Chinese immigrants should not be treated the same as other immigrant groups.

As passion and prejudice ruled the hour, easterners demonstrated that they did not think that, having survived the "depraved, slothful and brutal African" in their midst, they could manage the Chinese.[83] They showed their true colors in their vehement resistance to the employment of the Chinese. In the Northeast, they had marked similar boundary lines for African American laborers long before 1870. Following a tortuous course, American laborers had generally rejoiced at the downfall of slavery, but they were reluctant to support black demands for economic rights. The labor movement had been especially critical of radical Reconstruction and the Freedmen's Bureau, which was viewed as a "huge swindle upon the honest workingman." As late as 1869, the prominent labor organizer William H. Sylvis demanded that the "floating hordes" of southern idle blacks cease to be fed at federal expense and that they be taught they must work for a living or starve.[84] Whether in the North or in the South, African Americans met with discrimination, which barred their advance in the skilled trades. Many unions turned down their applications for membership. Paralleling discriminatory acts against Chinese labor in the West, not a few ordered their members to refuse to work in shops employing Negro mechanics. By 1870, collective and individual assault on black workers had taken a devastating toll; African American workers were almost totally absent from northern industrial workplaces.[85] Presiding over the first meeting of the National Colored Labor Union in 1869, Frederick Douglass exposed the limited opportunities offered blacks, mostly in the service and manual labor sectors. Pointing to his son's experiences, he declared that a black man was made "a transgressor for working at a low rate of wages by the very men who prevented his getting a higher rate."[86] This was a charge black workers shared with Chinese laborers.

Sampson did not turn to the more practical and economical solution of hiring African Americans to break the Crispins' strike. While there were only 57 African Americans in North Adams in 1870, there were 1,322 blacks in the Berkshire County. Given the pattern of irregular employment of African Americans in most cities, they could have constituted a very adequate labor pool for employers in search of workers and strikebreakers. However, there, as in the western region, Sampson and most employers did not recruit black laborers. For the previous thirty years, whiteness had been a prerequisite to economic employment in northern mills. In trying to remedy the labor shortage of the North, employers looked to white foreign labor. It is significant that while blacks constituted less than 1 percent of the population in Massachusetts in 1870, the foreign-born stood at 25 percent.[87] Sampson's decision to go to the distant West Coast for Chinese laborers, rather than the closer pool of African American workers, is reminiscent of similar choices made in western states. By doing so, Sampson reinforced the exclusionary movement vis-à-vis blacks in the North. Eastern laborers and their supporters, in their hostile reaction to his seventy-five Chinese employees, demonstrated their determination to maintain all-white workplaces by defining their identity as non-black *and* non-Chinese.

8. Chinese Immigrants, African Americans, and the Retreat from Reconstruction, 1870–74

As usual, you [Sumner] are in the van, the country in the rear.
—Frederick Douglass to Charles Sumner, July 6, 1870

FOR FIVE YEARS before North Adams, passion and prejudice had ruled the tense relations between the North and the South over Reconstruction policy. From 1870 on, the final round of Reconstruction was played with equal acrimony, and again the Chinese question emerged as an important element.

Far from being the crowning act of a radical conspiracy to promote black equality, as Democrats claimed, the Fifteenth Amendment actually took a moderate position. Like the Fourteenth Amendment, it was worded in the negative, limiting the power of national and state governments to deny African Americans the ballot. While it outlawed using race, color, or previous condition of servitude as a test for voting, the Fifteenth Amendment left to the states the freedom to restrict suffrage on any other basis. After its passage, many Republican congressmen pointed to the loophole in the amendment that allowed southern states to exclude black voters by imposing literacy tests, property qualifications, and poll taxes. Although these requirements were racially motivated, they could not be held unconstitutional because they allegedly applied to all voters.[1] Together with other congressmen, these Republicans were also alarmed at the reports of politically sponsored violence by the Ku Klux Klan and kindred organizations, such as the Knights of the White Camelia and the White Brotherhood.[2]

By 1870, these extralegal organizations were deeply entrenched in nearly every southern state. As the elections of 1870 drew nearer, terrorist activities became so pervasive that they threatened Republican ascendancy in the South. Furthermore, the larger Democratic delegation in the House of Representatives following the readmission of the southern states in 1868 and 1870, the increase of southern representation due to the repeal of the three-fifths clause, and the resurgent strength of the Democratic party at the polls in Virginia, North Carolina, and Georgia indicated the fragility of Reconstruction regimes in the South. Republicans decided to act before the ebb and flow of the political tide decreased their power and barred them from remedying the deficiencies of the Fourteenth and the Fifteenth amendments. In 1870 and 1871, they introduced legislation aimed at implementing the two amendments. The first of the so-called Enforcement Acts forbade state officials to discriminate among voters on the basis of race or color and outlawed the use of force, bribery, threats, intimidation, and conspiracies to prevent citizens from exercising their constitutional rights. The Ku Klux Klan Act of 1871 made it a federal offense to conspire to prevent citizens from holding office, serving on juries, enjoying equal protection of the laws, or voting.[3]

In assessing the intent and meaning of this legislation, scholars have usually omitted an important feature in the first Enforcement Act, that is, the section to enforce the equal protection clause on behalf of aliens, mainly Chinese aliens.[4] In February 1870, Senator William M. Stewart, a radical Republican from Nevada and an important member of the powerful Judiciary Committee, proposed a bill to extend the Civil Rights Act of 1866. The clause relevant to this discussion reads:

[That all] persons within the jurisdiction of the United States . . . shall have the same right . . . in the United States to make and enforce contracts, to sue, be parties, give evidence, and to the full and equal benefit of all laws and proceedings for the security of person and property as is enjoyed by white citizens, and shall be subject to like punishments, pains, penalties, taxes, licenses, and exactions of every kind, and none other, any law, statute, ordinance, regulation, or custom to the contrary notwithstanding. No tax or charge shall be imposed or enforced by any State upon any person emigrating thereto from a foreign country which is not equally imposed and enforced upon every person emigrating to such State from any foreign country, and any law of any State in conflict with this provision is hereby declared null and void.[5]

The language of this clause is very similar to section 1 of the Civil Rights Act of 1866. There is one major difference, though. While the 1866 act secured "all persons born in the United States" the equal protection of the laws, Stewart's bill extended that protection to citizens and noncitizens alike. When he introduced his bill, Stewart did not indicate concern for any specific group of aliens. In the course of the debate on the bill, however, he disclosed that his intent was to secure stronger guarantees for the civil rights of the Chinese in America.

By May 1870, the Judiciary Committee had greatly enlarged the scope of the proposed bill, which now aimed to enforce both the Fifteenth and Fourteenth amendments. Disagreeing with such a move, Senator John Sherman, a conservative Republican from Ohio, strongly objected to incorporating Stewart's bill into the enforcement bill. Such inclusion, he rebuked, would result in "dragging into the controversy the Chinese question and questions of that kind." In his rebuttal, Stewart insisted on not only the propriety of enforcing both amendments but also the necessity of a clause that would give the Chinese equal protection of the laws. For twenty years, he admonished, citizens on the Pacific Coast had violated every obligation of humanity, justice, and common decency toward the Chinese. By signing the Burlingame Treaty, America had pledged that the Chinese would be protected in their rights. It was thus the solemn duty of Congress to honor its pledge.[6]

On May 20, after an all-night session designed to break a Democratic filibuster, the enforcement bill, which by then included Stewart's amendment as section 16, was laid on the table and submitted to a vote. The Senate passed it by an overwhelming majority of 43 to 8.[7] Republican leaders had called on all members to settle their differences, emphasizing the need to pass the bill to thwart Democratic schemes in the upcoming fall elections. All the Republican senators representing the West Coast voted for the bill. Stewart then made what could be considered his last pro-Chinese remark. Long overdue, he stated, was the provision that extended the strong arm of the government to protect the Chinese. Little did Stewart know that, about six weeks later, he would be haranguing against the Chinese.[8]

In the House, the bill received much criticism from the larger Democratic delegation. While some congressmen expressed their concern over the effect of the bill on black-white relations,[9] James A. Johnson from California focused on the "Chinese menace." Pointing to the "immense, teeming, swarming, seething hive of degraded humanity" in the Chinese Empire, he warned that any lack of vigilance or any manifestation of leniency would turn that humanity loose upon America to destroy its institutions, religion, and race. Turning to the economic argument, Johnson stated that Chinese labor was even more degraded than African slaves because, unlike the slaves, they performed "voluntarily." Moreover, Johnson believed that it would be a mistake to suppose that the Chinese were coming to be drudges and fill the place of slaves. Already in California, he argued, the Chinese had started to take possession of American workshops, factories, and farms.[10] Johnson was particularly concerned about the implications of the bill for naturalization. Earlier, in January, he had used strong terms against radical Republicans because of their support for universal manhood suffrage. If these "friends of Chinese suffrage" went unchecked, he asserted, they would secure "the Hottentot, the cannibal from the jungles of Africa, the West India negro, the wild Indian, and the Chinaman" the right to vote and hold office. Soon America would have a "Chinese President, Hottentot Senate, cannibal House of Representatives, and a judiciary presided over by the pet lambs from San Domingo." Johnson believed that the Chinese constituted a greater threat to white supremacy than the other nonwhite groups. He explained that while the African groups would vote at random, the Chinese would always vote against the interest of whites.[11]

A few months later, when Johnson faced the imminent passage of a civil rights clause for the protection of the Chinese in the enforcement bill, he contended that the Fourteenth Amendment already gave the Chinese all the protection the law could give them. He suggested that the real intent of the "Chinese bill" was to make the Chinese a voter. Naturalization, he deplored, would be accomplished upon the passage of the enforcement bill. Once naturalized, the large Chinese male population in California would acquire political control of California. Who demanded Chinese naturalization, he asked, but Republican opportunists driven to champion Chinese suffrage in defense of not the Chinese but their own party? In agitating for the enfranchisement of the Chinese, he charged, these men were turning against their country and race.[12] Johnson's tirade notwithstanding, the House Republicans arrayed themselves in a solid column. The enforcement bill was passed by an overwhelming majority of 133 to 58.[13]

As expected, western Democratic representatives voted against the bill, while Republicans, notably Aaron A. Sargent from California and Thomas Fitch from Nevada, voted for it. Soon thereafter, however, Sargent and Fitch attempted to limit the scope of section 16 insofar as the Chinese were concerned. In June 1870, they gave vent to their anti-Chinese sentiment in a debate over a bill "to amend the naturalization laws and to punish crimes against the same," submitted to the House by Noah Davis (Republican from New York).[14] Initially intended to remedy the corruption and fraud that had crept into the ballot box of major eastern cities by means of unnaturalized or illegally naturalized European aliens, the bill soon became the center of a heated debate on citizenship. When it became clear that the pending naturalization bill would go beyond the original design, Fitch proposed amending it so that instead of stating that "any alien may become a citizen of the United States," the bill would say that "any aliens *except natives of China and Japan* may become citizens of the United States."[15] Fitch explained that, in general, the men who immigrated from Europe belonged to races stirred by the spirit of freedom and republicanism. In Asia, however, races were guided by a civilization totally incompatible with republican institutions. Sargent went beyond the common aspirations of Europeans and Americans, stressing that Europeans belonged to races from which Americans sprang.

For both Sargent and Fitch, Chinese immigrants were "slaves to exacting masters," both Chinese and American. Their indictment was, however, mostly directed at the Chinese laborers. Both men pointed to Massachusetts (North Adams), where the Chinese were already "supplanting" Americans in shoe manufacturing. Worse, Sargent added, the Chinese would ultimately weed out not only the white laborers but also their schools, churches, and all other characteristics of New England life. Turning to the political implications of the bill, Fitch warned that the Republican party in the West was at stake. In closing his harangue, Fitch reassured those who feared that his amendment might be deemed unconstitutional. Far from it, he exclaimed, it was in agreement with the Fifteenth Amendment, in that it was an exclusion not on account of race but on account of nativity or nationality. Nor did his amendment conflict with the Burlingame Treaty. In the original draft of the treaty, there had been no provision on naturalization, Sargent observed. But the question was pressing in Congress, and an objection was made that the treaty would be construed as allowing the naturalization of the Chinese. An amendment was thus offered and adopted—in the handwriting of Charles Sumner himself, he emphasized—to the effect that nothing in the treaty should be held to confer naturalization. Why was such a clause added, Sargent asked, if not to make sure that the Chinese could *not* claim naturalization?[16]

Less than a month after this colloquy, Senator Charles Sumner (radical Republican from Massachusetts) initiated an impassioned debate in the Senate when he offered to add this new section to the naturalization bill: "That all acts of Congress relating to naturalization be . . . amended by striking out the word 'white' wherever it occurs, so that in naturalization there shall be no distinction of race or color."[17] Following this motion, George Williams (Republican from Oregon) moved the following addition: "But this act shall not be construed to authorize the naturalization of persons born in the Chinese empire." He was supported by Stewart, the framer of section 16 of the Enforcement Act. Both senators complained that Sumner's motion was ill-timed and out of place in a bill aimed at regulating naturalization for persons entitled to receive it. This was not the case of the Chinese. The issue of their naturalization was, in Stewart's opinion, a "question of race and color," that is, "another question altogether." When he came to the Senate that afternoon, he had not, he stressed, made any agreement to extend naturalization to the Chinese on a bill to regulate naturalization. To Stewart, then, Sumner's motion was "a plain, palpable [and] clear violation" of the agreement among Republicans that no new motion should be appended to the bill being considered. Pointing to the fact that Sumner's amendment involved "the whole Chinese Question," Senator Oliver P. Morton (Republican from Indiana) cautioned that the country had just awakened to the enormous magnitude of the question. Morton was referring to the agitation following the arrival of the Chinese shoemakers in North Adams three weeks earlier.[18]

As passions flared among Republicans, Thomas McCreery (Democrat from Kentucky) seized the opportunity to offer another amendment to Williams's bill: "That the provisions of that act shall not apply to persons born in Asia, Africa, or any of the islands of the Pacific, nor to Indians born in the wilderness." While the motion aroused laughter in the chamber and was rejected without a vote, the tension among Republicans increased. Besides Stewart, Williams, and Morton, three other Republican senators expressed their intention to vote against Sumner's proposition.[19] Among them was the other radical senator from Massachusetts, Henry Wilson. Congress, Wilson stated, was desirous of securing a much-needed reform to guarantee the purity of the ballot box. He opposed Sumner's section not on principle but because it might endanger the passage of the bill. Most senators were not duped. Wilson's repeated attempts to curry favor with the Labor Reform party had caused him to lead a vocal campaign against Chinese labor. Sumner's amendment, however, was not about allowing or banning Chinese labor. It was about erasing the racial prerequisite from the naturalization statute as a means of providing the protection of law, regardless of race. Wilson's stand against it exposed his enduring nativist convictions.

Despite opposition from both sides of the political spectrum, Sumner's amendment prevailed with a vote of 27 to 22.[20] At Stewart's insistence that senators should reconsider the propriety of Sumner's amendment, however, senators decided the debate should resume two days later, on the Fourth of July. The debate turned out to be long and acrimonious. Senators Stewart and Williams professed to give the West Coast position on the Chinese question. The two senators from California were absent that day. Stewart's speech is interesting in view of his earlier pro-Chinese position. His first concern as he took the floor was to demonstrate that his opposition to Sumner's bill was consistent with his earlier position. While he had been instrumental in incorporating a Chinese protection clause in the Enforcement Act, at no time had he ever contemplated granting the Chinese citizenship and trusting them with political power. The problem with Sumner's bill, Stewart argued, was that it proposed handing over American institutions to foreigners who had no sympathy with republican institutions and American civilization. What followed was a long diatribe punctuated by specious expressions of friendship and compassion for the Chinese. While the Chinese were an honest and industrious people, they were above all pagans. Unlike European immigrants who "are of us, and assimilate rapidly, and aid in the development and progress of our country," the Asiatics had a civilization that was at war with American civilization. Until the Chinese became Christian and renounced their allegiance to China, it was imperative that senators fight any proposition to graft the Chinese onto the American body politic. What was more, he complained, the Chinese were brought to America under coolie contracts. Was it not the duty of a "humane Congress" first to see that no more coolies were imported to America?[21]

Stewart then set out to demonstrate that the Republican party had never committed itself to naturalizing the Chinese. There was nothing, he began, in the Republican record that made it necessary for Republicans to incorporate any other people in the body politic. Neither the Fifteenth Amendment nor even the Declaration of Independence meant that the Chinese had the same rights in this government that Americans had. "Because we did an act of justice, because we enfranchised the colored man," he asked, must we therefore necessarily abandon our institutions to the Chinese? While it was important that blacks should be enfranchised so that they might protect themselves, granting the Chinese naturalization and suffrage would bring chaos and violence. In fact, Stewart predicted, the Chinese would be "maltreated, murdered, [and] exterminated" before any one of them could be naturalized. Besides, the pending bill would wreak havoc in the Republican party of the West by giving ammunition to Democrats, who were claiming that Republicans wanted to trade in Chinese votes.[22]

Stewart's reasoning met with two major rebuttals from Senators Sumner and Lyman Trumbull (Republican from Illinois). If the Chinese were permitted to come to the United States, they countered, then they should be incorporated within the body politic rather than ostracized as slaves or inferiors. Pointing to the symbolic meaning of the date, the Fourth of July, Sumner reiterated his conviction that his bill was simply "the question of the Declaration of Independence." It was thus high time that the word *white,* which dishonored the Declaration, was expunged from the naturalization statutes. The greatest threat to the Republic, he thundered, came not from the Chinese but from disloyalty to its lofty ideals. In an attempt to divert attention away from the Chinese question, Sumner pointed to the practical bearing of his proposition on the southern Atlantic seaboard, where, he remarked, aliens of African ancestry, mainly from the West Indies, were barred from naturalization because of the word *white* in the naturalization laws.[23]

Williams then declared that he would have no objection to an amendment that would allow Africans specifically to be naturalized, because of the small number of such immigrants. The proposition before Congress was, however, whether the "mighty tide of pollution from Asia" should be allowed to continue. The Asiatic question, he warned, was huge. All the problems that had grown out of slavery, he added, dwindled into insignificance. To Williams, the Chinese question was first and foremost a racial question. No matter how long Mongolians stayed in the United States, they would never lose their identity as a separate people. They could, he maintained, never amalgamate with people of European descent. Williams believed that the senators only needed to consider the racial encounters and interaction with Native Americans and African Americans to ascertain the inevitably disastrous results of the contact between Euro-Americans and Asians. Was America prepared to welcome another racial group with all the danger that it entailed—"discord and collision"?[24]

Following these colloquies, Republican ranks sundered, with a small group supporting Sumner's motion and a larger group opposing it. Joining the Republican majority in dissent were three radicals: Wilson from Massachusetts, Charles D. Drake from Missouri, and Timothy O. Howe from Wisconsin. Most Republicans opposing Sumner's motion expressed their concern that it might jeopardize the passage of the pending bill.[25] Some, however, took sides in the controversy over Chinese naturalization. Senator Drake, for example, declared that he would vote for such a motion, when Sumner put it before the Senate by itself, or as part of a measure that would not be so vital to the interests of the country. Senator Wilson expressed his apprehensions about importing Chinese coolies to America. Already, he argued, the coolies were forcing the white men of the North and the colored men of the South to despair. It was therefore imperative to stop that trade first.[26] Senators Howe and Morton made a distinction between the natural rights established in the Declaration of Independence and the civil and political rights granted by the Constitution. The question of whether the Chinese should be naturalized was a question of policy, not natural right. Howe even went so far as to propose a proviso against the naturalization of "any person born in a pagan country, unless with his oath of allegiance the applicant shall take and file an oath abjuring his belief in all forms of paganism."[27]

On the opposite side were the senators who stood by Sumner as a question of principle and consistency: Trumbull, Samuel C. Pomeroy from Kansas, Matthew Carpenter from Wisconsin, and Carl Schurz from Missouri. Schurz was sorry that the excitement over the Chinese question had found its way onto the Senate floor. The exclusion of the Chinese from naturalization on the mere ground of nativity, he stressed, would be a great injustice. Following him, Carpenter delivered a blistering attack on the anti-Chinese position.

The cornerstone of American institutions, he explained, was that every man who was bound by the law ought to have a voice in making the law. When the Civil War ended with the emancipation of four million slaves, he recalled, the question confronting Congress had been whether they should be admitted to the full rights of citizenship. The Republican party had then bravely followed its principle. The question now was whether the party would stand by its principle or would permit the Chinese to constitute a class of inferiors. Strange as it was, he and Pomeroy remarked, the very men who had settled the question of citizenship for African Americans on principle now hesitated to apply the same principle to the Chinese. These senators were interposing the same objections to the enfranchisement of the Chinese that Democrats were still urging against black suffrage. At least, Pomeroy conceded, these vocal Sinophobes were not dodging the question, unlike those senators who intended to vote against Sumner's bill because it was on "the wrong kind of bill." The latter would find some other reason to vote against it when it was on the "right kind of bill." Pomeroy also expressed his concern about the repercussions of the decision to be made. If the senators chose to settle the naturalization of the Chinese by a policy at odds with the spirit of American Republicanism, then it would be no settlement at all. By taking the word *white* out of the naturalization statutes, however, Republicans would show their determination to complete the revolution that they had set in motion in the past years. To conclude, Carpenter warned that to deny the Chinese privileges because of their race would provide ammunition to the Democrats, who would again press their objections to the enfranchisement of the African.[28]

As Senator Trumbull stood to rebut the anti-Chinese position, he admitted that he had never been "extreme" in his political decisions.[29] Yet he could pride himself on having never abandoned the great principle of equal rights to all men. The Republican party, he stressed, had achieved its triumphs in the name of that principle. It was thus quite "extraordinary," he thought, that some Republicans should be so anxious about the presence of Chinese people in America that they would be willing to forsake the very foundation upon which they had stood for twenty years. Refuting the economic, political, cultural, and religious charges against the Chinese, he concluded that the opposition to the naturalization of the Chinese grew out of prejudice only: "They are Asiatics, and the color of their skin is yellow." Not so long ago, he observed, it was the color black that deprived individuals of their rights. With the adoption of the last three amendments to the Constitution, Republicans had repealed distinctions on account of race so far as blacks were concerned. Was it not a strange irony of fate that they were now engaged in resurrecting those distinctions for another race?[30]

Out of eight Democrats, only two participated in the debate. Willard Saulsbury from Delaware, a vehement opponent of black rights, showed his appreciation of the importance given to consistency and principles by moving
to amend Williams's proviso so that it would read, "*Provided,* that nothing
in this act shall be construed to authorize the naturalization of persons born
in the Chinese empire, *or persons of the negro race of foreign birth.*"[31] The
Democrats, Allen G. Thurman from Ohio observed, had taken hardly any
time during the debate, and he did not want to depart from that rule. Yet he
wished to note that it was very significant that a number of Republicans were
ready to sacrifice the great tenets on which their party was founded in order
to save a bill that, in his opinion, did nothing but pile up cumulative punishments for offenses already defined by the law. Henceforth, when Republicans talked about their lofty principles, he admonished, let it be remem-
bered that not all Republicans stood by them. So far as the Chinese question
was concerned, however, Thurman believed that senators had been very far
from getting to the root of the matter.[32]

Just before the vote to reconsider the favorable vote on his amendment,
Sumner made a final plea in behalf of the Chinese. He entreated fellow Republicans not to lose the opportunity to reshape the statutes in accordance
with the two great title deeds of the Republic. Sumner predicted that the
senators' refusal to sanction his amendment would result in opening at once
the flood gates of controversy. If they accepted his amendment, however, they
would have peace now and forever, and their Reconstruction policy would
be reinforced. Would Republicans, in the face of all that happened in the
previous years, retreat and retrace the steps they had already taken? he finally asked. When Sumner's amendment was submitted to a new vote, it lost,
by a vote of 14 to 30—with 28 not voting. Twenty-two out of the thirty nays
came from Republicans.[33]

Following the rejection, Willard Warner (Republican from Alabama) went
on to presume that there would be little objection to his motion: "That the
naturalization laws are hereby extended to aliens of African nativity and to
persons of African descent." Warner's amendment prevailed by a close vote
of 21 to 20. Twelve Republicans voted against the motion, eleven of whom
had also voted against Sumner's motion to extend naturalization to the
Chinese. Ten Republicans who had voted against Sumner's motion voted for
Warner's motion.[34] Thereafter, Trumbull entreated these ten senators to show
some consistency. By a single vote, he declared, they had struck out the word
white so far as it applied to the "pagan from Africa." How could they propose to deny the right of naturalization to the Chinaman, who was "infinitely
above the African . . . in every respect"? Warner's amendment, he clarified,

was not applicable to the American Negro. It was an amendment authorizing Africans—"the most degraded examples of man on the face of the
earth"—to come to America and be naturalized. Trumbull's entreaty was met
by Morton's and Williams's rebuttal that Warner's amendment would have
no significant effect. While a few Africans might come from the West Indies,
Africans from the continent, they insisted, would not come.[35] Still hopeful,
Trumbull offered an amendment to Warner's motion, extending it to "persons born in the Chinese empire." As expected, the motion was voted down
31 to 9, with 32 senators absent. A few days later, the naturalization statute
was amended to extend citizenship eligibility to "aliens of African nativity
and to persons of African descent."[36]

This revised naturalization statute of July 1870 was the first national anti-
Chinese legislation. The anti-Chinese vote cut across sectional lines. Moreover,
the measure was passed in the absence of the senators from California, both
absent on the second and more important day of the deliberations. As the
debates over naturalization followed their tortuous course, it soon became
clear that Sumner's motion would not result in a vote along party lines as far
as the Republicans were concerned. Realizing this, Senator Trumbull had expressed his consternation with his fellow Republicans' "attempt to reverse the
course of Reconstruction policy."[37] A few months earlier, in January 1870, Senator Drake had also complained that an "extraordinary" change had occurred
in congressional politics. While each party had until then arrayed itself in solid
column, Republican ranks were now divided, with several Republicans voting against Republican proposals.[38] The extent to which this development was
remarkable is, however, open to question. Prior to 1870, congressional Republicans had focused their attention on issues directly stemming from slavery,
the Civil War, and emancipation. In those years, Republicans never had to
choose between political expediency and political morality. Even so, the differences of opinion that arose in the context of the debates over the Fourteenth
and Fifteenth amendments had exposed the cracks in the Republican party's
apparent unity. Time and again, in the course of those debates, the broad language proposed by the radicals was opposed by conservatives who were concerned that it might lead to a change in the naturalization statutes and provide the means for Chinese equality. For about three and a half years before
July 1870, it was a Republican majority that had obstructed Sumner's earlier
proposals to rid the naturalization statutes of racial distinction.

What happened during the naturalization debates was not an "extraordinary reversal." The debates brought to light the deep-rooted rift between the
Republican minority, which saw the essence of the party in its devotion to
universal equality, and the majority, which saw it in a more limited and self-

serving commitment to equality for African Americans only. On both sides, the use of the theme of consistency showed their diverging perspectives. The senators who endorsed Sumner's call for universal naturalization did so because the policy of the Republican party was, in their opinion, to make all men free. They defended his amendment as the ultimate expression of the political morality called for by the Declaration of Independence and as the culmination of the reconstruction of the nation. Many Republicans, however, took strong issue with this position. Using the line of reasoning that had coursed through the discussion of black rights since 1865, they emphasized that the Declaration addressed the question not of *political rights* but of *natural rights:* the right to life, liberty, and the pursuit of happiness. The question of whether the Chinese should be entitled to naturalization was thus a question of policy, not natural right. Some senators went further, asserting that Republican policy in the past years had deliberately refrained from extending to the Chinese all the new rights granted to African Americans. As they expounded their position, these Republicans strove to dissociate the Chinese question from the Negro problem. The enfranchisement of the colored man was thus an act of justice, which was part of the national effort at redressing the great wrong perpetrated on native-born Americans of color.

While Sumner and his supporters spoke in terms of moral duty, their opponents responded in practical terms and acted on such terms. Most Republicans now saw political morality and political expediency as two options between which they could choose without jeopardizing their position or that of their party. When they defeated Sumner's amendment, they in effect "liberated" their party from the radical definition of its essence as total equality for all. Their success revealed the extent to which the few thorough racial egalitarians left had been stripped of their power, not only by conservative Republicans but also by erstwhile radicals, such as Henry Wilson from Massachusetts. Wilson had repeatedly advocated "equality for all" during the debates over Reconstruction. In 1870, Wilson's egalitarianism insofar as the Chinese were concerned may have been tempered by practical concerns. His senate seat depended on the outcome of state legislative races, and he therefore could not alienate labor support, especially in the context of the North Adams affair. Such concern, however, does not explain why Wilson voted against Warner's amendment, extending naturalization to persons of African descent. Nor can the avowed distress of Senators James W. Nye and William M. Stewart of Nevada over the imminent invasion of their state by "hordes of pagan coolies" explain their votes against the same motion. The double negative vote of these erstwhile radicals critically exposed the limitations of their moral principle.

To a certain extent, the Republican vote for Warner's motion reflected the continuous congruence of political morality and expediency insofar as persons of African ancestry were concerned. The first vote was a close one—21 yeas (all from Republicans), 20 nays (12 Republicans and 8 Democrats), and 31 absent. For the majority of the Republicans who voted for the motion, the extension of naturalization to Africans indicated that, despite their vote for continuing the use of the term *white* in the naturalization statutes, they could still profess a devotion to the principle of equality. As had been the case before 1870, the final vote on the naturalization bill was except for one vote (Senator Arthur I. Boreman, a Republican from West Virginia) a party vote— 33 yeas, 8 nays, and 31 absent.[39]

The importance of the anti-Chinese vote in the debate on naturalization cannot be overestimated. The extension of citizenship and thereby suffrage is an essential means of incorporating new groups into the nation. By keeping the word *white* in the statute, the Republican majority placed Chinese aliens in the category of persons ineligible for full membership in the national community. While the immediate postbellum Republican policy had produced tangible benefits for the Chinese in the form of the Fourteenth Amendment and section 16 of the Enforcement Act of 1870, Republicans decided that they would go no further and would not grant them full citizenship. The Naturalization Statute of 1870 concluded the piecemeal reversal of the *Dred Scott* decision by laying the ground for a new legal construction of American citizenship, one predicated on both whiteness and blackness. This expanded construction of American citizenship had critical implications for the nonwhite and nonblack. While the earlier act of 1790, confining naturalization to whites only, had been used by Chief Justice Taney in his infamous *Dred Scott* ruling, the 1870 statute would serve to legitimize the anti-Asian cast of American law and immigration policy for more than seventy years.

The anti-Chinese vote was but one symptom of an increasingly negative reaction to "radical Reconstruction." The year 1870 marked the beginning of the decline of Republican radicalism and the abandonment of southern Republicans. Historians have attributed various reasons to this decline: the deaths of radical Republicans, northern latent racism, an increasing commitment to federalism and laissez-faire, labor radicalism in the North, and the strength of reform-oriented Republicans.[40] As strong advocates of economic and constitutional liberalism, these reformers took a firm position against governmental waste, public control, and federal centralization. Although they had supported and even helped formulate the Reconstruction Acts and postwar amendments, they now insisted that with the principle of equal rights for southern African Americans secured, the government should move on to the "living issues" of the Gilded Age. Their attack on centralized power often included a criticism of the federal enforcement of Reconstruction measures. Just as radicalism had been the driving force of the party in the 1860s, liberalism and conservatism became more prevalent in the 1870s. As the debates on naturalization showed, a striking development was the ease with which some Republicans fell back upon racism to bolster their position.[41]

This retreat from radical Reconstruction affected African Americans. The Republican party had been straddling essential issues concerning the rights of African Americans before the debate on naturalization. In the early months of 1870, Sumner had introduced three bills to guarantee more protection for black Americans. These bills had been buried in the Judiciary Committee. The most critical of these bills aimed at forbidding discrimination in places of public accommodations, schools, juries, and church organizations.[42] The Republican majority did not support this civil rights bill, which languished in the committee for the next year and a half, until it became embroiled in political maneuvers connected with the Liberal Republican movement and the amnesty issue in the last months of 1871. The Republican majority then introduced the bill as an amendment to a general amnesty bill of ex-Confederates, expecting that it would ensure the defeat of the bill and that they would be able to blame Democrats for the defeat. It also hoped to check the Liberal Republicans, who were advocating complete amnesty for southerners in an attempt to attract support from southern whites and northern Democrats. In the course of the debates, these Republicans showed their lack of moral conviction by challenging the constitutionality of Sumner's civil rights bill and shearing it of the provisions regarding churches, jury duty, and state discrimination laws.[43]

The Republican majority also exposed its conservatism and prejudices by resisting Sumner's inclusion of what they called the "Chinese civil rights" section in his civil rights bill. Section 5 provided "[t]hat every law, statute, ordinance, regulation, or custom, whether national or State . . . making any discriminations against any person . . . by the use of the word 'white,' is hereby repealed and annulled." In February 1872, Senator John Sherman from Ohio objected to the section because it would enable Asians to become naturalized citizens of the United States. Sharing Sherman's apprehension, Cornelius Cole from California proposed an amendment to the bill, providing for the revocation of discrimination against *citizens* rather than *persons*.[44] The amendment was rejected 15 to 34, with 24 senators reported absent. He then offered a proviso that section 5 should not be construed to alter the naturalization laws. This new amendment was similarly rejected. Henry Corbett from Oregon then offered an amendment, which declared that section 5 should not be held to authorize the naturalization of the Chinese. His amendment was rejected by a vote of 13 to 32, with 28 absent. It would be wrong, however, to assume that these votes reflected a willingness to vote for Sumner's pro-Chinese section. Four days later, despairing of obtaining a favorable vote, Sumner modified his bill "so as to eliminate what may be compendiously called the Chinese question." He was then confident that the strenuous opposition to his civil rights bill would weaken.[45]

The Democrats were of course against Sumner's civil rights bill, and they were very much aware that the bill had been attached to the amnesty bill as a move to defeat the latter. In February and again in May 1872, the Senate approved Sumner's civil rights rider, shorn of its original section 5, by the tie-breaking vote of Vice-President Schuyler Colfax. Both times, however, a coalition of Democrats and radical and liberal Republicans defeated the combined amnesty–civil rights bill, some opposing amnesty and the rest opposing civil rights.[46] As the 1872 presidential election approached, political necessity made it vital for Republicans to separate the civil rights and amnesty measures. In May 1872, the Liberal Republican party held its convention in Cincinnati. Its platform attacked centralized power, endorsed local self-government and individual liberty, and called for immediate and universal amnesty for ex-Confederates. Fearful of defections, radical Republicans decided to pass an amnesty measure. In Sumner's absence, a separate civil rights bill, shorn of the school, jury, church, and cemetery clauses as well as the Chinese clause, was passed. They then passed the amnesty bill. The watered-down civil rights bill was then defeated in the House.[47] The deep division among Republicans in the House was made worse by the near unanimity of the Senate vote for amnesty. By its vote, however, the Senate solidified its moderate image in relation to Reconstruction.

When Congress convened in December 1872, the fate of Reconstruction was sealed.[48] Sumner's bill was reintroduced in its original form. Even though Republicans still had control of Congress by a two-thirds margin, the bill languished for the next two and a half years. When Sumner died in March 1874, the Senate passed a version of his bill, without, however, the original section 5 and the clause relating to churches.[49] The House did not pass it. In the congressional elections of 1874, more than half the Republican incumbents of the House were defeated. This defeat constituted the greatest reversal of partisan alignments in the nineteenth century, erasing the congressional majority that Republicans had enjoyed since secession and transforming the party's 110-vote margin in the House into a Democratic majority of 60 seats. While northern voters turned against the party in power as a reaction to the depression that had started in 1873, southern voters identified with the Democratic platform that emphasized white supremacy, low taxes, and control of the black labor force.[50] The civil rights bill had been an important element in the southern campaign. Following the elections, the lame-duck Republicans reintroduced the civil rights bill in its original form except for section 5. After a heated debate, Congress passed this last Reconstruction measure without the school desegregation clause and the cemetery provision.[51]

For many observers, the Civil Rights Act was harmless and unnecessary. For advocates of racial equality, their efforts to provide blacks with equal rights had turned into a hollow victory without the clause outlawing school segregation. In 1875, then, the hopes for racial equality and justice for African Americans and Chinese immigrants were highly compromised. Sumner's repeated attempts to lay the blueprint for a real social revolution were time and again defeated by his fellow Republicans' commitment to keep the foundational whiteness of American identity and their vacillating policy toward black Americans. The intentional exclusion of the Chinese from the purview of the new naturalization statute constituted a critical retreat. As a few radicals anticipated, this measure would pave the way for a reconsideration of the status of African Americans. In that process, rather than the Negroization of the Chinese question, it would be the Negro question that would be "Asianized."

9. Race Relations in California, 1870–74

In Washington men may talk; in Sacramento they must act. . . .
Face to face with a gigantic evil, the Californians have passed a
dozen laws in self-defence. . . . [San Francisco] has ceased to be a
free port in the sense in which New York is a free port.
—William H. Dixon, *White Conquest* (1876)

THE COMPLEX RACE relations situation in California had long set the stage for a conflation of the Negro and Chinese questions. After African Americans had won the right to testify in 1863, they had initiated a series of efforts to win the right to vote. Not until the ratification of the Fifteenth Amendment in February 1870, however, was the franchise extended to them. Henry H. Haight, California's Democratic governor, had opposed ratification of the Fifteenth Amendment on the ground that the Tenth Amendment reserved for the states the right to regulate suffrage laws. He warned the state senate that if it ratified the amendment, not only blacks but also the Chinese could be made electors. The legislature accepted his resolution calling for the rejection of the amendment, mainly because of its alleged effect on the status of Chinese immigrants.[1] While African Americans constituted only 0.8 percent of the state population, the Chinese amounted to about 8.8 percent. More than black suffrage, then, the Chinese vote had been a major concern in California since the Fifteenth Amendment was sent to the states. In 1869, the Democratic party platform made clear that its opposition to black suffrage was by and large overshadowed by a greater hostility to Chinese suffrage. Meanwhile, the Republican party pledged to support the Fifteenth Amendment but declared its opposition to Chinese suffrage.[2]

The ratification of the Fifteenth Amendment did not usher an era of equal treatment. African Americans were now able to join the ranks of California's electors by registering to vote; however, opposition to Chinese naturalization and suffrage persisted. While events in the East in 1870 temporarily shifted attention regarding the Chinese question from the West to the East, meetings of the unemployed on the West Coast triggered a decade of turbulent labor demonstrations. In 1869, California had suffered a mild recession. A year later, however, labor conditions worsened for various reasons, two of which were the great availability of laborers after the completion of the transcontinental railroad and the increased incorporation of California within the national economy. As in 1867, the presence of the Chinese seemed to be a ready explanation for the economic downturn.

Chinese entry into the manufacturing industries in the late 1860s was due to a scarcity of labor, following the increased opportunities afforded by the development of specific industries where their labor could be utilized.[3] Chinese immigration then increased (12,874 new arrivals in 1869 and 15,740 in 1870) in the largest continuous influx since 1854. These immigrants were readily absorbed in labor-intensive industries, such as construction, sweatshop industries, and agricultural work, as well as the lighter branches of industry usually allotted to women. A great number of Chinese workers also found employment as domestic servants and launderers. Until the spring of 1870, the Chinese did not face any major opposition from American laborers, but economic hardships reinvigorated the anti-Chinese feelings of white laborers. In their Sand Lot meetings in the early months of 1870, white unemployed laborers vented their bitterness at the business class and, more forcefully, Chinese laborers. Within four months, these meetings culminated in anti-Chinese mass demonstrations in San Francisco under the auspices of the Knights of Saint Crispin. Of the many trades represented, only one, the shoemaking trade, had recently suffered from Chinese competition. In 1869, the Chinese had entered the trade as a strikebreaking element. In their inflammatory addresses to the laborers in the midst of the North Adams controversy in July 1870, the president of the Mechanics' State Council (also co-secretary of the Central Pacific Anti-Coolie Association), the president of the San Francisco Crispins, state representatives, Henry George, and various public figures pointed to the fate of the cigar industry in California as a justification for strong anti-Chinese measures in the shoemaking trade and all other trades.[4]

The employment of the Chinese in the cigar industry, it will be recalled, preceded the discharge of Chinese laborers from the Central Pacific Railroad. After a short period of labor antagonism, agitation against the Chinese had stopped. Labor was then scarce, and labor conditions were still satisfactory. Upon learning the business of cigar making, many Chinese set up businesses for themselves, and they dominated the trade by 1870. Notwithstanding the fact that the Chinese did not displace American laborers who abandoned the trade to join more profitable trades, the leaders of the anti-Chinese demonstrations warned that this would be the fate of all the trades on the Pacific slope unless Chinese competition was suppressed. They resolved that if Congress refused to protect California from the "hordes of Chinese barbarian slaves," then Californians would either form a local military and civic organization for the protection of whites or enact exclusion laws. The racial undercurrent of this resolution was reinforced by expressions of cultural antagonism. The Chinese race was described as a "pestilence." Living like "hogs in a pen" and breeding filthy diseases, the Chinese were stained with all the abomination known to ancient and modern barbarism. The scope of the agitators' racial indictment extended to all Mongolians coming to America, except for commercial purposes. Subsequently, some ten thousand people gathered for a meeting, which resulted in the organization of the Anti-Chinese Convention of the State of California, whose object was to oppose Chinese immigration.

Political agitation was, however, compromised by Reconstruction policy, which had produced benefits to the Chinese in the form of the Fourteenth Amendment, the Burlingame Treaty, and section 16 of the Enforcement Act of 1870.[5] These measures began to grate on the customs and laws of California in the early 1870s. Between 1870 and 1873, the foreign miners' license law, the commutation tax of 1852, and the ban on Chinese testimony were all declared unconstitutional by the California Supreme Court.[6] In the face of cumulative obstacles to their efforts to discriminate against the Chinese, the Democratic-led state legislature and city authorities enacted a series of city ordinances and state statutes designed to discourage Chinese immigration. On March 18, 1870, before the local anti-Chinese labor campaign began in earnest, the California legislature passed two exclusion laws, ostensibly within the state's police powers: *An Act to Prevent the Importation of Chinese Criminals, and to Prevent the Establishment of Chinese Slavery* and *An Act to Prevent the Kidnaping and Importation of Mongolian, Chinese and Japanese Females, for Criminal and Demoralizing Purposes.* These acts left no doubt that their real intent was to make it increasingly difficult for even lawful Asian immigrants to be admitted to California. They provided that it was unlawful to bring into California "any Chinese or Mongolian . . . without first presenting to the Commissioner of Immigration, evidence satisfactory to him, that such [person] desires voluntarily to come into this state, and is a person of correct habits and good character, and thereupon obtaining from such Commissioner of Immigration, a license or permit, particularly describing such Chinaman or Mongolian, and authorizing [his or her] importation or immigration."[7] The acts were more spiteful than any of the "coolie bills" submitted to Congress. What was significant about them was the association of illegal entry and criminal activities with not only the Chinese but all Asians, with not only Asian males as criminals, malefactors, and slaves but also Asian women as prostitutes.

Like many other immigrant groups, the Chinese immigrated largely un-accompanied by women. The number of Chinese women entering the United Sates from 1854 to 1870 was only 5,544.[8] Although no consensus has been reached on the number of prostitutes among them, George Peffer estimates that half of the Chinese females living in San Francisco in 1870 were proba-bly not engaged in prostitution.[9] California was a predominantly bachelor society during the gold rush. Women from different parts of the world came there to meet the predictably large demand for prostitutes. Unlike the ma-jority of white prostitutes who came as independent professionals or worked in brothels for wages, Chinese women were generally imported as captives of an organized trade. Once in California, they were often subjected to ex-treme exploitation and abuse.[10] Like Chinese males, Chinese prostitutes were soon singled out for censure. Chinese prostitution was perceived as particu-larly hazardous because it supposedly infused "foul, contagious and poison-ous diseases in Anglo-Saxon blood." As early as 1866, the California legisla-ture had enacted a statute declaring Chinese houses of prostitution to be public nuisances.[11] The statute did not lead to an aggressive campaign for the abatement of Chinese prostitution, but it served to frame the Chinese woman question. While Chinese men were branded as "inveterate coolies," Chinese women would be stigmatized as "degenerate prostitutes." Anti-Chinese pro-pagandists shored up their assessment of Chinese moral depravity with a new and rigid stereotype—that of the Chinese prostitute. While all Chinese men were coolies, all their women must be prostitutes. By passing the 1870 stat-utes, the California legislature sanctioned this typology and showed its de-termination to abate the two aspects of the Chinese question. Both acts im-posed heavy penalties or an imprisonment term of two to twelve months. Although these acts were never enforced,[12] they reflected the legislators' deep racial animosity and a defiant behavior, akin to that of southerners in their dealing with African Americans.

Paralleling this state legislation, San Francisco passed ordinances targeting its Chinese residents. By the late 1860s, local health officials attributed most of the epidemic outbreaks in the city to living conditions among the Chinese.[13] In July 1870, the San Francisco Board of Supervisors passed the "lodging-house" or "cubic air ordinance," making it a misdemeanor for a landlord to lodge any person in a room where there was less than five hundred cubic feet of air for each person. The penalty was a fine (ten to five hundred dollars) or imprisonment for five days to three months. While the ordinance was not enforced with any degree of consistency or regularity, sporadic raids, especially at the height of anti-Chinese agitation, were made on the Chinese quarters. That same year, two other ordinances banned the employment of the Chinese in public works and prohibited any person from walking on the sidewalks while carrying baskets suspended from a pole resting across the shoulders. That ordinance was unquestionably aimed at the Chinese, who were accustomed to delivering vegetables, laundry, and merchandise in this manner.

In the midst of this persecution, Henry C. Bennett, the enumerator and compiler of the city of San Francisco, delivered a lecture before the San Francisco Mechanics' Institute in behalf of the Chinese. Despite frequent attempts to interrupt him and even wrest the podium from his control, Bennett managed to shed light on the "unpopular side" of the Chinese question. Far from being heathens incapable of assimilation, he stated, the Chinese were rapidly adopting American language and customs. He further noted that the charge of Chinese inferiority had one significant precedent—the cry of Negro inferiority. In the last decade, Bennett argued, the nation had grown more liberal, and African Americans were now equals with whites. So would it be with the Chinese, he predicted. When they were treated equitably, they would prove equal to that other "exotic race" and would increase the national prosperity. An important complaint against the Chinese, Bennett added, was that they worked for less wages than white laborers and thus deprived whites of employment and threatened social tranquility. The Chinese, he corrected, were chiefly employed at work that whites would not do for the wages manufacturers could afford to pay. For Bennett, however, racial prejudice was the greatest factor in singling out the Chinese among all other immigrants. Together with Democratic news organs, he contended, labor leaders were successful in persecuting the Chinese and those who employed them because they appealed to the racial prejudices of the working classes. He remarked that the Chinese became objectionable to politicians only after they were drawn into the state and national political forums as a substitute for the African American.[14]

The pro-Chinese thrust of Bennett's lecture was obviously buttressed by his anti-labor and anti-Democratic positions. It was also qualified by the fact that it reinforced the notion of the Chinese as a cheap laborer. To Bennett, it was not desirable that white laborers compete with the Chinese. In the natural order of things, the raw materials should be prepared by the "lowest races of men," but it required the higher intelligence of whites to increase their value by skill, enterprise, trade, and commerce. He was thus confident that the patient and plodding Chinese could contribute to the region's economy and progress. Bennett went further, predicting the use of the Chinese to achieve the manifest destiny of America. Once Americanized, the Chinese, who were more adapted than whites to the climate of Mexico and other similar regions, could be drafted into America's new possessions.[15]

As 1870 drew to a close, however, another blow was given to the Chinese in the form of a poem, "Plain Language from Truthful James," by Bret Harte.[16] The poem tells the story of three men, two Americans and a Chinese, playing cards and trying to cheat one another. In the beginning of the poem, Truthful James and Bill Nye get Ah Sin into a "small game of Euchre," which they were sure he did not understand. Bill Nye's sleeve was "full of aces and bowers," with the intent to deceive. Ah Sin, however, beat the two Americans at their own game and in the same way. Upon finding out that he, too, had cheated, Nye rose and said, "'Can this be? / We are ruined by Chinese cheap labor' / And he went for that heathen Chinee." Truthful James's conclusion was, "That for ways that are dark / And for tricks that are vain / The heathen Chinee is peculiar." Popular literature has always been a valuable gauge of opinion. The reaction to the poem was immediate. Popularly known as "The Heathen Chinee," the poem was hawked on the streets of San Francisco. It went into several editions in the United States, in Canada, and in England. Neither the irony nor the inference about American duplicity and hypocrisy caught the attention of most Americans.[17]

In a vitriolic speech entitled "The Heathen Chinese," delivered in the House in January 1871, Representative William Mungen (Democrat from Ohio) used lines from Harte's poem as an epigraph. Besides a tirade on the medical hazards posed by the Chinese, Mungen's disquisition is interesting in that it drew many parallels between the Chinese and African Americans. The importation of Chinese labor, Mungen expounded, had served to establish a virtual slaveholding oligarchy in the West. Furthermore, he argued, the Chinese were worse than African slaves because they assumed their position voluntarily. Mungen believed that the Chinese had become a political menace because of the Reconstruction amendments. All of them, he claimed, could now become voters and hold office. With a little incentive from their capitalist employers, the Chinese would soon realize that the vote could bring them advantages. The Chinese would then decide they would rather "sit a Senator in the United States Senate beside the honorable [Senator] REVELS" than return to the Celestial Empire, "to be bambooed by order of an official of sufficient rank." The choice of Senator Hiram R. Revels of Mississippi was, of course, not random. Revels was the first African American to serve in the U.S. Senate. Mungen concluded that a race war would ensue from Chinese citizenship and suffrage. The only way to avert it was to prohibit any further immigration of Chinese, except as travelers or merchants and under certain restrictions, notably that they be located in designated areas.[18]

THE CHINESE QUESTION.—[See Page 147.]

COLUMBIA.—"HANDS OFF, GENTLEMEN! AMERICA MEANS FAIR PLAY FOR ALL MEN."

"Columbia—'Hands off, Gentlemen! America means fair play for all men,'" the caption read. The anti-Chinese rioters in the illustration have just burned down a colored orphan asylum (a reference to the 1863 race riots in New York) in the background and are now on their way to assault a Chinese man. Their complaints as listed in the illustration give prominence to race as the main factor of antagonism. (Source: *Harper's Weekly*, February 18, 1871, 149. Courtesy of the Library of Congress)

Meanwhile, during the gubernatorial campaign of 1871, the Republican and Democratic parties adopted anti-Chinese planks in their platforms. Both parties had been contacted by a vigorously anti-Chinese association, the Industrial Reformers, which by 1871 numbered some ten thousand members. Meeting in June 1871, the Democratic party condemned Congress for preventing local authorities from handling their Chinese problem and for helping abrogate the foreign miners' license. In the two planks addressing the Chinese question, *importation of Chinese coolies* and *immigration of Chinese laborers* were used interchangeably. The Democrats opposed Chinese immigration on the ground that the labor of white people should not be brought into competition with the labor of a class of inferior people. Interestingly, the anti-Chinese plank included neither the earlier conflation of black and Chinese inferiority nor the double objection to black and Chinese suffrage. By separating the black and Chinese issues, the Democratic party in the West redefined the racial question in the region as the Chinese question.

The thrust of the 1871 Republican platform demonstrates that anti-Chinese sentiment among California Republicans had increased since the last convention in 1869. The employment of the Chinese, a plank declared, was offensive to the exalted idea of the dignity of labor and detrimental to the prosperity of the American laboring classes. The presence of a large number of Chinese laborers who were "incapable of assimilation with our own race" was a serious injury to the interests of the state. California Republicans were adamantly opposed to granting the Chinese citizenship. They also called on the federal government to adopt treaty regulations and legislation that would discourage the further immigration of the Chinese.[19]

Adopting a strong anti-monopolist position, especially anti-railroad, and a thorough anti-Chinese program, the Republicans were able to carry the elections. They elected the governor, his administration, and three congressmen, and they regained control of the lower house.[20] In the fall of 1871, however, a large-scale attack on the Chinese in Los Angeles led to the toning down of the anti-Chinese rhetoric. Los Angeles was then a frontier town of about 5,750 inhabitants, of which 3 percent were Chinese. The Chinese were concentrated in a few occupations, especially domestic service and laundry businesses, and did not compete for jobs with American laborers. Their quarters were in a deprived area, known as Nigger Alley (from its Mexican name, Calle de los Negros). Long before the arrival of the Chinese, the area had been a center of gambling, drinking, and prostitution. Until 1871, there was no wholesale public resentment against the Chinese. But on October 24, 1871, two officers were injured, and an American civilian was killed during a feud between two Chinese companies. Within a short time, a mob of five hundred

"Angels" stormed through the Chinese quarter, firing into houses; shooting, hanging, or burning to death the Chinese they caught alive; and appropriating over thirty thousand dollars in money and personal property. Nineteen Chinese were killed.[21] The best elements of the community condemned the massacre and decided to put an end to the deep-seated tradition of lawlessness in the city. In the state at large, the massacre exerted a sobering influence. Editors and Republican governor Newton Booth condemned the massacre in strong terms.[22] Earlier, Governor Booth had indicated that he harbored serious apprehensions about the Chinese. However, he believed that any local restriction on their immigration would be interfering with federal power and violating treaty and commercial agreements. In 1871, he was appalled by the Los Angeles riot. Mob violence, he stated, was a dangerous expression of lawlessness. The display of American brutality did a disservice to California's efforts to deal with the Chinese question. Such violence, he stressed, suggested that a coarse prejudice was the force behind these efforts. The Chinese, he insisted, would be given full protection of the law during their residence in California. In the meantime, the state government would strive to convince Congress of the need for restriction.[23]

In 1873, Chinese arrivals in the United States increased dramatically, amounting to a little more than 17,000.[24] Meanwhile, labor conditions remained poor. The situation was ripe for a resumption of anti-Chinese organizational efforts. In May, the Workingmen's Alliance of Sacramento, the Anti-Chinese League of San Francisco, and the Industrial Reformers joined to form the People's Protection Alliance, an anti-Chinese organization aiming to embrace the whole Pacific Coast in its activities. Condemning violence, the alliance resolved that petitioning Congress was the only way to obtain relief. In a later meeting, though, the California members of the alliance applauded the suggestion of the Oregon branch to add to the petition that riot and bloodshed would follow all along the Pacific coast if Congress turned a deaf ear to their demands.

These organizational endeavors of workers encouraged political parties and state and municipal authorities to fully enlist in the efforts to secure an exclusion or restriction law. Beginning in the fall of 1872, a strong anti-railroad party had grown up under the leadership of Governor Booth, who charged that the state Republican party was under the railroad influence and party managers who frequently misused power. Booth Republicans met in June 1873 and set up a new party, the Independent Taxpayers' party. The Independent and Democratic parties held conventions in 1873. The platforms of both parties contained an anti-Chinese plank. Regarding the presence of the Chinese as an unmitigated evil, the Democrats demanded that the incoming legislature, through enactments of its own and appeals to Congress, take steps to prevent the further influx of the "mongolian horde" in California and to secure the "speedy exodus of those already here." The Independent party concurred, urging that the whole legal and moral force of the state be used to oppose Chinese immigration because the Chinese were a "menace to the moral, physical, and pecuniary welfare of the people of this state."[25]

Meanwhile, in early June 1873, two orders—known as the Pagan Orders because they targeted the Chinese—were passed by the San Francisco Board of Supervisors. The laundry ordinance stipulated that laundries using a one-horse vehicle for delivery purposes pay a license fee of two dollars per quarter and those using a two-horse vehicle four dollars, while the laundries using no vehicle at all—that is, mainly laundries kept by the Chinese who used baskets—were required to pay a tax of fifteen dollars per quarter. In the spring of 1873, the San Francisco police had resumed its enforcement of the cubic air ordinance with renewed vigor. On May 23 and 25, seventy-five Chinese were arrested for violating the law. In July and August, 247 more arrests were made. Of the latter, 70 were discharged, 177 were convicted, and the amount of cash realized was $2,060.[26] Rather than pay the fines, many Chinese opted for prison sentences. Not satisfied with this act of resistance to taxation and aware that the enforcement of the ordinance would be limited to the capacity of the jails, the board of supervisors adopted the second of the Pagan Orders—known as the Bob-Tail or Queue-Cutting Order. This ordinance required the sheriff to cut to the length of one inch the hair of all persons committed to his care. The ordinance was particularly malicious because it was common knowledge that, for the Chinese, the preservation of one's hair was essential to one's standing.

Both ordinances were vetoed by Mayor William Alvord. The laundry ordinance, he charged, was unjust and would cause great hardship to those who delivered their own work. The "queue ordinance," he objected, was manifestly intended to inflict upon the Chinese a degrading punishment. In his veto message, he pointed out that the passage of the ordinance would be a clear violation of the Burlingame Treaty of 1868. Furthermore, the ordinance was contrary to the provisions of the Civil Rights Act of 1870 (sections 16 and 17 of the Enforcement Act). In substance and effect, he noted, the queue ordinance would be a special punishment inflicted on Chinese residents solely because of their race. Moreover, the order raised the larger issue of the interference with national policy on immigration. So long as Congress and the executive departments pledged to protect Asian citizens in the United States, he concluded, no state, much less a municipality, could legally and justifiably interfere with national policy.[27]

Although Alvord's veto of the queue ordinance was sustained, his veto of the ordinance on laundry businesses was overridden.[28] Significantly, the vetoes won strong approval from the leading state newspapers and the eastern press. While some western papers congratulated Mayor Alvord on his demonstration of the illegality of the proposed orders, others thanked him for rebuking the bigoted board of supervisors and relieving the West from the ignominy of a breach of treaty obligations and the violation of the principles of common justice and humanity.[29] For several eastern papers, the attempted municipal legislation had taken the form of downright persecution. Even people opposed to Chinese immigration, they remarked, approved of Mayor Alvord's action.[30] The pro-Chinese thrust of these reactions was often tempered by an admission that the Chinese posed a singular problem to America. If Californians wanted to find a remedy to cure the Chinese evil, however, this was not the way. The principles of Republicanism and the spirit of the treaties, the *New York Tribune* argued, had to be considered first. Moreover, it was "too late to attempt to stay any tide of immigration by special legislation discriminating against race or color."[31]

After Mayor Alvord's veto, the cubic air order was not enforced for the next three years, partly because of the Chinese willingness to accept jail sentences and partly because of an adverse decision made in a local court.[32] Agitation against the Chinese, however, went unabated among workers. In June 1873, M. B. Starr was appointed grand lecturer by the People's Protective Alliance, and money was raised to defray his expenses while lecturing throughout California and Oregon.[33] In a book published that same year, Starr gathered his thoughts about what he described as the coming struggle against the coolie invasion. This struggle, "in the name of God, our country, our wives and our children," he prophesied, threatened to wash America into another combat, more bloody and costly than the Civil War. For it to be averted, it was essential to nip the coolie trade in the bud and to prohibit the immigration of all the servile races of Asia.[34]

On the whole, what was impressive about Starr's slanted history was his articulation of the correlation between African slavery and Chinese coolieism. Notwithstanding the use of the specious name of "coolie" and the ostensible loosening of the right of property in coolies, he contended, the *imported* Chinese were "*virtually slaves* to their superiors." Coolieism would ultimately produce a caste society. In the same way that slavery had divided masters from the "poor white trash," coolieism would alienate "citizen labor." When all the avenues to decent employment were closed by the employment of Chinese coolies, the number of Christian homes would dwindle until the nation was overrun "with Chinese jungles, and 'Melicum harems.'" The only way of preserving America's institutions and civilization was to weed out the "Asiatic excrescences" at once. The earlier attempt to mix American free institutions with African slavery should have taught Americans that it was crucial to crush servile labor before it could draw nourishment from Congress. Ignoring the harsh lessons of the past, he argued, the American government had repeated the same error by ratifying a "coolie treaty" (the Burlingame Treaty). Furthermore, it was also wrong to assume that because the African was Americanized, the Asiatic would also acculturate. The imported Africans, he explained, had not been permitted to perform their former "stupid worship." Before long, they had forgotten the material religion of their ancestors and had embraced Christianity. For the protection of the public good, he added, Negroes had not been allowed to roam over the country at large and prowl about the neighborhood at night. They had been fettered by positive restrictions, which had gradually brought their minds up to the highest standard that their degraded condition as slaves would admit. In contrast, the debased Chinese were let loose as free agents of destruction. Besides this, he stated, the stock of the current "African chattel" was substantially improved because American Negroes often had the best southern blood in their veins and because no fresh addition from Africa had been made after 1807. With the present coolie system, however, America was cursed with unmitigated heathenism ad infinitum.[35]

This racial indictment found echo in a lecture delivered by a Jesuit priest of Native American origin, Father James Chrysostom Bouchard—"Chinaman or White Man—Which?"[36] In brief, this thoroughly assimilated priest argued that the Chinese belonged to an inferior, immoral, and pagan race, incapable of rising to the virtues of Christian civilization. Their presence in California was depriving white men of employment and reducing their wives to beggars, their sons to hoodlums, and their daughters to prostitutes. His lecture concluded with a juxtaposition of the inestimable blessings to be derived from European immigration and the impending ruin attendant upon the immigration of coolies.

Father Bouchard's lecture was met by a strong rebuke from the Reverend Otis Gibson, a missionary in China from 1855 to 1865, a minister to the Chinese in San Francisco since 1868, and the superintendent of the Methodist Episcopal Mission House in San Francisco from 1868 to 1885.[37] Gibson was repelled by Bouchard's coarse racism and demagoguery, which he ascribed to his devotion to "Popery." He repudiated the charges of cheap labor, servility, and inferiority against the Chinese. He conceded that the Chinese had helped reduce the price of labor; however, this was a benefit because the early rates had been excessive. Their regulation was essential to the development of California manufacturing enterprises. Instead of lessening the demand for white laborers, he added, the Chinese had actually stimulated the demand for more. Furthermore, by performing unskilled labor, the Chinese were lifting the white race to higher planes of industry. As to the charge of servility, he remarked that the Chinese abhorred the American system of African slavery. Chinese men, he averred, came voluntarily. Many of them received financial aid to emigrate, but immigration societies all over the country were importing Europeans on the same terms. With regard to the alleged inferiority of the Chinese race, Gibson hinted at the lost grandeur of Chinese civilization. After a long tirade against Bouchard's call for "European papists" to supplant Chinese immigrants, Gibson betrayed the limits of his pro-Chinese position. His lecture began by proclaiming that all avenues of industry should be open to all, without distinction of race or color. His eulogy of Chinese labor, however, contained the significant qualification that the Chinese were particularly suited for "mudsill labor." Moreover, while Gibson insisted that the Chinese should not be feared, he was still of the opinion that their immigration would entail "many evils" and that "the vices and ignorance" that they brought to America "should be dealt with vigorously."[38]

Gibson's denunciation of the "dangerous fallacies of the Priest of the Church of Rome" was to no good effect. Governor Booth, in his message to the California legislature in December 1873, expressed his apprehensions about the increased volume of Chinese immigration in the past year. The Chinese, he stated, constituted "a marked class, a distinctive element of society." He therefore declared his hope that the federal government would amend the Burlingame Treaty to permit his state to restrict their further immigration. In the meantime, he would strive to protect Chinese residents in the state from violence and persecution.[39] The governor's message was followed by renewed efforts on the part of the state legislature to pressure the federal government. In 1874, the Democrat-led senate passed two resolutions against Chinese immigration, and the Republican-led assembly concurred. Following these resolutions, the legislature passed an immigration act. Broader in scope than the acts of 1870 regarding Asian prostitutes and coolies, this act required the commissioner of immigration at any port of California to satisfy himself that none of the passengers on incoming ships was "lunatic, idiotic, deaf, dumb, blind, crippled, or infirm . . . or a lewd or debauched woman." Any person belonging to the specified classes would be excluded unless the master, owner, or consignee of the vessel that brought the person posted a five hundred dollar bond.[40]

On its face, the statute did not seem to have been designed to discriminate against the Chinese. Events following the landing of a Pacific Mail Steamship Company's liner *Japan* in August 1874 demonstrated otherwise. Boarding the ship, the commissioner interviewed about sixty Chinese women and decided that twenty-two of them had been brought to San Francisco for "immoral purposes" and were thus ineligible to land in California. The steamship company and the Chinese women refused to post the required bonds, and the women were ordered to be detained on board. The women then applied for a writ of habeas corpus to the state district court in San Francisco, alleging that their detention was in contravention of the Burlingame Treaty and in conflict with the U.S. Constitution and denying that they were either "lewd or debauched women." The court upheld the commissioner and remanded the women to the ship. The women then applied to the chief justice of the state for another writ of habeas corpus. The state supreme court sustained the ruling of the district court, holding that the statute under which the women were detained was valid and binding under the bilateral treaty and the Constitution and that the evidence justified the commissioner's finding on the character of the women.[41]

One woman, Ah Fong, sought a third writ of habeas corpus from the U.S. circuit court. Notwithstanding the adjudications of the state tribunals, Stephen J. Field (the presiding justice on circuit from the Supreme Court) declared that the petitioner was entitled to a hearing by a federal tribunal because she was a subject of a country having treaty relations with the U.S. government. In finding for the petitioner, Justice Field made it clear that the statute under which Ah Fong was restrained was an anti-Chinese statute, despite its general terms. It was true, he opined, that the right of a state to exclude any person deemed dangerous or injurious to the interests and welfare of its citizens had been asserted in previous decisions of the Supreme Court. Much of what was said about the power of a state in this respect, he observed, had grown out of the necessity felt by the southern states to exclude all free blacks from their limits. Currently, however, the power of a state to exclude a foreigner from its territory was limited to the right of self-defense. The legality of an exclusion measure against convicts, lepers, persons afflicted with incurable diseases, paupers, idiots, and lunatics could not be doubted. However, the California statute confounded persons widely variant in character and even went so far as to exclude persons who did not pose a threat to the state. What was more, the statute discriminated between different classes of foreigners. The intercourse of *all* foreigners with American institutions, he objected, was exclusively within the jurisdiction of the federal government. If the state apprehended that the ingress of foreigners might be injurious to its peace and that these foreigners might disregard the laws of the state, the remedy, he maintained, lay in the more vigorous enforcement of the local laws, not in the exclusion of these foreigners. Furthermore, if the possible violation of the laws by an immigrant and the supposed immorality of his or her past life or profession were used to determine a foreigner's right of immigration, then a door would be opened to all sorts of oppression against "other parties, besides low and despised Chinese women."[42]

Throughout his decision, Justice Field was mindful of the racial antagonism toward the Chinese. Californians, he stated, felt that the dissimilarities in the Chinese physical characteristics, religion, and habits would forever prevent them from assimilating. This opinion, however, could not justify any state or municipal legislation providing for their exclusion, especially if this legislation did not apply to the inhabitants of the most favored nations of the Caucasian race as well. While Justice Field recognized the need to adopt stringent measures to suppress prostitution, he had little respect "for that discriminating virtue which is shocked when a frail child of China is landed on our shores, and yet allows the bedizened and painted harlot of other countries to parade our streets and open her hells in broad day, without molestation and without censure." If Chinese immigration was to be restricted, he admonished, it would and should be by the federal government, where the whole power over immigration lay. At present, though, Justice Field declared that the detention of the petitioner was unlawful under the Burlingame Treaty, the Fourteenth Amendment, and section 16 of the Enforcement Act of 1870. Justice Field ordered that Ah Fong and the other women be released.[43]

This decision was important in that Justice Field verified that racial prejudice rather than a concern about the immorality of a class of foreigners was the force behind the setting apart of Chinese females and, more generally, Chinese immigrants from all other aliens. The range of discriminatory measures against Chinese residents in California revealed the racial aspect of American enmity and the definition of the race problem in California as the Chinese question. While African Americans had gained the right to participate fully in the political and judicial processes, the Chinese remained excluded from these rights (except for the right to testify) for want of eligibility for citizenship. In the domain of education, too, African Americans, unlike Chinese immigrants, had come a long way. Both groups had initially suffered the same treatment, that is, exclusion and segregation. In 1866, a new act had been passed, requiring that a separate school be provided where there were at least ten children of African, Mongolian, or Indian descent. It also stated that wherever education for these groups could not be provided for in that way, they might be permitted to attend the white children's schools. In 1870, the legislature amended the law by eliminating "Mongolian" children altogether from its benefits. In 1872, school districts were required to admit African and Indian children to the white schools if separate schools were not provided. Three years later, segregated education for African Americans was abolished. Chinese children remained excluded from the public schools, even though their parents paid their pro rata of the school tax, both state and municipal.[44] Finally, while the Chinese experienced greater economic opportunities than African Americans, the racism leveled at them showed no sign of abating.

10. Intensification of the Anti-Chinese Movement, 1874–80

"At Length!" exclaims a Senator in Sacramento . . . "Our Master in the White House [President Grant] has spared one moment from the contemplation of his Black agony on the Gulf to a consideration of our Yellow Agony on the Slope!"
—William H. Dixon, *White Conquest* (1876)

While Justice Stephen J. Field's decision in *In re Ah Fong* displeased anti-Chinese elements in California, it confirmed that relief could be afforded only by the federal government. Ignoring Field's scathing remarks about the racial intolerance embedded in the statute of 1874, however, Sinophobic Californians decided to use *Ah Fong* to vindicate their case at the national level. The last months of 1874 seemed to be an opportune moment to resume legislative efforts at the national level.

In 1873, the collapse of Jay Cooke and Company, a pillar of America's banking establishment, had ushered the first great economic crisis of industrial capitalism. As Eric Foner ably showed, the crisis had profound political and ideological consequences. The depression undermined assumptions at the core of the free labor ideology, exacerbated class conflict, and reshaped the nation's political agenda and balance of power between the parties. As the depression deepened, the tension between labor and capital loomed large as the main economic and political problem of the day. A new ideological consensus emerged, uniting northern conservatives with southern redeemers and a new generation of liberals or progressives, on the necessity of asserting the authority of capital over the laboring classes. While the depression shattered the mold of the two-party system in a number of western states, it was a major cause for the defeat of the Republicans in the elections of 1874. By abandoning the tenets of equal rights and the dignity of labor and adopting a conservative agenda for the defense of property and the economic status quo, the Republicans contributed to the electoral tidal wave that swept over the North.[1]

The Republican ideological shift affected prevailing attitudes toward Reconstruction and race. Following the publication of James S. Pike's classic indictment of radical Reconstruction, *The Prostrate State* (1874), a description of South Carolina as a state engulfed in political corruption and led by "a mass of black barbarism," even some erstwhile supporters of Reconstruction helped reinforce the idea that the cause of "corrupt misrule" in the South lay in "negro government."[2] Meanwhile, a growing spirit of sectional reconciliation in Congress had eroded the notion of equality of rights for African Americans as the essence of the Republican party's self-image. The retreat from Reconstruction policies was obvious in not only the Republicans' lack of support for Sumner's bills (see chapter 8) but also the lavishing of "respectable" southern Democrats with federal patronage, the curtailment by the Justice Department of prosecutions under the Enforcement Acts of the early 1870s, and the hasty pardons granted to many Klansmen. "Ironically," Foner commented, "even as racism waned as an explicit component of the Northern Democratic appeal, it gained a hold on respectable Republican opinion, offering a convenient explanation for Reconstruction's 'failure.'"[3]

This shifting tide of opinion affected attitudes toward not only African Americans but also Chinese immigrants. No other paper did more to combine anti-Chinese and anti-black sentiments than the *New York World*. In October 1874, in a spate of articles, the *World* conveyed the alarming prospect of a series of racial confrontations in America. In one issue, five of the six columns on the front page were devoted to "The BLACK LEAGUE/The Secret Society Doings of the Negroes in the South/Semi Barbarians Led into Horrible Excesses by the Very SCUM of Northern Carpetbaggism." The last column predicted an imminent and full-blown racial peril. Threatening American cities was the wave of "the scum of Asia," fed by Chinese coolies and prostitutes. White America was on the verge of total ruin because of the infiltration of black and yellow barbarians. It was the editor's opinion that the question of Chinese citizenship should be apprehended in broad terms. The question of whether Chinamen should vote, he explained three days later, amounted to asking whether Asia and Ethiopia should stretch out their hands and gain political rights in America. If the Chinese were granted such rights, he warned, then the other "darker races" would seek the same privileges.[4]

On December 7, 1874, President Ulysses S. Grant provided significant impetus to the anti-Chinese movement. In his sixth annual message to Congress, Grant called congressmen's attention to "the general conceded fact" that "the great proportion of the Chinese immigrants who come to our shores do not come voluntarily, to make their homes with us and their labor productive of general prosperity, but come under contracts with headmen, who own them almost absolutely. In a worse form does this apply to Chinese women. Hardly a perceptible percentage of them perform any honorable labor, but they are brought for shameful purposes, to the disgrace of the communities where settled and to the great demoralization of the youth of those localities." Grant vowed to enforce any regulation that Congress would pass to legislate against these evils.[5]

This devastating message marked a critical turning point in the executive attitude toward the Chinese question. Except for the special case of Andrew Johnson, the executive office had always insisted that the Chinese coming to America were voluntary immigrants. In all but his first annual message, President Grant himself had not seemed to harbor any apprehension about the "conceded facts" of Chinese coolieism and prostitution in the United States. In his first message in 1869, he had expressed his satisfaction with the prospect of increased relations with China as a result of Anson Burlingame's sagacity. Grant had then recommended the enactment of legislation that would forever preclude the enslavement of the Chinese on American soil and the involvement of American vessels in the transportation of coolies to any other country.[6] There was nothing in the message, however, that indicated that Grant believed that there were coolies in the United States. This was made clear in his communication to the Senate in the midst of the North Adams controversy, in which he affirmed that all the Chinese in the United States were voluntary immigrants.[7] In his next annual messages, the president pointed to the friendly relations between the United States and China and encouraged Congress to retain the good opinion of the Chinese in order to secure a share of the Chinese commerce. In December of 1873, President Grant added that some slight advance had been made toward suppressing "the infamous Chinese cooly trade" during the past year. He also advised Congress to inquire whether additional legislation was needed. Still, President Grant did not seem to have in mind Chinese immigrants. Neither these earlier messages nor Grant's papers give any indication as to what convinced him of the existence of Chinese coolies and prostitutes in the United States in 1874. Grant did not express any disquietude over the subject in his papers, and his later messages do not afford any clarification. In December 1875, after strongly indicting the Mormon practice of polygyny, he expressed uneasiness about the similarly flagrant crime of Chinese prostitution. In his last annual message, in December 1876, no mention whatsoever was made about either the evils or benefits of Chinese immigration.[8]

Unlike the *New York World*, whose invectives against the Chinese confirmed the notorious bigotry of the paper, Grant's 1874 message cannot be brushed off as a vulgar manifestation of prejudice or demagoguery or as pure propaganda. President Grant was neither a Californian nor a candidate for office when he made his anti-Chinese appeal. The Grant administration had, however, some interesting peculiarities that might shed some light on Grant's concern. Grant's two vice-presidents, Schuyler Colfax (1869–1873) and Henry Wilson (1873–1877), had both been prominent members of the anti-immigrant American (Know Nothing) party in the 1850s. President Grant himself had been a Know Nothing, even though he later insisted that he had joined solely out of curiosity and that he came to loathe the intolerant spirit of the Know Nothings. Notwithstanding this retraction, Grant's private letters indicate that he was uncomfortable with the increasing number of immigrants holding governmental offices.[9] By 1873, Wilson had long established himself as an advocate of Chinese restriction and ineligibility for citizenship. Colfax, a native of New York, began his political career as a Whig and ended it as a prominent Republican. Like Wilson and many others, Colfax made the transition into the Republican party after an active career in the American party. Another critical cabinet member was the attorney general from 1871 to 1875: none other than George H. Williams, former senator from Oregon and a vehement Sinophobe. Williams was one of the president's strongest supporters. As senator and attorney general, he was often called by the president for advice.[10] Although Grant did not say much in public about Chinese immigrants during his presidency, these three cabinet members' records suggest a far from liberal attitude.

It would be wrong, however, to ascribe Grant's 1874 message only to the manipulative power of these cabinet members. Grant did feel uneasy about Chinese immigration, even if he did not write about it. As a young army officer in the 1850s, Grant had served in California and witnessed the increasing antagonism toward Chinese immigrants. His early presidency coincided with the nationalization of the Chinese question following the introduction of Chinese labor in the East and the congressional debates on the status of Chinese immigrants. Following his presidency, Grant embarked on a world tour that took him to China, where he met with Li Huang-chang, the most important Chinese policymaker from the 1870s to the 1890s. In June 1879, Grant told him that the problem of Chinese immigration in the United States derived from the fact that the Chinese did "not come of their own free will." Grant urged that China not only stop "the slavery feature" of that emigration but also restrict voluntary emigration so that the Chinese would not "glut the market." His proposed solution, a three-to-five year suspension of emigration to the United States, also conveyed his racial reasoning. China, he recommended, could redirect its excess population to "wilderness areas," such as Borneo, New Guinea, or the Congo, where it could expect the support of the United States as it attempted to found "new Shangais and Cantons" in those regions.[11]

Grant's 1874 message might well have originated in his latent nativism, as well as that of his nativist or openly Sinophobic advisers.

Within the context of the depression, Grant's indictment of coolieism might also have been a smoke screen inspired by the political and economic crises affecting the country. No one could argue that the depressed condition of American laborers in the East was the result of competition with "cheap Chinese labor." It would have been difficult to divert the attention of the eastern laboring classes from the structural problems of inequality by pointing an accusing finger at the few Chinese immigrants in the region. This was certainly not Grant's intention. However, his condemnation of the Chinese as cheap and unfree labor revived the traditional notion of the dignity of labor, which had been seriously eroded by the depression. Besides this, the condemnation of "coolie immigration" could be interpreted as an attempt to mitigate the waning image of the Republican party as the party of freedom and equality. Even if the party had retreated from its commitment to racial equality, Grant's message implied that it was still the party of freedom—the party opposing all forms of slavery. Grant's recommendation regarding Chinese women may also be traced to the increasing influence of standards of respectability in society. In his strong denunciation of Chinese prostitution, President Grant may well have sought to convey his concern about this social ill and his commitment to the nineteenth-century temperance movement. What is certain, however, is that Schuyler Colfax was prominently known for his temperance principles and that Williams had long stood for the exclusion of Chinese women. Moreover, Grant's message was given after the *Ah Fong* decision, which had incensed anti-Chinese zealots. Justice Field's setting free of the "Chinese maidens" had caused them to take their case directly to President Grant. The provision about Chinese prostitutes in his message reflected the large scope of the anti-Chinese agenda— opposition to Chinese men (as coolies) and women (as prostitutes).

Whatever Grant's motivations, Congressman Horace F. Page (Republican from California) was prompt to seize the opportunity to renew his anti-Chinese efforts. The day after President Grant's message, he introduced a resolution requesting the Committee on Foreign Affairs to inquire whether any "new legislation was necessary to prevent the importation of Chinese coolies and prostitutes."[12] The committee advised Congress to protect American moral values by establishing a process of interrogation of all Chinese female emigrants attempting to leave China for the United States. Refusing to limit himself to the committee's recommendation, Page submitted a series of bills: previous bills calling for the exclusion of all Chinese immigrants and the alteration of the Burlingame Treaty and two new bills providing for the reg-

ulation of the immigration of Chinese prostitutes and the exclusion of the
Chinese from naturalization.[13] The Committee on Foreign Affairs was receptive to the bill focusing on Chinese prostitutes. However, Page was not satisfied
with a simple prostitution ban. In February 1875, he addressed the House on
the subject of treaty relations with China, and he introduced a more comprehensive bill for the regulation of Chinese prostitution and coolieism. While
Page thought the moral aspect of prostitution was important, he stressed that
the workers of California were also subjected to the degrading effects of coolie labor. To illustrate his point, he read a petition signed by more than sixteen thousand American laborers appealing to Congress to relieve them of the
"dreadful scourge" of the Chinese. The petitioners made clear that their objection to the Chinese was more than economic. While they harbored no "feeling inimical to the less advanced races," they felt compelled to oppose the
immigration of the Chinese, whether they came voluntarily or not. The Chinese, they complained, could never become homogeneous with Americans as
a people, and their vitiating influence would arrest American progress.[14]

Congress passed Page's bill with virtually no opposition.[15] This 1875 act
closely mirrored the provisions of the 1870 California statutes regarding Asian
coolies and prostitutes. The scope of the Page law was similarly broad, including any subject of any "Oriental country." Significantly, the Page law was passed
after a similar statute in California had been declared arbitrary and discriminatory by a U.S. circuit court in *Ah Fong*. Moreover, notwithstanding Page's
claim that his bill was in keeping with the terms of the Burlingame Treaty, at
no time did he refer to the other two major objections made by Justice Field
in his decision in *Ah Fong*—the Fourteenth Amendment and the Enforcement
Act of 1870. The disregard of these previous stumbling blocks in California's
anti-Chinese efforts reflected the retreat from Reconstruction. The highest
court itself was moving away from an expansive definition of federal power
and contributing to a piecemeal emasculation of the postwar amendments.
In the *Slaughter-House Cases* (1873), the Supreme Court's first attempt at in-
terpreting the Thirteenth and Fourteenth amendments, the court affirmed that
the "one pervading purpose" of these amendments was the protection of African Americans.[16] The impact of that decision was felt in the national legislature, where congressmen were debating the civil rights bill. The Page law was
passed two days after the passage of the civil rights bill on March 1, 1875. Deliberately shorn of a provision that would have provided the Chinese with the
means of vindicating their rights as immigrants and potential citizens, the Civil
Rights Act extended the Supreme Court's denial of the applicability of the
postwar amendments to whites in *Slaughter-House* to the Chinese. The absence
of objection to the Page law on the grounds that it might be in conflict with

these amendments demonstrates that the Chinese question was one of the first casualties of the Republican retreat from Reconstruction.

Although the Page law did not have the scope and impact of the Exclusion Act of 1882, it proved to be an effective measure to restrict Chinese women. Until recently, the immigration experience of Chinese women in nineteenth-century America was a neglected dimension of the historiography of the Chinese question. When it was not ignored entirely, it was an appendage of the sojourner theme or was confined to a discussion of Chinese prostitution.[17] Close examination of Chinese prostitution is, of course, important. Perhaps the majority of Chinese women immigrating to the United States in the nineteenth century were prostitutes; however, the substantial body of evidence on Chinese prostitutes cannot account for the scarcity of Chinese wives in nineteenth-century America. Explanations of the shortage of Chinese wives have favored the sojourner mentality of Chinese immigrants, political and economic events in China, and cultural idiosyncrasies. If these factors had constituted the only impediments, however, they would have hindered the emigration of Chinese women whatever their destination. Unlike the United States, Singapore, other parts of Southeast Asia, and Hawaii experienced an increase in the number of Chinese women immigrating there with each passing decade, leading to the strengthening of Chinese communities.[18] Obviously, factors within the host society must have contributed to the anomalous development of a "bachelor Chinese community" in America. Recent works have demonstrated that an inhospitable atmosphere and harsh legislation effectively stopped a budding immigration of Chinese wives. Because of the consular officials' overzealous methods of enforcing the Page law, the law turned out to be a deterrent to the immigration of Chinese women.[19] These consuls eventually reduced the immigration of Chinese women to the United States. From 1876 to 1882, the number of Chinese women entering the United States declined by 68 percent from the previous seven-year period—from 4,142 to 1,338. Meanwhile, from 1876 to 1882, the immigration of Chinese males amounted to 109,242 arrivals—almost 40,000 of them coming in the few months in 1882 prior to the enforcement of the Chinese Exclusion Act.[20] Like preceding legislation, the anti-coolie provision in the Page law did not halt the immigration of Chinese male laborers. Even so, it paved the way for the broader Exclusion Act of 1882. It was clear that no anti-coolie law could stop an immigration that was legitimate. Besides this, the Page law demonstrated that politicians in Washington had taken a critical step in their handling of the Chinese question, from wording civil rights legislation in the negative insofar as the Chinese were concerned to legislating expressly against them.

The Page law was a victory for the anti-Chinese movement on the Pacific Coast, even if it fell short of total exclusion. The law was not enough to reverse the political trend, though. Whereas the California Democrats chose to ignore the Page law in their 1875 platform, the Republicans were keen to refer to Page's congressional record, concluding that it commended the Republican party to the fullest confidence of the state.[21] The election returns in 1875 showed that the people of California thought otherwise. The Democrats regained power at the executive and legislative levels, also winning two seats in the House of Representatives. The Chinese issue does not seem to have influenced the voters. Like the national legislative elections of 1874, the California elections were symptomatic of the strong disaffection of the voters for the leading party rather than their confidence in the Democratic party's ability to alleviate the effects of the depression that were increasingly felt on the West Coast.

In March 1876, the U.S. Supreme Court announced its decision regarding the writ of error brought on behalf of Chy Lung, one of the Chinese women denied admission in 1874. In *Chy Lung v. Freeman,* Justice Samuel Miller confirmed Justice Field's decision in *Ah Fong,* ruling that the California statute under which she and the other women had been deprived of their right to immigrate was unconstitutional. Reviewing the provisions of the 1874 California statute (see chapter 9), he declared that it was an extraordinary statute, skillfully framed to place in the hands of a single man, the state commissioner of immigration, the power to prevent foreign passengers from landing in the United States "unless they submitted to systematic extortion of the grossest kind."[22] Miller's construction of the intent of the statute as extortion fell short of Field's condemnation of it as a blatant exclusion effort. Moreover, Miller did not allude to the Fourteenth Amendment or the Enforcement Act of 1870 to support his opinion. For these reasons, his decision was not met with as much resentment as *In re Ah Fong.* In *Chy Lung,* western Sinophobes simply found confirmation that they should be careful not to infringe on the exclusive right of Congress over commerce.[23]

Meanwhile, agitation against the Chinese in California increased in the beginning of 1876 because of the worsening economic situation. While thousands of American laborers were out of work, Chinese immigration increased significantly, reaching high-water marks in 1875 and 1876—16,473 and 22,781 new arrivals, respectively. Subsequently, mass anti-Chinese meetings were held, and pamphlets and circulars were printed and distributed. Laying out its new constitution and bylaws, the Anti-Chinese Union prided itself on including in its roster of honorary vice-presidents the governor and a host of Republican and Democratic politicians. Besides sanctioning the use of all lawful means to suppress Chinese immigration, the Anti-Chinese Union called on its members to strive for the expulsion of the Chinese, not by force but by a "starvation system," forbidding anyone to employ Chinese labor or purchase goods from any employer of Chinese laborers. Yet violence was often advocated in mass meetings. In April 1876, the state and municipal authorities, as well as the various anti-Chinese associations and clubs, united in the largest anti-Chinese demonstration that had yet taken place. The *Daily Alta California* estimated that twenty-five thousand people attended the meeting. Serving as chairman of the meeting and as keynote speaker, Governor William Irwin, a Democrat, stated that the Chinese question was everything that "goes to make up American civilization."[24] The legislature promptly responded to the rising anti-Chinese sentiment by passing a lodging house law similar to the San Francisco cubic air ordinance of 1870, while the board of supervisors reenacted the queue ordinance. More than five hundred Chinese were arrested for violating the law in the next three months.[25] The legislature also passed laws forbidding the employment of Mongolians in the construction of certain public projects.

Some of these measures had already been declared unconstitutional. Their reenactment was symptomatic of the newly gained confidence of the state legislature and municipal authorities that they could persecute the Chinese with total impunity from the federal government.[26] This confidence was actually vindicated when the two major political parties in the state and the nation at large included anti-Chinese planks in their platforms. The California Democrats simply renewed their commitment to demanding that all the powers of the national government be exerted to exclude the Chinese.[27] In the 1876 presidential campaign, the Democrats focused their attention on two major issues: the political corruption of the Grant administration and the depression. In their national convention in St. Louis, the Democratic delegates denounced the Republicans' manipulation of false issues by which they sought "to light anew the dying embers of sectional [hate]." The real issue, they hammered in, was the need for reform on all levels of government. While they affirmed their allegiance to the Union, the Constitution, and the Civil War amendments, they also pointed to the Reconstruction excesses, and they stressed their party's commitment to the supremacy of civil authority over military authority. In the midst of their cautiously worded planks, however, the Democrats inserted an anti-Chinese plank with an unmistakable racial message. "Reform," they bluntly declared, was necessary "to correct the omissions of a Republican Congress and the errors of our treaties and our diplomacy, which . . . has exposed our brethren of the Pacific Coast to the incursions of a race not sprung from the same great parent stock, and in fact now by law denied citizenship through naturalization as being unaccustomed to the traditions of a progressive civilization. . . ." They further denounced the policy that tolerated the Mongolian trade in women for immoral purposes and in servile laborers. The solution was a modification of the Burlingame Treaty and the enactment of legislation to prevent further importation and immigration of the Mongolian race.[28] By racializing the issue of Chinese immigration, the Democrats managed to convey their perennial adherence to white supremacy without referring to African Americans. They did not think that the Republicans would use this plank to kindle sectarian strife.

It would have been difficult for Republicans to condemn the Democrats' anti-Chinese plank when their party in California was displaying a similar antagonism. During their first meeting in April 1876, the California Republican delegates deprecated the presence of "hordes of servile Chinese" in their state. At their second convention, a few months later, they took a more extreme position. The Republican party, they pledged, would use every possible means to prevent the further immigration of the Chinese who, by reason of their "ingrained character and national antecedents," were unable to become American citizens or desirable members of American communities.[29]

After the first Republican state convention, Charles E. Pickett, a California pamphleteer and future spokesman of the Workingmen's Party of California, had delivered a scathing attack on the Republicans. For him, the Chinese question had matured into a question of "chickens coming home to roost" for the whole Republican party, not just its branch in California. The national Republican party, Pickett argued, had until then remained indifferent to the calls of its members in the West because it had to maintain its image as the party dedicated to equality. As of late, though, this image had become a political liability, and the Republicans had retreated from their commitment to black rights. Pickett believed that national Republicans would soon perceive the possibilities of anti-Mongolian agitation to further their retreat from Reconstruction. These "Universal Brotherhood crusaders," Pickett predicted, would eventually demand the repeal of the Reconstruction amendments as the only way to stop Chinese immigration. Under the pretense of dealing with the Chinese question, he admonished, these "hypocrites" who had always abhorred the "darkey" would simultaneously rid themselves of all responsibility to the African American.[30]

Meeting the following month at Cincinnati for their national convention, the Republican delegates proved right Pickett's assessment that the national Republican party favored some kind of action regarding the Chinese question. They requested that Congress fully "investigate the effects of the immigration and importation of Mongolians on the moral and material interests of the country."[31] As a Massachusetts delegate noted, however, this was the first time that the Republican party had included "a discrimination of race" in its platform. The "Mongolian plank" was much more than the expression of an objective concern about Chinese immigration. It served to reinforce the retreat from the party's earlier advocacy of equality for all races. This reactionary move was manifest in the 1870 Naturalization Act, the recent shearing of the "Chinese clause" from the Civil Rights Act of 1875, and the passage of the Page Act. Insofar as African Americans were concerned, it was embodied in the defeat of the 1875 "force" bill that would have expanded the president's power to suppress southern political violence and intimidation of voters, in the reluctance to send troops to the South for the defense of black rights, and in the *U.S. v. Cruishank* decision of 1876 that the postwar amendments empowered the federal government to prohibit violations of black rights by *states,* not by individuals.[32] During the 1876 presidential campaign, moreover, while the Civil War dominated Republican rhetoric, the defense of black rights played a secondary role. The political situation had so evolved that reference to the African American was no longer required, even when Republicans waved the bloody shirt. So far as the Chinese were concerned, the "Mongolian plank" indicated that the presence of Chinese, whatever their status, was perceived to be a problem—economic, cultural, and, above all, racial. Chinese immigration, Republicans had decided, deserved a plank separating it from European immigration. The plank preceding the anti-Chinese plank called for the modification of existing treaties with European governments to safeguard the status and rights of their citizens immigrating to the United States.

The electoral campaign of 1876 was followed by an electoral crisis when the Democratic candidate, Samuel Tilden, won the popular vote and undisputed title to 184 electoral votes, one short of victory, and the Republicans claimed victory on the basis of disputed returns from the three southern states still under Republican control—Louisiana, Florida, and South Carolina. Not until the spring of 1877 was the election decided, with Rutherford B. Hayes declared president. Hayes's inauguration marked the end of Reconstruction, a result that most contemporary historians agree was inescapable. The year 1877 symbolized the decisive retreat from the idea of a powerful national state protecting the fundamental rights of African Americans. For two major national publications, "the long controversy over the black man" had reached a "finality" in 1877.[33] If Negroes "disappeared" from the front burner of national racial politics, they were soon replaced by the Chinese. Starting in 1877, a plethora of anti-Chinese legislative reports, speeches, pamphlets, and articles gave a new prominence to the Chinese question.

In the summer of 1876, following the national Republican platform, Congress authorized the appointment of a joint congressional committee to proceed to California to investigate "the character, extent, and effect of Chinese immigration."[34] The congressional committee met in San Francisco and Sacramento to hear witnesses in the latter part of 1876. The composition of the investigating committee was such that objectivity could hardly be expected from most of its members. While the committee was chaired by Senator Oliver P. Morton (Republican from Indiana), the actual working members were Senator Aaron A. Sargent (Republican from California), Representative William A. Piper (Democrat from California), Senator Henry Cooper (Democrat from Tennessee), and Representative Edwin R. Meade (Democrat from New York). Within a year, Meade expressed his staunch opposition to the Chinese before the Social Science Association in New York. Both Sargent and Piper were honorary vice-presidents of the Anti-Coolie Union of San Francisco. Representing the city of San Francisco before the committee was Frank M. Pixley, a former state's attorney general who was notorious for his anti-Chinese activities and membership in the Anti-Coolie Union. Not only did Pixley believe that the Chinese were "the inferiors of any race God ever made," but also he had stated publicly that he would gladly stand on Telegraph Hill and see all of them hanged from the yardarms and the ships bearing them burned as they came into the harbor. The presence of these intransigent foes of the Chinese should have been deemed as improper as soliciting vehemently Negrophobic members—such as Ku Klux Klan members—for a committee to investigate the conditions of southern blacks. Assuming the role of prosecuting attorney, Pixley acted in collusion with Sargent, harassing pro-Chinese witnesses and flattering Sinophobic witnesses. In session for seven weeks, the investigating committee compiled a 1,200-page report containing the testimony of 128 witnesses, including men and women from all walks of life. Although no Chinese testified, Frederick A. Bee, a prominent San Francisco businessman with legal training, was hired by the Six Companies (see chapter 2) to act as a defense attorney during the hearings. The committee first heard persons opposed to Chinese immigration and then those favorable to it.[35] Due to the illness of Senator Morton, the majority report was written by Sargent.

On the whole, the report's indictment of the Chinese was cultural, political, and racial rather than economic. Its overriding theme was that the Chinese had none of the characteristics of a desirable population. They were described as an "indigestible mass in the community"—distinct in language, pagan in religion, and inferior in mental and moral qualities. The testimony, the report argued, indicated that the Pacific Coast must in time become either American or Mongolian. The report concluded that the exclusion of the Chinese from the ballot was necessary to the survival of republican institutions. At the same time, though, it recognized that the denial of suffrage deprived the Chinese of adequate protection. The only way to prevent the establishment of a caste system was to exclude them altogether.[36]

Notwithstanding Sargent's report, many local and national observers believed the testimony had demonstrated that the Chinese had greatly contributed to the prosperity of the West. Significantly, the report failed to establish the servile condition of Chinese immigrants.[37] All things considered, their presence in California was not as portentous as the hue and cry against them suggested.[38] That the charges against the Chinese were not supported by the testimony was reinforced by Senator Morton's assessment. Morton died before the final draft of the majority report was completed, but his notes were published posthumously in what became a minority report in 1878. Morton believed that the Chinese did not pose an economic threat. Much of the intelligent testimony, he noted, proved that the Chinese had increased demand for superior labor. It was because of the Chinese that California had become an inviting place for other immigrants and that workers were better paid there than in almost any other part of the country. Having laid to rest the alleged economic causes of the antagonism, Morton concluded that the only plausible reason for the persecution visited on the Chinese was race prejudice. He wrote, "If the Chinese in California were white people, being in all other respects what they are, I do not believe that the complaints and warfare made against them would have existed to any considerable extent." Their difference in color and culture, he added, had "more to do with this hostility than their alleged vices or any actual injury to the white people of California." Morton concluded that the animosity against the Chinese was like that against the Negro, belonging as it did "to the family of antipathies springing from race and religion."[39]

A review of the testimony shows that the two major investigators, Sargent and Pixley, were aware of the limitations of the economic argument. Time and again, they asked pro-Chinese witnesses to disregard the material advancement of the state as a result of Chinese labor and to consider the moral, social, and political welfare of the country. The heavy emphasis on the "social" aspect of the question actually afforded the possibility of racializing the issue. Chinese immigrants were used as a counterpoint to white Americans and European immigrants. The presence of the Chinese, the majority report stated, discouraged the migration of white Americans and white aliens who would strengthen the Caucasian race because they were of "cognate language, religion, habits, and traditions."[40]

Besides this, interesting analogies were drawn between the African/African American and the Chinese. James P. Dameron, a lawyer claiming to be "somewhat of a naturalist and ethnologist," stated that the Mongolian and the Negro were incapable of a free form of government because of the inferior brain capacity of their heads. While both races were objectionable, Dameron believed that the "Mongolian species" represented a greater threat because in his estimation they amounted to over 40 percent of the world population. Given the easy accessibility of their "hive," Mongolians would soon turn the United States into an Asiatic colony. The survival of the fittest would work in reverse, as the inferior but countless "vegetable-eating" Mongolians survived and the superior "flesh-eating" Caucasians perished.[41]

In his testimony, Henry George repeated the arguments he had used in his anti-Chinese letter to the *New York Tribune* in 1869. Like Dameron, George thought that both Negroes and the Chinese were incapable of attaining the state of civilization of the Caucasian. He thus had the same objection to the introduction of the Negro as to the importation of the Chinese. George stated, however, that an important difference between them was that the number of Negroes in the country was fixed, while the number of Chinese might increase indefinitely.[42] Sworn and examined after George, Henry H. Haight, the former Democratic governor of California, explained his opposition to Chinese immigration by drawing a parallel with African slavery. No one, he stated, would disagree that it had been a great misfortune that the Negro had been imported into the southern states. The recent importation of Chinese immigrants, he argued, was worse. The Chinese not only endangered the social and moral fabric with their vices but also were unable to understand constitutional liberty. Allow them to exercise the franchise, he warned, and you "might as well vote so many quadrupeds." Unlike the Chinese, Negroes were familiar with the working of republican government. Besides this, he argued, blacks in California were so few that Negro suffrage had not occasioned divergent opinions. Turning his attention to blacks in the old slave states, Haight believed that their larger numbers and inferior intelligence when compared with California Negroes called for an alternative course: a waiting period of twenty to twenty-five years, until they became informed enough to exercise the franchise.[43]

Whether the African American served as a counterpoint to the Chinese or whether both were used as a counterpoint to the white population, the message was clear: nonwhite races constituted an odd element in the American social fabric. This opinion was well encapsulated in Pixley's statement as he represented the municipality of San Francisco: "The Divine Wisdom has said that . . . to the Blacks He would give Africa; to the Red Man He would give

America; and Asia, He would give to the yellow races. He inspired us with the determination . . . to have stolen from the Red Man, America; and it is now settled that the Saxon, American or European groups of families, the White Race, is to have the inheritance of Europe and America and that the yellow races are to be confined to what the Almighty originally gave them. . . ."[44]

Even pro-Chinese witnesses expressed a certain ambivalence toward the Chinese. While this can be accounted for by the aggressive, indeed insulting, interrogation methods of Sargent and Piper, it was also a very candid expression of the witnesses' misgivings and cultural anxiety. One case in point is the railroad magnate Charles Crocker, who had employed thousands of Chinese laborers to build the transcontinental railroad (see chapter 4). During his testimony, Crocker was assailed by his interrogators, who strove to establish that his pro-Chinese position was mainly due to his interest in cheap labor and potential passengers on his Oriental Steamship Line, an auxiliary of his railroad. Throughout the examination, he strove to hold his ground, stating that Chinese labor had been a great contribution to all branches of industry, not just railroad building. Crocker insisted that the Chinese were very intelligent and endowed with a great aptitude for hard work. If he had a big contract and a limited time to fulfill it, he added cautiously, he would not hesitate to use Chinese labor, as he had in the 1860s. In response to repeated attacks on his integrity, Crocker clarified his position by stating that Chinese labor was "a mighty substitute for white labor" only when the whites were not available. Of course, he never meant to call into question the superiority of white labor. For this reason he wished to go on record as saying that white immigrants were, without any doubt, a better class of population than Chinese immigrants or any other nonwhite group. Above all, the European could become an American and "be a white man among white men." While the Chinese could not assimilate, they were, in Crocker's opinion, totally harmless. Their lack of interest in politics meant they could not affect American politics. Besides, they were far outnumbered by whites. A firm believer in the law of supply and demand, Crocker did not believe that Chinese immigration would increase dramatically. However, he assured Sargent that should the Chinese population get too "thick," he would join in preventing their coming. He concluded by saying that he certainly would not like to see as many Chinese as whites and that he was opposed "to [admitting] them to citizenship" as voters.[45]

The joint special committee's report was presented to Congress in February 1877, but Senator Morton's minority report was not included in the report. A year would pass before his notes would be appended as a miscellaneous document.

In 1876, the California senate had appointed its own committee to investigate the effects of Chinese immigration on California. In August 1877, the findings of the committee were published in a shorter, 300-page report entitled *Chinese Immigration: Its Social, Moral, and Political Effect.* More than ten thousand copies of the report were distributed to members of Congress, state governors, and leading national newspapers. As one would expect from a California committee, the report was extremely anti-Chinese. The roster of witnesses included sixteen Chinese and forty-two Americans. Most Americans held anti-Chinese views. More than half were public officials. There were no representatives of the large employers of Chinese laborers. The pro-Chinese testimony was ignored, emasculated, or falsified. The report included a "Memorial to the Congress of the United States" and an "Address to the People of the United States upon the Evils of Chinese Immigration," both drawing on the testimony to expound the "monstrous evils" of Chinese immigration. A number of essays, papers, and articles were also appended to substantiate further the general "repugnance" to Chinese immigrants.[46]

The committee opened with the declaration that the Chinese had come to California before Americans had time to consider the propriety of their admission. For twenty-five years, it argued, the Chinese had proved to be impregnable to Anglo-Saxon culture. Since they came from a completely antagonistic culture, there was no point of contact through which the Chinese could be Americanized. The committee was convinced that by nature and instinct, Chinese immigrants were "voluntary slaves." Departure from their natural condition as "hewers of wood and drawers of water," it deplored, was never upward. The change was from servitude to crime. As to Chinese women, their crime was prostitution. One-third of the witnesses were interrogated at length on Chinese prostitution, and one-fifth of the testimony was devoted to it. This sensational testimony was, of course, aimed at touching the right chord in those sensitive to moral delinquency. It also implied the need for a radical solution: exclusion of *all* Chinese, male and female. Like Chinese male laborers, Chinese prostitutes were charged with being cheaper. Besides being very affordable, Chinese prostitutes were considered to be much more immoral than white prostitutes because, unlike whites, they did not have the decency to refuse the patronage of young boys. Finally, Chinese prostitutes were arraigned for poisoning the next generation's bloodstream with venereal diseases of the worst type. The Chinese as a whole had brought other hazards to the health of American people—leprosy, smallpox, and opium smoking. The committee recognized that Chinese exclusion would initially result in the paralysis of the state's economy. This was, however, inconsequential when the broader aspect of the question was considered: "For after all, what is it that we are doing here upon the Pacific Coast? Are we engaged in building up a civilized empire, founded upon and permeated with . . . Caucasian culture; or are we merely planted here for the purpose of fighting greedily . . . ?" The Chinese question, the committee concluded, was not the issue of comparative wages. Rather, it was about the "Mongolianization or Americanization" of California and ultimately the United States.[47]

All the documents appended at the end of the report revolved around the racial incompatibility of the Chinese. One essay by John Boalt, a member of the San Francisco Bar, professed to give the final word on the impossibility of assimilation of the Mongolian race with the Caucasian race.[48] The two races, he began, were separated by marked physical peculiarities. The contact with the Mongolian excited in most Americans "an unconquerable repulsion" that would forever prevent any miscegenation of the races. Given the insuperable differences between the races, he called for Chinese exclusion, claiming that it would not conflict with American policy. Until the recent "Chinese invasion," he explained, only races in perfect concord with Americans had been a welcome addition to the population. The exception was, of course, the African, whose coming had been regretted ever since. "[The] Negro did come," he said, and "we just barely survived his coming." Could Americans afford to repeat the same mistake? Finally, Boalt rejected the notion that the opposition to Chinese immigration was mainly economic or confined to a few demagogues. This fallacy was readily apparent when one considered that some European groups were as cheap and industrious as the Chinese, yet there was no opposition against them. The real cause of antagonism, he concluded, was that "[w]e want no race which we cannot absorb."[49] Another appendix was an address by Edwin R. Meade, who had been a member of the congressional committee on the Chinese in 1876. This paper was certainly included to convey the national aspect of anti-Chinese feelings. Meade did not believe that America was bound to receive such an "unamalgamating, unassimilating unnatural element" as the Chinese race. The problem, as Meade saw it, was that the admission of the Chinese would inevitably result in their enfranchisement. Sooner than later, he maintained, the Chinese would have to be treated as equals, lest Americans must turn back the hands of time and reestablish a caste system. However, he warned, the extension of citizenship to the Chinese would invite the final stage of the irrepressible conflict of the races in America.[50]

This Cassandra-like prediction was a leitmotif throughout the report. All the other contributors stated that there was only one remedy to this "unarmed invasion" of a nonassimilative race. The national government should enact a law preventing further immigration from China. If Congress tarried, it could expect riots and sectional strife when free white laborers united and defied civil power.

The large distribution of the California senate and congressional reports gave new impetus to the Sinophobic campaign by providing anti-Chinese elements in California and in Congress with innumerable "facts" to vindicate their demands. Both reports embodied an insurgent racism directed at the "Mongolian races." The separation of Mongolian immigrants from the "European kindred races" reflected the classification of the Chinese with African Americans. To be sure, there were instances when the Chinese were presented as a counterpart to African Americans. The lack of genuine sympathy for African Americans was however soon evident. On most occasions, the reports lamented the presence of both African Americans and Chinese immigrants. Even when blacks were not mentioned, the commentary on Chinese nonassimilation had implications for all nonwhite groups. On the whole, the appeals for Chinese exclusion were presented as necessary to the survival and integrity of a white republic.

While the reports' predictions about insurrection and bloodshed by exasperated white workers were aimed at conveying a sense of urgency,[51] they obviously blotted out the long tradition of racial oppression in the West. Starting in the late 1860s, secret societies had been formed throughout the region under various names: Order of Caucasians, Anti-Chinese Union, and Anti-Coolie Club. In March 1869, a Nevada paper denounced these organizations, labeling them a type of "Ku-Klux-ism" and a "burning disgrace" to the nation. Whenever Sinophobes were in full cry after the Chinese, the members of these organizations would drill and march through the streets in western cities and towns with muslin transparencies, which exhibited skulls and crossbones and Mongolian heads caricatured in hideous forms. Chinese passersby would be knocked down and kicked in the most brutal manner.[52] By the mid-1870s, complacency on the part of western officialdom had led to a rapid growth in individual and collective violence against the Chinese. Only two weeks after the release of the congressional report, the brutal murder of four Chinese woodchoppers in Chico, California, confirmed the existence of a "crisis of violence" in the West. As early as 1867, Sinophobic sentiment in Chico had led to the renaming of the *Butte County Free Press,* which assumed the new title of *Chico Caucasian.* In 1872, a local secret society called the Order of the Caucasians was formed, which issued a statement declaring that all those who employed, defended, assisted, or rented property to Chinese laborers were public enemies. Dozens of anti-Chinese demonstrations were then organized by the order, with men carrying banners reading, "The Yellow Devils Must Go," and women wheeling their offspring in carriages and carrying signs reading, "We will have to stop having these unless the Chinese go." Within a few years, demonstrations were followed by violent acts. In 1877, there were several attempts to burn the Chinese quarter in Chico. On March 13, this reign of terror culminated in the savage attack, gunning down, and attempt to burn the bodies of four Chinese laborers.[53]

It was within such a context of long-held and deep-rooted racial enmity that the Workingmen's Party of California was formed.[54] The party had its inception in a combination of national and local economic forces: the depression finally reaching California and accentuating the effects of the drought of the winter of 1876–77, the large decrease in mining returns, and the stock crash. In the summer of 1877, meanwhile, a series of railroad strikes in the East led to major uprisings and violence. Workers in California held meetings to express their sympathy for eastern laborers and vent their frustrations at the declining economic opportunities. By October 1877, they organized into the Workingmen's Party of California. From then on, the party was a success story, electing mayors, assemblymen, and senators and taking an active and prominent part in the drafting and adoption of a new state constitution in 1879. The overriding assumption of the party was that the rich and the Chinese were engaged in a conspiracy to oppress white laborers. When the party was formed, the labor movement had already reached full maturity as a Sinophobic movement calling for total Chinese exclusion. In 1877, the party's slogan, "The Chinese Must Go!" indicated a radicalization of purpose (involving exclusion of potential immigrants and deportation of Chinese residents). This development can be traced to the fact that both national parties had enlisted in the anti-Chinese crusade. Besides this, the renewed statutory persecution of the Chinese in California had the effect of legitimizing extreme anti-Chinese activities and sentiment. Long before Denis Kearney, the notorious labor agitator dubbed by his critics as the "ranting knave,"[55] began to harangue the crowds of unemployed laborers on the Sand Lot, using violent and incendiary language and threatening in plain terms to burn and pillage the Chinese quarters, many propagandists had called for extreme measures to avert the imminent race war. In short, the coarse racism of the Workingmen's Party of California had its origin in the traditional racialization of the political discourse on the Chinese question.

Opposition to the Chinese appeared in each set of the party's resolutions.[56] These resolutions went beyond the expression of an economic antagonism. In January and April 1878, the party resolved that Chinese labor was a curse to America, degrading to the morals, and a menace to American liberties. During the large labor gatherings, a blatantly racist and inflammatory language was used. At a meeting in January 1878, for instance, Kearney declared, "Now we are ready to come right to the scratch, and expel every one of the moon-eyed lepers."[57] The propaganda literature of the party also gave full expression to the racial factor in the anti-Chinese sentiment of its members. In a pamphlet published shortly after the rise of the party, a series of sketches professed to inform the public about the Chinese. Three of the sketches exposed the sexual fears of the authors. The first two repeated the usual indictment of Chinese prostitution. Using a sensational approach, the last sketch focused on the Chinese male servant who brought "the luxury and debauchery of the Orient" into the houses of the rich. In short, John Chinaman had many shortcomings: he could not speak English; he was disgusting in his habits; he had no sense of decency; he was a liar and a thief; and he had all the "vices of slaves all the world over." Notwithstanding, he was "the pet of the household." The pamphleteers believed that it was high time that husbands understood their wives' immoral fascination for John Chinaman. Then followed a lengthy seduction scene, which reflected the sexual frustrations of the authors as much as their fear of the "Oriental art of love." At first, the Chinese servant was said to be a shy helper, so pliant that he was regarded by all as "a thing, a dog or a monkey." Accordingly, without a thought, he was asked to lace corsets and change stockings. Leaving the rest to the imagination of the readers, the authors lamented that the degradation of the mistress soon followed. They concluded that the Chinese servant must go and leave way to the poor Americans who had "sex, and shame, and [a] sense of propriety."[58]

By the middle of 1878, the Workingmen's Party of California burst into full blossom, having gained many political victories in the senate, the assembly, and municipal elections. The party managed to elect a third of the delegates to the second California constitutional convention. The seeming majority against the Workingmen's Party of California did not materialize because many of the other delegates, whether they were nonpartisan, Democrat, Republican, or Independent, demanded the same reforms that the party was urging.[59] This was especially the case for those concerning the Chinese. The constitutional convention assembled in Sacramento from September 28, 1878, to March 3, 1879. While the major racial question on the agenda of the first constitutional convention in 1849 pertained to the African American, it was now the status of the Chinese. The convention delegates agreed to send a memorial to Congress, urging it to take immediate measures against Chinese immigration. The reasons they gave for their opposition to the Chinese were mainly cultural, biological, and racial. Expression of racial antipathy came from all parties.[60]

While anti-Chinese propositions were discussed, many were abandoned. Overall, the delegates feared that extreme measures might weaken their position before the country and might be invalidated by the federal court. Some delegates, however, favored radical measures because they wanted to show eastern Americans that they were in earnest, even if, as one delegate argued, it took "Hottentot legislation" to achieve such aim.[61] Two anti-Chinese sections were finally included in the new constitution. In article 2, section 1, the Chinese were denied suffrage, together with "idiots," "insane" persons, or persons convicted of an infamous crime.[62] For several years, workers and others had called for a boycott of firms employing Chinese. Article 19 of the new constitution implemented this call for "exclusion by starvation." The article contained four sections. The first authorized the legislature to take all necessary measures to deal with aliens who might become vagrants, paupers, mendicants, criminals, invalids, affected with contagious diseases, or otherwise dangerous members of the community. The second prohibited the direct or indirect employment of Chinese or Mongolians by corporations, while section 3 extended the same prohibition to the state, counties, and municipalities. The fourth declared the presence of "foreigners ineligible to become citizens" dangerous to the well-being of this state. The state legislature was directed to discourage their immigration, and it was required to pass legislation to enforce these provisions.[63]

The constitutional convention exposed the ineffectiveness of the Workingmen's Party of California. Except for the anti-Chinese clauses and the support for the Granger amendments, the simplest, most traditional labor demands were ignored. Following the convention, a series of setbacks practically ended the party's leadership. But the seeds of a renewed general assault on the Chinese had been planted. In a move reminiscent of earlier referenda on African Americans, the subject of Chinese exclusion was submitted to the people of California in the election of September 3, 1879. In an unequivocal display of racial animosity, about 96.0 percent opposed the admission of the Chinese, 0.5 percent favored it, and 3.6 percent failed to vote on the issue.[64] Encouraged by the results, the largely Republican state legislature promptly pursued the mandate included in article 19 of the constitution by enacting in February 1880 an act prohibiting the employment of Chinese laborers or Mongolians by corporations, under penalty of fine and imprisonment.[65] The legislature passed a series of other anti-Chinese measures as well.[66]

After the enactment of the discriminatory employment legislation, many Chinese were discharged. The law was soon tested by the owner of a quicksilver mining company. The case went to the U.S. circuit court. In rendering his decision, Judge Ogden Hoffman went beyond the statute, holding void any section of article 19 upon which it was based and any law of California that was in conflict with the Burlingame Treaty. It was Hoffman's opinion that article 19 and the ensuing legislation were but the latest of a series of enactments designed to limit the right of the Chinese to immigrate to and reside in the United States, with all the privileges, immunities, and exemptions of subjects of a most favored nation. The California statute, he averred, was a violation of the fundamental right to labor. Rejecting Attorney General Augustus L. Hart's argument that the California policy was constitutional because it had in view the corporations' relations with the state, Hoffman maintained that the policy aimed to exclude the Chinese from a wide range of employment and that its ultimate end was to drive those already in California from the country and prevent others from coming. By depriving the Chinese of work, Hoffman admonished, Californians sought to reduce them to "vagrants, paupers, mendicants, and criminals" and thus provide the conditions for their removal from the state in accordance with section 1 of article 19. Hoffman declared that the constitutional article and the legislation ran afoul of the Burlingame Treaty and the Fourteenth Amendment to the U.S. Constitution. Pointing to the racialism of the statute, he observed that the legislation would have encountered a storm of indignation if the labor of the Irish or Germans had been similarly proscribed. The right of Europeans to support themselves by their labor stood on no higher ground than that of the Chinese, he reprimanded.[67] Following Hoffman's decision, other acts passed to enforce sections 3 and 4 of article 19 were declared unconstitutional. Municipal ordinances to enforce the first section of the article met with the same fate.

As in earlier legal decisions, however, Hoffman's opinion exposed the purely doctrinal basis of his decision.[68] He agreed with most thoughtful persons that "the unrestricted immigration of the Chinese to this country is a great and growing evil . . . , and that if allowed to continue in numbers . . . , it will be a menace to our peace and even to our civilization." Hence, the demand that the Burlingame Treaty be rescinded or modified was, in his opinion, "reasonable and legitimate." So long as the treaty existed, though, the Chinese had the same rights of immigration, residence, and labor as any other foreigners. Any attempt to abrogate those rights, he warned, would be met with firmness by the courts. Notwithstanding his castigation of the California legislature for its racist policy, Judge Hoffman's statements suggested he would not object to a similarly discriminatory course of action by the federal government.[69] He was not alone. In *Ah Fong* (1874) and in a later decision, *Ho Ah Kow v. Nunan* (1879), invalidating the "queue" ordinance of 1876, Justice Field denounced the racist impulses of the California statutes. In both cases, however, he called for federal action. In the second case, especially, he acknowledged the desirability of preventing the immigration of "vast hordes" of Chinese immigrants, susceptible to "giving rise to fierce antagonisms of race," but he insisted that only the federal government could achieve such an aim.[70]

Besides these cases, a critical judicial decision in 1878 on the right of naturalization was a major setback for the Chinese. The Naturalization Act of 1870, which extended the right of naturalization to "aliens of African descent or nativity," did not expressly disqualify Chinese immigrants from naturalization (see chapter 8). However, the 1870 congressional debate sparked by the proposition to strike the "white person" prerequisite from the naturalization law left no doubt about the intended prohibition of Chinese naturalization. In 1873, when the federal statutes were codified for the first time, the words "being a free white person" were "inadvertently" omitted.[71] The seemingly liberal statute encouraged Chinese immigrants to petition for naturalization. A Chinese was naturalized in 1873 in New York. At least thirteen Chinese applied for citizenship in California within the next three years. In response, anti-Chinese elements expressed their concern in lithographs representing Chinese men occupying diverse official positions, notably as assemblymen, judges, and governor; in editorials calling attention to the danger of being governed by the Chinese; and in a memorial sent to Congress to revise the naturalization law. Congress acceded to their demands by amending the act and reinserting the missing words in February 1875.[72]

Notwithstanding this, the right of a court to deny the Chinese naturalization had not been finalized. Some Chinese immigrants were therefore allowed to file declarations of intention to become citizens in 1875 and 1876. Not until 1878 would a legal decision address squarely the question of Chinese naturalization. In *In re Ah Yup,* Judge Lorenzo Sawyer ruled that the application of Ah Yup, "a native and citizen of the Empire of China, of the Mongolian race," for American naturalization was unacceptable because he was not a "white person" within the meaning of the naturalization statute. To come to that decision, Sawyer solicited opinions of members of the bar, and he used extensive "anthropological evidence" about racial classification. After carefully reviewing the history of the naturalization statute, he concluded that the debates over naturalization in 1870 made it clear that congressmen used the word *white* precisely to exclude the Chinese. The same concern was behind the reinsertion of the words *white person* in the revised statute, he added.[73]

Judge Sawyer's decision was a proper construction and interpretation of the naturalization statutes, fully in accordance with the intent of their framers. By declaring the Chinese ineligible for citizenship because they were "nonwhite," the U.S. circuit court upheld the law of the land. At the same time, the court paved the way for a new convergence of racism and national policy, after the brief hiatus inspired by Reconstruction idealism. Although the target had shifted from African Americans to the Chinese, the official exclusion of the Chinese from naturalization because they were "nonwhite" revealed the persistence of a white supremacist ideology and the token enfranchisement of African Americans. Moreover, the inclusion of Africans in the naturalization statutes was not viewed as a repudiation of racial thinking at all. The intent of the framers of the naturalization statute of 1870 was raised in another important decision. Two years after *Ah Yup*, Judge Matthew Deady denied the citizenship application of a man of white Canadian and Indian Canadian parentage, a resident of Oregon for sixteen years. Like Judge Sawyer, Deady referred to the naturalization law of 1870; unlike him, he discussed the statute insofar as Africans and African Americans were concerned. He made clear that the extension of "the boon of American citizenship to the comparatively savage and strange inhabitants of the 'dark continent,' while withholding it from the intermediate . . . red and yellow races," was but a "seeming inconsistency." In fact, he argued, Africans were not likely to immigrate, and extending naturalization to them was therefore "merely a harmless piece of legislative buncombe." In contrast, the Chinese were "only too willing to assume the mantle of American sovereignty."[74] The debates over Chinese exclusion verified the notion advanced by Deady that while naturalization was "ostentatiously offered to the African," it was essential to deny it to Asians.[75] To conclude, then, the California judiciary and legislature were not in basic conflict. Nor did these two branches of government clash with the strongly adverse public feeling that manifested itself in the anti-Chinese referendum of 1879.

11. The Politics of Racism in the Chinese Exclusion Debates, 1879–82

The [Chinese Exclusion] bill is founded on race hatred and panic.... [If] a whole race may be excluded from the national domain..., a whole enfranchised class may be excluded from the suffrage for the same reason.
—*Harper's Weekly*, April 1, 1882

WHILE THE California legislature was attempting "to remedy the evils of Chinese immigration" by state and municipal legislation, the Pacific states' congressmen were busy presenting their case to their eastern colleagues. The appointment of the joint congressional committee on Chinese immigration in 1876 had convinced western congressmen that a national hearing would follow the committee's presentation of its findings to Congress. When the report was submitted in February 1877, however, it was obscured by the Hayes-Tilden election controversy. Western congressmen continued to submit resolutions and bills to restrict the immigration of the Chinese, their employment, and naturalization, and they called on the administration to open correspondence with China for the abrogation of the Burlingame Treaty.[1] President Rutherford B. Hayes disappointed them by refusing to take a public stand on the issue. His responsibility as chief diplomat played an essential part in his handling of the Chinese issue. Together with Secretary of State William M. Evarts, the president was concerned that a unilateral abrogation of the treaty might harm commercial relations with China. While congressmen thought that the administration was insensitive to their calls, Hayes and Evarts were quietly striving to reach a diplomatic resolution through discussion with the U.S. minister in China and the newly established Chinese legation in Washington.[2] The president's initial efforts met with an unfavorable response from the Chinese legation, which expressed its determination to maintain the terms of the Burlingame Treaty. Hayes still hoped that a diplomatic remedy could be found. In his second annual message to

Congress on December 2, 1878, Hayes announced his satisfaction with the establishment of a permanent Chinese legation, which, he had no doubt, would "be of advantage to both nations in promoting friendly relations and removing causes of difference."[3]

President Hayes's hope for a diplomatic solution was shattered by the intensification of the anti-Chinese movement in the West and by the decision of the Pacific Coast delegation to take advantage of the November elections. With the Democrats controlling the House (153 to 140), the delegation felt that the time had come to take action. In January 1879, the House Committee on Education and Labor, to which different anti-Chinese resolutions, memorials, bills, and petitions had been referred, recommended a restriction bill, H.R. 2423 (the "fifteen passenger" bill), which provided that no master of a U.S. vessel could take aboard more than fifteen Chinese passengers, male or female, with the intent of bringing them to the United States. In presenting the bill to the House, the committee insisted that there was no principle on which Americans had to receive into their midst the natives of Asia or Africa. The problems that had resulted from the presence of the red and black races in America would be renewed and, indeed, "in a more aggravated and dangerous form by the yellow race." This was because, unlike the Indians, the Mongolians were brought in daily contact with the social and political life of the white community, and unlike the Africans, they did not surrender any of their "marked peculiarities" through contact. The committee concluded that it was neither possible nor desirable for two races as distinct as the Caucasian and the Mongolian to live under the same government.[4]

Martin Townsend (Republican from New York) offered the only substantial rebuttal during the brief debate that ensued in the House. Citing the economic benefits the Chinese had brought to California, he expressed his contempt for the Sinophobic demagogues and hoodlums of the West. For Townsend, the agitation against the Chinese was a new manifestation of Know-Nothingism. While there was a day when the cry was against the German and the Irish, the clamor was now against "the Heathen Chinee." By associating the anti-Chinese movement with this form of nativism, Townsend not only underscored the racial aspect of the current movement against the Chinese but also failed to rebuke the report's arraignment of Native Americans and African Americans.

Albert Willis (Democrat from Kentucky), the chairman of the House Committee on Education and Labor, responded to Townsend by focusing on the racial argument. Unlike European groups, who "freely" mingled in the stream of American life, the Chinese would always be an alien element in America, he argued. Twice before, he recalled, the United States had had to address questions arising from the differences of races. Now, he lamented, before the trials and difficulties with the Indian and black races were fully ended, another and more hazardous experiment with the yellow race was presenting itself. If the earlier experiences had foundered, he asked, what could Americans expect from the Mongolian who had neither the docility and humility of the one nor the consciousness of inferior civilization that distinguished the other? Willis was seconded by Horace Page (Republican from California), who upheld the pending bill by explaining that America's open immigration policy applied only to immigrants capable of assimilation. Page said he also wanted to expose the fallacious notion that extending naturalization to African Americans had a bearing on the Chinese question. The granting of citizenship to the African race, he contended, was made not because population from Africa was desired or expected but because it was a requisite for protecting the millions of Christianized people of African ancestry who already were in America.[5]

The vote was taken following this brief colloquy. The bill passed easily, with 155 yeas, 72 nays, and 61 not voting. Democrats overwhelmingly supported the bill with 104 yeas and 16 nays. Republicans were more equally divided, voting 51 yeas and 56 nays.[6] The bill reached the Senate a couple of weeks later. Unlike the House, the Senate debated vehemently for three days. The Senate was dominated by Republicans—39 to 36. Chief among the supporters of the bill were, of course, the western senators—Aaron A. Sargent (Republican from California), Newton Booth (Republican from California), La Fayette Grover (Democrat from Oregon), and John H. Mitchell (Republican from Oregon).[7] Besides elaborating on the constitutionality and propriety of the restriction of Chinese immigration by Congress, these senators strove to relieve the western anti-Chinese movement from the stigma of "Kearneyism." Pointing to the 1877 congressional investigation committee report (see chapter 10), Sargent stated that testimony from the bench, the pulpit, and the workshop alike had shown the same strong objection to the Chinese. Furthermore, western Americans were not alone in calling attention to the evils of Chinese immigration. Sargent furnished copies of articles from national newspapers and letters by major public figures in the East—notably, clergymen, college professors, and politicians of both parties—all supporting a restriction policy. The Chinese question, Mitchell added, had united in one solid phalanx men of every party and section. The Chinese question was one that rose above party alignment and appealed to American congressmen not as partisans striving for political supremacy but as conservators of the integrity of republican institutions in America.

Mitchell did not address his remarks to the Democrats because they were naturally inclined to discriminate on account of race and color. He directed his arguments at fellow Republicans, who had until then held more liberal racial views. Mitchell believed that a restraint of Chinese immigration as a measure of protection was not in conflict with the belief in the universal brotherhood of man. While every Republican should abide by the promises of life, liberty, and the pursuit of happiness for all and the inalienable right of expatriation of all, the first duty of an American statesman was to protect the social fabric within his jurisdiction against any disturbing element. Republican egalitarian beliefs, Mitchell stressed, would not stand a minute if eastern Republicans paused to reflect on the contaminating effects of the customs of Asiatic barbarians on America. They would decide that the promises of equal rights and privileges were meant to apply to people coming from the civilized nations of Europe, not the heathen nations of the world. Focusing on the incompatibility between the Mongolian and Caucasian races, Senator Grover expressed his concern that the Mongolian was "a man among us but not of us." The Chinese, he went on, "[was] not bone of our bone, nor flesh of our flesh, and never can be." Senator Booth was also of the opinion that the meeting of two civilizations as antagonistic as the Mongolian and the American would be totally destructive of America. Like Mitchell, Booth entreated fellow Republicans to set aside their unreasonable humanitarianism. "We do not want a conflict of races," he concluded, and "we do not want an amalgamation of races."[8]

Pronouncements about impending race conflicts resulting from the presence of two different races had, of course, bearing on race relations in the nation at large. If no law could promote harmony between the Caucasian and the Mongolian races, then Reconstruction racial policy could be said to have caused more harm than good for both African Americans and European Americans. For John T. Morgan (Republican from Alabama), the "unfortunate" Burlingame Treaty of 1868 was the culmination of the excessive philanthropy that characterized federal policy at the time of its ratification. The Chinese had been included in the midst of a "national craze" about the "regenerating" effect of inferior races on the social and political system. The most ill-conceived policies, Morgan lamented, were those that strove to place Negroes far above whites. At present, white southerners were still beset with difficulties in their efforts to preserve some of the remaining rights of their race. "For the sake of our own institutions which our fathers endeavored to build with the materials which they found in the white race, excluding Negroes and Indians," he admonished, "let us not take in charge the hordes of pagan China."[9]

Speaking on the third day, Senator James B. Eustis (Democrat from Louisiana) went beyond the issue at hand to present a plea on behalf of his white constituents. He made clear from the start that his support for the restriction bill had nothing to do with the specious desire to regulate the labor or habits of a class of immigrants. Representing a state afflicted by a race problem of "no modified type," he admitted that the Chinese question touched a very weak point in him. According to the Republican-dominated western delegation, Eustis said, the Anglo-Saxon race on the Pacific rim was on the verge of a fierce struggle with the Mongolian race. Comparing race relations in the West and in the South, he concluded that the charges against the Chinese were simply groundless: "The inferior race [in California] does not claim, as is the case in Louisiana . . . to control every interest which society holds dear and every right and privilege to which man is attached. . . ." If the mere presence of the Chinese in the West stimulated so much racial pride that whites used violence to extirpate them, Eustis wondered why Republicans should express surprise or indignation "that there should be occasionally a little violence or a little bloodshed in the State of Louisiana." There was a double standard in the Republican handling of race matters. While whites in his state were arraigned before the bar of public opinion for trying to regain political supremacy from Negroes, the white race of California was vindicated in its demand for the exclusion of a comparatively inoffensive inferior race. Compared with Californians, Eustis argued, the people of Louisiana should be complimented for having shown much restraint. They had never asked that African Americans be expelled from their state, as was being proposed for the Chinese.[10]

Eustis's major target for criticism was Senator James G. Blaine (Republican from Maine)—a politician whose popularity was such that he had been a serious contender for the presidency in 1876 and whose strong position in favor of the civil rights of African Americans had earned him commendation. In the debate over the fifteen passenger bill, Blaine provided perfect ammunition for the foes of the Republican party. The Chinese question was first and foremost a racial issue, he insisted. In essence, the Chinese question was whether America should be "the home and the refuge of our own people and our own blood" or be inevitably degraded by the immigration of servile Confucius worshipers. Blaine's argumentation indicates that the specter of the "failure" of Reconstruction bore heavily on his mind. Pointing to the recent past, he challenged fellow Republicans to "make light [of the race trouble]" and asked, "Does any man here to-day assume that we have so entirely solved and satisfactorily settled on a permanent basis all the troubles growing out of the negro race trouble that we are prepared to invite another one?" If congressmen upheld the principle of free immigration for the Chinese, he warned, the only way to maintain law and order would be, as in the South, through national military force. It was these statements that prompted Eustis's rebuke of the Republicans' self-serving racial policy.[11] Blaine retorted that there was no similarity between the Chinese question and the Negro problem. By birth and long settlement in Louisiana, the colored race, he explained, had rights that the Chinese aliens could not claim. He conceded that the troubles that sprang from the biracial situation in the South were serious, yet he did not agree that the remedy lay in the withdrawal of national authority from there and the establishment of white supremacy. The situation at the South, however, was a critical indication of the folly of inviting another inferior race.[12]

The opposition to the bill was led by a small group of Republican senators, notably George F. Hoar from Massachusetts, Stanley Matthews from Ohio, Roscoe Conkling from New York, and Hannibal Hamlin from Maine. These senators were mainly concerned about the consequences of a bill that basically abrogated articles of a bilateral treaty. They often cited the commercial and business interests that depended on friendly relations with China.[13] Senators Hoar and Hamlin went beyond these arguments, warning that the passage of the bill would dramatically reverse the country's tradition as an asylum for *all*. Neither man, however, expressly voiced the ideal of racial equality that had been Senator Sumner's leitmotif in his vain efforts to strike the word *white* from the federal statutes (see chapter 8). Hamlin's position in the 1870 debate over naturalization came back to haunt him. Blaine, in an attempt to divert attention from himself and to vindicate his restrictionist stand, criticized Hamlin for voting against Sumner's naturalization motion in 1870. Hamlin's initial response was that he had feared the election bill to which it was attached might not pass. He then conceded that there was another, more compelling reason for his and other Republicans' vote against the naturalization of the Chinese. Thinking that it would be unwise to add the Chinese to the four million newly enfranchised African Americans, they had decided to postpone consideration of Chinese naturalization to a more opportune time. In view of the current magnitude of the Chinese question, he confessed that had the Chinese been granted naturalization in 1870, there would be no Chinese question to discuss in 1879.

Concluding the debate, the Senate added a provision to the bill requiring the president to abrogate articles 5 and 6 of the Burlingame Treaty. The bill passed the Senate with 39 yeas, 27 nays, and 9 absent. Democrats overwhelmingly supported the bill, with a vote of 25 to 8. As in the House, Republicans split, 19 of them opposing the bill and 14 favoring it.[14] The vote reflected the partisanship behind it and the importance of the sectional factor. Republican and Democratic westerners were largely supported by southern Democrats. However, the debates showed the racial anxieties of many Republicans.

It would be incorrect to regard the negative Republican vote as evidence of a fundamental opposition to restriction. All the Republicans who expressed their opposition to the bill declared their willingness to seek a solution to the Chinese question through diplomacy. They were all ready to vote for a restrictive legislation that would be respectful of treaty obligations. Except for Blaine, Republicans did not refute the Democratic indictment of Reconstruction. Nor did they seem to find fault with the charges of inferiority and impossibility of assimilation made against African Americans.

In a letter to the *New York Tribune* sent on February 15, 1879, William Lloyd Garrison, the prominent abolitionist and humanitarian, reprobated the spirit of caste that lay behind the "unjust" and "absurd" fifteen passenger bill. To Garrison, the debate on the Chinese question had disgraced almost everyone who had participated in it. Above all, he was indignant about the zealous collusion of Republicans in such a "vulgar" measure, particularly Senator Blaine. Blaine, Garrison charged, was hoping to earn the support of the Pacific Coast for his presidential aspirations.[15] According to the *Nation,* the debate about the fifteen passenger bill had forced such declaimers as Senator Blaine to approach the race question in a practical way. The editor did not agree, however, with Blaine's contention that the Chinese problem bore little resemblance to the Negro problem. Both cases presented the same question: what was the best way for two different races to live peaceably together? If it was reasonable for Californians to threaten to burn and ravage unless they were rid of Chinese laborers, then southern whites were equally justified in objecting to being ruled by a majority of "ignorant Africans" just emancipated from a most degrading form of bondage.[16] Another article elaborated further on the "misfortune" of the Republicans trying to ride two horses at the same time. Republicans were defending Negro suffrage on the basis of human rights, while they assailed the Chinese—also human—on the basis of expediency. Notwithstanding, the *Nation* agreed that a massive Chinese immigration would certainly constitute a strain on American institutions. The magazine's shamelessly inegalitarian creed offered a glaring contrast to the Republicans' dissembling on it. "[The] Chinaman has no 'Divine patent,' . . . to come here and run or damage American society, even if he is willing to labor," it stated; nor does the Negro have a "'Divine patent' to wreck any machinery of civilized government there may be at the South."[17]

Soon after Congress passed the bill, the executive office was swamped with memorials, petitions, resolutions, letters, and telegrams. Newspaper editorials were also forwarded to President Hayes in an attempt to influence his decision. Overall, public opinion reflected the partisan and sectional pattern exhibited during the debates. Furthermore, the critics of the bill betrayed an ambivalent attitude, similar to that of congressmen. On the one hand, they favored a presidential veto because of the implications of the bill for Chinese-American relations and for the principle of free immigration. On the other hand, they expressed their support for a restriction of Chinese immigration that would be respectful of treaty obligations.

President Hayes vetoed the bill. His veto message demonstrates that he responded to the bill primarily as a diplomatic issue. Beginning with a review of the history and provisions of the Burlingame Treaty and the dangers of unilateral tampering with treaty obligations, Hayes concluded that he must reject the bill because its obvious intent was to repress the immigration of the Chinese to an extent approximating absolute exclusion. At the same time, however, Hayes indicated his own misgivings about what he called the "experiment" of Chinese immigration. Ten years after the negotiation of the Burlingame Treaty, he argued, the Chinese adherence to their "traits of race, religion, manners, and customs" and their obstinate segregation from American life stamped them as strangers and sojourners. In view of this, Hayes suggested that a careful reconsideration of the treaty might be necessary to shield America against a larger and more rapid infusion of that race than American society could assimilate with ease. He further indicated that "the very grave discontents of the people of the Pacific States" deserved the most serious attention from the American people and their government. The message was clear. Chinese immigration was problematic, and efforts to secure a diplomatic solution should precede any legislative action.[18]

Hayes's veto message reflected his sympathy with the demand for Chinese restriction and his belief that the principle of free immigration had limits, hinging on the perceived potential of foreigners for assimilation. This was confirmed in his diary, in which he declared that Chinese immigration amounted to a pernicious invasion that ought to be discouraged. What was more, Americans' past experiences with "weaker races" led him to conjure up a new cycle of racial oppression and conflict.[19] The president's major objection to the bill revolved around the possible disturbance of the treaties with China. At no time did Hayes evoke the ideals of equality and justice. Nor did he allude to the equal protection of the laws in the Fourteenth Amendment and the Enforcement Act of 1870 as a ground for declaring the bill unacceptable. In that respect, the president reinforced the narrow definition of the Chinese question as a matter of treaty relations and obligations. It is important to bear in mind that the modification of the Burlingame Treaty was construed as a means of institutionalizing the discriminatory treatment of the Chinese. The Chinese government's support of provisions that would allow the American government to regulate Chinese immigration would serve to obfuscate the racist undercurrent of the new bilateral relation. By agreeing to new terms, the Chinese government would seem to legitimate the separation of the Chinese from other immigrants of the most favored nations and their differential treatment.

Congress failed to override the president's veto.[20] As expected, the people of the Pacific Coast were very bitter about the veto. They expressed this by holding anti-Chinese mass meetings and voting overwhelmingly against the admission of the Chinese in the September referendum (see chapter 10). The California state and municipal authorities passed a plethora of laws and ordinances against the Chinese. Branding Chinese prisoners on the forehead with the letter *C* was even proposed.[21] In the East, meanwhile, western congressmen focused on quickly negotiating a new treaty with China.[22] Before the end of 1879, the Chinese government let it be known through George F. Seward, the American minister to China, that it would consent to the prohibition of criminals, prostitutes, diseased persons, and contract laborers.[23] But the U.S. government wanted much more than a redundant prohibition of these "undesirable classes." In June 1880, a special diplomatic mission appointed expressly for the purpose of securing a new treaty left for China. That same month, the two major parties held their national conventions for the forthcoming presidential election. They both included anti-Chinese planks in their platforms. The Democratic plank called for an amendment to the Burlingame Treaty and for a prohibition of all Chinese immigrants, except for travel, education, and foreign commerce—provided their presence was "carefully guarded." Regarding unrestricted immigration as a matter of grave concern, the Republican party pledged to support the enactment of restrictive legislation that would be "just, humane, and reasonable."[24]

Just two weeks before the election, a letter purported to have been written by the Republican candidate, James A. Garfield, to a certain Henry Morey was published in an attempt to discredit him. In the letter, Garfield allegedly advocated the free admission of Chinese laborers. That he had advised President Hayes to veto the fifteen passenger bill and had voted to sustain him made the authenticity of the letter plausible.[25] Although the letter was a forgery, it cost Garfield California and Nevada. Despite the "Morey letter" and the defections of these two states, the Republicans won the election.[26]

In his letter of acceptance, Garfield dispelled all the doubts about his alleged pro-Chinese position. He first expounded the tradition of hospitality to the immigrants who came to share the burdens and benefits of American life and intended to become an indistinguishable part of the population. The Chinese, he observed, had few such qualities. Their coming to the United States was too much like an "importation" and an "invasion." If the special mission to China failed to secure an adequate modification of the Burlingame Treaty, Garfield announced that Congress should pursue an appropriate course of action. Shortly after this declaration, on November, 17, 1880, a new treaty gave the United States the unilateral power to "regulate, limit, or suspend" the coming of Chinese laborers to the United States and their residence whenever it felt that Chinese immigration affected or threatened to affect American interests; however, it might not absolutely prohibit it. Furthermore, any limitation or suspension could apply only to Chinese *laborers* and it should be *reasonable*. Other immigrants, such as teachers, merchants, diplomats, or tourists, along with their personal servants, and Chinese laborers already in the Unites States were exempt. Under this treaty, the rights, privileges, and immunities of subjects of the "most favored nation" were restricted to the exempt classes. A second treaty was signed for the purpose of protecting American commercial interests in China.[27]

In 1881, President Garfield was fatally shot by an assassin, and Vice-President Chester A. Arthur succeeded him. In his first annual address on December 6, 1881, Arthur informed Congress that he would support some form of Chinese restriction if it was properly carried out.[28] The way was open for a new round of legislative debates on restricting Chinese immigrants. The Senate was then evenly divided between Republicans and Democrats (37 each and 1 Independent), and there was a Republican majority in the House—147 to 135, with 11 Independents. Almost twenty bills were introduced during the session of Congress following the ratification of the new treaty. Of these, Senate bill 71, offered by John F. Miller (Republican from California), received serious consideration in the Senate. The ostensible legitimacy of the bill was reflected in its title, "A Bill to Enforce Treaty Stipulations relating to the Chinese." It provided for the prohibition of the immigration of Chinese laborers for twenty years, beginning sixty days after the passage of the bill. It would not apply to the Chinese who were in the United States on November 17, 1880, or who would come during the sixty days following the passage of the act. Right of reentry was given to those who were lawfully in the United States and wanted to return to China, provided they obtained a certificate at the port of departure. Diplomatic and other government officers were exempted from the law. The bill also provided for an elaborate system of registration, certification, and identification, with imprisonment and deportation as penalties for fraud.[29]

The bill was heatedly debated in the Senate for seven days, February 28 to March 9, 1882, and in the House for another seven days, March 14 through 23. In the course of the debates, all the old arguments were reiterated. On the one hand, the restrictionists, mainly from the West and the South, expounded the economic, social, political, demographic, cultural, and racial dangers of Chinese immigration.[30] On the other hand, the congressmen who opposed the bill (for the most part, Republicans from the East) cited the economic benefits of Chinese immigration and trade and elaborated on the fact that the bill violated the spirit and letter of the newly ratified treaty by going far beyond the stipulations of the agreement.[31] For them, the object of the bill was not to "regulate" Chinese immigration but to "exclude" the Chinese. What was more, Senator Orville H. Platt (Republican from Connecticut) averred, the enforcement of the bill would amount to an "extirpation" of the Chinese from the United States. Within twenty years, the Chinese in the United States would have passed away, failing to be replaced by new immigrants. Not only was the time of suspension not "reasonable" within the meaning of the treaty, the critics of the bill argued, but also the bill struck at a class of laboring people, whose coming had not been injurious to the interests of society. By striking at both "servile" and "free" labor, the bill was unduly harsh, placing Chinese laborers on the same footing as paupers, prostitutes, and diseased persons.[32]

Most congressmen opposing the bill made it clear that they were not opposed to legislating against the Chinese. Indeed, they frequently deplored the presence of the Chinese and maintained that they would support a "just" and "reasonable" bill, which would provide for a shorter period of suspension (ten years) and would exempt skilled laborers. As during the debates over the fifteen passenger bill, these congressmen objected not to the principle or goal of restriction but to the means by which to reach it. Unlike the earlier debates, however, a few congressmen went beyond the argument that the bill was an infraction of the treaty by which it professed to be bound, eventually exposing the proposed bill as one based on racial prejudice.

In introducing his bill, Miller had argued that the Chinese and American races were radically antagonistic. Any close relation between them was, in his opinion, bound to merge in a mongrel race, "altogether mixed and very bad." While there was nothing new in Miller's Sinophobic hyperboles, the response of George F. Hoar (Republican from Massachusetts) marked a departure from the earlier skirting of the racist cast of the proposed anti-Chinese legislation. Hoar rebutted Miller's arguments by deploring that the old prejudice that had played its part in recent history was rearing its ugly head again. There was no argument against the Chinese that had not been heard against African Americans. Like the old "visionaries of the East [Abolitionists]," he noted, the opponents of the Chinese exclusion bill were accused of being "sickly philanthropists," who were meddling with social arrangements and standing at a distance to watch evils from which they were safe. In view of the recent history, he objected, who could be so bold as to deny that the "colored race" was fit for citizenship? Pointing to the political achievements of African Americans, Hoar concluded that twenty years after their emancipation from slavery, they had thoroughly vindicated their title to the highest privileges of citizenship.

During the debates over the fifteen passenger bill, African Americans' "lack of fitness" for the obligations of citizenship had been used as evidence against the Chinese. Yet neither Hoar nor any other member of the New England phalanx against the bill had raised any strong objection to this indictment of African Americans. By failing to do so, they had not only strengthened the position of the restrictionists but also provided the southern Democrats with a golden opportunity to vindicate the legitimacy of a return to white supremacy. In a delayed attempt to offset the Republicans' lack of reaction during the earlier debates, Hoar expressed his dismay by asking, "What has happened within thirteen years that the great Republic should strike its flag? What change has come over us that we should eat the bravest and truest words we ever spoke?" According to the census of 1880, he observed, the number of Chinese people in the United States was 105,000—that is, one-five-hundredth of the whole U.S. population. The number of immigrants of all nations in 1881 was 720,045. Of these, only 20,711 were Chinese. How could the country and the Republican party boast of their democracy if the presence of a hundred thousand Chinese caused them to put an end to their free immigration policy? If such change occurred, he deplored, America would reveal to the world that "the self-evident truth is a self-evident lie."[33]

Senator Platt shared Hoar's opinion that the old arguments against social equality between Negroes and whites were "resuscitated and rehabilitated for the occasion." The true intent and meaning of the bill, he said, was to declare that henceforth, "excepting only the Chinese now here and the colored people now here, no man shall work in the United States except he be a white man." While Senator Joseph R. Hawley (Republican from Connecticut) saw no problem with literacy, property, or any other qualification that would apply to everyone, irrespective of race and birthplace, he believed that a bill that excluded a person "because he is yellow, or because he is black, or because he was born in a certain place" would be a departure from the Republican doctrine. Failing to rekindle the fire of progressive Republicanism, he adverted to the postbellum amendments and deplored that the radical principles embodied in them were fading away.[34]

This burst of principled opposition was to no good effect. The majority of the Republicans who took a stand against the bill did so not on the grounds that it was a violation of their party's egalitarian principles. Indeed, some

Republicans justified their support for restriction by stressing that, through its candidate in 1880, the Republican party had committed itself to the restriction of Chinese immigration.[35] What was more, the lofty ideals expressed by Hoar and his supporters were censured by not only Democrats but also Republicans from both wings of the party—western and eastern. In the ensuing debates, it became obvious that party lines had blurred and that racial politics had transcended its association with Democrats and gained ascendancy and respectability among Republicans.[36]

From the western wing of the Republican party, Senator John P. Jones from Nevada asked his colleagues to think back to the time when the first shipload of Africans landed in the United States and imagine that someone had objected to their immigration because he believed that they could not amalgamate with Americans. By excluding Africans from the country, Jones argued, that man would have rendered the nation a great service. "Does anybody suppose for an instant that if the African were not in this country to-day, we should be anxious to welcome him?" he asked rhetorically. For Jones, the recent experiment of conferring on African Americans political rights had proved to be a "dismal failure." This, he believed, should be imputed neither to Republicans nor to the Negro but to the "human laws" that had irrevocably stamped on one race its superiority over the other. If this early experience failed to evidence the folly of permitting a new "tidal wave of barbarism," Jones had yet another reason. The Chinese race, he argued, belonged to a race that was less capable of assimilation than the Negro race.[37]

From the eastern wing of the party, Senator George F. Edmunds from Vermont expressed his opposition to the bill unless an amendment requiring a shorter suspension was passed. Like Senator Wilson in 1870 and Senator Blaine in 1879, Edmunds assumed at once the role of the eastern Republican star defector. In his exposition, however, Edmunds departed significantly from Wilson's and Blaine's reasoning by including both the Chinese and the African American in his expressions of racial contempt. Pointing to the statements of Senators Hoar and Henry L. Dawes (Republican from Massachusetts) that all humanity was of one kin, Edmunds objected that the two senators spoke only for themselves. Neither the people of Massachusetts nor the people of his own state, Vermont, could be said "to be hungry for an irruption of a million of the inhabitants of the continent of Africa to-day, or to-morrow, or next year. . . ." The defense of the rights of colored persons in the United States as citizens, not as slaves, he averred, had never meant that blacks should be equal with whites. The "curse of our southern sister states," he added, was the "want of homogeneity" and the impossible "coalescence" of its white and black population. If it was so with the Negro who had be-

come Americanized in the course of several generations, it was even more
so with the Chinese, whose racial superiority to blacks was complicated by
different habits and modes of thought.[38]

The racialization of the Republican line of reasoning encouraged Democrats to present their own racist views and to call for home rule.[39] Senator
James Z. George (Democrat from Mississippi), for example, carried the bill's
logic to what he thought was a reasonable inference. When the question over
the relations of the African race to the white race arose again, he expected
that white southerners would be given the same deference to their wishes as
had been given to the white people of California.[40] Senator Hoar could not
help but express his disbelief at George's extravagant yet alarming claim that
the citizenship rights of the African race in America were likely to be reconsidered in the near future.

The efforts of Senator Hoar and the few other principled Republicans were
doomed to fail. Their party had surrendered to racial politics by singling out
Chinese immigrants for particular treatment for more than a decade. Even
those who joined Hoar in his denunciation of the discriminatory intent of
the legislation concluded their rebuttals with a call for a shorter suspension
or one limited to unskilled laborers. Although the amendment for a ten-year
suspension instead of twenty years failed, two other amendments were accepted. One prohibited the naturalization of the Chinese, and the other
defined laborers as both skilled and unskilled. The protest of a few congressmen that the bill was now indicative of "a spirit of proscription" was not
enough to reverse the trend toward the institutionalization of the racialization of American immigration policy. As the exclusionists pointed out, the
naturalization clause was in agreement with the earlier policy on the status
of Chinese immigrants, from the Burlingame Treaty to the recent *Ah Yup*
decision by the U.S. Circuit Court of California.[41]

The bill passed in both chambers—by a Senate vote of 29 to 15, with 32
absent, and a House vote of 167 to 66, with 55 not voting.[42] In both cases, the
Democrats provided the main support for the bill. Since the House was con-
trolled by the Republicans, however, the bill could not have passed without
them. The same pattern emerged in the Senate, where eight Republicans
voted for the bill, thirteen against, and thirteen were reported absent. The
Republican western delegation (California and Nevada) was joined by the
four senators from Wisconsin and Colorado, Eugene Hale from Maine, and
Warner Miller from New York. Out of 37 Republicans, only 13 voted against
the bill. A thorough analysis of the vote shows that 9 senators declared their
pairing with absentees, which would have brought the final vote to 38 in favor of the bill and 24 against: 30 Democrats and 8 Republicans in favor of it,

and 22 Republicans, 1 Democrat, and 1 Independent opposing it.[43] On the basis of this enlarged figure, it is clear that more Republican senators were opposed to the bill than would seem from a superficial reading of the yeas and nays. Indeed, almost 60 percent of the Republican senators opposed the bill. Yet this tabulation of the Republican vote should not be interpreted to mean a majority took a principled opposition to the bill. In the course of the debates, most Republicans had expressed their objection to three stringent measures in the bill—the duration of restriction, the scope of the bill extending the ban on *all* laborers, and the prohibition of naturalization.

When President Arthur received the bill, he was in the same dilemma as his predecessor. Several organs of public opinion and Congress had endorsed a bill that would jeopardize America's relations with China.[44] Like Hayes's veto message, the one dispatched by Arthur to the Senate was extremely diplomatic.[45] In short, the president stated that the bill was a breach of the national faith. Neither the United States nor China had ever contemplated the passage of a twenty-year prohibition of immigration. The bill contained no provision for a transit across the United States of Chinese subjects residing in foreign countries, and the system of registration and passports was undemocratic and hostile to the spirit of American institutions. Having presented his objections, Arthur concurred with Congress that Chinese immigration endangered good order throughout the country. Both good faith and good policy, he agreed, required Congress to "suspend" the immigration of Chinese laborers. His hope was that Congress would modify the unreasonable features of the bill to meet the expectations of the people of the United States without coming in conflict with the rights of Chinese subjects and with American interests. Pointing to the contribution of the Chinese to the economy of the Pacific slope, Arthur stressed that Chinese labor had benefited both the capitalist and the laborer of Caucasian origin. There might come a time, he cautioned, when other sections of the country might use "that species of labor" without injury to white American laborers. He begged congressmen to remember that, if it should pass, the bill would result in driving the trade and commerce of all Oriental nations into friendlier hands. To conclude, Arthur opined that the wisest policy for the moment was to make a shorter experiment, with a view toward maintaining permanently only such features as time and experience might commend. Significantly, Arthur did not object to the broad definition of the term *laborer* and the ban on naturalization.[46]

The veto came near the end of the congressional session. The vote on passing the bill over the veto failed. Four exclusion bills were hurriedly introduced into the House and referred to the Committee on Education and Labor. House Resolution 5804 was well received. The bill differed from Senate Resolution 71 in its reduction of the suspension to ten years. It also substituted the word *certificate* for *passport* in an effort to obviate President Arthur's objections. Like the first bill, however, it denied the Chinese the right to become naturalized citizens, and it defined laborers in a broad sense as both skilled and unskilled.[47]

The debate that followed was brief and extremely disorderly, with many members shouting for recognition and rising to "parliamentary inquiries" and "points of order" and the Speaker of the House losing control. Thirty minutes were set aside for debate, equally divided between the friends and opponents of the bill. Albert S. Willis (Democrat from Kentucky), a member of the committee that had introduced the bill, spoke first. He announced that, although he was in favor of a longer suspension (fifteen years) and stricter enforcement measures, he would vote *for* the new bill. The problem was that he had required recognition from the Speaker as an *opponent* of the bill. Under the rule, Speaker J. Warren Keifer (Republican from Ohio)) decided that Willis had spoken for the opponents of the bill, and he proceeded to give the floor to Representative Page from California as the spokesperson for the supporters of the bill. For nearly an hour after that, some representatives attempted to prevent the Speaker from recognizing Page. Keifer held his own, reminding them that when he called for representatives seeking recognition for the purpose of opposing the bill, *only* Willis answered his call. When order was finally restored, Page yielded most of his time to John A. Kasson (Republican from Iowa). Kasson had voted against the first version of the bill, because of treaty obligations and commerce rights and because he believed that a twenty-year suspension would be detrimental to agricultural interests in the West. Now that the new bill proposed a "reasonable" time suspension, he supported it fully. The Republican party, he declaimed, was the party of liberty, justice, and hospitality to all the oppressed nationalities of the earth. Why then did he and other Republicans support restriction? They did so only for the sake of "a just trial" of the Chinese question. What was more, Kasson did not believe that the new bill went even "one hair's breadth" beyond the Republican principles of equality and justice.[48]

The vote for the bill demonstrated that the majority of the Republicans had no qualms about supporting a bill, the effect of which was to initiate a racially based immigration policy. The bill was quickly passed by a large majority (201 in favor, 37 against, and 53 not voting), an indication of the bipartisan support for Chinese exclusion. While the western and southern representatives voted unanimously for the bill, it was obvious that easterners and midwesterners who opposed the bill were in the minority. Together with the 7 westerners and 82 southerners, 53 representatives from the eastern states and 59 midwesterners voted for the measure. Only 24 easterners and 13 midwesterners voted against it. The Republicans approved the bill, 88 to 34 (with 24 not voting), the Democrats, 102 to 3 (with 28 not voting), and all other parties, 11 to 0.[49]

In the Senate, the debate on the bill turned into a political harangue. An outraged John T. Morgan (Democrat from Alabama) expatiated on the fact that two presidents had "thwarted and checked and destroyed the will of the American people." Furthermore, Arthur's veto message contained, in his opinion, a veiled threat to the southern states. In his speeches and letter of acceptance, Morgan recalled, the president had made loud professions of his friendship with the Negro race and his disaffection with the Chinese. Yet his veto message praised Chinese industry in California and reported that the Chinese could be employed in other regions, where they would not come into competition with Caucasian Americans. Given the anti-Chinese sentiment in most of the country, Morgan was convinced that the president meant the South. If not with Caucasians, Morgan inferred, the Chinese would have to compete with African Americans. Here, then, was a Republican president, a professed "negrophilist," who proposed to flood the South with Chinese labor and reduce his "Negro friends" to poverty. The strife arising from the competition between the African American and the Chinese would cause the destruction of the last vestige of civilization in the South. No, Morgan averred, southerners would not allow the Chinese to be let loose in their society.[50]

The following day, Senator Hawley repeated his earlier complaint that an exclusion based purely on race was "unphilosophical, unjust, and undemocratic." The people the bill proposed to exclude from immigration and naturalization, he admonished, were neither the political thugs of the world nor universal criminals. They were a peaceable, industrious, and economical class of people. When the proposed statute was read a hundred years hence, Hawley predicted, it would be read side by side with the anti-Negro legislation of the antebellum period. The twelfth section of the bill, which provided for the deportation of unlawful immigrants and put control of deportation in the hands of federal officers, was, in his opinion, but a new version of the old fugitive slave law of 1850.[51] Following Hawley's efforts, critics of the bill suffered repeated attacks by western and southern Democrats, notably James T. Farley from California and George G. Vest from Missouri. The vacillation of the Republican majority during the debates on Reconstruction and its potential effect on the Chinese, the reaction to the North Adams affair, the Republican vote against the naturalization of the Chinese in 1870, and the commitment of the Republican party to Chinese restriction since 1876 were used by the Democrats to embarrass the Republicans opposing parts or all of the bill. The attempts to underplay the anti-Chinese attitudes of the people of Massachusetts and such Republican leaders as Henry Wilson and Benjamin F. Butler in 1870 were easily dismissed by Vest, who pointed to the inclusion of extreme anti-Chinese planks in the platform of the Massachusetts Republican party at the 1870 convention. For Vest, however, this Sinophobic reaction to North Adams also proved the power of race to inflame the blood of every American, irrespective of political affiliation.[52]

The Senate passed the bill on April 28, 1882. Thirty-two senators voted in favor of the bill, 15 voted against it, and 29 were reported absent. As expected, the western and southern contingents voted unanimously for the bill. Miller from California and Jones from Nevada were joined, as in the earlier vote, by 7 Republicans from the Midwest and the East. Out of 38 Republicans, 15 voted against the bill. Nine senators declared their pairing with absentees, which would have brought the final vote to 41 in favor of the bill and 24 against—30 Democrats, 10 Republicans, and 1 Independent in favor of the bill, and 24 Republicans opposing it.[53]

Here again, the opposition to the bill of a little more than three-fifths of the Republican senators was due to their objection to some particular provisions of the bill (notably the ban on naturalization and the exclusion of both skilled and unskilled laborers), which they regarded as extremely harsh and unjust. Except for a handful of principled congressmen, the majority of the Republicans agreed with Democrats that Chinese immigration ought to be restricted. The vote on the exclusion bill shows that the bill went further than most Republicans desired. However, for the last sixteen years, the Republican majority had created the conditions for the passage of such an extreme bill. By wrangling among themselves over the soundness of extending their pro–African American policy to the Chinese, Republicans paved the way for the codification of racism in immigration policy. As Senator Hawley correctly pointed out in the final debate on the exclusion bill, it was too late to object to the harshness of the proposed bill. "What is the use of arguing the question at all?" he asked fellow Republicans. "If we have made up our minds to put this, in the middle of the nineteenth-century, on the statute-books of our country," he lamented, "let us do it in silence and in mourning."[54]

From 1866 onward, the Republican majority policy on the Chinese question had exposed the crack in its professed commitment to equal rights for all. In the first major national debate over the Chinese question in 1870, the Democrats had remained singularly silent, while some Republicans had denied or qualified the notion that their party adhered to total egalitarianism. By 1879, the Democrats had gained the necessary confidence to capitalize on the Republican retreat from Reconstruction policy. On March 6, 1882, Senator George of Mississippi was thus satisfied that, for the first time since the era of sectional strife, the subject of race relations could be discussed in "a calm and philosophical spirit."[55] If the problem of the Chinese race and its solution by exclusion failed to rekindle old sectional animosities, he and other southerners maintained, then the question of *all inferior races,* in and out of America, should be treated with the same detachment. Southern congress-men's confidence in the final round of the debates on exclusion in 1882 was justified. The majority of the Republicans not only failed to rebut their rac-ist invectives but also exposed their own racial prejudices. Above all, Repub-licans failed to denounce the southerners' statement that race relations had ceased to be a partisan or sectional issue. Hence, Senator Morgan of Alabama could say, without fear of being censured, that every congressman and the president would concur that the absolute moral and social necessity in 1865 should have been to expel the African American; the problem was that nei-ther branch of government had the power to do so then.[56] Finally, the Re-publican majority did not react to southerners' anticipation of the return of white supremacy in the South.[57]

House Resolution 5804 was sent to President Arthur, who signed it into law three days later, on May 6, 1882. Most congressmen and newspaper edi-tors had no doubt that the president would sign the bill. Although the law of 1882 contained some provisions that the president had held objectionable, Congress had met his most important objection. By reducing the suspension from twenty to ten years, it had acceded to his call for a reasonable suspen-sion of Chinese immigration—"a shorter experiment," as he called it.[58]

Conclusion

> [The Chinese Exclusion Bill] changes and revolutionizes the
> traditions and principles of this country. . . . I say to this country,
> that we know not when the next wall will be erected, nor where its
> foundations will be laid. . . . It is the first break in the levee. . . . I
> would deem the new country we will have after this bill becomes
> law as changed from the old country we have to-day as our country
> would have been changed if the Rebellion of 1861 had succeeded.
>
> —Representative Ezra B. Taylor, *Congressional Record*,
>   March 16, 1882

NOTWITHSTANDING the use of such terms as *short experiment* or *suspension* and the euphemistic title of the law—*An Act to Execute Certain Treaty Stipulations relating to Chinese*—the general perception of the law of 1882 was that it was the "Chinese Exclusion Law."[1] This first Chinese Exclusion Act reflected the extent to which racial politics had regained respectability in the national political discourse. The exclusion of the Chinese was intended to bar a "non-assimilating race" more than a "competitive coolie race." While racist thought legitimized the Chinese Exclusion Act, the ban on Chinese labor immigration would be used to sanction further racism in *all* matters related to race and even ethnic relations in the United States. By 1882, racial formation in America had developed into a complex process, involving the Negroization of the Chinese and the Asianization of African Americans.

During the congressional debates over anti-Chinese bills (1879–82), many revealing developments unfolded in the situation of African Americans. On January 16, 1879, two days after Congress began to consider the fifteen passenger bill, Senator William Windom (Republican from Minnesota) introduced a resolution for the appointment of a commission to examine the practicability of the partial migration of southern blacks to various states and territories. Such migration, he suggested, would concern only those blacks who could not exercise their right of suffrage. Fourteen years after the war, he lamented, Reconstruction enactments had failed to secure the rights of the freed persons in the southern districts where the black population was in the majority. Windom was careful, however, to indicate that he favored the migration of only a quarter of a million or less. Besides, only territories and states that expressed the desire to receive black migrants would be considered. Some regions, he suggested, seemed not only particularly adapted to the "nature and wants" of the black population but also capable of welcoming them warmly and respecting their rights: Arizona, New Mexico, and the Indian Territory.[2] Following the objection of Senator Eli Saulsbury (Democrat from Delaware) that the resolution contained an unfounded accusation against certain southern states, Windom refrained from pressing his resolution further.[3]

While black migration from the South remained a major staple in the racist propaganda of the postbellum North, the number of southern blacks who moved north during Reconstruction remained small. In general, the formerly

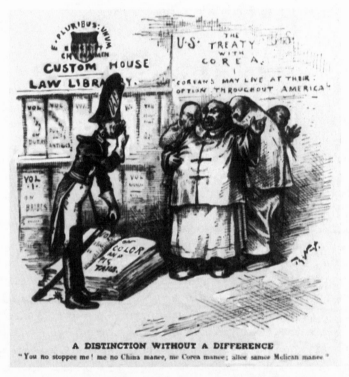

A DISTINCTION WITHOUT A DIFFERENCE
" You no stoppee me ! me no China manee, me Corea manee ; allee samee Melican manee "

The racist cast of the Chinese Exclusion Act is reflected in this cartoon, which anticipates the broadening of the Chinese exclusion movement into an Asian exclusion movement. (Source: *Harper's Weekly,* August 19, 1882, 527. Courtesy of the Library of Congress)

enslaved African Americans showed very little inclination to seek their fortunes in the North. What they desired most was land of their own to cultivate and the opportunity to obtain an education. However, as Nell Irvin Painter has noted, when the Republicans decided not to confiscate plantations and redistribute land among the freed persons, they effectively foreordained an "unfinished revolution."[4] Reconstruction did not bring about significant changes in the economic status of southern blacks. By the late 1870s, most were still working the white man's land, with the white man's plow drawn by the white man's mule.[5] Moreover, African Americans throughout the country, but especially in the South, were victims of prejudice, discrimination, segregation, and sometimes violence. An increasing number of discontented blacks began advocating voluntary colonization

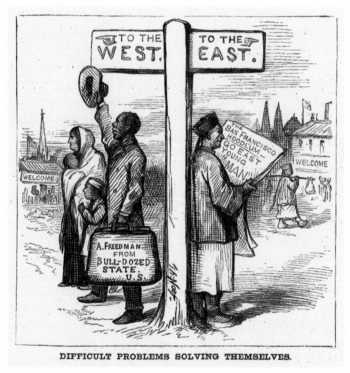

DIFFICULT PROBLEMS SOLVING THEMSELVES.

This illustration shows not only the conflation of the Chinese question and the Negro problem in 1879 but also the implications of the racialization of the Chinese question in the postbellum period for the handling of the "Negro problem." (Source: *Harper's Weekly,* March 29, 1879, 256)

overseas. After failing to obtain federal assistance for emigration to Liberia, some black leaders began to turn their attention to domestic migration. In the spring of 1879, a few weeks after Senator Windom proposed his resolution, a land rush to Kansas began, involving ten to forty thousand African Americans, mostly from the lower Mississippi valley states of Louisiana and Mississippi but also from states further east, including Alabama, Georgia, and the Carolinas.[6] Led by two charismatic leaders, Benjamin "Pap" Singleton and Henry Adams, the so-called Exodusters proved that African Americans did not resign themselves to economic exploitation and white political domination. Although Kansas was no Canaan, the Exodusters fared better there, economically and politically, than in the South. Racial prejudice was, however, prevalent there as well. Reports of white violence, peonage, abuse of black women, inadequate facilities, and political intimidation abounded. Labor conflict between white Kansans and Exodusters was frequent. Interestingly, the *New Orleans Times* expressed its sympathy for white laborers in Kansas, condemning black migrants for underbidding them and "pushing in like the Chinese."[7]

The Kansas exodus was the first significant post–Civil War out-migration of black southerners. It attracted much attention on the part of northerners and southerners alike. Southern white reaction was one of mixed emotions: puzzlement, bitterness against the "ungrateful" migrants, resentment especially toward the young Negro generation, a "good riddance" attitude, and lamentations about the flight of labor. Meanwhile, blacks held conventions in which they discussed the progress of the migrants, passed resolutions favoring relocation away from the South, and asked for federal assistance to carry it out. Some whites reacted to this endorsement by warning potential migrants that Kansas offered no real economic opportunities. Above all, a Louisiana paper affirmed, northern and western whites had incurable antipathy toward nonwhites. A Mississippi weekly went further, stating that the Sinophobic campaign and its war cry, "The Chinese must go!" should teach blacks a good lesson. That slogan, the paper predicted, would apply to blacks once they left their southern homes and attempted to settle in the North.[8] Anticipating a labor shortage, a few southerners advocated using Chinese workers as a substitute labor force.[9] This proposed scheme was soon condemned as an attempt to import, as one newspaper put it, "a race vastly more alien than the Negro was, even in his aboriginal barbarism."[10]

In the North, the Exodusters had the sympathy and support of old-time abolitionists.[11] Many congressmen, however, were circumspect. In December 1879, Senator Daniel W. Voorhees (Democrat from Indiana) presented a resolution for the appointment of a committee to investigate the cause of the migration of a few hundred blacks from North Carolina to his state. In the course of the debate, his resolution was enlarged to embrace the exodus of all African Americans from the South. Voorhees's purpose, as he stated it, was to ascertain whether Negroes were driven from their southern homes because of the injustice and cruelty of the whites or because of a conspiracy to disturb the peace and tranquility of the nation. Disclaiming any ill-will toward blacks, he averred that Indiana was a liberal state open to all, "black, white and red," provided they came "in the natural and legitimate order of things." Using a significant analogy, he observed that Indianians, however, did "no more want this population [freed persons] colonized upon [them] in large squads, battalions, regiments, divisions, and corps than the people of California want the Chinese landed upon them through organized societies of emigration."[12]

Senator Windom seized the opportunity of Voorhees's motion to pursue his earlier resolution to investigate means of promoting partial black migration. The destinations that he offered for the emigrants were now limited to the *territories*. Windom's amendment was rejected by a vote of 18 to 25, with 33 reported absent. The debate over Voorhees's resolution was not over yet. Senator George G. Vest (Democrat from Missouri) proposed solving the race problem in the South by sending blacks to the Indian Territory. A portion of that territory, he stressed, had been set aside for freed blacks at the time that the treaties were made. Having inquired of the Department of Interior whether that land was still available, Vest was satisfied that this land was awaiting them. He went on to ask, "Why then were Negroes carried to the northern states?" Why should Indiana, a state unsuited to their "peculiar idiosyncrasies," be selected for their resettlement, when the government had provided a place elsewhere specifically for them?[13] Interestingly, while touring the country in 1878, Representative Charles M. Shelley (Democrat from Alabama) had suggested that the Chinese who refused to leave the United States should be put on reservations.[14]

In 1880, the senatorial investigation committee issued a 1,700-page report about the causes for southern black out-migration. The majority report concluded that conditions in the South were better than expected and that the rights of African Americans were not being denied. Besides validating the idea of a Republican/black conspiracy, the report expressed its satisfaction at the short-lived migrations of the last months and anticipated no such migration as the Kansas exodus in the near future. The minority report, however, pointed to the economic and political plight of southern blacks and the abridgment of their rights.[15] Congress opted to cement the ebbing away from Reconstruction by simply ignoring the minority report and refusing to legislate further to protect the rights of African Americans. Three years later, the Supreme Court went one step further when it partially invalidated the last Reconstruction measure. In the *Civil Rights Cases* (1883), the Court held that the public accommodations sections of the Civil Rights Act of 1875 were unconstitutional. Justice Joseph Bradley stated in his ruling that the special conditions created by slavery in American society no longer existed. Acts of discrimination against African Americans could no longer be traced to slavery. The role of the federal government in the protection of black rights was thus purely secondary and corrective.[16]

As Loren Miller has argued, this Court decision was more than a simple abrogation of a law that only prohibited discrimination against blacks in places of public accommodation. It took a long step backward by implicitly holding that the Constitution tolerated and protected racial distinctions among citizens.[17] While the Court did not deny the reality and pervasiveness of racial discrimination, its ruling meant that Congress lacked the power to prohibit racial discrimination and that the states could regain control of civil rights. Justice John Marshall Harlan, the sole dissenter in the case, averred that "the one underlying purpose of congressional [Reconstruction] legislation [had] been to enable the black race to take the rank of mere citizens." The Civil Rights Act was still necessary to secure African Americans the enjoyment of privileges belonging to all citizens under the law. "Today," he argued, "it is the colored race [African Americans] which is denied, by corporations and individuals . . . rights fundamental in their freedom and citizenship." At some future time, he anticipated, it might be "some other race that will fall under the ban."[18] Harlan's remark is interesting in view of the concurrent treatment of Chinese immigrants. Justice Harlan must have been aware of the fate of Chinese immigrants. The racialization of American immigration policy since the 1882 Chinese Exclusion Act indicated that the Chinese had already fallen "under the ban." However, Justice Harlan was concerned about the abridgment of the rights of *citizens* rather than aliens. Besides this, despite the liberal stance of his extensive dissent in this and other cases, Harlan had no sympathy or respect for the Chinese.[19]

The decision in the *Civil Rights Cases* is often considered to be a landmark in Reconstruction history for its invalidation of parts of the Civil Rights Act of 1875 and, by the same token, its sapping of the Fourteenth Amendment's broad scope. However, this critical retreat of the judicial branch had a precedent in the courts' handling of the Chinese question. Time and again, in the 1870s, Chinese litigants had successfully used the Enforcement Act of 1870 and the Fourteenth Amendment (as well as the Burlingame Treaty) to vindicate their rights. By 1879, however, U.S. circuit courts in California had established that, while they would still use Reconstruction measures to strike out *state* discriminatory legislation against the Chinese, they would acquiesce to any such statute emanating from the federal government. It is significant that the Page Act and the Chinese Exclusion Act were passed after court decisions had invalidated similar measures passed by the state of California because of their unconstitutionality and blatant discriminatory nature. By the early 1880s, then, national politics reflected the resurgence of old and deep-seated racial animosities. In the case of the Chinese aliens, it culminated in an exclusion act. In the case of African Americans, the hopes of southern congressmen that Chinese exclusion would be a catalyst for a reconsideration of the relation of the black race to the white race materialized one year later in the *Civil Rights Cases.* These two decisions gave legitimacy to not only the southern clamor for a return to home rule but also the call for racial homogeneity and white supremacy at the national level. As the *Nation* put it, if nothing else, the unanimous approval of these decisions revealed that the extravagant expectations aroused by the Civil War had died out.[20]

While the Chinese Exclusion Act signified there were two legal categories of aliens—white and Asian, separate and unequal[21]—the *Civil Rights Cases* implied there were two categories of citizens—white and black, with the former enjoying more rights than the latter. The immediate consequence of this racial order was that racial discrimination increased by leaps and bounds. Racial disdain was manifest in writings questioning black suffrage, calling for its abolition and even the repeal of the Fifteenth Amendment.[22] Negro-baiting and lynching became increasingly virulent, pervasive, and barbarous. With the removal of the federal government's oversight, the drive to reinstitute white dominance was given great impetus. The most significant catalyst in this process was the disfranchisement of blacks in the South through legal means and physical intimidation. Once that was accomplished, the path was cleared for the enactment of the entire array of Jim Crow measures designed to separate blacks and whites in almost all areas of social life. In 1896, the Supreme Court decision in *Plessy v. Ferguson* upheld the "separate but equal" doctrine. Racial segregation in the South was then securely in place. In the North, antebellum patterns of segregation and discrimination endured after the war.

Insofar as the Chinese were concerned, the Exclusion Act of 1882 marked the beginning of increasingly harsh legislation. An often neglected dimension of the act was its effect on Chinese female immigration. Only the wives of members of the exempt classes were granted the right to join their husbands in the United States. Between 1882 and 1904, additional Chinese exclusion acts were passed (see below for details). The effectiveness of these laws in limiting Chinese immigration and contributing to the decline of the Chinese American community is illustrated by the fact that only 35,676 Chinese immigrated to the United States during this twenty-two-year period. If the Chinese laborers had been allowed to bring in their wives during that period, the Chinese American community would have survived and expanded. The exclusion of the Chinese laborers' wives suggests that the goal of Chinese exclusion was the abatement of the Chinese presence in the United States over a generation.[23]

Besides barring Chinese laborers and their wives and imposing restrictions on the reentry of Chinese immigrants, the acts placed the Chinese residents in the United States outside the political and civil community and dealt with them as an alien group from a most favored nation yet ineligible for citizenship. As such, they could be treated differently from native white Americans and white aliens. The restriction on naturalization makes it impossible to accept at face value the economic and political arguments used to justify the Chinese Exclusion Act. The postbellum congressional debates reveal the extent to which racial prejudices permeated the treatment of Chinese immigrants. By 1882, the time for dissembling and convolutions was over; it was time to expressly forbid the immigration of Chinese laborers and the naturalization of all Chinese residents. From then on, Congress and the courts took a course of action that indicated they believed that their imposition of permanent alien status on Chinese immigrants had effectively prevented them from claiming all the safeguards of life, liberty, and property guaranteed by the Bill of Rights.

The passage of the ten-year exclusion bill in 1882 did not bring an end to anti-Chinese agitation. In its wake, a brutal season of anti-Chinese activity and violence unparalleled in American history began.[24] The following years saw not only the adoption of discriminatory local and federal laws but also instances of vicious mob actions. The most spectacular anti-Chinese outbreak took place at Rock Springs, Wyoming, in the summer of 1885, when a mob of white citizens attacked the local Chinese community, burning and destroying homes and attacking Chinese miners. When the race riot subsided, twenty-eight Chinese were dead, fifteen were seriously injured, and many others had been driven from their homes. Paralleling these mob actions, Congress carried out a program of legislative harassment and discrimination. In 1884, Congress passed a series of amendments to the 1882 act, in the hope of curbing its "loopholes." One amendment extended the provisions of the act to all Chinese, irrespective of their country of origin. The certificates of the exempt classes, which now included "merchants" and "travelers," were made more elaborate, and the word *merchant* was defined to exclude hucksters, peddlers, and fishermen. The certificates, which had to be verified by the U.S. diplomatic officer at the port of departure, were made the only evidence admissible for the right of reentry.

By late 1886, the Chinese government, of its own accord, had proposed prohibiting emigration to the United States and the return of laborers who had gone back to China, unless they had family and property in the United States. This proposition originated in the violent anti-Chinese outbreaks in the American West and the persistent demand for even stricter exclusion laws. China realized that American Sinophobes had actually become even more vehement. In exchange for a new treaty, the Chinese government asked that the United States take new steps to protect the Chinese lawfully residing in the United States. The negotiations were arduous and long. The United States unilaterally added amendments to tighten up the provisions of the treaty. Before the treaty was ratified, Congress passed an extremely harsh act in 1888 to amend the 1882 act. The Scott Act prohibited permanently the coming of Chinese laborers and made no allowance whatsoever for the return of laborers with property holdings or families. In 1892, the Geary Act was passed, specifying that all existing laws would continue for another ten years. All Chinese laborers in the United States had to secure certificates within one year, and if anyone was found without a certificate, the person was liable to deportation unless "one credible *white* witness" could testify that that person was a resident of the United States and had failed to register because of some "unavoidable" cause. Furthermore, any Chinese found in the United States illegally was liable to imprisonment at hard labor for up to a year before being deported. In a collective act of civil disobedience, the majority of the Chinese residents did not register. In May 1893, the Supreme Court ruled the Geary Act constitutional, and a bill was then passed to extend the period of registration for six months. That same year, an amendment to the 1892 act (known as the McCreery amendment) provided for the partial repeal of the racial limitation on the right to testify in deportations cases. To prove residency, a Chinese now needed "one credible witness *other than Chinese.*" In 1894, negotiations between China and the United States ended in a new treaty that provided for the exclusion of all Chinese laborers for ten years and a more lenient treatment of the exempt classes. In 1904, when China refused to renew the treaty of 1894, Congress again reenacted the old exclusion laws, this time, on an *indefinite basis.*[25]

Throughout this lengthy and increasingly implacable legislative assault on Chinese immigrants, American congressman and their constituents did not believe they were bound by treaties when it came to the Chinese. The standard practice of renegotiating unilaterally and violating the treaties forced on Native Americans was transferred to the treaties entered into by the Chinese government under duress, by virtue of American dominance. The Chinese, in both China and the United States, denounced and vigorously fought these draconian laws.[26] However, there was nothing much they could do to reverse the exclusionist and expulsionist trends. The courts, to which the Chinese often appealed to challenge the adverse local and federal laws, provided the legal basis for their oppression by articulating the notion that the Chinese residing in the United States did so as a "matter of permission or indulgence" rather than a matter of right. Such dispensation was granted to them not by treaties, because treaties were on no higher ground than federal laws; rather, it was granted by Congress and could thus be revoked by this body. The Scott Act's denial of their right to leave the United States and return was therefore held constitutional. It is significant that the effect of this act was to make it impossible for any Chinese laborer then in the United States to visit China and return to the United States.

The immigration decisions of the federal courts are striking because they endorsed the right of Congress to exclude not only new immigrants but also Chinese residents in the United States if they left the country. Such disregard of the right of Chinese legal immigrants to move freely between the United States and their native land was made possible because of their permanent alien status. Time and again, in legal cases brought by the Chinese to test the constitutionality of the federal exclusion acts, justices speciously insisted that alien Chinese had never been recognized as citizens of the United States or authorized to become such under the naturalization laws.[27] This argument is reminiscent of the reasoning in the *Dred Scott* (1857) decision about blacks' ineligibility for citizenship. While Chief Justice Taney had claimed that African Americans had never been and could never be U.S. citizens, Justice Benjamin R. Curtis, in his extensive dissent, evidenced that blacks in the early history of the Republic had been voters and hence citizens. Similarly, not everyone agreed with the opinion that the Chinese had never been constituent members of the nation. In *In re Rodriguez* (1897), a federal court in Texas held that a "pure-blooded Mexican" who had been excluded from naturalization because of his color should be admitted.[28] The court based part of its argument on the first case sanctioning the racial prerequisite to naturalization (*In re Ah Yup*) and the 1882 Chinese Exclusion Act. Until 1882 and despite the opinion of the federal court in *Ah Yup*, the Texas court stated, the term *free white persons* could not be interpreted as expressly withholding the right of naturalization from the Chinese. If the Chinese had been denied such right under laws existing when *Ah Yup* was decided, the Texas court asked, why did Congress enact the naturalization prohibition in the Chinese Exclusion Act? While the court affirmed that up until 1882, the Chinese had had the legal right to obtain naturalization, it did not go further and did not question the denial of naturalization in the 1882 act; nor did it argue that because the Chinese had been constituent members of the nation prior to the act, they should not have been denied the right to claim citizenship.

The consequence of permanent alien status was, of course, extreme vulnerability. The eloquent and articulate arguments of the Chinese community and the Chinese government that the exclusion laws and legal decisions violated every principle of justice, equity, and fair dealing between two friendly powers won no hearing. The most the Chinese could hope for in their litigation struggles was some mitigation in the severity of the exclusion laws and the protection of the rights of their children who were born in the United States and thus were citizens.[29] There were, however, instances when citizenship failed to protect Chinese Americans. This was the case of American-born women who married noncitizens. In 1907, Congress recognized and mandated a practice under which many such women were stripped of their U.S. citizenship. Under pressure, Congress partially repealed the act in 1922. Its provision was now indicative of the interplay between gender and racial restrictions in that it required the expatriation of any American woman married to a foreigner racially barred from citizenship. This act remained in force until 1931, when Congress repealed it.[30] The loss of birthright citizenship was particularly harsh for American women of Chinese and, more generally, Asian ancestry because their race made them ineligible to regain citizenship through naturalization. Another instance of the failure of citizenship to protect the rights of Chinese American citizens was in the decision rendered by the U.S. Supreme Court regarding the rights of citizens of Chinese ancestry in *U.S. v. Ju Toy* (1905), the year after the enactment of indefinite Chinese exclusion. This decision completed the cycle of judicial oppression of the Chinese by depriving a citizen, Ju Toy, of the protection that the Constitution guarantees all citizens. Returning to the United States after a temporary absence, Ju Toy was denied admission on the grounds of the Chinese exclusion acts. The highest court of the land affirmed the constitutionality of the order of exclusion against Ju Toy. In his dissent, Justice David J. Brewer stated that exclusion laws were applicable to aliens and that the only reason behind the denial of due process of law was that Ju Toy belonged to "an obnoxious race." The effect of this decision has yet to be assessed by historians.[31] The same line of racial reasoning would be used thirty-eight years later, when not even citizenship would protect Japanese Americans from being rounded up and sent to concentration camps.

This "flagitious and ferocious legislation" buttressed by the courts, the forceful eviction of Chinese residents from many areas in the West, and other

forms of violence and anti-Chinese local statutes reflected that the turn of
the century was the "nadir" of not only the black odyssey in America but also
that of the Chinese.[32] Notwithstanding the trickling of Asian immigration
at the turn of the century, a plethora of extravagant writings projected images of America being taken over by a "flood of Asiatics." By the early 1890s,
the Chinese question was already subsumed within the "Mongolian question" or "yellow peril" theme. All the economic, cultural, political, and biological arguments used in the earlier anti-Chinese campaigns were extended to other Asian immigrants as they entered the United States. By 1920, one

"The Wedding of the Chinee and the Coon," music by Bob
Cole and words by Billy Johnson, was released in 1907, three
years after the passage of the last exclusion act, banning Chinese immigration indefinitely. The song marked the culmination of the conflation of African Americans and Chinese immigrants. (Courtesy of Brown University Library)

of the most notorious advocates of white supremacy, Lothrop L. Stoddard, expressed his opinion that Asiatic migration was "a universal peril, menacing every part of the white world." He warned that "unless the [white man] erected and maintained barriers, he would perish."[33] In 1920, when he made that ominous prediction, there were only 135,199 Asians in the United States.[34]

As Roger Daniels has argued, the Chinese exclusion acts constituted "the hinge on which all immigration policy turned."[35] Congress passed an act excluding all Asians (except for Japanese) in 1917, and it included a section in the Immigration Act of 1924 that implicitly excluded Japanese immigrants through a familiar catchphrase—"ineligible for citizenship."[36] Besides completing the exclusion cycle for Asian immigration to the United States, the 1924 act provided for the restriction of European immigration. An essential element in the campaign for the restriction of the "new immigrants" (eastern and southern Europeans) at the turn of the century was their racialization. While the Chinese had been Negroized, the new immigrants were "Asianized." This conflation of Asians and new immigrants reflected the relatively narrow gap, as some nativists saw it, between these two groups. For some labor leaders and their rank and file and for some politicians, judges, and scholars, it was an easy step to claim that, like the Chinese, not only the Japanese, East Asians, Koreans, and Filipinos but also European immigrants had been imported under contract. The "Asiatics" were not the only "social degenerates" liable to destroy American civilization and republican institutions; the inferior new immigrants were, too. Abetted by a new surge of racist theories involving the division of Europeans in a superior Nordic type and two inferior racial types (Alpine and Mediterranean), the Asianization of the new immigrants was conveyed in the habitual "imported labor," "degraded labor," or "degraded race/s" allegations but even more directly in the description of the new immigrants as "Continental Chinese."[37]

This being said, the conflation between Asian and European aliens had limits. Through the fluctuations of the complex and many-faceted processes of racial formation, public opinion on the "new immigration issue" drew a line between Asian and European immigrants. While European immigrants were subsumed under the category "immigration problem," Asians immigrants were relegated beyond the pale with the phrases "Chinese question," "Japanese question," and "Asiatic/Oriental problem." It is therefore not surprising that the processes of racialization for European immigrants were different from those affecting Asians and that racialization for Europeans did not have the same consequences as for Asian immigrants. It is significant that while blacks and Chinese (and all nonwhites) had been subjected to racial discrimination because of their color, European immigrants shared the color of the white American dominant group. Notwithstanding the division of Europeans into several "races," all European immigrants were thought to be and were accepted as *white* by the courts, the U.S. Census, unions, employers, and political parties and institutions. Unlike Asian immigrants, European immigrants were thought to have the capacity to assimilate. By not enacting an exclusion law for the new immigrants, American legislators not only paved the way for their subsequent de-racialization but also demonstrated in no uncertain terms the persistence of the old racist ideology that had shored up *white* dominance in the United States.[38] As Mae Ngai has shown, the Immigration Act of 1924 did more than rank European immigrants in a hierarchy of desirability; it codified the principle of racial exclusion of the peoples of all the nations of the Far East by incorporating it for the first time into general immigration law. It also codified the rule of racial ineligibility for citizenship for all Asians. Meanwhile, Europeans' eligibility for citizenship remained unchallenged. Besides relegating Asians to the status of permanent foreigners, the 1924 Immigration Act allowed only two hundred immigration slots for black Africans.[39]

"The memorable agitation of the '70s for Chinese exclusion," the white supremacist Madison Grant wrote in 1934, "is now only a historical event, but it was important as helping to lay the foundation for a wise immigration policy in the United States."[40] Not until the 1950s would the winds of change cause the U.S. government to look back at the anti-Asian movement and other foundational events and begin the slow and protracted revision of its racist policies, culminating in the mid-1960s in the overturning of decades of constitutional infringements on the rights of African Americans and Asian Americans. The struggle for the complete equality of these groups continues. Meanwhile, a growing international immigration has brought more colors upon the American loom, stirring much public controversy and an insurgent nativism reminiscent of the anti-Asian movements.

Notes

Introduction

1. See Daniels's review of the historiography in "Westerners from the East," 375; and Daniels, *Asian America,* 3–7.

2. See, for example, Daniels and Kitano, *American Racism;* Lyman, *The Asian in North America;* L. Cohen, *Chinese in the Post–Civil War South;* Takaki, *Strangers from a Different Shore;* Chan, *This Bittersweet Soil;* and Tchen, *New York before Chinatown.*

3. Daniels, *Asian America,* 6; Chan, "European and Asian Immigration"; Ng, "The Sojourner."

4. See also Cole and Chin, "Emerging from the Margins."

5. Given the comparative scope of this study, the treatment of the organizational and associational efforts of the Chinese (and African Americans) in their fights against discrimination had to be limited. On Chinese efforts, see McClain, *In Search of Equality;* and Cole and Chin, "Emerging from the Margins."

6. See the positive review of Coolidge's book in the *Nation,* Dec. 1909, 574. Coolidge's book was withdrawn from sale a few days after publication for several weeks because it contained too much criticism of the policy of Chinese exclusion and the way exclusion laws were enforced.

7. Coolidge, *Chinese Immigration,* 82, 180, 233, 335–75.

8. Ibid., 29, 40, 253, 267.

9. Ibid., 182 (second quote), 233 (first quote).

10. See, for example, Eaves, *A History of California Labor Legislation,* 6, 105–96; Perlman, *A History of Trade Unionism,* 62; and Cross, *A History of the Labor Movement in California,* 73–129.

11. Sandmeyer, *The Anti-Chinese Movement in California,* 41, 58, 78, 82, 97.

12. Ibid., 22–24 (quote on 22).

13. Ibid., 109–10.

14. Chiu, *Chinese Labor in California,* xi (first quote), xii (second quote), 15, 30, 52, 102, 137.

15. Saxton, *The Indispensable Enemy*, 1, 2, 19; see also Lyman, *Chinese Americans*.

16. S. Miller, *The Unwelcome Immigrant*, 201.

17. Almaguer, *Racial Fault Lines*, 6–7.

18. Ibid., 38–41.

19. On this historiographical deficiency, see de Graaf, "Recognition, Racism, and Reflections."

20. The sociologists Michael Omi and Howard Winant use the expression *racial formation* to describe "the process by which social, economic, and political forces determine the content and importance of racial categories, and by which they are in turn shaped by racial meanings." Omi and Winant, *Racial Formation*, 61.

21. "John Chinaman—What Shall We Do with Him?" *New York Times*, June 29, 1869.

22. The term *racialization* is from Omi and Winant, *Racial Formation*, 64.

23. The term *Negroization* is from Caldwell, "The Negroization of the Chinese." On the use of the term, see also Haney López,, *White by Law*, 51–52. At times, the Chinese were "Indianized." See, for example, *People v. Hall*, 4 Cal. 399, 400–402 (1854).

24. A variation of the coolie theme was recently resurrected in Gyory's *Closing the Gate*. In this polemical study, Gyory challenged the conventional wisdom about the connection between the labor and anti-Chinese movements by arguing that American workers opposed not the *immigration* of Chinese laborers but rather their *importation*. Like earlier historians who took for granted the "cheap labor" charge leveled against the Chinese, however, Gyory did not examine critically the historical significance of the "imported labor" allegation. Nor did he attempt to verify its validity. For a thorough critique of Gyory's argument on the attitudes of the American working class toward the Chinese, see Lyman, "The 'Chinese Question' and American Labor Historians."

25. Benedict, "Preserving the Constitution."

26. On nativism in America, see Higham's classic account, *Strangers in the Land*. In this work, *nativism* refers to the third form of nativism in his classification—i.e., *racial nativism*, or mobilization for the defense of Anglo-Saxon/white American identity and supremacy.

27. Douglass, "The Composite Nation" (1869), 215–31.

Chapter 1: Racial Nativism in America until 1850

1. Naturalization Act of Mar. 26, 1790, *U.S. Statutes at Large* 1 (1845): 103, repealed and superseded by Act of Apr. 14, 1802, *U.S. Statutes at Large* 2 (1845): 153. The racial prerequisite remained in force until 1952. Immigration and Nationality Act of 1952, *U.S. Statutes at Large* 66 (1953): 239.

2. George Julian quoted in E. Foner, *Politics and Ideology*, 78.

3. Meier and Rudwick, *From Plantation to Ghetto*, 67–68.

4. Litwack, *North of Slavery*; Berwanger, *The Frontier against Slavery*; Voegeli, *Free but Not Equal*.

5. The compromise had three parts: Maine entered the Union as a free state, Missouri entered as a slave state, and, finally, slavery was "forever prohibited" in all the federal territories north and west of Missouri. *An Act to Authorize the People of the Missouri Territory to Form a Constitution and State Government* (Mar. 6, 1820), *U.S. Statutes at Large* 3 (1846): 545–48 (quote on 548).

6. Swisher, *History of the Supreme Court,* 379.

7. Ibid., 379–82 (Taney quoted on 380).

8. *Passenger Cases,* 48 U.S. (7 How.) 283, 333 (quote) (1849).

9. Ibid., 424, 426, 428–29.

10. He was alluding to *Groves v. Slaughter,* 40 U.S. (15 Pet.) 449 (1841); and *Prigg v. Pennsylvania,* 41 U.S. (16 Pet.) 539 (1842).

11. *Passenger Cases,* 48 U.S. (7 How.) 283, 492 (quotes) (1849).

12. Sullivan, "Annexation," 7.

13. P. Foner and Lewis, eds., *The Black Worker,* 70–109, 152–59, 165–79.

14. See, for example, Bonacich, "Abolition, the Extension of Slavery, and the Position of Free Blacks"; and Saxton, "Race and the House of Labor."

15. For an excellent discussion of working-class formation and the systematic development of its sense of "whiteness," see Roediger, *The Wages of Whiteness.*

16. Kerber, "Abolitionists and Amalgamators," 34–35; Runcie, "'Hunting the Nigs' in Philadelphia," 198–201.

17. Kerber, "Abolitionists and Amalgamators," 28–39 (quote on 32); Richards, *Gentlemen of Property and Standing,* 114–15.

18. Quoted in Runcie, "'Hunting the Nigs' in Philadelphia," 215.

19. Ibid., 210.

20. Act of Mar. 26, 1790, *U.S. Statutes at Large* 1 (1845): 103. This first statute required a two-year residence before naturalization. On March 3, 1813, the act was amended to require a five-year residence.

21. Van Dyne, *Citizenship of the United States,* 111.

22. Haas, *Conquests and Historical Identities,* 13–44, 204; Pitt, *The Decline of the Californios,* 1–25.

23. *Daily Alta California,* Jan. 25, Feb. 22, and Mar. 22, 1849.

24. Shaw, *Golden Dreams and Waking Realities,* 86.

25. *Californian* (San Francisco), Mar. 15, 1849; *San Francisco California Star,* Mar. 25, 1849.

26. Browne, *California Constitutional Convention,* 43–44.

27. Ibid., 44, 48–49, 61–76, 137–52, 331–40.

28. Ibid., 48.

29. Ibid., 48, 137 (second quote), 138, 152 (first quote), 332, 334–35.

30. Ibid., 143–44, 146–47, 151, 152, 332–33, 335.

31. Ibid., 49–50.

32. Ibid., 139 ("free men of color" and "expediency" quotes), 140, 141 ("free" and "liberal" quotes), 145–46, 149 ("simply because" quote), 150 ("Negro citizen" quote), 151.

33. Ibid., 330–38.

34. See especially Jones's, Lippitt's, and Botts's statements in ibid, 333–34, 336, 338, respectively.

35. Ibid., 340–41. The proceedings of the debates do not give the first vote on the measure. Ibid., 152.

36. State of California, *Journal of the Senate of the State of California* [hereafter *Journal of the Senate*], 1st sess. (1850), 38–39.

37. State of California, *Journal of the Assembly of the State of California* [hereafter *Journal of the Assembly*], 1st sess. (1850), 723, 729, 873, 1223, 1232; State of California, *Journal of*

the Senate, 1st sess. (1850), 337, 338, 347. Several months later, a similar bill met with the same fate. State of California, *Journal of the Assembly,* 2d sess. (1851), 1315, 1440.

38. Act of Apr. 16, 1850, ch. 99, §14, *California Statutes* (1850): 229, 230.

39. *Civil Practice Act of 1851,* ch. 5, §394, *California Statutes* (1851): 51, 114.

40. *An Act Regulating Marriages,* section 3, *California Statutes* (1850): 424.

41. Berwanger, "The 'Black Law' Question in Ante-Bellum California," 214; Thurman, "The Negro in California," 69; Swett, *History of the Public School System in California,* 205.

42. Bancroft, *History of California,* 2–3.

43. U.S. Census Office, *A Compendium of the Eleventh Census, 1890,* part 1, 472.

44. Loosley, *Foreign Born Population of California,* 5–7.

45. *Passenger Cases,* 48 U.S. (7 How.) 283 (1849).

46. California Constitution (1849), article 1, section 17.

47. Browne, *California Constitutional Convention,* 141, 150 (quotes).

48. Thomas J. Green, "Report on Mines and Foreign Miners," in State of California, *Journal of the Senate,* 1st sess. (1850), Appendix S, 493–97.

49. State of California, *Journal of the Assembly,* 1st sess. (1850), 805–11.

50. Act of Apr. 13, 1850, ch. 97, §1, *California Statutes* (1850): 221–22. By a vote of 22 to 2, the state assembly decided to petition Congress to bar from the mines all persons of foreign birth, including naturalized citizens. State of California, *Journal of the Assembly,* 1st sess. (1850), 803–11; State of California, *Journal of the Senate,* 1st sess. (1850), 1013–18.

51. *Daily Alta California,* July 26, 1849; *Sonora Herald,* July 27, 1850; Shinn, *Mining Camps,* 244; Browne, *California Constitutional Convention,* 140–41, 150–51.

52. *Daily Alta California,* May 28, 1850; *San Francisco Daily Picayune,* Aug. 14, 1850; *Daily Pacific News,* May 28, 1850; *Stockton Times,* May 25, May 30, and June 1, 1850.

53. In their initial interaction with white Americans, Australian and French miners were categorized as objectionable, despite their whiteness. See Aarim, "Chinese Immigrants," 73–78.

54. Browne, *California Constitutional Convention,* 61–74 (quote on 63).

55. Ibid., 62–74, 305–7; California Constitution (1849), article 2, section 1 (quote).

56. On the persistence of the racialization of Californios, see Peterson, *Manifest Destiny in the Mines;* and Almaguer, *Racial Fault Lines,* 51–65.

57. Royce, *California,* 363–64. *Greaser* is an abusive term for Spanish-speaking people, including "mestizos," persons of mixed Indian and Spanish background.

Chapter 2: The Beginning of the Negroization of the Chinese in California, 1850–53

1. Tinker, *A New System of Slavery;* Look Lai, *Indentured Labor.*

2. The first shipment of Chinese laborers under contract with foreigners was made from Amoy in a French vessel to the Isle of Bourbon (Réunion Island) in 1845. The first vessels taking Chinese to Cuba and Peru were in 1847 and 1849, respectively. Wang, *The Organization of Chinese Emigration,* 39–40. On the coolie trade, see ibid., 39–256; Campbell, *Chinese Coolie Emigration;* and Irick, *Ch'ing Policy toward the Coolie Trade.*

3. On the horrific treatment of Chinese emigrants in Cuba, see the Cuba Commission, *Report of the Commission Sent by China to Ascertain the Condition of Chinese Coolies in Cuba.*

4. Although some Chinese brought in a few contract laborers to California, they soon gave up the practice as unprofitable and ill-suited to the American environment. Zo, *Chinese Emigration into the United States,* 88–98.

5. Emigrants were loaned seventy dollars for their passage and were expected to return two hundred. Wang, *The Organization of Chinese Emigration,* 105; Daniels, *Not like Us,* 5.

6. Capron, *History of California,* 277.

7. Wang, *The Organization of Chinese Emigration,* 110–12; S. Wu, *One Hundred Years of Chinese in the United States and Canada,* 14–19; Hunt, *The Making of a Special Relationship,* 64–69.

8. Hoy, *The Chinese Six Companies.*

9. Lapp, *Blacks in Gold Rush California,* 78–81, 272.

10. State of California, *Journal of the Senate,* 3d sess. (1852), 15.

11. *Daily Alta California,* Mar. 6 and 8, 1852.

12. Nor did McDougal consider Native Americans as an option, although they had been a main source of labor prior to American annexation. Hurtado, "'Hardly a Farm House— A Kitchen without Them.'"

13. Browne, *California Constitutional Convention,* 142, 339.

14. S.B. 63, in State of California, *Journal of the Senate,* 3d sess. (1852), 168. See also *Daily Alta California,* Mar. 8, 1852.

15. Tingley's nativistic feelings reemerged in 1855 when he was nominated as a Know-Nothing candidate for the position of attorney general. He eventually became a campaign speaker for Abraham Lincoln in 1860. Davis, *History of Political Conventions in California,* 7, 8, 23, 43–44, 49, 126.

16. Philip A. Roach, "Minority Report of the Select Committee on S.B. 63 for an 'Act to Enforce Contracts and Obligations to Perform Work and Labor or Contracts for Foreign Laborers,'" in State of California, *Journal of the Senate,* 3d sess. (1852), Appendix, 667–75.

17. State of California, *Journal of the Senate,* 3d sess. (1852), 305–7.

18. California Legislature, Committee on Mines and Mining Interests, "Report," in State of California, *Journal of the Assembly,* 3d sess. (1852), Appendix, 829, 830 (quotes), 835.

19. Ibid., 829, 831, 834.

20. In 1836, Chancellor James Kent had argued that "it was a matter of doubt, whether under the provision [of the Naturalization Act of 1870], any of the tawny races of Asia [could] be admitted to citizenship." Kent, *Commentaries on American Law,* 39.

21. Shinn, *Mining Camps,* 244.

22. "Report of the Committee on the Governor's Special Message in regard to Asiatic Emigration," in State of California, *Journal of the Senate,* 3d sess. (1852), Appendix, 731–37.

23. "Governor Bigler's Special Message in Regard to Chinese Coolie Emigration," in State of California, *Journal of the Senate,* 3d sess. (1852), 373.

24. In this text, all Chinese immigration numbers are from Coolidge, *Chinese Immigration,* 498.

25. Canfield, *The Diary of a Forty-Niner,* 222–23 (entry for May 2, 1852, "getting to be" quote on 222), 232 (entry for May 16, 1852, all other quotes).

26. Act of May 4, 1852, ch. 37, *California Statutes* (1852): 84.

27. Pitt, *The Decline of the Californios,* 58–68.

28. Act of May 3, 1852, ch. 36, *California Statutes* (1852): 78, amended by Act of Apr. 2, 1853, ch. 51, *California Statutes* (1853): 71.

29. Coolidge, *Chinese Immigration,* 70–71, 431, 447. The act applied to passengers arriving in the ports of the state of California, not to immigrants who arrived in California using the overland routes. While the Chinese arrived by sea, a substantial number of European immigrants landed on the East Coast and traveled to California by land.

30. Quoted in Shaw, *Golden Dreams and Waking Realities,* 86.

31. Canfield, *The Diary of a Forty-Niner,* 223 (entry for May 2, 1852).

32. The letter was published in *Daily Alta California,* May 5, 1852. On Asing, see McClain, *In Search of Equality,* 11–12; and Jackson, *Gold Dust,* 291–92.

33. U.S. Census Office, *A Compendium of the Ninth Census, 1870,* vol. 1, 5.

34. *An Act Respecting Fugitive Slaves from Labor, and Slaves Brought To This State Prior to Her Admission into the Union,* ch. 33, *California Statutes* (1852): 67–69.

35. *In the Matter of Carter Perkins and Robert Perkins,* 2 Cal. 424, 438–59 (quotes on 438) (1852).

36. State of California, *Journal of the Assembly,* 3d sess. (1852), 159.

37. State of California, *Journal of the Senate,* 3d sess. (1852), 438; *Journal of the Assembly,* 3d sess. (1852), 703–4, 711.

38. California Legislature, Committee on Mines and Mining Interests, "Report on the Chinese Population," in State of California, *Journal of the Assembly,* 4th sess. (1853), Document No. 28, Appendix, 9.

39. Ibid., 5.

40. Act of Mar. 30, 1853, ch. 44, §6, *California Statutes* (1853): 62, 63; Act of Apr. 12, 1853, *California Statutes* (1853): 82, in C. Wu, *"Chink!"* 25–26.

41. California Legislature, "Report on the Chinese Population," in State of California, *Journal of the Assembly,* 4th sess. (1853), Document No. 28, Appendix, 7–10. On this early complaint by the Chinese leadership, see McClain, *In Search of Equality,* 13–16.

42. Quoted in Bennett, *Chinese Labor,* 18.

43. Speer, *China and California.* On the Reverend Speer and the Chinese, see Tseng, "Ministry at Arms' Length," 36–50.

44. On the attitudes of American mainline Protestant leaders toward the Chinese and the anti-Chinese movement, see Tseng, "Ministry at Arms' Length"; and Daniels, *Asian America,* 43, 51.

45. Speer, *China and California,* 4–10, 13 ("Asiatic multitudes" quote), 15 ("sub-worker" quote).

46. Ibid., 11, 15 ("Sons of Han/Ham" quotes), 16, 20 ("with a thousand" quote), 26 ("[God] has selected us" quote).

Chapter 3: *"The Copper of the Pacific" and "The Ebony of the Atlantic"*

1. *Daily Alta California,* Mar. 28, 1853.

2. Ibid., May 12, 1851, Feb. 17, 1852, and Mar., 28, 1853.

3. Ibid., May 21, June 4, June 15, and July 29, 1853.

4. Ibid., June 4, 1853.

5. Act of May 13, 1854, ch. 49, *California Statutes* (1854): 55.

6. California Congressional Resolution of May 13, 1854, *California Statutes* (1854): 230.

7. *People v. Hall,* 4 Cal. 399 (1854). On the case, see McClain, *In Search of Equality,* 20–23.

8. *People v. Hall,* 4 Cal. 399 ("[n]o black" quote), 403 ("domestic" and "a policy" quotes), 405 ("differing" quote) (1854).

9. Lai, "Remarks of the Chinese Merchants."

10. Lapp, *Blacks in Gold Rush California,* 197–98.

11. On the mining industry, see Rodman, *Mining Frontiers of the Far West.*

12. California Legislature, Assembly Select Committee on Foreign Miners, "Majority Report on Assembly Bills Nos. 206, 207, and 208," in State of California, *Journal of the Assembly,* 6th sess. (1855), Document No. 19, Appendix [hereafter "Majority Report," 1855], 5–8 (quote on 8); and California Legislature, Senate Select Committee, "Minority Report on Resolutions of Miner's Convention of Shasta County," in State of California, *Journal of the Senate,* 6th sess. (1855), Document No. 16, Appendix [hereafter "Minority Report," 1855], 3–7.

13. California Legislature, Assembly Select Committee on Foreign Miners, "Majority Report," 1855, 5, 6 (second quote), 8 (first quote). See also California Legislature, Senate Select Committee, "Minority Report," 1855, 3, 5–7.

14. See, for example, the statement of Representative Henry C. Murphy from New York in the *Congressional Globe,* 30th Cong., 1st sess., Appendix (May 16, 1848): 579–81; and State of Indiana, *Report of the Debates and Proceedings of the Convention for the Revision of the Constitution of the State of Indiana,* vol. 2, 1792.

15. California Legislature, Assembly Select Committee on Foreign Miners, "Majority Report," 1855, 7 (first quote); California Legislature, Senate Select Committee, "Minority Report," 1855, 4 (second quote).

16. State of California, *Annual Message of the Governor of California, Jan. 1, 1855.*

17. California Concurrent Resolution of May 13, 1854, *California Statutes* (1854): 230.

18. California Legislature, Assembly Select Committee on Foreign Miners, "Majority Report," 1855, 5 (quote), 6.

19. Ibid., 5.

20. Ibid., 7.

21. California Legislature, Senate Select Committee, "Minority Report," 1855, 4 (quote), 5–6, 7.

22. Act of Apr. 28, 1855, ch. 153, *California Statutes* (1855): 194.

23. Ibid.; *People v. Downer,* 7 Cal. 169 (1857).

24. Act of Apr. 30, 1855, ch. 174, *California Statutes* (1855): 216.

25. Tseng, "Ministry at Arms' Length," 75.

26. On Helper's racism, see Fredrickson, *The Arrogance of Race,* 28–53 (quote on 28).

27. Helper, *The Land of Gold;* Helper, *Dreadful California.*

28. Helper, *The Land of Gold,* 39, 47, 86, 115, 226 (first quote), 227 (second quote).

29. Helper, *Dreadful California,* 70–77 ("Celestials" and "xanthous" quotes on 70, "semibarbarians" on 75, "subordinate" on 77).

30. Helper, *The Land of Gold,* 96.

31. On Chinese stereotypes, see S. Miller, *The Unwelcome Immigrant.*

32. Horace Greeley, "Chinese Immigration to California," *New York Tribune,* Sept. 29, 1854.

33. California Legislature, Senate Committee on Mines and Mining Interests, "Minority Report," in State of California, *Journal of the Senate,* 7th sess. (1856), Appendix [hereafter "Minority Report," 1856], 3–6; California Legislature, Assembly Committee on Mines and Mining Interests, "Report," in State of California, *Journal of the Assembly,* 7th sess. (1856), Appendix [hereafter "Report," 1856], 3–16.

34. California Legislature, Senate Committee on Mines and Mining Interests, "Minority Report," 1856, 6.

35. California Legislature, Assembly Committee on Mines and Mining Interests, "Report," 1856, 7, 9 (quote), 11.

36. Ibid., 3–9 (quote on 7), 12, 14–15.

37. Ibid., 15.

38. Speer, *An Humble Plea.*

39. Ibid., 4–6, 12 (second quote), 13 (first quote), 33–35, 37–38.

40. Ibid., 32.

41. Act of Apr. 19, 1856, ch. 119, *California Statutes* (1856): 141.

42. On the American party at the national and local levels, see Anbinder, *Nativism and Slavery;* and Hurt, "The Rise and Fall of the 'Know Nothings,'" 16–49, 99–128.

43. From 1847 to 1854, German immigrants numbered 684,654 and Irish immigrants 853,484. *Congressional Globe,* 33d Cong., 2d sess. (Jan. 15, 1855): 95, (Dec. 18, 1854): 51.

44. Anbinder, *Nativism and Slavery,* ix.

45. Hurt, "The Rise and Fall of the 'Know Nothings,'" 33, 45–46.

46. Higham, *Strangers in the Land;* Anbinder, *Nativism and Slavery,* viii, 56–57. Even Hurt's study, "The Rise and Fall of the 'Know Nothings,'" points to the peculiarities of Californian nativism (38, 117–18).

47. Davis, *History of Political Conventions in California,* 42 (quotes); Hurt, "The Rise and Fall of the 'Know Nothings,'" 39, 44–45.

48. Pitt, *The Decline of the Californios,* 136. Anti-Californio planks included calls for the "speedy settlement of [American] land titles" and a "liberal and just legislation in favor [of settlers upon Spanish grants]." Davis, *History of Political Conventions in California,* 43 (second quote), 51 (first quote), 82.

49. Davis, *History of Political Conventions in California,* 60. Obviously, more research is needed on western nativism. The new studies should begin from the premise that nativism in California did not start in 1855 and that anti-Chinese sentiment is a form of nativism.

50. The whole Massachusetts delegation to the Thirty-fourth Congress, which included Representative Anson Burlingame, belonged to the American party.

51. *Congressional Globe,* 33d Cong., 2d sess., Appendix (Dec. 18, 1854): 52.

52. Ibid., (Jan. 15, 1855): 95.

53. E. Foner, *Free Soil,* 125–29.

54. Anbinder, *Nativism and Slavery,* 273–74.

55. E. Foner, *Free Soil,* 12, 29, 39, 56–59.

56. *New York Tribune,* Oct. 15, 1856.

57. Finkelman, "Rehearsal for Reconstruction," 4–5, 11–12.

58. State of California, *Journal of the Assembly,* 8th sess. (1857), 811, 823, 824.

59. State of California, *Journal of the Senate,* 8th sess. (1857), 285, 294, 336.

60. *Dred Scott v. Sandford,* 60 U.S. (19 How.) 393 (1857). On *Dred Scott,* see Swisher, *History of the Supreme Court,* 592–630; and Fehrenbacher, *Slavery, Law, and Politics.*

61. See Justice Benjamin R. Curtis's dissenting opinion that blacks had been constituent members of the nation in a number of states at the founding and that some states currently granted citizenship rights to their black residents. *Dred Scott v. Sandford,* 60 U.S. (19 How.) 393, 572–73 (1857).

62. Ibid., 407 (first quote), 408–9, 410 (second quote), 412–16, 419–22. See also L. Miller, *The Petitioners,* 62–81; and Lively, *The Constitution and Race,* 6–7, 27–31.

63. Fehrenbacher, *The Dred Scott Case,* 229–343.

64. Litwack, *North of Slavery,* 62.

65. Van Evrie, *The Dred Scott Case Decision,* iii.

66. Carey, *The Oregon Constitutional Proceedings and Debates,* 324 (first two quotes); Constitution of the State of Oregon (1857), article 2, section 6, in *The Federal and State Constitutions,* comp. and ed. Thorpe, 3000 (last quote).

67. Carey, *The Oregon Constitutional Proceedings and Debates,* 361–62 (quotes). In 1860, there were 128 blacks, 177 "civilized Indians," and 52,160 white residents. Compiled from U.S. Census Office, *Population of the United States in 1860,* 405; and U.S. Census Office, *A Compendium of the Ninth Census, 1870,* vol. 1, 3, 4, 5.

68. Berwanger, *The Frontier against Slavery,* 93.

69. *Congressional Globe,* 35th Cong., 1st sess. (May 5, 1858): 1966.

70. Ibid., (May 18, 1858): 2205.

71. Ibid., 2204.

72. Angle, *Created Equal?* v–xxx.

73. Douglas quoted in Fehrenbacher, *Slavery, Law, and Politics,* 243; Lincoln, *Abraham Lincoln's Complete Works,* ed. Nicholay and Hay, 82–84; Lincoln, *Collected Works of Abraham Lincoln,* ed. Basler, 398, 400, 402.

74. Douglas at Chicago, July 9, 1858, in *Created Equal?* ed. Angle, 22 (quotes), 23.

75. Lincoln at Chicago, July 10, 1858, ibid., 40.

76. See, for example, his speeches in Springfield (July 17, 1858) and Ottawa (Aug. 21, 1858), ibid., 64–65, 111.

77. Douglas and Lincoln at Jonesboro, Sept. 15, 1858, ibid., 201 (quote), 204–23.

78. State of California, *Journal of the Assembly,* 9th sess. (1858), 342, 408, 444–45; State of California, *Journal of the Senate,* 9th sess. (1858), 553, 661, 663–64.

79. Compiled from U.S. Census Office, *A Compendium of the Seventh Census, 1850,* 394; and U.S. Census Office, *A Compendium of the Ninth Census, 1870,* vol. 1, 5.

80. Compiled from U.S. Census Office, *A Compendium of the Ninth Census, 1870,* vol. 1, 3, 8.

81. Act of Apr. 26, 1858, *California Statutes* (1858): 295, in Hittell, *The General Laws of the State of California,* 521.

82. On anti-Chinese legislation and attitudes in the early Pacific Northwest, see Wynne, *Reaction to the Chinese in the Pacific Northwest,* 41–105.

83. *Daily Alta California,* May 21, 1853. See also "What Is to Be Done with the China-man?" *Shasta Courier,* Dec. 3, 1853.

84. S. Miller, *The Unwelcome Immigrant.*

85. Spratt, "Report on the Slave Trade to the Southern Convention"; De Bow, "The Coolie Trade"; Wright, "The Coolie Trade."

86. Speer, *China and California,* 15.

87. See, for example, California Legislature, Assembly Committee on Mines and Mining Interests, "Report," 1856, 3, 8–9, 13; Helper, *The Land of Gold,* 257; and "The World in California."

88. Quoted in S. Miller, *The Unwelcome Immigrant,* 235.

89. "Life in Hong Kong."

90. *New York Times,* Apr. 21, 1850; *Daily Alta California,* Aug. 17, 1852.

91. Hirata, "Free, Indentured, Enslaved," 24.

92. "The World in California." See also Caldwell, "The Negroization of the Chinese."

93. On the history of education for nonwhites in California, see Low, *The Unimpress-ible Race;* and Hendrick, *Education of Non-Whites in California.*

94. *Sacramento Daily Union,* Jan. 30, 1855.

95. "Free School for Colored Children," reprinted from *Sacramento Daily Union* in *Liberator,* Dec. 14, 1855.

96. See, for example, *San Francisco Daily Evening Bulletin,* Feb. 24, 1858. On the case, see Lapp, *Blacks in Gold Rush California,* 169–71.

97. *California Statutes* (1860): 325, in Hittell, *The General Laws of the State of California,* 998.

98. State of California, Superintendent of Public Instruction, *Eighth Annual Report,* 14–15.

Chapter 4: Race Relations in the Civil War Era

1. E. Foner, *Free Soil,* 261–300.

2. On Republican disclaimers of any intention to challenge white supremacy, see Berwanger, *The Frontier against Slavery,* 123–37; and Litwack, *North of Slavery,* 267–72.

3. E. Foner, *Free Soil,* 266–67.

4. Among the framers of these colonization plans were such dignitaries as Representatives Francis Blair Jr. from Missouri, Edward Bates from Missouri, and Montgomery Blair from Maryland and Senator James Doolittle from Wisconsin. *Congressional Globe,* 35th Cong., 1st sess. (Jan. 14, 1858): 293–98, (June 14, 1858): 3034.

5. Trefousse, *The Radical Republicans,* 29–31.

6. Voegeli, *Free but Not Equal,* 3.

7. Lincoln at Charleston, Illinois, Sept. 18, 1858, in *Created Equal?* ed. Angle, 235. On Lincoln's racial attitudes, see Fredrickson, *The Arrogance of Race,* 54–72; and Sinkler, *The Racial Attitudes of American Presidents,* 29–62.

8. *New York Tribune,* Aug. 19, 1862.

9. Franklin, *The Emancipation Proclamation;* Trefousse, *The Radical Republicans,* 203–30.

10. Quoted in Woodward, *The Burden of Southern History,* 81.

11. *Columbus Crisis* (Ohio), July 11 and Aug. 22, 1861, and Jan. 29, 1862; *Chicago Times,* Oct. 8, 1861, and Mar. 18, Apr. 18, and May 22, 1862; *Detroit Free Press,* Dec. 10, 1861, and Apr. 13 and June 15, 1862.

12. James S. Pike, "What Shall We Do with the Negro?" *New York Tribune,* Mar. 13, 1860.

13. *Congressional Globe,* 37th Cong., 2d sess. (Jan. 14, 1862): 332, (Jan. 22, 1862): 441, (Mar. 6, 1862): 1107; "A Little Common Sense"; *Chicago Tribune,* Aug. 28 and Nov. 5, 1862, and Jan. 12 and Apr. 16, 1863.

14. Abraham Lincoln, "Second Annual Message" (Dec. 1, 1862), in *A Compilation of the Messages and Papers of the Presidents,* vol. 5, comp. Richardson, 3328–29.

15. Quoted in *Sacramento Daily Union,* June 9, 1859.

16. *San Francisco Daily Evening Bulletin,* Apr. 15, Apr. 21, and May 13, 1858; *Sacramento Daily Union,* Apr. 16, 1858; *San Francisco Daily Herald,* June 6, 1858; *Daily Alta California,* Apr. 20, 1858. See also Winks, *The Blacks in Canada,* 272–87.

17. Lapp, *Blacks in Gold Rush California,* 239.

18. The law was struck down in an unpublished opinion. On February 15, 1860, California adopted a revised version of the Immigrant Act of 1852—*Act concerning Passengers Arriving in the Ports of This State*—which provided for the appointment of a superintendent of immigration to be located at San Francisco to supervise the landing, admission, and exclusion of aliens. Hittell, *The General Laws of the State of California,* 523–27; U.S. Immigration Commission, *State Immigration and Alien Laws,* 533.

19. Revenue Act of May 17, 1861, *California Statutes* (1861): 447, in Hittell, *The General Laws of the State of California,* 456, 895–97.

20. Act of Apr. 26, 1862, ch. 339, *California Statutes* (1862): 462. Similar capitation taxes were levied on Chinese residents in the Pacific Northwest. See Wynne, *Reaction to the Chinese in the Pacific Northwest,* 44–45, 49, 53–55, 58, 61–62.

21. Notwithstanding the emphasis on the Chinese in the law's caption, section 1 provided for the taxation of all persons of the Mongolian race, male and female. Hittell, *The General Laws of the State of California,* 521.

22. Loosley, *Foreign Born Population of California,* 10.

23. California Legislature, "Report of the Joint Select Committee relative to the Chinese Population of the State of California," in State of California, *Journal of the Senate,* 13th sess. (1862), Appendix, 6, 7.

24. *Daily Alta California,* Sept. 14, 1859.

25. Chiu, *Chinese Labor in California,* 119–20.

26. *Daily Alta California,* Nov. 2, 1859.

27. Ibid., Sept. 14 and Nov. 2, 1859.

28. Archbald, *On the Contact of Races,* 7 (second quote), 8–9, 10 (first quote), 13, 26 (last quote).

29. Stout, *Chinese Immigration,* 5, 8.

30. Ibid., 7 (first quote), 12, 13 (second quote), 16, 18–19.

31. State of California, *Journal of the Senate,* 13th sess. (1862), 99.

32. California Legislature, "Report of the Joint Select Committee relative to the Chinese Population of the State of California," in State of California, *Journal of the Senate,* 13th sess. (1862), Appendix, 4, 6–7.

33. Ibid., 6.

34. State of California, *Journal of the Assembly*, 13th sess. (1862), 544–50.

35. State of California, *Journal of the Senate*, 13th sess. (1862), 362.

36. *Sacramento Daily Union*, Mar. 24, 1862.

37. U.S. House, *Memorial of 242 Free Colored Persons of California, on Colonization.*

38. *Congressional Globe*, 37th Cong., 2d sess. (June 25, 1862): 2938.

39. *Lin Sing v. Washburn*, 20 Cal. 534 (1862). On this case and two earlier cases involving Chinese litigants successfully challenging the foreign miners' license tax, see McClain, *In Search of Equality*, 27–28, 29.

40. *Lin Sing v. Washburn* 20 Cal. 534, 554–55, 575 (1862).

41. "Annual Message of Leland Stanford, Governor of the State of California," in State of California, *Journal of the Senate*, 14th sess. (1863), 30.

42. Voegeli, *Free but Not Equal*, 13–29.

43. Ibid., 80–90.

44. Ibid., 5–7, 15; Man, "Labor Competition"; Jones, *American Work*, 273–97.

45. Bernstein, *The New York City Draft Riots*, 119–20; Gilje, *The Road to Mobocracy*, 143–70.

46. The figure 105 is Adrian Cook's revision of the earlier inflated estimates of a thousand or more casualties. If doubtful cases are included, the figure increases to 119. Cook, *The Armies of the Streets*, 193–95.

47. Bernstein, *The New York City Draft Riots*, 5, 28–30.

48. On these changes, see Jones, *American Work*, 273–97.

49. *New York Herald*, July 17, 1863, 1.

50. Ibid., July 14, 1863, 1, 5, 8, July 17, 1863, 1. See also Bernstein, *The New York City Draft Riots*, 34, 296n83, 299n132.

51. *Congressional Globe*, 38th Cong., 1st sess. (May 11, 1864): 2218 (quotes), Appendix (July 2, 1864): 249.

52. Voegeli, *Free but Not Equal*, 122–23 (quote), 161–62; E. Foner, *Reconstruction*, 7–10, 28.

53. E. Foner, *Reconstruction*, 60–61.

54. Act of Mar. 18, 1863, ch. 70, *California Statutes* (1863): 69.

55. *Congressional Globe*, 38th Cong., 1st sess. (Feb. 16, 1864): 672–75 (quote on 674).

56. May, "Continuity and Change in the Labor Program of the Union Army," 247 (first and second quotes); *Liberator*, Mar. 3, 1863 (last quote). See also *Liberator*, Mar. 11, 1864; and *National Anti-Slavery Standard*, May 14, 1864.

57. On the wartime labor programs of the Union army in Louisiana and the concepts of free labor/free contract, see Messner, *Freedmen and the Ideology of Free Labor*, xi–xii, 32–113.

58. Voegeli, *Free but Not Equal*, 175–76; *Congressional Globe*, 39th Cong., 1st sess. (Jan. 12, 1866): 129, (Jan. 22, 1866): 316.

59. John Usher, "Report of the Secretary of Interior," in *Congressional Globe*, 38th Cong., 1st sess., Appendix (Dec. 5, 1863): 26.

60. *An Act to Encourage Immigration* (July 4, 1864), *U.S. Statutes at Large* 13 (1866): 385–87.

61. *An Act to Prohibit the "Coolie Trade" by American Citizens in American Vessels* (Feb. 19, 1862), *U.S. Statutes at Large* 12 (1863): 340–41.

62. On the attempts by American commissioners to raise the attention of the U.S. government, see Meagher, *The Introduction of Chinese Laborers,* 319–22; McLeod, "New Views on the Coolie Trade," 66–82; and L. Cohen, *Chinese in the Post–Civil War South,* 26–45.

63. Quoted in L. Cohen, *Chinese in the Post–Civil War South,* 32–33.

64. *An Act in Addition to "An Act to Prohibit the Introduction (Importation) of Slaves into Any Port or Place within the Jurisdiction of the United States . . ."* (Apr. 20, 1818), *U.S. Statutes at Large* 3 (1846): 450–53.

65. Meagher, *The Introduction of Chinese Laborers,* 322; L. Cohen, *Chinese in the Post–Civil War South,* 37–39.

66. McLeod, "New Views on Coolie Trade," 105.

67. See, for example, "The American Coolie Trade," *New York Times,* Apr. 17, 1860; De Bow, "The Coolie Trade"; and Wright, "The Coolie Trade."

68. *An Act to Prohibit the "Coolie Trade" by American Citizens in American Vessels* (Feb. 19, 1863), *U.S. Statutes at Large* 12 (1863): 340–41.

69. H.R. 109, in *Congressional Globe,* 37th Cong., 2d sess. (Jan. 15, 1862): 350–52.

70. *An Act to Encourage Immigration* (July 4, 1864), *U.S. Statutes at Large* 13 (1866): 386.

71. *Congressional Globe,* 40th Cong., 2d sess. (July 23, 1868): 4362; U.S. Immigration Commission, *State Immigration and Alien Laws,* 69.

72. *Congressional Globe,* 38th Cong., 1st sess., Appendix (Dec. 5, 1863): 26.

73. Ibid., 37th Cong., 2d sess. (June 25, 1862): 2938–39; ibid., 38th Cong., 1st sess. (Apr. 9, 1864): 1490.

74. See Charles Crocker's testimony in U.S. Senate, *Report of the Joint Special Committee to Investigate Chinese Immigration,* 666–68; and that of his superintendent, James H. Strobridge, ibid., 723–28. See also Yen, "Chinese Workers and the First Transcontinental Railroad," 28–29, 96–146.

75. U.S. Senate, *Report of the Joint Special Committee to Investigate Chinese Immigration,* 667–68.

76. Ibid., 677.

77. Yen, "Chinese Workers and the First Transcontinental Railroad," 31.

78. Compiled from U.S. Census Office, *A Compendium of the Ninth Census, 1870,* vol. 1, 3, 5, 8.

79. The Act of Apr. 16, 1850, ch. 99, §14, *California Statutes* (1850): 229–30, was amended by the Act of Mar. 18, 1863, ch. 70, *California Statutes* (1863): 69. The Civil Practice Act of 1851, ch. 5, §394, *California Statutes* (1851): 51, 114, was amended by the Act of Mar. 16, 1863, ch. 68, *California Statutes* (1863): 60.

80. Act of Apr. 6, 1863, *California Statutes* (1863): 210, in Hittell, *The General Laws of the State of California,* 998.

81. Wynne, *Reaction to the Chinese in the Pacific Northwest,* 41–105.

82. Quoted in Kraus, "Chinese Laborers and the Construction of the Central Pacific," 45.

83. Crocker in U.S. Senate, *Report of the Joint Special Committee to Investigate Chinese Immigration,* 669.

84. *Sacramento Daily Union,* July 1, 1867, 2.

85. *National Anti-Slavery Standard,* Nov. 6 and 13, 1869; Wilson, *The Black Codes,* 72, 97.

86. *Sacramento Daily Union,* July 3, 1867.

87. U.S. Senate, *Report of the Joint Special Committee to Investigate Chinese Immigration,* 670, 678–79.

88. Saxton, "Army of Canton in the High Sierra," 152.

Chapter 5: Congressional Reconstruction and the Race Questions, 1865–69

1. Kaczorowski, "To Begin the Nation Anew," 50–51.

2. Benedict, *A Compromise of Principle,* 21–58, 325–26; Kaczorowski, "Searching for the Intent of the Framers of the Fourteenth Amendment."

3. Benedict, *A Compromise of Principle,* 22, 48, 326 (first quote), 327 (second quote).

4. E. Foner, *Reconstruction,* xxiv–xxvi, 278 (first quote), 279 (last two quotes).

5. For this discussion of the legal reconstruction of the American polity, an important source has been Avins, *The Reconstruction Amendments' Debates.*

6. U.S. Senate, *Report of Maj. Gen. Carl Schurz on Condition of the South.*

7. *Congressional Globe,* 39th Cong., 1st sess. (Jan. 12, 1866): 211.

8. Ibid., (Jan. 29, 1866): 474–75 (quote on 474).

9. Ibid., (Jan. 19, 1866): 322, (Jan. 29, 1866): 474–76.

10. Ibid., (Jan. 29, 1866): 475, (Jan. 30, 1866): 497–98 (quote on 497).

11. Ibid., (Jan. 30, 1866): 498–99 (quotes on 498).

12. Ibid., (Feb. 1, 1866): 569.

13. Ibid., (Feb. 2, 1866): 606–7.

14. Ibid., (Feb. 27, 1866): 1063–65, (Feb. 28, 1866): 1083, 1087, 1094–95, (Mar. 1, 1866): 1123–24, (Mar. 2, 1866): 1151–57, (Mar. 8, 1866): 1262–66. See also ibid., Appendix (Mar. 8, 1866): 156–59.

15. Ibid., (Mar. 27, 1866): 1679–81 (quotes on 1679).

16. Ibid., (Apr. 6, 1866): 1809, (Apr. 9, 1866): 1861.

17. Ibid., (May 23, 1866): 2764–67.

18. Gypsies were a tiny percentage of the population when Cowan expressed his opposition to them in the 1860s. While most Gypsy immigrants to the United States came between 1855 and 1885, those who settled in Pennsylvania came as early as the 1830s. Natives of Germany, these Gypsies, called Black Dutch or Chickeners, were naturally drawn to Pennsylvania German communities. There, as elsewhere in the East, anti-Gypsy attitudes and legislation were common. Sutherland, *Gypsies.*

19. *Congressional Globe,* 39th Cong., 1st sess. (May 30, 1866): 2890–91.

20. Ibid., 2891–92.

21. Ibid., (Feb. 27, 1866): 1054, 1056 (quote).

22. Ibid., (May 23, 1866): 2765–66.

23. Ibid., (Feb. 27, 1866): 1056, (June 16, 1866): 3214, Appendix (Mar. 8, 1966): 158.

24. Ibid., (May 23, 1866): 2766.

25. Ibid., (Jan. 23, 1866): 376, 383, 385–86, (Jan. 24, 1866): 406, (Jan. 25, 1866): 427, (Feb. 6, 1866): 673, 675, 684; Appendix (Jan. 24, 1866): 298, 299. African American leaders also took exception to the proposition. See U.S. House, *Address of the Colored Citizens of Chi-*

cago on *Civil Rights;* and U.S. Senate, *Memorial of a Delegation of Colored People against the Passage of Joint Resolution Proposing to Amend the Constitution.*

26. *Congressional Globe,* 40th Cong., 2d sess. (Dec. 5, 1867): 38–40, 49–51, (Jan. 11, 1868): 466, (Jan. 31, 1868): 876–77, (June 11, 1868): 3054. See also Fishel, "Northern Prejudice and Negro Suffrage," 19–22.

27. *Congressional Globe,* 39th Cong., 1st sess. (Jan. 22, 1866): 357.

28. *An Act to Provide for the More Efficient Government of the Rebel States* (Reconstruction Act of Mar. 2, 1867), *U.S. Statutes at Large* 14 (1868): 428–29; Supplementary Reconstruction Act of Mar. 23, 1867, *U.S. Statutes at Large* 15 (1869): 2–5; Supplementary Reconstruction Act of July 19, 1867, *U.S. Statutes at Large* 15 (1869): 14.

29. *Congressional Globe,* 40th Cong., 2d sess. (Feb. 8, 1868): 1067.

30. Ibid., (May 13, 1868): 2450.

31. Ibid., (June 6, 1868): 2898–99.

32. Republican platform, 1868, in Franklin, "Election of 1868," Appendix, 1270.

33. *Congressional Globe,* 40th Cong., 3d sess. (Feb. 5, 1869): 911–12.

34. Ibid., (Jan. 28, 1869): 668–72, 673, (Jan. 29, 1869): 707–8, (Feb. 4, 1869): 855, 860, 862–63, (Feb. 5, 1869): 912 (quote).

35. Ibid., (Feb. 5, 1869): 899–901 (quotes on 901).

36. Carey, *Oregon Constitutional Proceedings,* 361–62.

37. *Congressional Globe,* 40th Cong., 3d sess. (Feb. 5, 1869): 909–12.

38. Ibid., Appendix (Feb. 6, 1869): 167–68.

39. Ibid., (Feb. 6, 1869): 938. The amendment would have read, "The right of *natural-born* citizens of the United States to vote and hold office shall not be denied or abridged by the United States or by any State on account of race, color, or previous condition of servitude." Ibid.

40. Ibid., 939.

41. Ibid., (Feb. 8, 1869): 978–79.

42. Ibid., Appendix (Feb. 8, 1869): 287.

43. Ibid., 40th Cong., 2d sess. (Feb. 25, 1868): 1416, (June 10, 1868): 2999–3008.

44. Ibid., 40th Cong., 3d sess. (Feb. 8, 1869): 986–90.

45. Ibid., 990.

46. Ibid., 1008–9.

47. Ibid., 1009.

48. Ibid., 1012.

49. Ibid., 1011.

50. Ibid., 1012.

51. Ibid., (Feb. 9, 1869): 1030 (first quote), 1031 (second quote).

52. Ibid., 1033–34 (quote on 1033). Morton's anti-Chinese statements are interesting in view of his change of outlook in 1876, which is discussed in chapter 10.

53. Ibid., 1034–35 (quote on 1035).

54. Ibid., 1035.

55. Ibid., 1036.

56. Ibid., 1035, 1036, 1040.

57. Ibid., 1038.

58. Ibid., 1043–44.

59. Ibid., 1040, (Feb. 15, 1869): 1226.

60. Ibid., (Feb. 25, 1869): 1563–64, (Feb. 26, 1869): 1641.

61. Three representative works are Van Evrie, *White Supremacy*; J. Hayes, *Negrophobia*; and Dixon, *New America*.

62. Helper, *Nojoque*, 253–54.

63. Ibid., 78–79 (quotes on 78).

64. Ibid., 71 (first quote), 72 (next two quotes), 73–77, 236.

Chapter 6: *Americans and the Chinese Question, 1865–69*

1. Davis, *History of Political Conventions in California*, 213–40.

2. Cross, *A History of the Labor Movement in California*, 29–59, 79–80; Saxton, *The Indispensable Enemy*, 68–75.

3. In these two years, there was a net loss of 71 Chinese immigrants. The following year, 1867, the loss was 205. Coolidge, *Chinese Immigration*, 498.

4. Quoted in Melendy and Gilbert, *The Governors of California*, 129–42 (quotes on 133).

5. Cross, *A History of the Labor Movement in California*, 79; Saxton, *The Indispensable Enemy*, 72.

6. Cross, *A History of the Labor Movement in California*, 79–80.

7. The trades represented included wine merchants, carpenters, plumbers, masons, tinners, stevedores, carriage-makers, shoemakers (the Chinese entered this field after 1867), and lumbermen. Chiu, *Chinese Labor in California*, 53.

8. Gorham's letter in Davis, *History of Political Conventions in California*, 241–42.

9. Ibid., 248–49.

10. Ibid., 264–65 (quote on 265).

11. Ibid., 259–60.

12. On the elections of 1867, see Benedict, *A Compromise of Principle*, 257–78.

13. The address is available in C. Wu, *"Chink!"* 109–13 (first two quotes on 110, last two on 112).

14. Davis, *History of Political Conventions in California*, 270, 277–80, 282, 285.

15. Quoted in *San Francisco Daily Evening Bulletin*, Apr. 29, 1868.

16. *Daily Alta California*, May 8, 1868.

17. "Treaty of Trade, Consuls, and Emigration between China and the United States [Additional Articles to the Treaty between the United States of America and China of June 18, 1858]" (July 28, 1868), *U.S. Statutes at Large* 16 (1871): 739–41.

18. *New York Times*, Feb. 25, 1871.

19. Earlier treaties were the Treaty of Peace, Amity, and Commerce, July 3, 1844, and the Treaty of Peace, Amity, and Commerce, June 18, 1858. Malloy, *Treaties, Conventions, International Acts*, 196–206, 211–21.

20. Williams, *Anson Burlingame*, 146, 156–57. Seward had received many inquiries from business sources about the possibility of legally importing Chinese laborers.

21. Quoted in Tsai, *China and the Overseas Chinese*, 25.

22. "Treaty of Trade, Consuls, and Emigration between China and the United States" (July 28, 1868), *U.S. Statutes at Large* 16 (1871): 740.

23. Ibid.

24. Van Dyne, *Citizenship of the United States*, 327–62.

25. *An Act concerning the Rights of American Citizens in Foreign States,* in *Congressional Globe,* 40th Cong., 2d. sess., Appendix (July 27, 1868): 561–62.

26. Mark Twain, "The Treaty with China," *New York Tribune,* Aug. 9, 1868.

27. *Daily Alta California,* July 30 and Aug. 31, 1868; *Sacramento Daily Union,* July 16, 1868.

28. *San Francisco Daily Evening Bulletin,* July 31, 1868; *Sacramento Daily Union,* July 16, 1868.

29. *Daily Alta California,* July 30, 1868.

30. Cross, *A History of the Labor Movement in California,* 40–45, 60–72; Eaves, *A History of California Labor Legislation,* 11–26, 198–214.

31. George, "What the Railroad Will Bring Us."

32. Henry George, "The Chinese on the Pacific Coast," *New York Tribune,* May 1, 1869.

33. Of course, adherence to Whiggism and later Republicanism does not mean that Greeley was pro-Chinese. In the 1850s, Greeley had taken a strong anti-Chinese position. See chapter 3; and S. Miller, *The Unwelcome Immigrant,* 169–72.

34. Adams, "The Protection of the Ballot," 91–111 (first quote on 106, second on 110).

35. "The Growth of the United States through Emigration—The Chinese," *New York Times,* Sept. 3, 1865.

36. Godkin, "The Chinese Treaty."

37. *New York Times,* June 7, 1868.

38. See, for example, *New York Times,* June 29, July 14, July 16, and July 24, 1869; *New York Herald,* July 22, July 24, Aug. 3, Oct. 7, and Oct. 25, 1869; *New York Tribune,* July 7, Aug. 10, and Sept. 14, 1869; *Albany Evening Journal,* July 21, 1869; and *New York Sun,* July 12, 1869. Previously, events in China attracted the attention of eastern editors.

39. "John Chinaman—What Shall We Do with Him?" *New York Times,* June 29, 1869.

40. "Our Celestial Negro," *New York Independent,* Aug. 19, 1869.

41. Godkin, "The Coming of the Barbarian."

42. *San Francisco Daily Herald,* May 24, 1869.

43. Davis, *History of Political Conventions in California,* 290.

44. Ibid., 293–94 (quote on 293).

45. "Sambo versus John Chinaman—The California Republicans," *New York Herald,* July 24, 1869.

Chapter 7: Chinese Labor in the South and New England, 1865–70

1. *New York Herald,* Aug. 3, 1869.

2. Davis, *History of Political Conventions in California,* 293.

3. W. Cohen, *At Freedom's Edge,* xiii–xvi.

4. *Congressional Globe,* 39th Cong., 1st sess. (June 16, 1866): 3215.

5. W. Cohen, *At Freedom's Edge,* 108.

6. Loewenberg, "Efforts of the South to Encourage Immigration," 369–71.

7. Brandfon, "The End of Immigration."

8. Williamson, *The Crucible of Race,* 44–46, 250, passim; W. Cohen, *At Freedom's Edge,* xvi, 3–22.

9. U.S. Senate, *Report of Maj. Gen. Carl Schurz on Condition of the South,* 17–18.

10. L. Cohen, *Chinese in the Post–Civil War South,* xi–xii.

11. *Galveston Daily News* (Texas), July 12, 1865, and *Mobile Daily Advertiser and Register,* Oct. 24, 1865, letters quoted in L. Cohen, *Chinese in the Post–Civil War South,* 46–48.

12. "Coolies as a Substitute for Negroes," 215.

13. U.S. House, *Report of the Commissioner of Immigration, February 28, 1866*, 6.

14. U.S. Attorney General Henry Stanbery asked District Attorney Samuel H. Torrey to investigate whether the vessel had also violated the Thirteenth Amendment and section 2 of the Act of 1864 to Encourage Immigration.

15. Bradish Johnson, quoted in *New Orleans Commercial Bulletin,* Oct. 21, 1867.

16. L. Cohen, *Chinese in the Post–Civil War South,* 76.

17. George W. Gift, quoted in Burwell, "Science and the Mechanic Arts," 567 (first quote), 568 (second quote).

18. Quoted in ibid., 568.

19. "The Coming Laborer," *Vicksburg Daily Times,* June 30, 1869.

20. "The Chinaman," *New Orleans Daily Picayune,* June 5, 1869 (quote); "Chinese Immigration," *New Orleans Daily Picayune,* July 7, 1869.

21. "The Chinamen and the Negroes," *New Orleans Daily Picayune,* July 13, 1869.

22. *Montgomery Weekly Mail,* June 23, 1869.

23. "The Coming Laborer," *Vicksburg Daily Times,* June 30, 1869.

24. *Lexington Observer and Reporter,* July 12, 1869.

25. *Memphis Daily Appeal,* July 15, 1869.

26. On the issue of Chinese immigration at Memphis and other conventions, see Anders, "The Coolie Panacea," 78–149. For the Memphis proceedings, see *Memphis Daily Appeal,* July 14, 15, 16, and 17, 1869.

27. *Memphis Daily Appeal,* July 14 and 16, 1869.

28. Hellwig, "Black Attitudes," 152–54; Shankman, *Ambivalent Friends,* 10–12.

29. Douglass, "Composite Nation" (1869), 220–21 (quotes on 20).

30. Quoted in Krebs, "John Chinaman," 373–75.

31. *Montgomery Daily Appeal,* Oct. 3, 1866.

32. "The Gothic, African, and Chinese Races," *Journal and Guide* (Norfolk, Va.), reprinted in *De Bow's Review* 5, no. 10 (1868): 943–45 (quote on 944).

33. Burwell, "Science and the Mechanic Arts"; "Cooley-ite Controversy."

34. Burwell, "Science and the Mechanic Arts," 557–58, 560 (last quote), 562, 564, 569 (first two quotes).

35. "The Cooley-ite Controversy," 709, 710 ("far more docile," "soldiers," and "best friends" quotes), 715 ("autochtones" quote), 717 ("overloaded" quote), 720 ("pagans" quote), 721, 723, 724 ("importation" quote).

36. Krebs, "John Chinaman," 377–78.

37. Quoted in Shankman, *Ambivalent Friends,* 11.

38. State of Tennessee, *Journal of the House,* 36th Assembly, 1st sess. (1869), 228; State of Tennessee, *Acts of Tennessee,* 36th Assembly, 1st sess. (1869), 188–89.

39. Quoted in Barth, *Bitter Strength,* 194 (quote), 283n24.

40. "Immigration and Labor."

41. Rudolph, "Chinamen in Yankeedom," 16, 19.

42. *Springfield Republican,* June 17, 1870; *Boston Commonwealth,* June 25, 1870.

43. *New York Times,* July 6 and 7, 1870.

44. *Springfield Republican,* June 17, 1870; *Boston Evening Transcript,* June 25, 1870; *Boston Commonwealth,* June 25, 1870.

45. Daniels, *Asian America,* 43.

46. Gyory, *Closing the Gate,* 41–44, 46–47.

47. *Workingman's Advocate,* Feb. 6, June 2, and Aug. 7, 1869. Another case was Adolph Douai, who was to play a crucial role in American Marxist organizations. See *Die Arbeiter-Union* (New York), May 25, 1869.

48. *Boston Investigator,* July 6, 1870, 78.

49. Erickson, *American Industry,* 31, 50–53.

50. *Springfield Republican,* June 17, 1870.

51. *Boston Investigator,* July 6, 1870 (quotes); *New York Tribune,* July 18, 1870.

52. *Workingman's Advocate,* Aug. 7, 1869 (quotes); Commons et al., *History of Labour,* 148; Commons et al., *A Documentary History of American Industrial Society,* 221–23, 237.

53. "Immigration and Labor"; *Louisville Courier-Journal,* Aug 3, 1869; C. Brooks, "The Chinese Labor Problem," 416–18.

54. Commons et al., *History of Labour,* 149–50.

55. After the Civil War, radical Republicans had selectively embraced labor reforms, shunning reforms behind which lurked the specters of class warfare and "special legislation." Montgomery, *Beyond Equality,* 230–386.

56. Rudolph, "Chinamen in Yankeedom," 25–26; Baum, "Woman Suffrage," 73–75.

57. *Congressional Globe,* 41st Cong., 2d sess. (Dec. 13, 1869): 86. A couple of months later, he introduced a somewhat modified version of the bill. Ibid., (Feb. 18, 1870): 5162.

58. *National Anti-Slavery Standard,* May 29, 1869.

59. See, for example, *National Anti-Slavery Standard,* Mar. 5, Mar. 19, Mar. 26, Apr. 2, and Apr. 16, 1870.

60. Quoted in ibid., Apr. 16, 1870.

61. Wendell Phillips, "The Chinese," *National Anti-Slavery Standard,* July 30, 1870.

62. S. Miller, *The Unwelcome Immigrant,* 177.

63. Godkin, "The Chinese Invasion."

64. Godkin, "Tertullian at the Amphitheatre," 187.

65. Godkin, "The Chinese Invasion."

66. Compiled from U.S. Census Office, *A Compendium of the Ninth Census, 1870,* vol. 1, xvii, 8; U.S. Census Office, *A Compendium of the Eleventh Census, 1890,* part 1, 472, 516–24; and U.S. Bureau of the Census, *Fifteenth Census of the United States: 1930,* vol. 2, 233. According to the census of 1870, twenty-three states and eight territories contained over 63,200 Chinese residents.

67. Woodhull, "Labor and Capital."

68. "What Shall Be Done with John Chinaman?" *New York Times,* Mar. 3, 1870.

69. *New York World,* July 10, 1870.

70. U.S. Senate, *Presidential Message on Importation of Chinese Coolies into the United States.*

71. On these two experiments, see Barth, *Bitter Strength,* 197–98, 204–6, 208–9. While only a handful of Chinese workers remained in North Adams after 1875, a few dozen Chinese laborers were brought to Boston to rebuild the city after the devastating fire of 1872. On the Chinese in Boston at the turn of the century, see Rogers, "Chinese and the Campaign to Abolish Capital Punishment."

72. Quoted in "Great Anti-Chinese Demonstration in San Francisco, California, July 1870, under the Auspices of the Knights of St. Crispin," *San Francisco Daily Examiner,* July 9, 1870.

73. Ibid.

74. *American Workman,* July 2 and 23, 1870.

75. *New York Tribune,* June 30, 1870, 1–2.

76. *Congressional Globe,* 41st Cong., 2d sess. (Dec. 6, 1869): 3, (Dec. 13, 1869): 86.

77. H.R. 102, ibid., (Jan. 10, 1870): 338.

78. S.R. 973, ibid., (June 1, 1870): 4126.

79. Ibid., (July 8, 1870): 5382, 5384–85.

80. Ibid., (Jan. 25, 1870): 752–53 (quote on 752).

81. Ibid., (July 8, 1870): 5382–84.

82. Ibid., 5385 ("Chinese treaty" quote), 5386 ("eject" and "other hordes" quotes), 5389 ("pestilence" quote).

83. *New York Herald,* June 27, 1870.

84. Sylvis, *The Life and Speeches,* 333–36 (entry for Feb. 13, 1869, quotes on 333).

85. Jones, *American Work,* 258–97.

86. Douglass, *Douglass Papers,* 232–34.

87. Compiled from U.S. Census Office, *A Compendium of the Ninth Census, 1870,* vol. 1, 165, 568.

Chapter 8: Chinese Immigrants, African Americans, and the Retreat from Reconstruction, 1870–74

1. On Republican's exposition on the loopholes in the Fifteenth Amendment, see *Congressional Globe,* 41st Cong., 2d sess. (Jan. 20, 1870): 598–600, (Feb. 17, 1870): 1363.

2. On these organizations, see Trelease, *White Terror;* and E. Foner, *Reconstruction,* 425–44.

3. *An Act to Enforce the Right of Citizens of the United States to Vote in the Several States of the Union* (May 31, 1870), *U.S. Statutes at Large* 16 (1871): 140–46; *An Act to Enforce the Provisions of the Fourteenth Amendment to the Constitution of the United States* (Anti–Ku Klux Klan Act, Apr. 20, 1871), ibid., 17 (1873): 13–15.

4. For a critique of the historiography and a short discussion of the relevance of the Enforcement Act to the Chinese, see McClain, *In Search of Equality,* 36–42.

5. *Congressional Globe,* 41st Cong., 2d sess. (Feb. 24, 1870): 1536. Stewart had been the prosecutor in *People v. Hall.*

6. Ibid., (May 18, 1870): 3570, (May 20, 1870): 3656, 3658, (May 23, 1870): 3701, (May 24, 1870): 3758.

7. Ibid., (May 20, 1870): 3690.

8. Ibid., (May 25, 1870): 3807–8. On Stewart's fluctuating attitudes toward the Chinese, see McClain, *In Search of Equality,* 37–41.

9. *Congressional Globe,* 41st Cong., 2d sess. (May 27, 1870): 3874, 3876, Appendix (May 27, 1870): 400.

10. Ibid., 3878 (first quote), 3880 (second quote).

11. Ibid., (Jan. 25, 1870): 755–56 ("Hottentot" quote on 756, all other quotes on 755).

12. Ibid., (May 27, 1870): 3878–80.

13. Ibid., 3884. Section 16 was reinforced by two sections: sections 17 and 18.

14. Ibid., (Mar. 24, 1870): 2201.

15. Ibid., (June 9, 1870): 4277 (emphasis added).

16. Ibid., 4275–79.

17. Ibid., (July 2, 1870): 5121.

18. Ibid., 5122.

19. Ibid., 5121, 5124.

20. Ibid., 5124.

21. Ibid., 5125 (second quote); (July 4, 1870): 5152 (first quote).

22. Ibid., (July 4, 1870): 5152 (first quote), 5173 (second quote).

23. Ibid., 5154–55.

24. Ibid., 5155–58 (quotes on 5157).

25. Ibid., 5153.

26. Ibid., 5161–63, 5167.

27. Ibid., 5161–63, 5175 (quote).

28. Ibid., 5158–59, 5160–61, 5168, 5169 (quotes).

29. Ibid., 5165. For instance, Trumbull had opposed the fundamental conditions appended to the readmission of Virginia. Ibid., (Jan. 21, 1870): 643. As they had done in 1867, Republicans imposed conditions for the readmission of the remaining states—that is, the obligation to include in their constitutions the right to vote without discrimination on the basis of, for example, literacy or property; the right to hold office and sit on juries; and the right to receive school funds. Trumbull opposed these conditions on the ground that Congress could not dictate the contents of southern state constitutions. Avins, *The Reconstruction Amendments' Debates,* 418–19, 421–23.

30. *Congressional Globe,* 41st Cong., 2d sess. (July 4, 1870): 5163, 5164 ("They are Asiatics" quote), 5165 ("extraordinary" quote).

31. Ibid., 5160 (emphasis added).

32. Ibid., 5175–76.

33. Ibid., 5173, 5176. At a later stage of the proceedings, Sumner renewed his motion. It was again rejected—12 to 26, with 34 not voting.

34. Ibid., 5176.

35. Ibid., 5177.

36. *An Act to Amend the Naturalization Laws and to Punish Crimes against the Same* (July 14, 1870), *U.S. Statutes at Large* 16 (1871): 254–56.

37. *Congressional Globe,* 41st Cong., 2d sess. (July 4, 1870): 5164.

38. Quoted in E. Foner, *Reconstruction,* 453. Drake made this observation following the defection of 19 senators and 37 representatives in the vote for the conditions appended to the admission of Virginia (see note 29 above).

39. *Congressional Globe,* 41st Cong., 2d sess. (July 4, 1870): 5176–77.

40. E. Foner, *Reconstruction,* 449–53, 475–84, 488–505, 512–24, 582–87.

41. Another good illustration of this can be found in the racist statements made by Republican congressmen during the debates on the proposition to annex the Dominican Republic.

42. *Congressional Globe,* 41st Cong., 2d sess. (May 13, 1870): 3434, (July 7, 1870): 5314. For a review of Sumner's efforts in 1870, as well as 1871 and 1872, see ibid., 42d Cong., 2d sess. (Feb. 5, 1872): 821.

43. *Congressional Globe,* 42d Cong., 2d sess. (Dec. 20, 1871): 240–45, (Dec. 21, 1871): 272–74, 279–80, (Jan. 15, 1872): 381–86, (Jan. 17, 1872): 429–34, (Jan. 30, 1872): 706, (Jan. 31, 1872): 726–31, (Feb. 1, 1872): 759–63, (Feb. 2, 1872): 788–91, (Feb. 5, 1872): 819–21.

44. Ibid., (Dec. 20, 1871): 244 (quote), (Feb. 8, 1872): 901.

45. Ibid., (Feb. 8, 1872): 901, (Feb. 9, 1872): 909–12, 918, (Feb. 13, 1872): 985 (quote).

46. The amendment bill required a two-thirds majority to pass. Ibid., (Feb. 9, 1872): 919, 928–29, (May 9, 1872): 3268, 3270.

47. Ibid., (May 21, 1872): 3730–39, (May 28, 1872): 3932, (June 7, 1872): 4322.

48. Gillette, "Election of 1872," 1320–21, 1330.

49. *Congressional Record,* 43d Cong., 1st sess. (May 22, 1874): 4175–76.

50. E. Foner, *Reconstruction,* 523–24, 549–50.

51. *Congressional Record,* 43d Cong., 2d sess. (Feb. 3, 1875): 938, 943–60, (Feb. 4, 1875): 977–92, 996–1012, (Feb. 26, 1875): 1791, 1795–99, (Feb. 27, 1875): 1861–70; *U.S. Statutes at Large* 18 (1875): 336–37.

Chapter 9: *Race Relations in California, 1870–74*

1. State of California, *Journal of the Senate,* 18th sess. (1869–70), 149–50, 244; State of California, *Journal of the Assembly,* 18th sess. (1869–70), 295–96.

2. Davis, *History of Political Conventions in California,* 290, 293–94.

3. Chiu, *Chinese Labor in California,* 52, 55.

4. *San Francisco Daily Examiner,* July 9, 1870.

5. That Californians were aware of the possible effects of these measures on state policy regarding the Chinese was obvious in the media coverage of congressional policy. See *Daily Alta California:* "The Civil Rights Bill and Chinese Testimony," Nov. 19, 1867, and Jan. 15, 1869; "The Tax on Chinese Miners," Jan. 18, 1868; "Novel View of the Chinese Question," July 8, 1869; "Citizen John Chinaman," July 24, 1869; "The Very Latest: Washington," May 24, 1870; "The Very Latest—Congressional," May 25, 1870; and *Occidental,* "The Radicals and Chinese Suffrage," May 17, 1867.

6. On legal test cases in the 1870s, see McClain, *In Search of Equality,* 40–76.

7. Acts of Mar. 18, 1870, ch. 230–ch. 231, *California Statutes* (1869–70): 330, 332.

8. Coolidge, *Chinese Immigration,* 498, 502.

9. On the disparities in recorded Chinese prostitute populations prior to 1875, see Peffer, *If They Don't Bring Their Women Here,* 7, 112, 124n13.

10. Hirata, "Free, Indentured, Enslaved"; Yung, *Chinese Women,* 18–23; Chan, *This Bitter Soil,* 387–91; Tong, *Unsubmissive Women,* 3–77.

11. James Johnson (Democrat from California) in *Congressional Globe,* 41st Cong, 2d sess. (Jan. 25, 1870): 752; Act of Mar. 31, 1866, ch. 505, *California Statutes* (1866): 641–42.

12. Their enforcement would have led to a challenge in the courts. Furthermore, the state did not have the means to provide for their enforcement.

13. On the role of anti-Chinese prejudice in public health policy, see Trauner, "The Chinese as Medical Scapegoats"; and McClain, *In Search of Equality,* 234–76.

14. Bennett, *Chinese Labor.*

15. Ibid., 3–4, 8–15, 19, 22, 23 (quote), 24–34, 37, 40–41.

16. Harte, "Plain Language from Truthful James," 287–88.

17. On Harte's attitudes toward the Chinese, see Moy, *Marginal Sights,* 23–34.

18. *Congressional Globe,* 41st Cong., 3d sess. (Jan. 7, 1871): 351–60 (quote on 358).

19. Davis, *History of Political Conventions in California,* 299–300, 307 (quote), 308.

20. Delmatier, McIntosh, and Waters, *The Rumble of California Politics,* 60, 449–55.

21. Locklear, "The Celestials and the Angels," 243–44.

22. State of California, *Journal of the Senate,* 19th sess. (1871–72), 115–16; *Los Angeles Star,* Oct. 26, 1871; *Daily Alta California,* Oct. 26, 1871.

23. State of California, *Journal of the Senate,* 19th sess. (1871–72), 115–16.

24. In 1871 and 1872, the numbers were, respectively, 5,540 and 9,770.

25. Davis, *History of Political Conventions in California,* 321–24, 327 (first two quotes), 334 (last quote).

26. Friends of International Right and Justice, *How the U.S. Treaty with China Is Observed,* 7.

27. The whole veto message is available in ibid., 8–13.

28. The "laundry order" was, however, not enforced for a year and was then declared unconstitutional.

29. *Contra Costa Gazette,* June 14, 1873; *Oakland Daily Transcript,* June 11, 1873; *Los Angeles Evening Express,* June 13, 1873; *Santa Barbara Press,* June 14, 1873; *San Francisco Daily Evening Bulletin,* June 24, 1873; *Daily Alta California,* June 24 and 25, 1873.

30. *Boston Journal,* June 11, 1873; *Hartford Courant,* June 14, 1873; *Albany Evening Journal,* June 10, 1873.

31. *New York Tribune,* June 11, 1873.

32. Cross, *A History of the Labor Movement in California,* 82, 317n39.

33. *Daily Alta California,* June 12, 1873.

34. Starr, *The Coming Struggle,* 5.

35. Ibid., 13, 17, 19, 20 ("stupid worship" quote), 21, 38–39, 41 ("virtually slaves" quote), 42, 44–45, 64 ("poor white trash" and "citizen labor" quotes), 66, 67 ("African chattel" quote), 68, 69 ("with Chinese jungles" quote), 88 ("Asiatic excrescences" quote), 91, 126.

36. Bouchard, *Chinaman or White Man?*

37. Gibson, *Chinaman or White Man, Which?*

38. Ibid., 5, 9–11, 12, 13–14, 16 ("European papists" quote), 18 ("mudsill" quote), 28 ("Popery" quote), 29 ("many evils" and "the vices" quotes).

39. Ibid., 6; Booth quoted in *Congressional Record,* 43d Cong., 2d sess., Appendix (Feb. 10, 1875): 42.

40. *Political Code of California* (1874), title 7, chap. 1, section 2952.

41. This synopsis is drawn from *Power of the State to Exclude Foreigners,* 5–7.

42. Ibid., 17.

43. Ibid., 8, 12–20 (quote on 17).

44. Becker, *Humors of a Congressional Investigating Committee,* 25–31; Lapp, *Blacks in Gold Rush California,* 171, 181–82, 183.

Chapter 10: Intensification of the Anti-Chinese Movement, 1874–80

1. This summary discussion is drawn primarily from E. Foner, *Reconstruction,* 512–31; and Slotkin, *The Fatal Environment,* 287–90.

2. Pike, *The Prostrate State,* 12, 67 (quote); *Harper's Weekly,* Mar. 14, 1874, 229–30. On the shift of Republican opinion, see E. Foner, *Reconstruction,* 524–27 (quotes on 526).

3. E. Foner, *Reconstruction,* 527.

4. *New York World,* Oct. 14, 1874 ("The Black League" issue); "Shall Chinamen Vote?" ibid., Oct. 17, 1874 ("darker races" quote).

5. Richardson, *A Compilation of the Messages and Papers of the Presidents,* vol. 6, 4242.

6. Ibid., 3991.

7. U.S. Senate, *Presidential Message on Importation of Chinese Coolies into the United States.*

8. Richardson, *A Compilation of the Messages and Papers of the Presidents,* vol. 6, 3991, 4050, 4096, 4138, 4189, 4309, 4353.

9. Anbinder, *Nativism and Slavery,* 274.

10. Teiser, "Life of George H. Williams."

11. Quoted in Hunt, *The Making of a Special Relationship,* 121; Gyory, *Closing the Gate,* 186–87.

12. *Congressional Record,* 43d Cong., 2d sess., (Dec. 8, 1874), 19.

13. H.R. 4146, ibid., (Dec. 22, 1874): 224.

14. Ibid., Appendix (Feb. 10, 1875): 40–45 (quotes on 44). On Horace Page and the "Page Law," see Peffer, *If They Don't Bring Their Women Here,* 33–37, 115–17.

15. *An Act Supplementary to the Acts in relation to Immigration* (Mar. 3, 1875), *U.S. Statutes at Large* 18 (1875): 477.

16. *Slaughter-House Cases,* 83 U.S. 36, 71 (1873).

17. On the lacunae of the early historiography and a new interpretation of Chinese women's history, see Peffer, "From Under the Sojourner's Shadow"; and Peffer, *If They Don't Bring Their Women Here.*

18. Peffer, *If They Don't Bring Their Women Here,* 12–27.

19. Ibid., 43–56. All Chinese women were subjected to a rigid interrogation, involving up to three examinations that included such questions as "Do you go to the United States for the purpose of prostitution? Are you married or single? What are you going to the United States for? Have you lived in a house of prostitution in Hong Kong, Macao, or China? Have you engaged in prostitution in either of the above places? Are you a virtuous woman? Do you intend to live a virtuous life in the United States?" Ibid., 45–46. Although Chinese prostitutes applying for passports might have been prepared for such an ordeal, a Chinese wife would likely be baffled by such questions and would feel humiliated by the implicit assumption of immorality in these examinations.

20. Coolidge, *Chinese Immigration,* 498, 502.

21. Davis, *History of Political Conventions in California,* 341, 352.

22. *Chy Lung v. Freeman,* 92 U.S. 275, 278 (quote) (1876).

23. *Congressional Record,* 44th Cong., 1st sess., (Feb. 4, 1876): 901, (May 1, 1876): 2850, (May 15, 1876): 3087, (June 12, 1876): 3763.

24. Quoted in *Daily Alta California,* Apr. 6, 1876.

25. Friends of International Right and Justice, *How the U.S. Treaty with China Is Observed,* 4–7; B. Brooks, *Brief of the Legislation and Adjudication Touching the Chinese.* On the legal challenges to the lodging house law and the queue ordinance, see McClain, *In Search of Equality,* 65–69.

26. Friends of International Right and Justice, *How the U.S. Treaty with China Is Observed,* 16; Layres, *The Other Side of the Chinese Question,* 32.

27. Davis, *History of Political Conventions in California,* 358, 361.

28. Democratic platform in Pomerantz, "Election of 1876," Appendix, 1437–40 (quotes on 1439).

29. Davis, *History of Political Conventions in California,* 357 (first quote), 363, 364 (second quote).

30. Pickett, *Pickett's Pamphlet,* 17–20 (first quote on 18, all other quotes on 17).

31. Republican platform in Pomerantz, "Election of 1876," Appendix, 1442.

32. E. Foner, *Reconstruction,* 530–31, 560–63, 569; *U.S. v. Cruishank,* 92 U.S. 542 (1876).

33. "The Political South Hereafter," 202 (quote); "Solving the Southern Problem," *New York Tribune,* Apr. 5, 1877.

34. *Congressional Record,* 44th Cong., 1st sess. (July 6, 1876): 4421. On western congressmen's exhortations that Republicans act on their commitment regarding the Chinese questions, see ibid., (July 6, 1876): 4418–21, (July 10, 1876): 4507, (July 17, 1876): 4671–72, 4678, (July 18, 1876): 4705, (July 20, 1876): 4772, (July 28, 1876): 4910, (Aug. 2, 1876): 5060, (Aug. 15, 1876): 5697.

35. U.S. Senate, *Report of the Joint Special Committee to Investigate Chinese Immigration,* iii, 370 (quote), 876. On the testimony, see Daniels, *Asian America,* 45–54.

36. U.S. Senate, *Report of the Joint Special Committee to Investigate Chinese Immigration,* iii–viii (quote on v).

37. Ibid., 1243–53. See also the testimony of Thomas H. King and Thomas Hart Hyatt, ibid., 121, 758–61.

38. Becker, *Humors of a Congressional Investigation Committee;* Chinese Consolidated Benevolent Association, *Memorial of the Six Chinese Companies;* Layres, *Evidence of Public Opinion;* Kennedy, *Argument in Senate.*

39. U.S. Senate, *Character, Extent, and Effect of Chinese Immigration to the United States,* 4. The authenticity of the report was challenged by advocates of Chinese exclusion. Whitney, *The Chinese,* 58.

40. U.S. Senate, *Report of the Joint Special Committee to Investigate Chinese Immigration,* vi. See the testimony of Henry George and John F. Swift, ibid., 275–88, 951–68.

41. Ibid., 1043–51 ("somewhat" quote on 1043, "Mongolian" and "hive" quotes on 1050, "vegetable-eating" and "flesh-eating" quotes on 1051).

42. Ibid., 282, 287, 289. See also the testimony of Charles W. Brooks, John Swift, Lewis M. Foulke, and the Reverend Samuel V. Blakeslee, ibid., 942, 961, 1133–34, 1241–48.

43. Ibid., 290–94.

44. Ibid., 31.

45. Ibid., 667, 670, 672, 676, 677 ("mighty substitute" quote), 678, 679 "to [admitting]" quote), 680 ("thick" quote), 681–684, 685 ("be a white" quote).

46. State of California, Senate, *Chinese Immigration,* 5, 6 (quotes), 59.

47. Ibid., 53 ("For after all" and "Mongolianization" quotes), 62 ("hewers" quote), 63 ("voluntary slaves" quote).

48. John Boalt, "The Chinese Question—A Paper Read before the Berkeley Club, August 1877," ibid., 253–62.

49. Ibid., 253, 254–55, 257 ("an unconquerable" quote), 258–59, 260 ("Chinese invasion" and "[The] Negro" quotes), 261 ("[w]e want" quote). See also H. Clement's essay, "Caucasion vs. Mongolian," 265–84.

50. Ibid., 293–302 (quote on 300). See also "Address of Rev. S. V. Blakeslee," ibid., 241–49.

51. U.S. Senate, *Report of the Joint Special Committee to Investigate Chinese Immigration*, v, 849–51, 936, 1215–24; State of California, Senate, *Chinese Immigration*, 56, 64, 243–44, 248, 261–62, 268, 274, 281–82, 295.

52. U.S. Senate, *Report of the Joint Special Committee to Investigate Chinese Immigration*, 926–27, 1088–89, 1169–72; *Daily Territorial Enterprise* (Virginia City, Nev.), Mar. 17, 1869 (quotes); Lingenfelter, *Hardrock Miners*, 107–27.

53. Quoted in Book, *The Chinese in Butte County*, 52.

54. On the Workingmen's movement in California, see Davis, *History of Political Conventions in California*, 365–93; Eaves, *A History of California Labor Legislation*, 27–33; Cross, *A History of the Labor Movement in California*, 88–129; and Saxton, *The Indispensable Enemy*, 113–32.

55. *New York Tribune*, Mar. 14, 1880. Born in County Cork in 1847, Kearney came to San Francisco in 1868 as a cabin boy. In 1872, he decided to remain there as a driver of carts. Early on, he was sympathetic to capital, but he moved to labor after unsuccessful business speculation, ultimately assuming a leading role in the Workingmen's campaign and party. His talent for fluent and abusive speech earned him the suspicion of eastern papers. When he visited the East in 1878, the papers chronicled his voyage as the "rake's progress." *Boston Advertiser*, July 12 and 13, 1878. Speaking of Kearney as a "most ignorant, profane, strife-engendering and besotted disclaimer," W. L. Garrison concluded that he was "much more entitled to be in a lunatic asylum than running at large." *New York Tribune*, Feb. 17, 1879.

56. Davis, *History of Political Conventions in California*, 366, 367, 368, 369, 370, 374, 379, 384, 385.

57. *San Francisco Daily Evening Bulletin*, Jan. 10, 1878.

58. *The Great Problem of the Day*, 22–27 ("vices" quote on 24, "the pet" quote on 26, all other quotes on 25).

59. Six months before the election of delegates to the convention, some Democrats and Republicans agreed to a "non-partisan" fusion to prevent the domination of the convention by "communist Kearneyites." Davis, *History of Political Conventions in California*, 390–92.

60. Sandmeyer, *The Anti-Chinese Movement in California*, 67–72.

61. Quoted in Eaves, *A History of California Labor Legislation*, 155.

62. California Constitution (1879), article 2, section 1.

63. Ibid, article 19, sections 1, 2, 3, and 4.

64. Eaves, *A History of California Labor Legislation*, 158. The same question was taken to the people of Nevada: 18,397 were in favor of restrictive measures, and 183 were against them.

65. *An Act to Amend the Penal Code by Adding Two New Sections Thereto, to Be Known as Sections 178 and 179, Prohibiting the Employment of Chinese by Corporations* (Feb. 13, 1880), ch. 10, *California Statutes* (1880): 6.

66. Eaves, *A History of California Labor Legislation*, 158; Sandmeyer, *The Anti-Chinese Movement in California*, 74.

67. *In re Tirbucio Parrott*, 1 F. 481–521 (quote on 494) (1880). On the case, see McClain, *In Search of Equality*, 87–92.

68. On Judge Hoffman and the Chinese, see Fritz, *Federal Justice in California,* 210–49.

69. *In re Tirbucio Parrott,* 1 F. 481, 498 (quotes) (1880).

70. *In re Ah Fong,* in *Power of the State to Exclude Foreigners,* 17 (on the case, see chapter 9); *Ho Ah Kow v. Nunan,* 12 F. Cas. 252, 256 (quotes) (1879).

71. In 1878, Judge Sawyer declared, "Upon the revision of the statutes, the revisors, probably inadvertently, as Congress did not contemplate a change of the laws in force, omitted the words 'white persons.'" *In re Ah Yup,* 1 F. Cas. 223 (1878). The revised statute read, "Sec. 2169. The provisions of this Title shall apply to aliens of African nativity and to persons of African descent." Quoted in Van Dyne, *Citizenship of the United States,* 56.

72. Act of Feb. 18, 1875, *U.S. Statutes at Large* 18 (1875): 318; Van Dyne, *Citizenship of the United States,* 56–57; U.S. Senate, *Report of the Joint Special Committee to Investigate Chinese Immigration,* 288; McClain, *In Search of Equality,* 70–72.

73. *In re Ah Yup,* 1 F. Cas. 223–25 (quote on 223) (1878). On the case, see McClain, *In Search of Equality,* 72–73; and Haney López, *White by Law,* 54–55, 63–64.

74. *In re Camille,* 6 F. 256, 258 (quotes) (1880).

75. Ibid., 258.

Chapter 11: *The Politics of Racism in the Chinese Exclusion Debates, 1879–82*

1. *Congressional Record,* 45th Cong., 2d sess. (Dec. 7, 1878): 68, (Dec. 10, 1878): 81, 98, (Jan. 10, 1879): 271, (Jan. 14, 1879): 318, 320, (Jan. 17, 1879): 383, (Mar. 7, 1879): 1544–1545, (Apr. 11, 1879): 2439–40, (June 8, 1879): 4328–32.

2. Hune, "Politics of Chinese Exclusion," 11–12. See also Tsai, *China and the Overseas Chinese,* 38–42.

3. Richardson, *A Compilation of the Messages and Papers of the Presidents,* vol. 6, 4448.

4. H.R. 2423, in *Congressional Record,* 45th Cong., 3d sess. (Jan. 28, 1879): 791–93 (quotes on 793).

5. Ibid., (Jan. 28, 1879): 793, 794–96, 798–99.

6. Ibid., 799–801.

7. Ibid., (Feb. 13, 1879): 1264–76, (Feb. 14, 1879): 1299–1316, (Feb. 15, 1879): 1383–89.

8. Ibid., (Feb. 13, 1879): 1267 (first two quotes), 1271 (last two quotes).

9. Ibid., 1273–74.

10. Ibid., (Feb. 15, 1879): 1387–88.

11. Ibid., (Feb. 14, 1879): 1299–1303 (first quote on 1303, others on 1302).

12. Ibid., (Feb. 15, 1879): 1388.

13. Ibid., (Feb. 13, 1879): 1274–75, (Feb. 14, 1879): 1305, 1307–9, 1312–13, 1315, (Feb. 15, 1879): 1383–87.

14. Ibid., (Feb. 15, 1879): 1388–1400.

15. *New York Tribune,* Feb. 17, 1879. See ibid., Feb. 23, 24, and 27, 1879, for the ensuing debate between Blaine and Garrison. See also Blaine's response in Blaine, *Political Discussions,* 236–45.

16. "The Chinese Debate," 130.

17. Godkin, "Sand-Lot Ratiocination."

18. Richardson, *A Compilation of the Messages and Papers of the Presidents,* vol. 6, 4466–72 (first quote on 4469, second on 4470).

19. R. Hayes, *Hayes,* 186–92.

20. *Congressional Record,* 45th Cong., 3d sess. (Mar. 1, 1879): 2276–77. In the House, only 110 members voted for the bill, while 96 voted against it.

21. *San Francisco Examiner,* Mar. 17, 1880.

22. *Congressional Record,* 46th Cong., 2d sess. (Dec. 17, 1879): 143, 151, (Jan. 7, 1880): 221, (Jan. 12, 1882): 286, (Feb. 2, 1882): 646, (Feb. 3, 1882): 678.

23. Hunt, *The Making of a Special Relationship,* 87–88.

24. Democratic and Republican platforms in Dinnerstein, "Election of 1880," Appendix, 1518 (first quote), 1520 (second quote).

25. Quoted in Smith, *Life and Letters of James Abram Garfield,* 677.

26. Dinnerstein, "Election of 1880," 1514. On the Morey letter, see Hinckley, "Politics of Sinophobia," 388–93.

27. "Treaty of Immigration between the United States and China" (Nov. 17, 1880), *U.S. Statutes at Large* 22 (1883): 826; "Supplemental Treaty between U.S. and China, concerning Commercial Intercourse and Judicial Procedure" (Nov. 17, 1880), ibid., 828.

28. Richardson, *A Compilation of the Messages and Papers of the Presidents,* vol. 7, 4629–30.

29. *Congressional Record,* 47th Cong., 1st sess. (Feb. 28, 1882): 1480–81.

30. Ibid., 1481–86, (Mar. 2, 1882): 1545–47, (Mar. 6, 1882): 1637–38, (Mar. 9, 1882): 1739–46, (Mar. 15, 1882): 1932–36, (Mar. 16, 1882): 1977–78.

31. Ibid., (Mar. 1, 1882): 1515–21, (Mar. 6, 1882): 1639–43, (Mar. 7, 1882): 1667, 1669–70, (Mar. 8, 1882): 1702–7, (Mar. 9, 1882): 1746–49, (Mar. 15, 1882): 1937–41, (Mar. 16, 1882): 1980–82.

32. Ibid., (Mar. 1, 1882): 1517, (Mar. 7, 1882): 1669–70, (Mar. 8, 1882): 1702 ("extirpation" quote), 1705–6, (Mar. 9, 1882): 1748, (Mar. 16, 1882): 1980.

33. Ibid., (Mar. 1, 1882): 1518.

34. Ibid., 1517–18, (Mar. 8, 1882): 1705 (Platt's quote), 1706, (Mar. 15, 1882): 1939–40 (Hawley's quote on 1940). See also Ohio Representative Ezra B. Taylor's statements, ibid., (May 16, 1882): 1980–81.

35. Ibid., (Mar. 7, 1882): 1674–75, (Mar. 8, 1882): 1712, (Mar. 15, 1882): 1936.

36. Ibid., (Mar. 2, 1882): 1546, (Mar. 9, 1882): 1740–41, 1747, (Mar. 15, 1882): 1932, 1936.

37. Ibid., (Mar. 9, 1882): 1744–45. See also the statements of Henry M. Teller (Republican from Colorado), ibid., (Mar. 8, 1882): 1712–13.

38. Ibid., (Mar. 7, 1882): 1674.

39. Ibid., (Mar. 6, 1882): 1637–38, (Mar. 8, 1882): 1707.

40. Ibid., (Mar. 6, 1882): 1637.

41. Ibid., (Mar. 8, 1882): 1707, (Mar. 9, 1882): 1746–53 (quote on 1746), (Mar. 15, 1882): 1937–41, (Mar. 16, 1882): 1980–81.

42. Ibid., (Mar. 9, 1882): 1753, (Mar. 23, 1882): 2228.

43. Pairing is a procedure whereby two senators on opposite sides agree to withhold their votes on roll calls so their absence from Congress does not affect the outcome of record voting. The Democrat opposing the bill was Joseph E. Brown from Georgia. On Brown's position, see ibid., (Mar. 6, 1882): 1639–41.

44. On public opinion, see Eaves, *A History of California Labor Legislation,* 178; *New York Times,* Apr. 5 and 14, 1882; *New York Herald,* Apr. 5 and 6, 1882; *New York Tribune,* Apr. 5, 1882; "The Chinese Bill"; *Harper's Weekly,* Apr. 15 and 22, 1882; *Nation,* Mar. 16 and Apr. 6, 1882; *San Francisco Examiner,* Mar. 29 and Apr. 3, 5, 6, and 7, 1882; and *San Francisco Morning Call,* Apr. 5, 6, 7, and 8, 1882.

45. *Congressional Record,* 47th Cong., 1st sess. (Apr. 4, 1882): 2551–52. See also the appended documents, 2553–62.

46. Ibid., 2551–52, 2562.

47. Ibid., (Apr. 5, 1882): 2607–17, (Apr. 17, 1882): 2967. See sections 1, 14, and 15 of the bill.

48. Ibid., (Apr. 17, 1882): 2972–73.

49. Ibid., 2973–74.

50. Ibid., (Apr. 25, 1882): 3266–71 (first quote on 3271, last two on 3269).

51. Ibid., 3264, Appendix (Apr. 26, 1882): 183–86 (quote on 184).

52. Ibid., (Apr. 26, 1882): 3308–12, (Apr. 27, 1882): 3351–58.

53. Ibid., (Apr. 28, 1882): 3411–12.

54. Ibid., (Apr. 25, 1882): 3264.

55. Ibid., (Mar. 6, 1882): 1637.

56. Ibid., (Apr. 25, 1882): 3267.

57. Ibid., (Apr. 27, 1882): 3359.

58. Ibid., (May 9, 1882): 3777. Chinese Exclusion Act of May 6, 1882, ch. 126, *U.S. Statutes at Large* 22 (1883): 58–61.

Conclusion

1. "The Senate and the Chinese"; "The Chinese Bill"; "The Chinese Panic"; Godkin, "The Republican Party and the Chinese Bill"; *Nation,* May 4, 1882, 369–70, 380–81.

2. *Congressional Record,* 45th Cong., 3d sess. (Jan. 16, 1879): 483, (Feb. 7, 1879): 1077–82 (quote on 1078).

3. Ibid., (Feb. 24, 1879): 1808.

4. Painter, *Exodusters,* xi.

5. Woodward, *Origins of the New South,* 105, 106.

6. Estimates of the migration range between 6,000 and 82,000. Hawkins, "Trends in Black Migration," 141.

7. Quoted in Athearn, *In Search of Canaan,* 195.

8. *New Orleans Daily Picayune,* Aug. 3, 1879; *Weekly Clarion* (Jackson, Miss.), Apr. 2, 1879 (quote).

9. *Weekly Clarion,* May 14 and Aug. 13, 1879. Conversely, there were calls for the use of African Americans to replace Asian laborers in California and Hawaii. Ochs, *A History of Chinese Labor;* Daws, *Shoal of Time.*

10. *New Orleans Daily Picayune,* Apr. 26, 1879; *New Orleans Times,* Mar. 11, 1880 (quote).

11. Athearn, *In Search of Canaan,* 109–30.

12. *Congressional Record,* 46th Cong., 2d sess. (Dec. 18, 1879): 155.

13. Ibid., (Dec. 16, 1879): 124–25, (Dec. 18, 1879): 159 (quotes).

14. *New York Times,* Feb. 4, 1878, cited in S. Miller, *The Unwelcome Immigrant,* 243n130.

15. U.S. Senate, *Investigation of Causes of Migration of Negroes from Southern to Northern States.* See Senator Windom's comments, *Congressional Record,* 46th Cong., 2d sess. (June 14, 1880): 4518, 4519, 4520–27.

16. *Civil Rights Cases* (1883), in *Supreme Court Reporter,* ed. Desty, 18–32.

17. L. Miller, *The Petitioners,* 144.

18. *Civil Rights Cases,* in *Supreme Court Reporter,* ed. Desty, 57.

19. Daniels, *Not like Us,* 18; Chin, "The Plessy Myth" and "The First Justice Harlan by the Numbers."

20. "The Chinese Debate" and Godkin, "Sand-Lot Ratiocination" (in response to the Fifteen Passenger Bill); "The End of the Civil Rights Bill" (in response to the *Civil Rights Cases*).

21. Two months after the passage of the Chinese Exclusion Act, Congress passed a general federal immigration law, purporting to regulate immigration, imposing a tax of fifty cents on all immigrants and barring the landing of persons convicted of crime, the mentally ill, and those who might become a public charge. Act of Aug. 3, 1882, ch. 376, *U.S. Statutes at Large* 22 (1883): 214–15. Still, the act reinforced the notion of *open immigration* for Europeans.

22. See, for example, Wickliffe, "Negro Suffrage, a Failure"; "Disfranchising a Race"; and "Ought the Negro to Be Disfranchised? Ought He to Have Been Enfranchised?"

23. Studies of Chinese American history have yet to assess the significance and full impact of Chinese women exclusion. Peffer's excellent monograph, *If They Don't Bring Their Women Here,* is bound to be a catalyst for a deeper investigation of such exclusion.

24. Daniels, ed., *Anti-Chinese Violence;* Wunder, "Anti-Chinese Violence in the American West."

25. Act of Apr. 27, 1904, *U.S. Statutes at Large* 33 (1905): 428 (emphases added).

26. On the lengthy litigation battles initiated by the Chinese community and Chinese attempts to seek federal protection against mob violence, see McClain, *In Search of Equality,* 150–219.

27. See, for example, *Fong Yue Ting v. United States,* 149 U.S. 698 (1893); *In re Hong Yen Chang,* 84 Cal. 163 (1890); and *United States v. Wong Kim Ark,* 169 U.S. 649 (1898).

28. *In re Rodriguez,* 81 F. 337 (1897).

29. In *U.S. v. Wong Kim Ark* (1898), Chief Justice Melville W. Fuller ruled that native-born children of aliens, even those permanently barred by race from acquiring citizenship, were birthright citizens of the United States.

30. Act of Mar. 2, 1907, *U.S. Statutes at Large* 34 (1907): 1228; Act of Sept. 22, 1922, *U.S. Statutes at Large* 42 (1923): 1021–22; Act. of Mar. 3, 1931, *U.S. Statutes at Large* 46 (1932): 1511.

31. *U.S. v. Ju Toy,* 198 U.S. 253, 279 (quote) (1905). The decision eventually contributed to the Chinese boycott of goods in 1905. On the case, see Konvitz, *The Alien and the Asiatic,* 40–43; and Salyer, *Laws as Harsh as Tigers,* 162–66.

32. On the "nadir" for African Americans, see Logan, *The Negro in American Life.*

33. Quoted in Daniels and Kitano, *American Racism,* 55.

34. The total number of foreigners was 13,920,692; and the U.S. total population was 105,710,620.

35. Daniels, *Not Like Us,* 17.

36. Filipinos constituted a special case. On the Asian exclusion movement, including Filipinos, see Daniels, *Asian America;* and Takaki, *Strangers from a Different Shore.*

37. Quoted in Lane, *Solidarity or Survival?* 85. Another example is Canadian French immigrants in New England factory towns, who came to be called the "Chinese of the Eastern States." Oberholtzer, *A History of the United States,* 406.

38. In this study, I have chosen to use *de-racialization* rather than *whitening* with respect to the dynamic involved in the changing status of European immigrants. Over the past decade, the theme of the "racialization and de-racialization" of European immigrants in nineteenth- and twentieth-century America has been the subject of several studies falling under the category of "whiteness studies" (Roediger's *Wages of Whiteness,* Ignatiev's *How the Irish Became White,* Brodkin's *How the Jews Became White Folks,* and Jacobson's *Whiteness of a Different Color*). Two important themes in these works are the nonwhite status of specific groups of European immigrants and the processes by which they became *white.* While whiteness studies have contributed to the inclusion of European immigration within the paradigms of "racial formation" and "racialization," to name the de-racialization of European immigrants "whitening" is problematic. In a recent critical assessment of the historiography of whiteness studies, Eric Arnesen has challenged the assertions of the nonwhite status of Europeans and has affirmed that notions of racial and cultural inferiority and notions of nonwhiteness were two different concepts. The historian Tom Guglielmo has called for a distinction between *race* and *color.* This comparative analysis of the Chinese question and the Negro problem points in the same direction and demonstrates the need to reexamine the processes by which European immigrants were marginalized and de-marginalized. Arnesen, "Whiteness and the Historians' Imagination," 88; Guglielmo, cited in Carstairs, "Defining Whiteness," 205. On the range of opinions on whiteness studies, see "Scholarly Controversy."

39. Ngai, "The Architecture of Race in American Immigration Law," 70, 73.

40. Grant, *The Conquest of a Continent,* 251.

Bibliography

State and Federal Documents

Congressional Globe. 29th Cong., 2d sess.

——. 30th Cong., 1st sess.

——. 31st Cong., 1st sess.

——. 35th Cong., 1st sess.

——. 36th Cong., 1st sess.

——. 37th Cong., 2d sess.

——. 38th Cong., 1st sess.

——. 39th Cong., 1st and 2d sess.

——. 40th Cong., 1st, 2d, and 3d sess.

——. 41st Cong., 2d and 3d sess.

——. 42d Cong., 2d and 3d sess.

Congressional Record. 43d Cong., 1st and 2d sess.

——. 44th Cong., 1st and 2d sess.

——. 45th Cong., 2d and 3d sess.

——. 46th Cong., 2d sess.

——. 47th Cong., 1st sess.

——. 61st Cong., 3d sess.

State of California. *Annual Message of the Governor of California, Jan. 1, 1855.* San Francisco: G. K. Fitch and V. E. Geiger, 1855.

——. *California Statutes, 1850–82.*

——. *Journal of the Assembly of the State of California, 1850–82.*

——. *Political Code of California, 1874.*

——. *Journal of the Senate of the State of California, 1850–82.*

——, Senate. *Chinese Immigration: Its Social, Moral and Political Effect: Report to the California State Senate of Its Special Committee on Chinese Immigration.* Sacramento: State Office, 1878.

————, Superintendent of Public Instruction. *Eighth Annual Report.* Sacramento: State Printer, 1858.

State of Indiana. *Report of the Debates and Proceedings of the Convention for the Revision of the Constitution of the State of Indiana.* Vol. 2. Indianapolis: A. H. Brown, 1850–51.

State of Tennessee. *Acts of Tennessee, 1869–70.*

————. *Journal of the House,* 1869.

U.S. Bureau of the Census. *Fifteenth Census of the United States: 1930.* Washington, D.C.: Government Printing Office, 1931.

U.S. Census Office. *A Compendium of the Seventh Census, 1850.* Washington, D.C.: Government Printing Office, 1854.

————. *A Compendium of the Ninth Census, 1870.* Washington, D.C.: Government Printing Office, 1872.

————. *A Compendium of the Eleventh Census, 1890.* Part 1, *Population.* Washington, D.C.: Government Printing Office, 1892.

————. *Population of the United States in 1860, Compiled from the Original Returns of the Eighth Census.* Washington: Government Printing Office, 1864.

U.S. House. *Address of the Colored Citizens of Chicago on Civil Rights.* 39th Cong., 1st sess., 1866. House Miscellaneous Document No. 109. Serial 1271.

————. *Memorial of 242 Free Colored Persons of California, on Colonization.* 37th Cong., 2d sess., 1862. House Miscellaneous Document No. 31. Serial 1141.

————. *Report of the Commissioner of Immigration [H. N. Congar], February 28, 1866.* 39th Cong., 1st sess., 1866. House Executive Document No. 66. Serial 1256.

U.S. Immigration Commission. *State Immigration and Alien Laws: Report.* Immigration Commission Report, vol. 39. 61st Cong., 3d sess., 1911. Senate Document No. 758. Serial 5879.

U.S. Senate. *Character, Extent, and Effect of Chinese Immigration to the United States.* 45th Cong., 2d sess., 1878. Senate Miscellaneous Document No. 20. Serial 1785.

————. *Investigation of Causes of Migration of Negroes from Southern to Northern States: Report and Testimony.* 46th Cong., 2d sess., 1880. Senate Report No. 693. Serial 1899 (Part 1), 1900 (Parts 2 and 3).

————. *Memorial of a Delegation of Colored People against Passage of Joint Resolution Proposing to Amend the Constitution.* 39th Cong, 1st sess., 1866. Senate Miscellaneous Document No. 56. Serial 1239.

————. *Presidential Message on Importation of Chinese Coolies into the United States.* 41st Cong., 2d sess., July 15, 1870. Senate Executive Document No. 116. Serial 1407.

————. *Report of the Joint Special Committee to Investigate Chinese Immigration, Feb. 27, 1877.* 44th Cong., 2d sess., 1877. Senate Report 689. Serial 1734.

————. *Report of Maj. Gen. Carl Schurz on Condition of the South. . . .* 39th Cong., 1st sess., Dec. 19, 1865. Senate Executive Document No. 2. Serial 1237.

U.S. Statutes at Large. Washington, D.C.: 1845–1932.

Newspapers, Magazines, and Periodicals

Albany Evening Journal
American Workman
Boston Commonwealth

Boston Investigator
Boston Journal
Boston Evening Transcript
Californian (San Francisco)
Chicago Times
Chicago Tribune
Columbus Crisis (Ohio)
Contra Costa Gazette
Daily Alta California (San Francisco)
Daily Pacific News (San Francisco)
Daily Territorial Enterprise (Virginia City, Nev.)
De Bow's Review
Detroit Free Press
Die Arbeiter-Union (New York)
Galveston Daily News (Texas)
Harper's Weekly
Hartford Courant
Hutching's California Magazine
Journal and Guide (Norfolk, Va.)
Lexington Observer and Reporter
Liberator
Los Angeles Evening Express
Los Angeles Star
Memphis Daily Appeal
Montgomery Daily Appeal
Montgomery Weekly Mail
Nation
National Anti-Slavery Standard
New Orleans Daily Picayune
New York Herald
New York Independent
New York Sun
New York Times
New York Tribune
New York World
Oakland Daily Transcript
Occidental
Sacramento Daily Union
San Francisco California Star
San Francisco Daily Evening Bulletin
San Francisco Daily Examiner
San Francisco Daily Herald
San Francisco Morning Call
San Francisco Daily Picayune
Santa Barbara Press

Shasta Courier
Sonora Herald
Springfield Republican (Boston)
Stockton Times
Vicksburg Daily Times
Weekly Clarion (Jackson, Miss.)
Woodhull and Claflin's Weekly
Workingman's Advocate

Books, Articles, Pamphlets, Theses, and Dissertations

Aarim, Najia, "Chinese Immigrants, African Americans and the Problem of Race in the United States, 1848–1882." Ph.D. diss., Temple University, 1996.

Adams, Charles Francis Jr. "The Protection of the Ballot in National Politics." *Journal of Social Science* 1 (June 1869): 91–111.

Almaguer, Tomás. *Racial Fault Lines: The Historical Origins of White Supremacy in California.* Berkeley: University of California Press, 1994.

Anbinder, Tyler. *Nativism and Slavery: The Northern Know Nothings and the Politics of the 1850's.* New York: Oxford University Press, 1992.

Anders, Steven E. "The Coolie Panacea in the Reconstruction South: A White Response to Emancipation and the Black 'Labor Problem.'" M.A. thesis, Miami University, 1973.

Angle, Paul M., ed. *Created Equal? The Complete Lincoln-Douglas Debates.* Chicago: University of Chicago Press, 1958.

Archbald, John. *On the Contact of Races Considered Especially with relation to the Chinese Question.* San Francisco: Towne and Bacon, 1860.

Arnesen, Eric. "Whiteness and the Historians' Imagination." *International Labor and Working Class History* 60 (Fall 2001): 3–32.

Athearn, Robert G. *In Search of Canaan: Black Migration to Kansas, 1879–1880.* Lawrence: Regents Press of Kansas, 1978.

Avins, Alfred, comp. *The Reconstruction Amendments' Debates: The Legislative History and Contemporary Debates in Congress on the 13th, 14th, and 15th Amendments.* Richmond: Virginia Commission on Constitutional Government, 1967.

Bancroft, Hubert H. *History of California.* Vol. 6. San Francisco: History Company, 1891.

Barth, Gunther Paul. *Bitter Strength: A History of the Chinese in the United States, 1850–1870.* Cambridge, Mass.: Harvard University Press, 1964.

Baum, Dale. "Woman Suffrage and the 'Chinese Question': The Limits of Radical Republicanism in Massachusetts, 1865–1876." *New England Quarterly* 56, no. 1 (1983): 60–77.

Becker, Samuel. *Humors of a Congressional Investigating Committee: A Review of the Report of the Joint Special Committee to Investigate Chinese Immigration.* Washington, D.C.: n.p., 1877.

Benedict, Michael Les. *A Compromise of Principle: Congressional Republicans and Reconstruction, 1863–1869.* New York: W. W. Norton, 1974.

———. "Preserving the Constitution: The Conservative Basis of Radical Reconstruction." *Journal of American History* 61, no. 1 (1974): 65–90.

Bennett, H. C. *Chinese Labor: A Lecture, Delivered before the San Francisco Mechanics' Institute in Reply to Hon. F. M. Pixley.* San Francisco: n.p., 1870.

Bernstein, Iver. *The New York City Draft Riots: Their Significance for American Society and Politics in the Age of the Civil War.* New York: Oxford University Press, 1990.

Berwanger, Eugene H. "The 'Black Law' Question in Ante-Bellum California." *Journal of the West* 6, no. 2 (1967): 205–20.

———. *The Frontier against Slavery: Western Anti-Negro Prejudice and the Slavery Extension Controversy.* Urbana: University of Illinois Press, 1967.

Blaine, James G. *Political Discussions: Legislative, Diplomatic, and Popular, 1856–1886.* Norwich, Conn.: Henry Bill, 1887.

Bonacich, Edna. "Abolition, the Extension of Slavery, and the Position of Free Blacks: A Study of Split Labor Markets in the United States, 1830–1863." *American Journal of Sociology* 81, no. 3 (1975): 601–28.

Book, Susan W. *The Chinese in Butte County, 1860–1920.* San Francisco: R. and E. Research Associates, 1976.

Bouchard, James C. *Chinaman or White Man—Which?* San Francisco: n.p., 1873.

Brandfon, Robert L. "The End of Immigration to the Cotton Fields." *Mississippi Valley Historical Review* 50, no. 4 (1964): 591–611.

Brodkin, Karen. *How the Jews Became White Folks and What That Says about Race.* New Brunswick, N.J.: Rutgers University Press, 1998.

Brooks, B. S. *Brief of the Legislation and Adjudication Touching the Chinese Question Referred to the Joint Commission of Both Houses of Congress.* San Francisco: Women's Co-Operative Printing Union, 1877.

Brooks, Charles Wolcott. "The Chinese Labor Problem." *Overland Monthly* 3, no. 5 (1869): 407–19.

Browne, J. Ross. *California Constitutional Convention: Report of the Debates in the Convention of California on the Formation of the State Constitution in September and October, 1849.* Washington, D.C.: John T. Towers, 1850.

Burwell, William M. "Science and the Mechanic Arts against Coolies." *De Bow's Review* 6, no. 7 (1869): 557–71.

Caldwell, Dan. "The Negroization of the Chinese Stereotype in California." *Southern California Quarterly* 53, no. 2 (1971): 123–31.

Campbell, Persia Crawford. *Chinese Coolie Emigration to Countries within the British Empire.* London: D. S. King and Son, 1923.

Canfield, Chauncey L., ed. *The Diary of a Forty-Niner [Diary of Alfred T. Jakson, Norfolk, Connecticut].* Boston: Houghton Mifflin, 1920.

Capron, E. S. *History of California.* Boston: J. P. Jewett, 1854.

Carey, Charles H., ed. *The Oregon Constitutional Proceedings and Debates of the Constitutional Convention of 1857.* Salem, Oreg.: State Printing Department, 1926.

Carstairs, Catherine. "Defining Whiteness: Race, Class, and Gender Perspectives in North American History." *International Labor and Working Class History* 60 (Fall 2001): 203–6.

Chan, Sucheng. "European and Asian Immigration into the United States in Comparative Perspective." In *Immigration Reconsidered: History, Sociology, and Politics,* edited by Virginia McLaughlin, 37–75. New York: Oxford University Press, 1990.

———. "The Exclusion of Chinese Women, 1870–1943." In *Entry Denied: Exclusion and the Chinese Community in America, 1882–1943,* edited by Sucheng Chan, 94–146. Philadelphia: Temple University Press, 1991.

————. *This Bittersweet Soil: The Chinese in California Agriculture, 1860–1910.* Berkeley: University of California Press, 1986.

Chin, Gabriel. "The Plessy Myth—Justice Harlan and the Chinese Cases." *Iowa Law Review* 82, no. 1 (1996): 151–83.

————. "The First Justice Harlan by the Numbers—Just How Great Was 'the Great Dissenter?'" *Akron Law Review* 32, no. 3 (1999): 629–60.

"The Chinese Bill." *Harper's Weekly,* Apr. 1, 1882, 194.

Chinese Consolidated Benevolent Association. *Memorial of the Six Chinese Companies: An Address to the Senate and House of Representatives of the United States; Testimony of California's Leading Citizens before the Joint Special Congressional Committee.* San Francisco: Alta, 1877.

"The Chinese Debate." *Nation,* Feb. 20, 1879, 130.

"The Chinese Panic." *Harper's Weekly,* May 20, 1882, 306–7.

Chiu, Ping. *Chinese Labor in California, 1850–1880: An Economic Study.* Madison: State Historical Society of Wisconsin for the Department of History, University of Wisconsin, 1963.

Cohen, Lucy M. *Chinese in the Post–Civil War South: A People without a History.* Baton Rouge: Louisiana State University Press, 1984.

————. "Entry of Chinese to the Lower South from 1865 to 1870: Policy Dilemmas." *Southern Studies* 17 (Spring 1978): 5–37.

Cohen, William. *At Freedom's Edge: Black Mobility and the Southern White Quest for Racial Control, 1861–1915.* Baton Rouge: Louisiana State University Press, 1991.

Cole, Richard P., and Gabriel J. Chin. "Emerging from the Margins of Historical Consciousness: Chinese Immigrants and the History of American Law." *Law and History Review* 17, no. 2 (1999): 325–64.

Commons, John R., Ulrich B. Phillips, Eugene A, Gilmore, Helen L. Sumner, and John B. Andrews, eds. *A Documentary History of American Industrial Society.* Vol. 9, *Labor Movement, 1860–1880.* Cleveland: Arthur H. Clark, 1910.

Commons, John R., David J. Saposs, Helen L. Sumner, E. B. Mittelman, H. E. Hoagland, John B. Andrews, and Selig Perlman. *History of Labour in the United States.* Vol. 2. New York: Macmillan, 1918.

Constitution of the Anti-Chinese Association. San Francisco: Anti-Chinese Association, July 1870.

Cook, Adrian. *The Armies of the Streets: The New York City Draft Riots of 1863.* Lexington: University Press of Kentucky, 1974.

"The Cooley-ite Controversy." *De Bow's Review* 6, no. 8 (1869): 709–24.

Coolidge, Mary. *Chinese Immigration.* New York: Holt, 1909.

"Coolies as a Substitute for Negroes." *De Bow's Review* 2, no. 2 (1866): 215–17.

Cross, Ira B. *A History of the Labor Movement in California.* Berkeley: University of California Press, 1935.

Cuba Commission. *Report of the Commission Sent by China to Ascertain the Condition of Chinese Coolies in Cuba (1874).* Taipei: Ch'eng Wen, 1970.

Daniels, Roger. *Asian America: Chinese and Japanese in the United States since 1850.* Seattle: University of Washington Press, 1988.

————. *Not Like Us: Immigrants and Minorities in America, 1890–1924.* Chicago: Ivan R. Dee, 1997.

————. "Westerners from the East: Oriental Immigrants Reappraised." *Pacific Historical Review* 35, no. 4 (1966): 373–83.

————. ed. *Anti-Chinese Violence in North America.* New York: Arno, 1979.

Daniels, Roger, and H. L. Kitano. *American Racism: Exploration of the Nature of Prejudice.* Englewood Cliffs, N.J.: Prentice-Hall, 1970.

Davis, Winfield. *History of Political Conventions in California, 1849–1892.* Sacramento: California State Library, 1893.

Daws, Gavan. *Shoal of Time: A History of the Hawaiian Islands.* Honolulu: University Press of Hawaii, 1968.

De Bow, J. D. B. "The Coolie Trade." *De Bow's Review* 23, no. 1 (1857): 30–35.

Delmatier, Royce, Clarence McIntosh, and Earl Waters. *The Rumble of California Politics, 1848–1870.* New York: John Wiley, 1970.

Desty, Robert, ed. *Supreme Court Reporter.* Vol. 3, *Cases Argued and Determined in the United States Supreme Court, October Term 1883.* Saint Paul: West Publishing, 1884.

Dinnerstein, Leonard. "Election of 1880." In *History of American Presidential Elections, 1789–1968,* vol. 2, edited by Arthur Schlesinger, 1491–1558. New York: Chelsea House, 1971.

"Disfranchising a Race." *Nation,* May 16, 1898, 398–99.

Dixon, William Hepworth. *New America.* Philadelphia: J. B. Lippincott, 1867.

————. *White Conquest.* London: Macmillan, 1876.

Douglass, Frederick. "Composite Nation" (1869). In *Racism, Dissent, and Asian Americans from 1850 to the Present: A Documentary History,* edited by Philip Foner and Daniel Rosenberg, 215–31. Westport, Conn.: Greenwood, 1993.

————. *The Frederick Douglass Papers.* Vol. 4, *1864–80.* Edited by John W. Blassingame. New Haven, Conn.: Yale University Press, 1979.

Eaves, Lucile. *A History of California Labor Legislation, with an Introductory Sketch of the San Francisco Labor Movement.* Berkeley: University of California Press, 1910.

"The End of the Civil Rights Bill." *Nation,* Oct. 18, 1883, 326.

Erickson, Charlotte. *American Industry and the European Immigrant, 1860–1885.* Cambridge, Mass.: Harvard University Press, 1957.

Fehrenbacher, Don E. *The Dred Scott Case: Its Significance in American Law and Politics.* New York: Oxford University Press, 1978.

————. *Slavery, Law, and Politics: The Dred Scott Case in Historical Perspective.* New York: Oxford University Press, 1981.

Finkelman, Paul. "Rehearsal for Reconstruction: Antebellum Origins of the Fourteenth Amendment." In *The Facts of Reconstruction: Essays in Honor of John Hope Franklin,* edited by Eric Anderson and Alfred Moss, 1–27. Baton Rouge: Louisiana State University Press, 1991.

Fishel, Leslie H. "Northern Prejudice and Negro Suffrage, 1865–1870." *Journal of Negro History* 39, no. 1 (1954): 8–26.

Fleming, Walter. "Historic Attempts to Solve the Race Problem in America by Deportation." *Journal of American History* 4, no. 2 (1910): 197–213.

Foner, Eric. *Free Soil, Free Labor, Free Men: The Ideology of the Republican Party before the Civil War.* New York: Oxford University Press, 1970.

————. *Politics and Ideology in the Age of the Civil War.* New York: Oxford University Press, 1980.

————. *Reconstruction: America's Unfinished Revolution, 1863–1877*. New York: Harper and Row, 1988.

Foner, Philip S., and Ronald L. Lewis, eds. *The Black Worker: A Documentary History from Colonial Times to the Present*. Vol. 1, *The Black Worker to 1869*. Philadelphia: Temple University Press, 1978.

Franklin, John Hope. "Election of 1868." In *History of American Presidential Elections, 1789–1968*, vol. 2, edited by Arthur Schlesinger, 1247–1300. New York: Chelsea House, 1971.

————. *The Emancipation Proclamation*. Garden City, N.Y.: Doubleday, 1963.

Fredrickson, George M. *The Arrogance of Race: Historical Perspectives on Slavery, Racism, and Social Inequality*. Middletown, Conn.: Wesleyan University Press, 1988.

The Friends of International Right and Justice. *How the U.S. Treaty with China Is Observed in California for the Consideration of the American People and Government*. San Francisco: n.p., 1877.

Fritz, Christopher G. *Federal Justice in California: The Court of Ogden Hoffman, 1851–1891*. Lincoln: University of Nebraska Press, 1991.

George, Henry. "What the Railroad Will Bring Us." *Overland Monthly* 1, no. 4 (1868): 297–306.

Gibson, Otis. *"Chinaman or White Man, Which?" Reply to Father Buchard [sic], Delivered in Platt's Hall, San Francisco, Friday Evening, March 14, 1873*. San Francisco: Alta, 1873.

Gilje, Paul A. *The Road to Mobocracy: Popular Disorder in New York City, 1763–1834*. Chapel Hill: University of North Carolina Press, 1987.

Gillette, Howard. "Election of 1872." In *History of American Presidential Elections, 1789–1968*, vol. 2, edited by Arthur Schlesinger, 1303–75. New York: Chelsea House, 1971.

Godkin, E. L. "The Chinese Invasion." *Nation*, July 14, 1870, 20.

————. "The Chinese Treaty." *Nation*, Sept. 10, 1868, 206.

————. "The Coming of the Barbarian." *Nation*, July 15, 1869, 44–45.

————. "The Republican Party and the Chinese Bill." *Nation*, Mar. 16, 1882, 222–23.

————. "Sand-Lot Ratiocination." *Nation*, Feb. 27, 1879, 145.

————. "Tertullian at the Amphitheatre." *Nation*, Sept. 22, 1870, 186–88.

"The Gothic, African, and Chinese Races." *Journal and Guide* (Norfolk, Va.), reprinted in *De Bow's Review* 5, no. 10 (1868): 943–45.

de Graaf, Lawrence B. "Recognition, Racism, and Reflections on the Writing of Western Black History." *Pacific Historical Review* 44, no. 1 (1975): 22–51.

Grant, Madison. *The Conquest of a Continent or the Expansion of Races in America*. New York: Charles Scribner's Sons, 1934.

The Great Problem of the Day, the Labor Agitators; or, The Battle for Bread, the Party of the Future: The Workingmen's Party of California, Its Birth and Organization—Its Leaders and Its Purposes; Corruption in Our Local and State Governments; Venality of the Press. San Francisco: G. W. Greene, n.d.

Gyory, Andrew. *Closing the Gate: Race, Politics, and the Chinese Exclusion Act*. Chapel Hill: University of North Carolina Press, 1998.

Haas, Lisbeth. *Conquests and Historical Identities in California, 1769–1936*. Berkeley: University of California Press, 1995.

Haney López, Ian F. *White by Law: The Legal Construction of Race*. New York: New York University Press, 1996.

Harte, Bret. "Plain Language from Truthful James," *Overland Monthly* 5, no. 3 (1870): 287–88.

Hawkins, Homer C. "Trends in the Black Migration from 1863 to 1960." *Phylon* 34, no. 2 (1973): 138–45.

Hayes, J. R. *Negrophobia "On the Brain," in White Men; or An Essay upon the Origin and Progress, Both Mental and Physical of the Negro Race, and the Use to Be Made of Him by the Politicians in the United States.* Washington, D.C.: Powell, Gink, 1869.

Hayes, Rutherford B. *Hayes: The Diary of a President, 1875–1881.* Edited by T. Harry Williams. New York: David McKay, 1964.

Hellwig, David. "Black Attitudes toward Immigrant Labor in the South, 1865–1910." *Filson Club History Quarterly* 54, no. 2 (1980): 151–68.

Helper, Hinton Rowan. *Dreadful California: Being a True and Scandalous Account of the Barbarous Civilization, Licentious Morals, Crude Manners and Depravities, Inclement Climate and Niggling Resources, Together with Various Other Offensive and Calamitous Details of Life in the Golden State.* 1855. Reprint, Indianapolis: Bobbs-Merrill, 1948.

———. *The Impending Crisis of the South: How to Meet It.* New York: A. B. Burdick, 1860.

———. *The Land of Gold: Reality versus Fiction.* Baltimore: H. Taylor, 1855.

———. *Nojoque: A Question for a Continent.* New York: George W. Carleton, 1867.

Hendrick, Irving G. *The Education of Non-Whites in California, 1849–1970.* San Francisco: R. and E. Research Associates, 1977.

Higham, John. *Strangers in the Land: Patterns of American Nativism, 1860–1925.* New Brunswick, N.J.: Rutgers University Press, 1955.

Hinckley, Ted C. "The Politics of Sinophobia: Garfield, the Morey Letter and the Presidential Election of 1880." *Ohio History* 89, no. 4 (1980): 381–99.

Hirata, Lucie Cheng. "Free, Indentured, Enslaved: Chinese Prostitutes in Nineteenth-Century America." *Signs* 5, no. 1 (1979): 3–29.

Hittell, Theodore. *The General Laws of the State of California from 1850 to 1864 Inclusive.* Vol. 1. 2d ed. San Francisco: H. H. Bancroft, 1870.

Holland, Frederic May. *Frederick Douglass: The Colored Orator.* New York: Funk and Wagnalls, 1891.

Hoy, William. *The Chinese Six Companies: A Short Historical Résumé of Its Origins, Function, and Importance in the Life of the California Chinese.* San Francisco: Chinese Consolidated Benevolent Association, 1942.

Hune, Shirley. "Politics of Chinese Exclusion: Legislative-Executive Conflict, 1876–1882." *Amerasia* 9, no. 1 (1982): 5–28.

Hunt, Michael H. *The Making of a Special Relationship: The United States and China to 1914.* New York: Columbia University Press, 1983.

Hurt, Peyton. "The Rise and Fall of the 'Know Nothings' in California." *California Historical Society Quarterly* 9, no. 1 (1930): 16–49; 9, no. 2 (1930): 99–128.

Hurtado, Albert A. "'Hardly a Farm House—A Kitchen without Them': Indian and White Households on the California Borderlands Frontier in 1860." *Western Historical Quarterly* 13, no. 3 (1982): 245–70.

Ignatiev, Noel. *How the Irish Became White.* New York: Routledge, 1995.

"Immigration and Labor: Coolies." *De Bow's Review* 4, no. 2 (1867): 151–52.

Irick, Robert. *Ch'ing Policy toward the Coolie Trade, 1847–1878.* San Francisco: Chinese Materials Center, 1982.

Jackson, Donald D. *Gold Dust.* New York: Alfred A. Knopf, 1980.

Jacobson, Matthew F. *Whiteness of a Different Color: European Immigrants and the Alchemy of Race.* Cambridge, Mass.: Harvard University Press, 1998.

Jones, Jacqueline. *American Work: Four Centuries of Black and White Labor.* New York: W. W. Norton, 1998.

Kaczorowski, Robert. "Searching for the Intent of the Framers of the Fourteenth Amendment." *Connecticut Law Review* 5 (Winter 1972–73): 368–98.

———. "To Begin the Nation Anew: Congress, Citizenship, and Civil Rights after the Civil War." *American Historical Review* 92, no. 1 (1987): 45–68.

Kennedy, Joseph C. G. *Argument in Senate of the United States Adverse to Bills 409 and 477 to Restrict the Immigration of the Chinese to the United States. . . .* 45th Cong., 2d sess., Feb. 25, 1878, Miscellaneous Document No. 36.

Kent, James. *Commentaries on American Law.* Vol. 2, 10th ed. Boston: Little, Brown, 1860.

Kerber, Linda K. "Abolitionists and Amalgamators: The New York City Race Riots of 1834." *New York History* 48, no. 1 (1967): 28–39.

Knobel, Dale. *"America for Americans": The Nativist Movement in the United States.* New York: Twayne, 1996.

Konvitz, Milton R. *The Alien and the Asiatic in American Law.* Ithaca, N.Y.: Cornell University Press, 1946.

Kraus, George. "Chinese Laborers and the Construction of the Central Pacific." *Utah Historical Quarterly* 37, no. 1 (1969): 41–57.

Krebs, Sylvia. "John Chinaman and Reconstruction Alabama: The Debate and the Experience." *Southern Studies* 21, no. 4 (1982): 369–83.

Lai, Chun-Chuen. "Remarks of the Chinese Merchants of San Francisco, upon Governor Bigler's Message, and Some Common Objections; with Some Explanations of the Character of the Chinese Companies to the Legislature of California, in Behalf of the Immigrants from the Empire of China to This State." In *An Humble Plea Addressed to the Legislature of California, in Behalf of the Immigrants from the Empire of China to This State,* by William Speer, 29–31. San Francisco: Office of the Oriental, 1856.

Lane, A. T. *Solidarity or Survival? American Labor and European Immigrants, 1830–1924.* New York: Greenwood, 1987.

Lapp, Rudolph M. *Blacks in Gold Rush California.* New Haven, Conn.: Yale University Press, 1977.

Layres, Augustus. *Evidence of Public Opinion on the Pacific Coast in Favor of Chinese Immigration.* San Francisco: n.p., 1879.

———. *The Other Side of the Chinese Question in California: Appendix II, Documentary Evidence of Public Sentiment in California on the Other Side of the Chinese Question before the Present Agitation.* San Francisco: Taylor and Nevin, 1876.

"Life in Hong Kong." *Harper's Weekly,* Jan. 30, 1858, 68.

Lincoln, Abraham. *Abraham Lincoln's Complete Works Comprising His Speeches, Letters, State Papers, and Miscellaneous Writings.* Edited by John G. Nicholay and John Hay. New York: Century, 1894.

———. *Collected Works of Abraham Lincoln.* Vol. 2. Edited by Roy P. Basler. New Brunswick, N.J.: Rutgers University Press, 1953.

Lingenfelter, Richard E. *The Hardrock Miners: A History of the Mining Labor Movement in the American West, 1863–1893.* Berkeley: University of California Press, 1974.

"A Little Common Sense." *Harper's Weekly,* Aug. 23, 1862, 530–31.

Litwack, Leon F. *North of Slavery: The Negro in the Free States, 1790–1860.* Chicago: University of Chicago Press, 1961.

Lively, Donald E. *The Constitution and Race.* New York: Praeger, 1992.

Locklear, William R. "The Celestials and the Angels: A Study of the Anti-Chinese Movement in Los Angeles to 1882." *Historical Society of Southern California* 42, no. 2 (1960): 239–56.

Loewenberg, Bert James. "Efforts of the South to Encourage Immigration, 1865–1900." *South Atlantic Quarterly* 33 (Oct. 1934): 363–85.

Logan, Rayford W. *The Negro in American Life and Thought: The Nadir, 1877–1901.* New York: Dial, 1954.

Look Lai, Walton. *Indentured Labor, Caribbean Sugar: Chinese Indian Migrants to the British West Indies, 1838–1918.* Baltimore: Johns Hopkins University Press, 1993.

Loosley, Allyn C. *Foreign Born Population of California, 1848–1920.* San Francisco: R. and E. Research Associates, 1971.

Low, Victor. *The Unimpressible Race: A Century of Educational Struggle by the Chinese in San Francisco.* San Francisco: East/West Publishing, 1982.

Lyman, Stanford M. *The Asian in North America.* Santa Barbara, Calif.: American Bibliographic Center–Clio, 1977.

———. *Chinese Americans.* New York: Random House, 1974.

———. "The 'Chinese Question' and American Labor Historians." *New Politics* 7, no. 4 (2000): 113–48.

Malloy, William M. *Treaties, Conventions, International Acts, Protocols and Agreements between the United States and Other Powers, 1776–1909.* 61st Cong., 2d sess., Senate Document No. 357.

Man, Albon. "Labor Competition and the New York Draft Riots of 1863." *Journal of Negro History* 36, no. 4 (1951): 375–405.

May, Thomas. "Continuity and Change in the Labor Program of the Union and the Freedmen's Bureau." *Civil War History* 17, no. 3 (1971): 245–54.

McClain, Charles J. *In Search of Equality: The Chinese Struggle against Discrimination in Nineteenth-Century America.* Berkeley: University of California Press, 1994.

McLeod, William F. Jr. "New Views on the Chinese Coolie Trade, 1845–1860." M.A. thesis, Georgia State University, 1976.

Meagher, Arnold J. *The Introduction of Chinese Laborers to Latin America: The "Coolie Trade," 1847–1874.* San Francisco: Chinese Materials Center, 1978.

Meier, August, and Elliott M. Rudwick. *From Plantation to Ghetto: An Interpretive History of American Negroes.* New York: Hill and Wang, 1966.

Melendy, Howard B., and Benjamin F. Gilbert. *The Governors of California: Peter H. Burnett to Edmund G. Brown.* Georgetown, Calif.: Talisman, 1965.

Messner, William F. *Freedmen and the Ideology of Free Labor: Louisiana, 1862–1865.* Lafayette: University of Southwestern Louisiana, 1978.

Miller, Loren. *The Petitioners: The Story of the Supreme Court of the United States and the Negro.* New York: Pantheon Books, 1966.

Miller, Stuart C. *The Unwelcome Immigrant: The American Image of the Chinese, 1785–1882.* Berkeley: University of California Press, 1969.

Montgomery, David. *Beyond Equality: Labor and the Radical Republicans, 1862–1872.* New York: Vintage Books, 1967.

Moy, James S. *Marginal Sights: Staging the Chinese in America.* Iowa City: Iowa University Press, 1993.

Ng, Franklin. "The Sojourner, Return Migration, and Immigration History." *Chinese American History and Perspectives* 2 (1987): 53–71.

Ngai, Mae M. "The Architecture of Race in American Immigration Law: A Reexamination of the Immigration Act of 1924." *Journal of American History* 86, no. 1 (1999): 67–92.

Oberholtzer, Ellis Paxson. *A History of the United States since the Civil War.* Vol. 4. New York: Macmillan, 1931.

Ochs, Patricia M. *A History of Chinese Labor in San Luis Obispo County.* San Luis Obispo, Calif.: San Luis Obispo Historical Society, 1970.

Omi, Michael, and Howard Winant. *Racial Formation in the United States: From the 1960's to the 1980's.* New York: Routledge and Kegan Paul, 1987.

"Ought the Negro to Be Disfranchised? Ought He to Have Been Enfranchised?" *North American Review* 128 (Mar. 1879): 225–83.

Painter, Nell Irvin. *Exodusters: Black Migration to Kansas after Reconstruction.* Lawrence: University Press of Kansas, 1986.

Peffer, George A. "From under the Sojourner's Shadow: A Historiographical Study of Chinese Immigration to America, 1852–1882." *Journal of American Ethnic History* 11, no. 3 (1992): 41–67.

———. *If They Don't Bring Their Women Here: Chinese Female Immigration before Exclusion.* Urbana: University of Illinois Press, 1999.

Perlman, Selig. *A History of Trade Unionism in the United States.* 1922. Reprint, New York: A. M. Kelley, 1950.

Peterson, Richard H. *Manifest Destiny in the Mines: A Cultural Interpretation of Anti-Mexican Nativism in California, 1848–1853.* San Francisco: R. and E. Research Associates, 1975.

Pickett, Charles. *Pickett's Pamphlet, on the Railway, Chinese, and Presidential Questions.* San Francisco: n.p., 1876.

Pike, James S. *The Prostrate State: South Carolina under Negro Government.* New York: D. Appleton, 1874.

Pitt, Leonard. *The Decline of the Californios: A Social History of the Spanish-Speaking Californians, 1846–1890.* Berkeley: University of California Press, 1966.

"The Political South Hereafter." *Nation,* Apr. 5, 1877, 202–3.

Pomerantz, Sidney I. "Election of 1876." In *History of American Presidential Elections, 1789–1968,* vol. 2, edited by Arthur Schlesinger, 1379–1487. New York: Chelsea House, 1971.

Power of the State to Exclude Foreigners from Its Limits, and to Prevent Their Landing, on Account of the Immorality of Their Past Lives, Considered. Opinion of Mr. Justice Field, of U.S. Supreme Court Delivered September 21st, 1874, in the Case of Ah Fong, a Chinese Woman, Brought before the Circuit Court of the United States, for the District of California, on a Writ of Habeas Corpus. San Francisco: Edward Bosqui, 1874.

Richards, Leonard. *Gentlemen of Property and Standing: Anti-Abolition Mobs in Jacksonian America.* New York: New York University Press, 1971.

Richardson, James D. *A Compilation of the Messages and Papers of the Presidents, 1789–1908.* Vols. 5–7. New York: Bureau of National Literature and Art, 1910.

Rodman, Paul W. *Mining Frontiers of the Far West, 1848–1880.* Albuquerque: University of New Mexico Press, 1974.

Roediger, David R. *The Wages of Whiteness: Race and the Making of the American Working Class.* Rev. ed. London: Verso, 1999.

Rogers, Alan. "Chinese and the Campaign to Abolish Capital Punishment in Massachusetts, 1870–1914." *Journal of American Ethnic History* 18, no. 2 (1999): 37–72.

Royce, Josiah. *California from the Conquest in 1846 to the Second Vigilance Committee in San Francisco.* Boston: Houghton, Mifflin, 1886.

Rudolph, Frederick. "Chinamen in Yankeedom: Anti-Unionism in Massachusetts in 1870." *American Historical Review* 53, no. 1 (1947): 1–29.

Runcie, John, "'Hunting the Nigs' in Philadelphia: The Race Riot of August 1834." *Pennsylvania History* 39, no. 2 (1972): 187–218.

Salyer, Lucie. *Laws as Harsh as Tigers: Chinese Immigrants and the Shaping of Modern Immigration Law.* Chapel Hill: University of North Carolina Press, 1995.

Sandmeyer, Elmer C. *The Anti-Chinese Movement in California.* 1939. Reprint, Urbana: University of Illinois Press, 1990.

Saxton, Alexander. "The Army of Canton in the High Sierra." *Pacific Historical Review* 35, no. 2 (1966): 141–52.

———. *The Indispensable Enemy: Labor and the Anti-Chinese Movement in California.* Berkeley: University of California Press, 1971.

———. "Race and the House of Labor." In *The Great Fear: Race in the Minds of White America,* edited by Gary B. Nash and Richard Weiss, 98–120. New York: Holt, Rinehart and Winston, 1970.

"Scholarly Controversy: Whiteness and the Historians' Imagination." *International Labor and Working Class History* 60 (Fall 2001): 1–92.

"The Senate and the Chinese." *Harper's Weekly,* Mar. 18, 1882, 162–63.

Shankman, Arnold M. *Ambivalent Friends: Afro-Americans View the Immigrant.* Westport, Conn.: Greenwood, 1982.

Shaw, William. *Golden Dreams and Waking Realities: Being the Adventures of a Gold-Seeker in California and the Pacific Islands.* London: Smith, Elder, 1851.

Shinn, Charles H. *Mining Camps: A Study in American Frontier Government.* New York: Charles Scribner's Sons, 1885.

Sinkler, George. *The Racial Attitudes of American Presidents from Abraham Lincoln to Theodore Roosevelt.* New York: Doubleday, 1971.

Slotkin, Richard. *The Fatal Environment: The Myth of the Frontier in the Age of Industrialization, 1800–1890.* New York: Atheneum, 1985.

Smith, Theodore C. *The Life and Letters of James Abram Garfield.* New Haven, Conn.: Yale University Press, 1925.

Speer, William. *China and California: Their Relations, Past and Present, a Lecture in Conclusion of a Series in Relation to the Chinese People.* San Francisco: John O'Meara, 1853.

———. *An Humble Plea Addressed to the Legislature of California, in Behalf of the Immigrants from the Empire of China to This State.* San Francisco: Office of the Oriental, 1856.

Spratt, L. W. "Report on the Slave Trade to the Southern Convention." *De Bow's Review* 24, no. 6 (1858): 473–91.

Starr, M. B. *The Coming Struggle; or, What the People on the Pacific Coast Think of the Coolie Invasion.* San Francisco: Bacon, 1873.

Stout, Arthur. *Chinese Immigration and the Physiological Causes of the Decay of a Nation.* San Francisco: Agnew and Deffenbach, 1862.

Sullivan, John L. "Annexation." *United States Magazine and Democratic Review* 17 (July 1845): 5–10.

Sutherland, Anne. *Gypsies: The Hidden Minorities.* New York: Free Press, 1975.

Swett, John. *History of the Public School System of California.* San Francisco: A. L. Bancroft, 1876.

Swisher, Carl Brent. *History of the Supreme Court of the United States.* Vol. 5, *The Taney Period, 1836–64.* New York: Macmillan, 1974.

Sylvis, James. *The Life and Speeches, Labors and Essays of William H. Sylvis, Late President of the Iron-Moulders' International Union; and Also of the National Labor Union.* Philadelphia: Claxton, Remsen, and Haffelfinger, 1872.

Takaki, Ronald. *Strangers from a Different Shore: A History of Asian Americans.* Boston: Little, Brown, 1989.

Tchen, John Kuo Wei. *New York before Chinatown: Orientalism and the Shaping of American Culture.* Baltimore: Johns Hopkins University Press, 1999.

Teiser, Sidney. "Life of George H. Williams: Almost Chief-Justice." *Oregon Historical Quarterly* 47, no. 3 (1946): 255–80; 47, no. 4 (1946): 417–40.

Thorpe, Francis, comp. and ed. *The Federal and State Constitutions, Colonial Charters, and Other Organic Laws of the States, Territories, and Colonies Now and Heretofore Forming the United States of America.* Washington, D.C.: Government Printing Office, 1909.

Thurman, A. Odell. "The Negro in California before 1890." *Pacific Historian* 20, no. 1 (1976): 62–72; 20, no. 2 (1976): 177–88.

Tinker, Hugh. *A New System of Slavery: The Export of Indian Labour Overseas, 1830–1920.* London: Hansib, 1993.

Tong, Benson. *Unsubmissive Women: Chinese Prostitutes in Nineteenth-Century San Francisco.* Norman: University of Oklahoma Press, 1994.

Trauner, B. "The Chinese as Medical Scapegoats in San Francisco, 1870–1905." *California History* 57, no. 1 (1978): 70–87.

Trefousse, Hans L. *The Radical Republicans: Lincoln's Vanguard for Racial Justice.* New York: Alfred A. Knopf, 1969.

Trelease, Allen W. *White Terror: The Ku Klux Klan Conspiracy and Southern Reconstruction.* Baton Rouge: Louisiana State University Press, 1971.

Tsai, Shih-Shan Henry. *China and the Overseas Chinese in the United States, 1868–1911.* Fayetteville: University of Arkansas, 1983.

Tseng, Timothy. "Ministry at Arms' Length: Asian Americans in the Racial Ideology of American Mainline Protestants, 1882–1952." Ph.D. diss., Union Theological Seminary, 1994.

Van Dyne, Frederic. *Citizenship of the United States.* Rochester, N.Y.: Lawyers' Co-Operative Publishing, 1904.

Van Evrie, J. H. *The Dred Scott Case Decision: Opinion of Chief Justice Taney.* New York: Van Evrie, Horton, 1860.

———. *White Supremacy and Negro Subordination; or, Negroes a Subordinate Race, and (So-Called) Slavery Its Normal Condition.* New York: Van Evrie, Horton, 1868.

Voegeli, Victor Jacque. *Free but Not Equal: The Midwest and the Negro during the Civil War.* Chicago: University of Chicago Press, 1967.

Wang, Sing-wu. *The Organization of Chinese Emigration, 1848–1888.* San Francisco: Chinese Material Center, 1978.

Whitney, James. *The Chinese and the Chinese Question.* New York: Thompson and Moreau, 1880.

Wickliffe, John. "Negro Suffrage, a Failure: Shall We Abolish It?" *Forum* 14 (Feb. 1893): 797–804.

Williams, Frederick Wells. *Anson Burlingame and the First Chinese Mission to Foreign Powers.* 1912. Reprint, New York: Russell and Russell, 1972.

Williamson, Joel. *The Crucible of Race: Black-White Relations in the American South since Emancipation.* New York: Oxford University Press, 1984.

Wilson, Theodore B. *The Black Codes of the South.* University, Ala.: University of Alabama Press, 1967.

Winks, Robert W. *The Blacks in Canada: A History.* Montreal: McGill–Queen's University Press, 1971.

Woodhull, Victoria. "Labor and Capital: Chinese Labor." *Woodhull and Claflin's Weekly,* July 9, 1870, reprinted in *Racism, Dissent, and Asian Americans from 1850 to the Present: A Documentary History,* edited by Philip S. Foner and Daniel Rosenberg, 167–69. Westport, Conn.: Greenwood, 1993.

Woodward, C. Vann. *The Burden of Southern History.* 1968. Reprint, Baton Rouge: Louisiana State University Press, 1993.

———. *Origins of the New South, 1877–1913.* Baton Rouge: Louisiana State University Press, 1951.

"The World in California." *Hutching's California Magazine* 1, no. 9 (1857): 385–93.

Wright, W. W. "The Coolie Trade; or, The Encomienda System of the Nineteenth Century." *De Bow's Review* 27, no. 3 (1859): 296–321.

Wu, Cheng-Tsu, ed. *"Chink!" A Documentary History of Anti-Prejudice in America.* New York: World Publishing, 1972.

Wu, Shangying. *One Hundred Years of Chinese in the United States and Canada.* Hong Kong: Chia lo yinshua Yu Hsien, Kung ssu, 1954.

Wunder, John. "Anti-Chinese Violence in the American West." In *Law for the Elephant, Law for the Beaver: Essays in the Legal History of the North American West,* edited by John McLaren, Hamar Foster, and Chet Orloff, 212–36. Pasadena, Calif.: Ninth Judiciary Circuit Historical Society, 1992.

Wynne, Robert E. *Reaction to the Chinese in the Pacific Northwest and British Columbia, 1850 to 1910.* New York: Arno, 1978.

Yen, Tzu-Kuei. "Chinese Workers and the First Transcontinental Railroad of the USA." Ph.D. diss., St. John's University, 1976.

Yung, Judy. *Chinese Women of America: A Pictorial History.* Seattle: University of Washington Press, 1986.

Zo, Kil Young. *Chinese Emigration into the United States, 1850–1880.* New York: Arno, 1978.

Index

abolition. *See* Emancipation Proclamation

abolitionists, 53, 131, 202, 206, 218; as advocates of racial equality, 20, 75; and decline of Sinophobia, 5; on labor programs of Union Army, 76; as targets in riots, 20–21. *See also* amalgamation

An Act concerning the Rights of American Citizens in Foreign States, 111

An Act for the Protection of Foreigners, 37

Act to Discourage the Immigration to This State [California] of Persons Who Cannot Become Citizens Thereof, 47

An Act to Execute Certain Treaty Stipulations relating to Chinese. See Chinese exclusion legislation: Exclusion Act of 1882

An Act to Prevent the Further Immigration of Chinese and Mongolians to This State [California], 59, 66

An Act to Prevent the Importation of Chinese Criminals, and to Prevent the Establishment of Chinese Slavery, 158–59

An Act to Prevent the Kidnaping and Importation of Mongolian, Chinese and Japanese Females, for Criminal and Demoralizing Purposes, 158–59

An Act to Prohibit the "Coolie Trade" by American Citizens in American Vessels, 77, 78–79

An Act to Protect Free White Labor against Competition with Chinese Coolie Labor, and to Discourage the Immigration of the Chinese into the State of California. See Chinese police tax

Adams, Charles F., Jr., 114

Adams, Henry, 218

"Address to the People of the United States upon the Evils of Chinese Immigration." *See Chinese Immigration: Its Social, Moral, and Political Effect*

Africa, 18, 24, 26, 94, 98, 143, 145

African Americans: activism during Civil War, 74–75; in border states, 64; compared with aliens, 27; and Constitution, 15, 86, 87; disaffection with race relations, 55, 71, 218; disfranchisement of, 16, 91, 215, 219; and *Dred Scott,* 54–55; free blacks, seen as threat to racial order, 19; hostility toward, 7, 10, 16, 21–22, 48, 73–74, 138, 218; limited opportunities of, in the northern states, 16, 25, 32, 73–74, 119, 138–39; limited rights of, in the northern states, 16, 25, 39, 45, 54, 55, 71, 75, 91, 119; migration of, from South, 119, 218; organizational efforts of, in California, 39; and *People v. Hall,* 45; racial stereotypes of, 10–11, 20, 23–24, 48, 54, 64, 68, 75, 108, 123, 185, 198, 208; reaction of, to recruitment of Chinese workers, 123; and Reconstruction, 153–55, 173, 182, 216–17; restrictions of rights of, in postbellum South, 86, 119; status of, in postbellum South, 122–23; subordination of, 48, 55; and three-fifths clause, 15, 91; as unassimilable, 7, 10, 64–65, 189, 208. *See also* anti-black attitudes; anti-black legislation; black codes; black colonization; black labor; California;

citizenship; emancipation; Northeast; Reconstruction; slavery; Southeast; testimony restrictions

Africans, 44, 96, 114, 198, 228; and immigration, 94, 147, 150, 195

Ah Fong (In re Ah Fong), 169–70, 172, 176, 177, 179, 193. *See also Chy Lung v. Freeman*

Ah Yup (In re Ah Yup), 194–95, 209, 224

Almaguer, Tomás, 7–8

Alvord, William, 165

amalgamation, 65, 69, 75, 127, 167; abolitionists and, 21; of Chinese and blacks, 226; of Chinese and whites, 34, 38, 46, 69, 83, 115, 124, 136, 188, 199, 206; Douglas on, 57–58; and emancipation, 72; Republicans as alleged advocates of, 63; and school segregation, 62; statutes banning, 62; white fears of, 21, 38, 73–74, 136. *See also* sexual vigilantism

American creed, 7, 48; African and Native Americans excluded from, 7, 15; Chinese excluded from, 12

American identity, 7, 8; criteria for, 7–8, 14, 15, 152, 194–95; and immigration, 7; incompatible with Asianness, 152, 185, 194–95; incompatible with blackness, 15, 185; and Republicanism, 15; and westward expansion, 7, 22. *See also* citizenship; whiteness

American party (Know Nothing party), 175; anti-Asian attitudes of, 51–52; anti-Californio attitudes of, 51, 236n48; attitudes of, toward immigrants, 50–53; decline of, 52–53; Republicans' ties with, 52, 53, 131, 175, 233n15; rise of, 50–51

American Workman, 136

amnesty, 85, 86, 153, 154

anti-Asian legislation, 2, 227, 228. *See also* anti-Chinese legislation

anti-black attitudes, 7, 10, 50, 55; and black colonization plans, 64, 217–18; in California, 23–24, 25, 27, 33, 39, 79; and Chinese exclusion, 197, 199–200, 202, 208–9, 212; effect of, on other nonwhites, 8, 13; following emancipation, 73–74, 75, 101, 138; following Reconstruction, 217–18, 221; and recruitment of Chinese in the South, 122–23; of Republicans, 64, 75, 99–100; and southern migrants, 218; varieties of, 16, 20, 221. *See also* African Americans

anti-black legislation, 6, 16, 21, 46, 54, 62; in California, 25, 39; dismantling of, 14, 74,

228; in post-Reconstruction South, 221. *See also* black exclusion

anti-Catholicism, 51, 167, 168

anti-Chinese convention, 158

anti-Chinese legislation: actors in, 14; and black-white relations, 8, 14; and California constitution, 192; Chinese resistance to, 1–2, 47, 165, 166, 225; dismantling of, 14, 158, 228; immigration acts (California), 37, 59, 66, 158; immigration acts (U.S.), 176–77, 213; lodging-house law, 159–65; in Pacific Northwest, 56, 59; reaction to, 166; severity of, 5, 8, 9, 59, 165, 225; following veto of fifteen passenger bill, 204. *See also* California; capitation tax; Chinese exclusion legislation; Chinese police tax; commutation tax; "exempt classes"; foreign miners' licence laws/taxes; Geary Act; *names of acts;* queue-cutting ordinance; San Francisco; schools; Scott Act

anti-Chinese movement: and American party, 51–52; and Burlingame mission and treaty, 109; in California, 45–47, 49–50, 70, 104, 156–61, 163–71, 179–80, 187–89, 190–95, 204; and call for Chinese exclusion, 35–36, 40, 49, 50, 69, 126–27, 130, 136–37, 158, 161, 163, 165, 181, 184, 187, 190, 196; Chinese reaction to, 1–2, 38–39, 40, 70; compromised by Reconstruction legislation, 158; directed at Chinese women, 176–78; Douglass on, 14; and fear of massive Chinese immigration, 35, 37, 38, 40, 43, 46, 48, 96, 97, 99, 101, 113, 130, 132–33, 134, 142, 144, 166, 173, 185, 205, 226; historiography of, 1–6, 9–10; importation versus immigration in rhetoric of, 130–33, 204, 230n24; motivations behind, 2, 3–5, 6–7, 8, 14, 43, 59, 135–36, 170, 206; in Northeast, 48–49, 60–62, 127–33, 135; in Pacific Northwest, 59, 189–90, 197; and provisions of Treaty of 1880, 205; and reports on Chinese, 189, 198; secret societies in, 189; stimulated by Tingley bill, 33–34, 37–38; violence of, 189–90, 222. *See also* Chinese; racial violence; Reconstruction; Sinophobia, Workingmen's Party of California

Anti-Chinese Movement in California (Sandmeyer), 3

Anti-Chinese Union, 179, 189

Anti-Coolie Association, 105

Anti-Coolie Club, 189
Anti-Coolie Union, 183
anti-Hispanic attitudes, 28–29
Anti-Slavery Society, 131
Archbald, John, 68
Arthur, Chester A., 205; signs Chinese Exclusion Act (1882), 214; vetoes first Chinese exclusion bill, 210, 212
Asia, 26, 34, 94, 113, 145, 173
Asianization: of African Americans, 148, 155, 215, 218, 219; of European immigrants, 227
Asing (As-sing), Norman, 38–39

Baltimore Statesman, 124
Banks, Nathaniel P., 52, 76
Bayard, James A., 94
Beck, James, 92
Bee, Frederick A., 183
Benedict, Michael L., 12, 84–85
Bennett, Gordon, 118, 119
Bennett, Henry C., 160
Berrien, John M., 17
Bigler, John, 35–36, 38, 45, 46, 47
black citizenship. *See* citizenship; *Dred Scott v. Sandford*; Fourteenth Amendment; Naturalization Act of 1790; Naturalization Act of 1870; Reconstruction
black codes (post–Civil War), 82, 86, 88, 120
black colonization (deportation): to Central and South America, 19, 64, 219; as panacea for race relations, 19, 41, 64, 75, 97; plans under Lincoln administration, 66; repeal of Republican colonization acts, 74; and Republican party, 64
black exclusion, 17, 19, 46, 49, 65, 71; California bills for, 25, 39–40, 54, 66; and California constitutional convention, 23–24; and fear of "black tide," 24, 25, 66; in Florida, 17; in Illinois, 43; in Iowa, 17; from mines in California, 23; from Oregon, 56; as precedent for Chinese exclusion, 43, 46
black labor: alleged degrading effect of, 19–20, 24; autonomy of, 120; Chinese labor as substitute for, 41–42, 50; compared with Chinese labor, 122–23; conditions of, 86, 120; and dual labor market, 32, 138; economic plight of, 16, 20, 32, 73–74, 86, 104–5, 138; excluded from labor movement, 138; opposed by white labor, 19, 20, 73–74, 138; as panacea for labor problem in postbellum South, 125; programs affecting, 76, 120; resistance of, 120; as scapegoat, 73;

shunned, 33, 80, 138–39; stigmatized as inferior, 10, 11, 20, 23, 38, 68, 81; as strikebreakers, 73; unity with white labor, 20; and upgrading of white labor, 67. *See also* black codes
black mobility, 16, 119, 125, 216; efforts to curb, 17, 21, 39, 46, 54, 65, 75–76, 79, 199; efforts to encourage, 76–77, 79; and family reunion, 120; fear of, 65–66, 72–73, 75, 119, 120, 134, 216, 219; resettlement proposals, 64, 215–16, 219; significance of *Passenger Cases* for, 18–19. *See also* black out-migration; Lincoln, Abraham
blackness. *See* whiteness
black out-migration, 39, 66, 71, 217–18
black suffrage: referenda on, 91; Republican position on, 99–101, 146, 150–51; resistance to, 74, 156. *See also* Fifteenth Amendment; Republican party
Blaine, James G., 200, 202, 208
Boalt, John, 188
Booth, Newton, 164, 168, 198, 199
Boreman, Arthur I., 152
Borneo, 175
Boston, 73
Boston Commonwealth, 126, 127
Boston Evening Transcript, 127
Bouchard, James C., 167
Bradley, Joseph, 220
Brewster, David J., 225
Burlingame, Anson, 108, 236n50
Burlingame mission, 108–9, 174
Burlingame Treaty, 109–12, 133, 137, 142, 144, 167, 177, 199, 203, 205; call for abrogation or modification of, 112, 130, 163, 168, 176, 193, 196, 201, 204, 205, 206; and coolie issue, 110; migration rights of Chinese in, 109–10; and naturalization, 110–11, 144; reaction to, 111–12, 115; as tool against anti-Chinese statutes, 111, 158, 165, 169, 170, 192, 220; and treaties with Europe, 110, 111; Twain on, 111–12
Burnett, Peter H., 25
Burwell, William M., 124–25
Butler, Benjamin F., 76, 213
Butte County Free Press, 189

California: American party in, 51–52; before annexation, 22; anti-Chinese movement in, 33, 107, 179; diversity of population in, 25–27, 47; economy of, 2, 4, 45, 104, 157; election of 1867, 103–4, 105; failure of contract labor in, 32; gold rush in, 23; labor movement in, 104; labor shortage in, 32, 33, 41; nativism in, 26, 27–29; and Reconstruction legislation, 117, 156; status of African Americans in, 23, 25, 79, 156; and whiteness, 25

—legislature: black exclusion bills in, 25, 39–40, 54, 58; Chinese exclusion bills in, 40, 49, 58–59, 158–59; Chinese immigration hearings by, 187–89; Chinese police tax by, 67–68; discriminatory employment legislation by, 192–93; fugitive slave law by, 39; immigration acts by, 37, 47, 49, 58–59, 168, 177, 179; lodging-house law by, 159, 165, 180; refuses petition from African Americans, 39; reports on Chinese by, 34–35, 40, 45–47, 49–50, 67, 70; and restriction of Chinese immigration, 43–44, 46, 164, 168, 188. *See also* anti-black legislation; anti-Chinese legislation; foreign miners' licence laws/taxes; schools; testimony restrictions

California Constitutional Convention (1849): 25, 35; and Hispanic Americans, 28–29; "Negro question" in, 23–24, 191; status of foreigners in, 26–27

California Constitutional Convention (1878–79), 191–92

Californian, 15

California State Convention of Colored Citizens, 80

California Workingmen's party. *See* Workingmen's Party of California

Californios, 22, 33; discrimination against, 28, 29; whitening of, 7, 28–29. *See also* Hispanics

Cameron, Andrew, 127

Cameron, Simon, 98

Canada, 39

capitation tax, 44, 47, 50, 59

Carpenter, Matthew, 147

Casserly, Eugene, 137

"Celestial Ladies," 60–61

"Celestial Negro," 115

Central Pacific Anti-Coolie Association, 157

Central Pacific Railroad, 66, 69, 79–83, 112, 157; and Chinese laborers, 80–82; and dual labor market, 79. *See also* Crocker, Charles

certificates of freedom, 16

certificates of residence, 223

Chase, Salmon P., 64

Chico Caucasian, 189

China, 30, 36, 44, 52, 70, 94, 105; American accounts of, 6, 48, 60; efforts of, to restrict emigration, 204, 223; reaction of, to Sinophobic legislation, 224; U.S. trade with, 5, 40, 41, 46, 108, 115, 117, 174, 196, 201; U.S. treaties with, 56, 89, 109, 166, 205, 223

Chinese: alien status of, 33, 37; associations of, 31, 40, 109; categories of emigrants, 30–31; compared with African Americans, 8, 38, 41, 43, 44, 45, 72, 81–82, 90, 95, 96, 98, 108, 113–14, 119, 122, 123, 124, 125, 134, 142, 143, 167, 170–71, 185, 186, 195, 197, 198, 200, 208, 209, 218; compared with Euro-Americans, 45, 48, 49, 52, 108, 110, 122, 133, 160, 184, 191, 199; compared with Europeans, 1, 79, 113, 119, 122, 134, 143–44, 167, 182, 184, 188, 193, 197, 227–28, 258n21; compared with Gypsies, 89; compared with Native Americans, 119, 197, 198; contributions to economy by, 4, 50, 67, 70, 160, 167, 184, 197, 210; criminalization of, 187; cultural incompatibility of, 35, 44, 45, 48, 71, 72, 89, 124, 136, 144, 145, 147, 170, 183, 200; eastern editors on, 48–49, 60, 115–16; emigration of, 30; extension of black restrictions to, 62; Indianization of, 230n23; as "indispensable enemies," 4; in Massachusetts, 126, 129; merchants, 70; as organizational tool for labor, 4, 157–58, 160, 181, 190–92; as outsiders, 32; in the Pacific Northwest, 56, 59; as perceived biological threat, 159, 187; as perceived political threat, 114, 116, 133, 136, 143, 144, 145, 146, 161, 184, 185, 188; as perceived sexual threat, 136, 159, 167, 191; as perceived threat to American civilization, 35, 60, 69, 89, 94, 97, 113, 136, 137, 142, 144, 146, 166–67, 180, 185, 188, 193; perceived vices of, 6, 35, 45, 46, 48, 49, 72, 113, 136, 158, 159, 167, 168, 170, 185, 187; praise for, 30, 32, 70, 122; protection of, in Burlingame Treaty, 110; social status of, 45, 70, 71, 121–22, 142; stereotypes of, 3, 4, 6, 10–11, 13, 35, 48, 49, 60–62, 68, 70, 108, 113–14, 123, 124, 125, 127, 129, 132, 137, 159, 161, 173, 174, 176, 185, 187, 191, 198; as unassimilable, 3, 37, 48, 49, 70, 71, 72, 113–14, 146, 147, 163, 167, 168, 177, 181, 183, 186, 187, 188, 197, 199, 200; women, 159, 178, 221–22, 252n19. *See also* anti-Chinese legislation; anti-Chinese movement; California; citizenship; conflation; Negroization; North Adams; Southeast; testimony restrictions

"Chinese civil rights bill," 153. *See also* Civil Rights Act of 1875
Chinese exclusion legislation: and black-white relations, 13, 209, 214, 215, 221; effects of, 227; Exclusion Act of 1882, 2, 5, 11, 214, 221; Exclusion Acts (1884–1904), 221, 222–23; debates on, 205–14; and Negro question, 207–8, 212–14; provisions of, 205, 209, 211; racist cast of, 196, 206–7, 212, 213, 215, 216, 221, 223; as violation of treaty obligations, 206, 210; vote on, 209, 211–12, 213; women in, 221–22. *See also* California; citizenship; fifteen passenger bill; naturalization; Page law
Chinese Immigration (Coolidge), 2
Chinese Immigration: Its Social, Moral, and Political Effect, 187–89
Chinese labor: benefits of, 41, 46, 116, 186; as cheap labor, 3–4, 33, 34, 83, 116, 122, 133, 160; compared with black labor, 41, 68, 81; compared with white labor, 34, 41, 81, 113, 122; and competition with white labor, 34, 35, 71, 105, 112, 157, 163, 166; and dual labor market, 32, 33, 67, 69, 105, 160, 168; excluded from white trades, 67–68, 105; harsh treatment of, 81–82; in mines, 36, 45; Negroization of, 38, 41–42, 122; as perceived deterrent to white migrants, 35, 70, 184; praise for, 81, 82, 89, 160, 167–68, 186; preferred over other workers, 11, 32, 33, 41, 80–81, 122, 138–39; recruitment of, 121–23, 126, 129; as solution to labor shortage, 41, 186; in the South, 121–23, 125; stigmatized as coolie labor, 11, 35, 43, 60, 72, 121, 127, 129, 130, 134–35, 146, 161, 166, 175–77; stigmatized as inferior labor, 32, 38, 41, 49, 68, 81, 113, 160, 166; stigmatized as servile/unfree labor, 6, 10, 11, 34, 35, 38, 43, 45, 60, 67, 68, 71, 121, 129–30, 134–35, 142, 161, 187; as strikebreakers, 104, 126, 157; strike by, 81–82, 113; as substitute for black labor, 41, 50, 60, 121, 122–23; as threat to labor, 3, 113, 166–67; as tool of capital, 43, 104, 113, 133, 135, 190; and upgrading of white labor, 67, 80, 168, 184, 186; violence against, 36, 40, 45, 81–82; white opposition to, 32, 36, 68, 68, 157. *See also* anti-Chinese legislation; anti-Chinese movement
"The Chinese must go" (calls for Chinese exclusion/removal), 35, 36, 38, 46, 104, 165, 180, 189, 190, 218
Chinese police tax, 67–68, 71, 72

Chinese question, 3; in California, 37, 163, 170, 188, 190, 191; compared with "Negro problem," 48, 115, 118, 124, 131–32, 137, 147, 148, 160, 166, 184, 185, 188, 197, 200, 203, 206, 207; in Congress, 12–13, 71–72, 93–101, 136, 140, 141–55, 176–77, 182; and the courts, 44, 169–70, 193–95, 224; nationalization of, 4–5, 72, 138, 177, 182; in Northeast, 126–39; party alignments and, 125–26; and Reconstruction, 177–78; and Republicans, 12, 101, 114, 181, 202; in Southeast, 125–26; and treaty obligations, 201, 203; unpopularity of, 160
Chinese restriction acts. *See* Chinese exclusion legislation
Chinese Six Companies, 109
Chinese women. *See* Chinese; prostitution
Chiu, Ping, 3–4
Chy Lung v. Freeman, 179. See also *Ah Fong*
Cigar Makers' Association of San Francisco, 68. *See also* People's Protective Union
citizenship, 16, 22, 152; of African Americans, 7, 16, 18, 22, 25, 54–55, 81, 86, 90–91, 101, 123, 152, 198, 207; of Chinese, 30, 34, 35, 45, 52, 59–60, 69, 81, 87, 89, 90–91, 92, 93, 94–99, 123, 145, 152, 173, 181, 188, 194, 224, 225; and civil rights acts, 86, 87, 142; and *Dred Scott*, 18, 54–55; of European immigrants, 22; loss of, 225; of Mexicans in annexed territory, 28–29; and mining rights, 29, 35, 36, 37, 43; and Reconstruction, 85, 198. *See also* American identity; citizenship; Fourteenth Amendment; naturalization
—ineligibility: of African Americans, 10, 59; of Asians, 227, 228; of Chinese, 10, 13, 35, 46, 47, 59, 194–95, 222, 224–25; legally constructed, 59, 100–101, 195; used to discriminate against Chinese and other Asians, 35, 225, 227; of West Indians, 146. *See also Dred Scott v. Sandford;* whiteness
civil rights: defined, 86; different from political rights, 86, 88, 147
Civil Rights Act of 1866, 86, 87, 88, 141
Civil Rights Act of 1870 (Enforcement Act): and anti-Chinese statutes, 152, 158, 165, 170, 177, 203, 220; Chinese and, 141–42; and naturalization, 142–43, 145; vote on, 142, 143 *See also* Stewart, William P.
Civil Rights Act of 1871 (KKK Act), 141, 173
Civil Rights Act of 1875, 173, 177, 179, 182; and Chinese question, 153–54; partial invalidation of, 220; passage of, 155

Civil Rights Cases (1883), 220–21

Civil War, 65, 84, 148. *See also* African Americans; black colonization; black labor; Reconstruction

coercive measures: against African Americans, 76, 82, 86; against Chinese, 82

Cole, Cornelius, 94, 96, 153

Colfax, Schuyler, 154, 175, 176

commerce clause, 16; and Negro seamen acts, 17; and *Passenger Cases*, 18, 19. *See also* immigration

commissioner of immigration: in California, 47, 158, 168, 169, 179; U.S., 121

Committee on Foreign Miners, 46. *See also* California

Committee on Mines and Mining Interests, 34–35, 40, 70. *See also* California

commutation tax, 37, 59; declared unconstitutional, 158; in *Passenger Cases*, 17

Compromise of Principle (Benedict), 84–85

conflation: of Chinese and new immigrants, 227; of nonwhites, 88, 94, 102

—of Chinese and African Americans, 8–11, 13, 32, 34, 38, 39, 44, 45, 48–49, 50, 56–57, 59–62, 66, 68–69, 71–72, 74, 81, 82, 90–91, 92, 94, 101, 103, 112, 114, 124, 136, 137, 143, 156, 161, 166, 173, 185, 189, 202, 207, 217, 226; Chinese rejection of, 38–39, 45; exceptions to, 11, 54, 72, 81, 84, 89, 151, 163, 167, 170, 189, 195, 201. *See also* Helper, Hinton; Speer, William; Wade, Benjamin

congressional debates: on Chinese exclusion, 197–214; on Chinese question, 87–93, 96–101, 141–55. *See also* naturalization; Reconstruction

Congressional Globe, 15, 43, 63, 84, 103

Congressional Record, 1

Conkling, Roscoe, 91, 201

Connecticut, 16, 51, 93

Conness, John, 89, 90, 94

Conscription Act (1863), 73

Constitution (U.S.), 15, 16, 17, 49, 147, 149. *See also Dred Scott;* Fifteenth Amendment; Fourteenth Amendment; Thirteenth Amendment

constitutional conventions, 55. *See also* California Constitutional Convention (1849); California Constitutional Convention (1878–79); Oregon

"Continental Chinese," 227

contract labor, 31; advocates of Chinese, 32, 37; in California, 31, 32, 33, 168; and labor control, 33; labor opposition to, 127, 129;

to stimulate immigration, 32, 77, 120, 168. *See also* anti-Chinese movement

Contract Labor Act (1864), 77, 78, 120, 129

Coolidge, Mary Roberts, 2, 3, 229n6

coolie acts: of 1862 (U.S.), 77, 78–79, 121, 177; of 1870 (California), 158

coolie labor: allegations of, in U.S., 68, 121, 137, 146, 166, 173–75, 181; in Cuba and Latin America, 31, 60, 77, 78, 121; legislation against, 136–37. *See also* Chinese labor; Grant, Ulysses S.; North Adams, Mass.; Southeast

"coolie theme," 11, 68, 101, 101, 105, 135; in Asian American historiography, 11, 230n24

coolie trade, 77–78; defined, 30–31, 78; legislation against, 31, 77; and slave trade, 31, 77, 78. *See also* coolie acts

Cooper, Henry, 183

Corbett, Henry, 94, 98, 153

Cowan, Edgar, 87, 89, 102

Crispins. *See* Knights of Saint Crispin

Crocker, Charles W., 79, 80, 82, 83; testimony of, 186

Cross, Ira, 112

Cuba, 78, 121

cubic air ordinances. *See* lodging-house legislation

Curtis, Benjamin R., 224

Daily Alta California (San Francisco): on adaptation of Chinese immigrants, 30; on anti-Chinese demonstration, 180; on Chinese immigration, 36; on citizenship of Chinese, 59; on Illinois black law, 43; on Know Nothings, 51; prejudices against Chinese in, 43

Daily Arkansas Gazette, 119

Dallas Herald, 125

Dameron, James P., 185

Daniels, Roger, 127, 227

Davis, Cushman K., 1

Davis, Garrett, 76, 95, 137

Davis, J. C. B., 122

Davis, Noah, 143

Dawes, Henry L., 208

Deady, Matthew, 195

De Bow's Review, 121, 124

Declaration of Independence: and African Americans, 95; assessments of, 146, 147, 151; and equal justice, 149; Lincoln on, 58; Sumner on, 97, 146, 149

Democratic party, 141; and Chinese exclusion

debates, 197–98, 199–200, 204, 205, 209, 212; and Chinese labor in the South, 124, 126; and Chinese question, 4, 181, 207, 209, 212–14; and election of 1868, 92–93; and Kansas-Nebraska Act, 53; in Massachusetts, 213; on naturalization bill of 1870, 149; platforms of, 155, 180–81, 204; race-baiting by, 63, 65; racial attitudes of, 74, 101; rehabilitation of, 107; on Republicans' racial policies, 89–92, 94, 95, 149, 200–201, 212
—in California, 105, 108, 117, 179, 191; anti-Chinese platforms of, 107, 117, 163, 164–65, 180; and Chinese question, 160; and conflation of black and Chinese issues, 105, 108, 117; rehabilitation of, 107
Dimmick, Kimball, 24, 27
discrimination. *See* African Americans; anti-black legislation; anti-Chinese legislation
Dixon, William H., 156, 172
Doolittle, James R., 96–97, 102
Douai, Adolph, 247
Douglas, Stephen A., 57–58
Douglass, Frederick, 14, 123, 138, 140
draft riots, 74–74, 162
Drake, Charles D., 147
Dreadful California (Helper), 47–48
Dred Scott v. Sandford, 17, 18, 56, 57, 87–88; and citizenship, 18, 55, 224; impact of, 55–59; and Reconstruction legislation, 152; and slavery, 54, 55
dual labor market: blacks in, 20, 32, 67; Chinese in, 32, 34, 67, 79–81, 104, 157; and Chinese police tax, 71; exploitation of nonwhites in, 33, 34

Eaves, Lucile, 112
Edmunds, George F., 95, 208
Eliot, Thomas D., 78
emancipation: of African Americans, 11, 65, 72, 74, 75, 119; of American Indians in colonial Mexico, 22
Emancipation Proclamation, 65, 72–73
Enforcement Acts. *See* Civil Rights Act of 1870; Civil Rights Act of 1871
European immigrants, 7, 22, 50, 79; and *Passenger Cases*, 17–18, racialization of, 227–28; southern efforts to attract, 120. *See also* Contract Labor Act
Eustis, James B., 199–201
Evarts, William M., 196
Exclusion Acts (1882–1904). *See* Chinese exclusion legislation

"exempt classes," 5, 205, 222
Exodusters, 218

Farley, James T., 212
Field, Stephen J., 169–70, 176
fifteen passenger bill, 196–202, 205, 207
Fifteenth Amendment, 93–99, 117, 131, 144, 146, 156, 215, 221; and Chinese, 93–101; loophole in, 140; political expediency in, 94, 99–101
Filipinos, 259n36
Fish, Hamilton, 135
Fitch, Thomas, 143–44
Foner, Eric, 85, 172, 173
"force" bill, 182
foreign miners' licence laws/taxes, 27, 36, 43, 47, 50, 66, 67, 163; declared unconstitutional, 158; discriminatory collection of, 28; effect of, on Latin American miners, 37; as exploitation device, 46–47, 67; and foreigners' civil rights, 37, 40; as revenue source, 37, 40, 46, 47, 50, 67; targeting of Chinese by, 35, 40; violence and fraud in enforcement of, 37
Fourteenth Amendment, 88–91, 92, 103, 140, 143, 177, 179, 220; and Chinese question, 88–91; Chinese use of, 152, 170; and due process for Chinese, 117, 143, 158, 177, 193, 203. *See also jus soli;* privileges and immunities clause
Freedmen's Bureau, 74, 76, 120, 138
Freedom's Phalanx, 51
free labor: and coercive measures, 120; differentiated from black labor, 11, 18–20, 38, 54, 139; differentiated from Chinese or Asian labor, 11, 34, 38, 67, 68, 139; ideology of, 19–20, 53–54, 64, 172; and Union Army, 76, 120
Frelinghuysen, Frederick T., 94
fugitive slave laws, 39, 212

Garfield, James A., 204–5
Garrison, William Lloyd, 202
Geary Act (1892), 223
George, Henry, 112–14, 116, 117, 157; testimony of, 185
George, James Z., 209, 214
Germans, 50, 52, 83, 96, 122, 193
Gibson, Otis, 167–68
Gilbert, Edward, 24, 27
Godkin, E. L., 115–16, 133–34
Gorham, George, 105, 106
Goulding, Charles, 122

Grant, Madison, 228
Grant, Ulysses S., 92, 135, 172, 180; and Chinese, 173–76
"greaser," 29, 232n57
Great Britain, 30, 109, 110. *See also* Negro seamen acts
Greeley, Horace, 48, 65, 113
Green, Thomas J., 27
Grover, La Fayette, 198, 199
Gwin, William M., 43, 57
Gypsies, 88, 89

Haight, Henry H.: attitudes toward African Americans, 185; attitudes toward Chinese, 41, 107–8, 109
Hale, John P., 56, 209
Harlan, John M., 220
Harper's Weekly, 9, 60, 61, 83, 116, 128, 162, 196, 216, 217
Hart, Augustus L., 193
Harte, Bret, 161
Hawley, Joseph R., 212, 213
Hayes, Rutherford B., 204; and Burlingame Treaty, 196–97; and fifteen passenger bill, 202, 203–4; misgivings about Chinese, 203
Hayes-Tilden Controversy, 196
heathen (pagan): black stereotype, 41, 90, 149; Chinese stereotype, 34, 36, 41, 60, 90, 125, 146, 161, 167, 197, 199, 200
Helper, Hinton R., 47–48, 101–2, 112
Hendricks, Thomas A., 95
Highby, William, 89–90
Hispanics: citizenship of, 28; as perceived threat to Anglo dominance, 33; as targets of Californian nativism, 27–29, 48, 51
historiography: of anti-Chinese movement, 1–6, 9–10; of Asian immigration and exclusion, 1–6, 178; of race relations, 13; of Reconstruction, 11–12, 84–85, 100
Ho Ah Kow v. Nunan, 193
Hoar, George F., 201, 206, 207, 208, 209
Hoffman, Ogden, 192–93
Hopkins, Mark, 82
Hottentots, 98, 99, 101, 143
Howard, Jacob M., 88, 90, 95, 96, 97
Howe, Timothy O., 147
Hubbs, Paul, 62
Huntington, Collis, 82
Hutching's California Magazine, 62

Illinois black law, 43
immigration: conventions, 123; desire for, of

Europeans, 22, 77; post–1965, 14; Immigration Act of 1924, 227, 228; protected by Congress, 18, 19, 26, 27, 56, 72, 164, 165, 169, 179, 194. *See also* Burlingame Treaty; Chinese; Chinese exclusion legislation; commissioner of immigration; Contract Labor Act; coolie acts
The Impending Crisis of the South (Helper), 47
Independent Taxpayers' party, 164, 165
The Indispensable Enemy (Saxton), 4
Industrial Reformers, 163, 164
intermarriage, 25, 62. *See also* amalgamation
In re Ah Yup. See *Ah Yup*
In re Rodriguez, 224
In re Tirbucio Parrott, 192–93
In Search of Equality (McClain), 1–2
In the Matter of Carter Perkins, 39
Irish, 2, 50, 52, 79, 83, 96, 134; and blacks, 20; and Chinese, 122, 193
Irwin, William, 180

Jacksonianism, 4, 5
Japan (steamship), 169
Japanese, 44, 69, 79, 94, 127, 143; internment of, 225
Jim Crow, 221
Joint Congressional Committee to Investigate Chinese Immigration, 183–86, 196, 198
Johnson, Andrew, 81, 86, 92, 96, 103, 108, 174; and Civil Rights Act, 88
Johnson, James A., 92, 137, 142
Jones, John P., 208
jus soli, 87, 88, 89, 90

Kansas exodus, 218
Kansas-Nebraska Act, 53
Kasson, John A., 211
Kearney, Denis, 190–91, 254n55
Kearneyism, 198
Keifer, J. Warren, 211
Knights of Saint Crispin: in North Adams, Mass., 126, 130, 138; in San Francisco, 157
Knights of the White Camelia, 140
Know Nothingism, 197
Know Nothing party, 44. *See also* American party
Ku Klux Klan, 140, 183, 189. *See also* Civil Rights Act of 1871
Kwong, Chong, Wing & Co., 129

labor movement: anti-Chinese rhetoric of, 104, 127–30, 190–91; anti-Orientalism and rise of, 2, 3, 4, 157–58, 190; ignores Chinese strike, 82; mobilizes against Chinese, 127–30, 157, 164, 190–91; and nonwhite labor, 104–5, 138; pro-Chinese voices in, 127; and Reconstruction policies, 138. *See also* anti-Chinese movement; Chinese labor; Sand Lot meetings; Workingmen's Party of California

Labor Reform party, 131, 145

The Land of Gold (Helper), 47–48

Lane, James H., 75

Latin Americans, 26, 31, 60, 64, 77, 80

Laundry ordinance, 165, 166

legislation. *See* anti-Asian legislation; anti-black legislation; anti-Chinese legislation; Chinese exclusion legislation; *individual acts*

Legree, Simon, 136

Liberal Republican party, 153, 154

Liberty party, 53

Li Huang-chang, 175

Lincoln, Abraham, 86; and black colonization, 66; on black out-migration, 66; on *Dred Scott*, 57; and issues of nonwhites; 58; on labor programs of Union Army, 76; racial attitudes of, 64–65; on Reconstruction plan, 85

Lincoln-Douglas debates, 57–58, 64

Lin Sing v. Washburn, 240n40

Lippincott's Geographical Dictionary of the World, 60

literacy: as voting requirement, 140

Litwack, Leon, 55

lodging-house legislation, 159, 165, 180

Los Angeles riot (1871), 163–64

Louisiana, 121, 122, 123, 182

Low, Frederick F., 104

McCarver, Morton, 23

McClain, Charles, 1

McCreery, Thomas, 145

McCreery amendment, 223

McDougal, John, 32–33

Malays, 46, 69, 127

Manchu court, 108–9

"Manifest Destiny." *See* Mexican-American War

Marcy, William, 77

Massachusetts, 17, 51, 52, 126

Massachusetts Labor Reform party, 132

Matthews, Stanley, 201

Maynard, Horace, 72

Meade, Edwin R., 183, 188

Mechanics' State Council, 157

"Memorial to the Congress of the United States." *See Chinese Immigration: Its Social, Moral, and Political Effect*

Memphis Immigration Convention (1869), 123

merchants, Chinese: exempt from exclusion acts, 5; reaction to Sinophobia, 47

Methodist Episcopal Mission House (San Francisco), 167

Mexican-American War, 7, 22–23; and "Manifest Destiny," 19

Mexicans. *See* Californios; Hispanics

Mexico, 27, 39, 161

Miller, John F., 205

Miller, Loren, 220

Miller, Samuel, 179

Miller, Stuart C., 6

Miller, Warner, 209

miscegenation. *See* amalgamation; sexual vigilantism

Missouri Compromise, 16, 230n5

Mitchell, John H., 198, 199

"Mongolian plank," 182

mongrelization, 94, 206. *See also* amalgamation

Morey, Henry, 204

Morgan, John T., 199, 212, 214

Morton, Oliver P., 97, 183, 243n52; opposes Chinese naturalization, 145, 147, 150; pro-Chinese minority report by, 184, 186

Moulder, Andrew, 62

Mungen, William, 161

Murray, Hugh C.: ruling in *In the Matter of Carter Perkins*, 39; ruling in *People v. Hall*, 44, 59

Nation, 115–16, 133–34, 202, 221

National Anti-Slavery Standard, 131, 132

National Colored Labor Union, 138

National Labor Union, 127, 129, 130

Native Americans, 7, 10, 81, 91, 145, 170–71, 185; and amalgamation, 69; and American nationality, 15; compared with Chinese, 147, 197; conflation of, with blacks, 69, 95; history of, 22; sexual vigilantism against, 74; stereotypes of, 198; as unassimilable, 7

nativism, 13, 14, 15, 28–29, 230n26, 236n49; affecting post-1965 immigration, 14; of

American party, 50–53; anti-Chinese, 13, 14, 35, 51–52; anti-Hispanic, 28–29; in California, 26–29; and European immigration, 13, 50, 227–28. *See also* American party

naturalization, 22, 55, 70, 152; ban on, in Chinese exclusion acts, 209, 224–25; and Burlingame Treaty, 110–11; consequences of excluding Chinese from, 148, 194–95, 222; as factor for tax exemption, 35; Know Nothings on, 52; opposition to Chinese, 48, 117, 133, 143; in Reconstruction debates, 85, 97, 143–50; significance of 1870 debate over, 12, 152–53. *See also* citizenship; Civil Rights Act of 1870; Fifteenth Amendment

Naturalization Act of 1790, 15, 35, 44, 55

Naturalization Act of 1870: and Chinese question, 12–13, 111, 143–52; interpretation of, 194, 195, 198; significance of anti-Chinese vote on, 148, 149, 150–51, 152, 181, 201; votes on, 145, 149, 150, 152

natural rights versus *political rights*, 75, 147, 151

Negroization of Chinese, 10, 30, 32, 38, 41–42, 44, 46, 48, 56, 60–62, 67, 68, 71, 81, 121, 155, 189, 191, 207, 208–9, 215, 227; Chinese resistance to, 38, 39, 40, 47, 81–82. *See also People v. Hall;* racialization

Negrophobia, 20

Negro seamen acts, 16–17

new immigrants, 228

New Orleans Commercial Bulletin, 122

New Orleans Daily Picayune, 122

New Orleans Times, 218

New York, 16, 17, 26, 51, 93, 107, 128. *See also* New York City; race riots

New York City: draft riots in, 73–74, 162; racial violence in, 20–21, 104

New York Herald, 74

New York Independent, 103, 115

New York Times, 136; on North Adams, 127, 134; on racial questions, 114, 115; on Republican racial policies, 118

New York Tribune, 48, 54, 111, 112, 136, 185, 202; on Pagan Orders, 166

New York World, 173, 174

Ngai, Mae, 228

Niblack, William, 89–90

Nojoque (Helper), 101

Norfolk Journal and Guide (Virginia), 124

Noriega de la Guerra, 28–29

Norris v. City of Boston. See Passenger Cases

North Adams, Mass., 126–36, 140, 144, 157, 174, 213; reaction to Chinese strikebreakers in, 126–33, 135, 136, 212

Northeast: attitudes toward Chinese immigration in South, 120–21, 126; job competition in, 73–74; reaction to Chinese in, 128, 130–39; restrictions on blacks in, 16, 75, 138. *See also* African Americans; black mobility

Nye, James W., 151

Ohio, 53, 56, 128

Opium Wars, 30

Order of Caucasians, 189

Oregon, 54, 57, 93, 96; black exclusion bill in, 56; Chinese and Negro questions in admission of, 55–56; discrimination against Chinese in, 56, 59

Pacific Coast Anti-Coolie Association, 104

Pacific Islanders, 26, 28, 44

Pacific Northwest. *See* anti-Chinese legislation; anti-Chinese movement

Pagan Orders, 159–60, 165–66

Page, Horace F., 176–77, 198, 211

Page law, 176–77, 182, 221. See also *An Act to Prevent the Kidnaping . . . Purposes*

Painter, Nell I., 217

Parker, Peter, 77

Passenger Cases, 17–18, 26, 52; and black mobility, 17–19; as precedent for Chinese exclusion, 49

Patterson, James W., 92, 99

"Peculiar Institution." *See* slavery

Peffer, George, 159

peonage, 105; alleged status of Hispanics, 29

People's Protection Alliance, 164, 166

People's Protective Union, 68

People v. Downer, 47

People v. Hall, 44, 46, 47, 49, 54, 59; Chinese reaction to, 45

Phillips, Wendell, 131–33

Pickett, Charles E., 181

Pike, James S., 173

Piper, William A., 183, 186

Pixley, Frank M., 72, 183, 184, 185

Platt, Orville H., 206, 207

Plessy v. Ferguson, 221

police power. *See* states, police power of

Polk, James K., 34

poll taxes, 140

Pomeroy, Samuel C., 64, 147

population statistics: on African Americans, 27, 39, 56, 58, 66, 75, 80, 138, 156; on aliens, 6, 25–26, 50, 67, 134, 139, 207; in California, 25–26, 67, 157; on Chinese, 6, 58, 70, 80, 112, 134, 156, 157, 159, 164, 178, 207, 222, 227; on Chinese immigration, 36, 40, 43, 45, 58, 66, 112, 157, 164, 178, 179; on Chinese women, 159, 178; comparing Chinese and Europeans, 6; on Hispanics, 23, 26, 33; on Native Americans, 23

"Prayer of Twenty Millions" (Greeley), 65

prejudices. *See* African Americans; Chinese

privileges and immunities clause, 89, 90. *See also* Fourteenth Amendment

property qualifications, 140

prostitution, 61–62, 159: of Chinese women, 62, 159, 170, 174, 176, 178, 181, 204; comparison of Chinese and white prostitutes, 159, 170, 187; legislation against Chinese, 158–59, 177, 178; number of Chinese women in, 62; stereotypes of Chinese women in, 155, 187; and stigmatization of Chinese women, 48, 159. *See also* Page law

The Prostrate State (Pike), 173

queue-cutting ordinance, 165, 180. See also *Ho Ah Kow v. Nunan*

race riots: anti-black, 20–21, 73–74; anti-Chinese, 73, 104, 162, 163–64, 189–90, 222

racial anxiety, 14; and African Americans, 65; and Chinese, 10, 14, 36, 37, 100–101, 186, 201; during Civil War, 65–66. *See also* African Americans; anti-black attitudes; anti-Chinese movement; Chinese; Grant, Ulysses; Hayes, Rutherford; Northeast; Republican party; Southeast

racial formation: in antebellum America, 7–8, 21, 46, 47, 48, 62, 70; definition of, 230n20; and expansion, 22; in postbellum America, 82, 122–23, 173, 194–95, 215; in revolutionary America, 15; and white supremacy, 8, 21, 82, 195

racialization: of Chinese/Asians, 10, 34, 35, 36, 40, 41, 43, 44, 45–46, 49, 59–62, 67, 68, 69, 101, 110, 124, 133, 136, 137, 144, 158, 159, 173, 188, 189, 197, 212, 227, 228; of Chinese question, 38, 45, 47, 48, 70, 100–101, 111, 115, 137, 144, 147, 162, 167, 173, 175, 176, 181, 184, 190–91, 203, 207–8; definition of, 10; of European immigrants, 227–28, 259n38;

of Hispanics, 29; of immigration policy, 47, 78–79, 177; reaction of Chinese to, 38–39, 40, 47

racial violence, 70, 189–90, 218, 221, 222. *See also* race riots

racism. *See* anti-black attitudes; anti-black legislation; anti-Chinese legislation; anti-Chinese movement; Mexican-American War; race riots; Republican party; whiteness

racist writings, 101–2, 191, 221, 226, 227. *See also* Helper, Hinton; Grant, Madison; Stoddard, Lothrop

radical Republicans, 152. *See also* Republican party

Reconstruction: Acts of 1867, 92; and blacks, 87–101, 150–51, 173; and Chinese question, 12, 85, 87–101, 141–55, 158; conflation of black and Chinese issues in, 12, 87, 148; congressional, 12, 84–101, 140–55; failure of, 215, 217; and Hayes's inauguration, 182; implications of, in California, 103, 108, 161; intent of framers of, 12, 14, 84–85, 99–101, 148, 150–51; Johnson's plan for, 86; Lincoln's plan for, 85; and Naturalization Act of 1870, 12–13, 150–53; political expediency in, 118, 146, 150–51; racial politics in, 12–13, 94, 137, 148, 153, 155, 173; and readmission of southern states, 141; retreat from, 13, 140, 148, 149, 150, 153–55, 173, 177, 182, 213, 219–20. *See also* Republican party

Reconstruction (Foner), 85

Reed, William, 77–78

referenda: on black exclusion, 56; on Chinese issues, 56, 192

registration papers, 58,

Republican party: on African Americans, 54, 64, 65–66, 74–75, 146, 198; and black migration, 65–66, 75–76; and black rights, 54, 92, 154–55, 173; and Chinese question, 12, 72, 87–101, 142–55, 182, 201, 202–13; on Chinese labor in the South, 123, 126; and Civil Rights Act (1875), 153–55; creed of, 148, 149, 150–51, 155, 173, 182, 199, 207, 213–14; decline of radicalism in, 152–55; dissociates civil and political rights, 75, 84, 91, 92, 146, 147; election of 1874, 154, 172; founding of, 53; and free labor ideology, 53–54, 64, 172; moderates versus radicals in, 75, 84–85, 98, 150–51; platforms/agenda of, 53, 54, 63, 65–66, 74, 75, 92, 172, 181–82,

204; racial attitudes of members of, 12, 53, 54, 64, 74–75, 94, 100, 118, 148, 151, 155, 173, 181, 182, 200, 208; reaction to *Dred Scott*, 55; on slavery, 53, 54, 63, 64; as "white man's party," 63. *See also* American party
—in California, 103, 191; anti-Chinese planks of, 105, 107, 117, 163, 180, 181; attitudes toward Chinese and African Americans, 54, 156; and black rights, 54, 71, 79, 103, 105, 107, 117; platforms of, 105, 107, 108, 117, 156, 163, 179
Revels, Hiram R., 161
Roach, Philip A., 34
Royce, Josiah, 29

Sacramento, 156, 183
Sacramento Daily Union, 1
Sampson, Calvin, 126, 138. *See also* North Adams
San Francisco, 47–48, 183; anti-Chinese ordinances (Pagan Orders) in, 159–60, 165–66; board of supervisors in, 159, 165, 166; Chinese arrivals in, 36, 43; prostitution in, 159. *See also Daily Alta California*
San Francisco Daily Herald, 117
San Francisco Examiner, 34
San Francisco Mechanics' Institute, 160
Sand Lot meetings, 157, 190–91
Sandmeyer, Elmer, 3
Sargent, Aaron A., 71–72, 143, 144, 183, 184, 186, 198
Saulsbury, Eli, 149, 216
Sawyer, Lorenzo, 194–95
Saxton, Alexander, 4
schools: black access to, 62, 170–71; black exclusion from, 25, 62, 81; Chinese exclusion from, 81, 170–71; racial segregation in, 62, 153–55
Schurz, Carl, 147
Scott Act, 223, 224
Section 16. *See* Civil Rights Act of 1870
segregation: in antebellum North, 20. *See also* Jim Crow
Seward, George F., 204
Seward, William H., 15, 98, 109
sexual vigilantism, 21, 62, 73–74, 136
Seymour, Horatio, 92
Shannon, William, 24
Shaw, William, 23
Shelley, Charles M., 219
Sherman, John, 142, 153

Singleton, Benjamin "Pap," 218
Sinophobia, 2, 3–4, 5, 8, 10, 13, 14, 40, 97, 113, 148, 189. *See also* anti-Chinese movement
Slaughter-House Cases, 177
"Slave Power," 63
slavery, 16, 82, 105; banning of, in California, 23, 39; and Civil War, 65; and coolieism, 77–78; Republican advocacy of nonextension of, 53, 63; Taney on, 54–55
slave trade: congressional act against, 77; and coolie trade, 31, 60, 77, 78; and U.S. Constitution, 49
Smith, Persifor, 26
Smith, William R., 52
Smith v. Turner. *See Passenger Cases*
South Carolina, 123, 173, 182; Negro seamen act of, 16–17
Southeast: African Americans in, 16; Chinese labor in, 41–42, 60, 120–21, 122–26, 218; efforts to maintain white supremacy in, 86, 122–23; racial anxiety over Chinese immigration in, 124–26; status of Chinese in, 120–21, 126, 134; unattractive to immigrants, 120, 122. *See also* African Americans; Reconstruction
Southern Farmer, 122
Speer, William, 41–42, 50
split labor market. *See* dual labor market
Springfield (Mass.) Republican, 126–27, 129
Stanford, Leland H., 66; anti-Chinese attitude of, 69–70, 72; pro-Chinese attitude of, 81
Starr, M. B., 166
states, police power of: and black issues, 17, 169; and immigration issues, 17–18, 36, 46, 49–50, 52, 58
stereotypes. *See* African Americans; Chinese
Stevens, Thaddeus, 64, 71, 91
Stewart, William M., 95, 137; anti-Chinese position of, 144–45, 151; and Enforcement Act of 1870, 141–42
Stoddard, Lothrop L., 227
Stout, Arthur B., 69
Sullivan, John, 19
Sumner, Charles, 140; on "Chinese civil rights bill," 153–54; on Fifteenth Amendment, 97–98; on Naturalization Act of 1870, 144, 147, 149, 151; and racial justice, 155
Swinton, John, 136
Sylvis, William H., 138

Taiping Rebellion, 30

Taney, Roger B.: and black mobility, 17, 18; opinion on African Americans, 17, 54–55, 87; opinion in *Dred Scott*, 54–55, 57, 152, 224; opinion on Negro seamen laws, 17; opinion on *Passenger Cases*, 18, 49–50

testimony restrictions: affecting blacks, 10, 25, 44, 54, 59, 71; affecting Chinese, 10, 40, 44, 54, 59, 81; affecting Native Americans, 81; call for repeal of, 54; Chinese reaction to, 40, 45; effect of, 44–45, 70; in *People v. Hall*, 44; repeal of, 81, 156, 158. *See also* Civil Rights Act of 1870

Thirteenth Amendment, 74, 86, 87, 88, 177

Thurman, Allen G., 149

Tilden, Samuel, 182

Tingley, George B.: contract labor bill of, 33–34, 36, 38; nativistic feelings of, 27, 33, 233n15

Townsend, Martin, 197

treaties of 1880 (between China and the U.S.), 205

Treaty of Guadalupe Hidalgo, 22, 28, 33

Treaty of Trade, Consuls, and Emigration. *See* Burlingame Treaty

Trumbull, Lyman, 76; on civil rights bill (1866), 86, 87, 88; on Fifteenth Amendment, 98; on naturalization bill (1870), 146, 147, 148, 149–50,

Twain, Mark, 111–12, 113

The Unwelcome Immigrant (Miller), 6

U.S. Congress. *See* Chinese exclusion legislation; immigration; *individual civil rights acts*; Reconstruction

Usher, John, 77, 79

U.S. v. Cruishank, 182

U.S. v. Ju Toy, 225

Van Winkle, Peter G., 87

Vest, George G., 212–13, 219

Vicksburg Daily Times, 122, 123

Voegeli, Victor J., 64

Voorhees, Daniel W., 218–19

Wade, Benjamin F., 56, 64

Ward, John E., 78

Warner, Willard, 95–96, 149, 150

Wayne, James M., 18

"The Wedding of the Chinee and the Coon" (Johnson), 226

West Indies, 31, 60, 77, 143, 150

Whig party, 53

whipping, 81–82

White Brotherhood, 140

White Conquest (Dixon), 172

whiteness: and access to California mines, 29, 35, 36, 37, 48; and American nationality/identity, 15, 22, 25, 60, 152, 194–95; in American West, 16, 19, 21–22, 48, 54; black colonization and, 64; and blackness defined, 44; and Chineseness/Mongolianness, 67; and Civil Rights Act of 1875, 155; and conflation of Asians and new immigrants, 228, 259n38; in Lincoln-Douglas debates, 58; and naturalization, 35, 194–95; and Naturalization Act of 1870, 12, 144, 146, 148, 152, 194; as prerequisite for employment, 139; significance of Chinese police tax for ideology of, 67. *See also* African Americans; amalgamation; American identity; Chinese; Hispanics; Native Americans

white supremacy, 7–8, 19, 48, 60, 63, 82, 127, 221

Willey, Waitman T., 76, 93

Williams, George H., 93, 94, 95, 137, 144, 145, 150, 175, 176

Willis, Albert, 197–98, 211

Wilson, Henry, 98–99, 175, 208, 213; in American party, 131, 175; and anti-Chinese bills, 131; on naturalization bill, 145, 147, 151; on North Adams, 130–31, 137

Windom, William, 215–16, 218, 219

Wirt, William, 17

Wisconsin, 26, 53

Woodhull, Victoria Claflin, 134

Workingman's Advocate, 127

Workingmen's Alliance of Sacramento, 164

Workingmen's Party of California, 181, 190–92. *See also* Kearney, Denis

Wozencraft, Oliver, 24

"yellow peril," 135, 173, 188, 226, 227

NAJIA AARIM-HERIOT graduated from the Université de Toulouse-le-Mirail in France and received her M.A. in British studies from the Université de Grenoble III and her Ph.D. in American history from Temple University. She is currently an assistant professor of history at the State University of New York at Fredonia. Her research focuses on African American and Asian American history and ethnicity and race in the global context.

The Asian American Experience

The Hood River Issei: An Oral History of Japanese Settlers in Oregon's
  Hood River Valley   *Linda Tamura*
Americanization, Acculturation, and Ethnic Identity: The Nisei Generation
  in Hawaii   *Eileen H. Tamura*
Sui Sin Far/Edith Maude Eaton: A Literary Biography   *Annette White-Parks*
Mrs. Spring Fragrance and Other Writings   *Sui Sin Far; edited by Amy Ling and
  Annette White-Parks*
The Golden Mountain: The Autobiography of a Korean Immigrant, 1895–1960
  Easurk Emsen Charr; edited and with an introduction by Wayne Patterson
Race and Politics: Asian Americans, Latinos, and Whites in a Los Angeles Suburb
  Leland T. Saito
Achieving the Impossible Dream: How Japanese Americans Obtained Redress
  Mitchell T. Maki, Harry H. L. Kitano, and S. Megan Berthold
If They Don't Bring Their Women Here: Chinese Female Immigration
  before Exclusion   *George Anthony Peffer*
Growing Up Nisei: Race, Generation, and Culture among Japanese Americans of
  California, 1924–49   *David K. Yoo*
Chinese American Literature since the 1850s   *Xiao-huang Yin*
Pacific Pioneers: Japanese Journeys to America and Hawaii, 1850–80   *John E. Van Sant*
Holding Up More Than Half the Sky: Chinese Women Garment Workers in
  New York City, 1948–92   *Xiaolan Bao*
Onoto Watanna: The Story of Winnifred Eaton   *Diana Birchall*
Edith and Winnifred Eaton: Chinatown Missions and Japanese Romances
  Dominika Ferens
Being Chinese, Becoming Chinese American   *Shehong Chen*
Chinese Immigrants, African Americans, and Racial Anxiety in the
  United States, 1848–82   *Najia Aarim-Heriot*

The University of Illinois Press
is a founding member of the
Association of American University Presses.

Composed in 10.5/13 Minion
with Minion display
by Jim Proefrock
at the University of Illinois Press
Manufactured by Thomson-Shore, Inc.

University of Illinois Press
1325 South Oak Street
Champaign, IL 61820-6903
www.press.uillinois.edu